American Literary Scholarship
1971

American Literary Scholarship

An Annual / 1971

Edited by J. Albert Robbins

Essays by John C. Broderick, Nina Baym, Merton M. Sealts, Jr., Bernice Slote, Hamlin Hill, William T. Stafford, Michael Millgate, Jackson R. Bryer, J. A. Leo Lemay, M. Thomas Inge, Patrick F. Quinn, Warren French, James H. Justus, Richard Crowder, A. Kingsley Weatherhead, Walter J. Meserve, John T. Flanagan, G. R. Thompson.

Duke University Press, Durham, North Carolina, 1973

Foreword

If you have looked at the first eight volumes of *American Literary Scholarship* on a shelf, a glance will tell you that *ALS* has been getting fatter. *ALS 1963* ran to 224 pages; *ALS 1970*, to 401. Over the years chapter 12 (Fiction: 1900 to the 1930s) has tripled in length, just to cite one example. It is not that *ALS* contributors are being more garrulous; they just have more scholarship to contend with. It is easy to document this growth by looking into the annual *MLA International Bibliography*. In 1963 there were 1,541 items in the American literature section; in 1970, 2,425—and these figures are too low, because the bibliography uses "block" entries to save space (a special Robert Frost issue of a journal with fifteen articles is cited as only one item). Because of this glut, I and the contributors have tried this year to cut and condense, but there is a limit beyond which excision diminishes the value of the enterprise. Scholarly inflation seems as resistant to control as fiscal inflation.

It is always an occasion of sadness to see faithful and able contributors resign from the series, but individuals do tire of the task or assume other commitments that require shedding this one. This year represents the final appearance of four valued contributors: John C. Broderick (Emerson, Thoreau and Transcendentalism), Merton M. Sealts, Jr. (Melville), Patrick F. Quinn (Poe and Nineteenth-Century Poetry), and A. Kingsley Weatherhead (Poetry: The 1930s to the Present). We thank each for his good work. Their replacements for *ALS 1972* are, respectively, Ralph H. Orth (University of Vermont), Hershel Parker (University of Southern California), G. R. Thompson (Washington State University), and Linda W. Wagner (Michigan State University). Thompson, who has so ably done the Themes, Topics, and Criticism chapter for three years, replaces Quinn for chapter 11 and George Monteiro (Brown University) replaces Thompson for chapter 18. Richard Crowder (Poetry: 1900 to the

1930s) will be on leave during the 1973–1974 academic year and his chapter for *ALS 1972* will be written by my colleague, Alvin Rosenfeld. To those leaving, my thanks for jobs well done. To those arriving, welcome. As always, I urge authors of articles to send reprints to me or to the appropriate chapter contributor.

We thank Jackson Bryer, who, this year as last, provided us with specially typed lists of items in his *MLA Bibliography* card file. With the *Bibliography* still badly off its usual publication schedule, this is an essential service to *ALS* contributors.

Finally, 1971 reaches a milestone of sorts. This year produced a four-letter "obscenity" in the title of an article. Scholarship moves forward with the times.

J. Albert Robbins

Indiana University

Table of Contents

Key to Abbreviations

A-A / Klaus Lanzinger, ed., *Americana-Austriaca: Beiträge zur Amerikakunde*, Vol. 2 (Vienna, Wilhelm Braumüller, 1970).
ABC / *American Book Collector*
ACF / *Annali di Ca' Foscari* (Venice)
A Cheerful Nihilism / Richard Boyd Hauck, *A Cheerful Nihilism: Confidence and "The Absurd" in American Humorous Fiction* (Bloomington, Ind. Univ. Press)
Agenda
AI / *American Imago*
AL / *American Literature*
ALR / *American Literary Realism, 1870–1910*
ALS / *American Literary Scholarship: An Annual*
A Many-Windowed House / Henry Dan Piper, ed. *A Many-Windowed House: Collected Essays on American Writers and American Writing*, by Malcolm Cowley (Carbondale, So. Ill. Univ. Press)
Americana Norvegica / Harald S. Naess and Sigmund Skard, eds., *Americana Norvegica, Vol. 3, Studies in Scandinavian-American Interrelations* (Oslo, Universitetsforlaget)
American Dreams / David Madden, ed., *American Dreams, American Nightmares* (Carbondale, So. Ill. Univ. Press, 1970)
AmerS / *American Studies* (formerly *Midcontinent American Studies Journal*)
AN / *Acta Neophilologica* (Ljubljana)
AN&Q / *American Notes and Queries*
AntigR / *Antigonish Review*
AQ / *American Quarterly*
AR / *Antioch Review*

Ariel / *Ariel: A Review of International English Literature*
ArlQ / *Arlington Quarterly*
ArQ / *Arizona Quarterly*
AS / *American Speech*
Athanor (Le Roy, N.Y.)
Atlantic Brief Lives / Louis Kronenberger, ed. *Atlantic Brief Lives: A Biographical Companion to the Arts* (Boston, Little, Brown)
AtM / *Atlantic Monthly*
ATQ / *American Transcendental Quarterly*
AW / *American West*
BaratR / *Barat Review* (Barat Coll.)
BARev / *Black Academy Review: Quarterly of the Black World*
BBr / *Books at Brown*
BC / *Book Collector*
BCB / *Boletín Cultural y Bibliográfico* (Bogotá)
BlackW / *Black World*
BNYPL / *Bulletin of the New York Public Library*
BRMMLA / *Bulletin of the Rocky Mountain Modern Language Assn.*
BSUF / *Ball State University Forum*
BuR / *Bucknell Review*
BYUS / *Brigham Young University Studies*
Cabellian / *The Cabellian: A Journal of the Second American Renaissance*
CC / *Cross Currents*
CE / *College English*
CEAA / Center for Editions of American Authors
CEJ / *California English Journal*
CentR / *The Centennial Review* (Mich. State Univ.)
Challenges / Ray B. Browne, Larry N. Landrum, and William K. Bottorff,

eds. *Challenges in American Culture* (Bowling Green, Ohio, Bowling Green Univ. Popular Press, 1970)

CimR / Cimarron Review (Okla. State Univ.)

CLAJ / CLA Journal (Coll. Language Assn.)

CLQ / Colby Library Quarterly

CLS / Comparative Literature Studies

ColQ / Colorado Quarterly

Comment (Univ. of Alabama)

Commentary

Commonweal

ConL / Contemporary Literature

ConnR / Connecticut Review

ContempR / Contemporary Review

CP / Concerning Poetry (Western Wash. State Coll.)

CQ / The Cambridge Quarterly

CR / Critical Review (Melbourne)

CRAS / Canadian Review of American Studies (Montreal)

Crit / Critique: Studies in Modern Fiction

Criticism (Wayne State Univ.)

CritQ / Critical Quarterly

CWCP / Contemporary Writers in Christian Perspective (Grand Rapids, Mich., William B. Eerdmans)

DAI / Dissertation Abstracts International

DN / Dreiser Newsletter

DR / Dalhousie Review

Dram / Dramatics

EA / Etudes anglaises

EAL / Early American Literature

ECS / Eighteenth-Century Studies

EDB / Emily Dickinson Bulletin

Edda (Oslo)

EIC / Essays in Criticism (Oxford)

Eight American Authors / James Woodress, ed. *Eight American Authors, A Review of Research and Criticism* (New York, Norton).

EigoS / Eigo Seinen [The Rising Generation] (Tokyo)

EIHC / Essex Institute Historical Collections

EJ / English Journal

ELH / ELH, Journal of English Literary History

ELN / English Language Notes

ELT / English Literature in Transition (1800–1920)

Encounter (London)

EngR / English Record

ErasmusR / Erasmus Review (Bayside, N.Y.)

ES / English Studies

ESA / English Studies in Africa (Johannesburg)

ESALL / Essays and Studies on American Language and Literature (Uppsala, Lundequistska, 1969), No. 18

ESQ / Emerson Society Quarterly

ESRS / Emporia State Research Studies

Essays /Thomas A. Kirby and William J. Olive, eds. *Essays in Honor of Esmond Linworth Marilla* (Baton Rouge, La. State Univ. Press)

Ethnomusicology

ETJ / Educational Theatre Journal

Expl / Explicator

Extracta: Resumeer af Specialeopgaver fra det Filosofiske Fakultet ved Københavns Universetet (Copenhagen)

Extrapolation

Festschrift Rudolf Stamm / Eduard Kolb and Jörg Hasley, eds., *Festschrift Rudolf Stamm* (Bern, Francke, 1969)

FHA / Fitzgerald-Hemingway Annual

FHS / Fort Hays Studies, new series, Bibliographical Series (Fort Hays, Kans. State Coll.)

Fifteen American Authors / Robert A. Rees and Earl N. Harbert, eds., *Fifteen American Authors Before 1900: Bibliographic Essays on Research and Criticism* (Madison, Univ. of Wis. Press).

FLang / Foundations of Language (Dordrecht, Netherlands)

FMLS / Forum for Modern Language Studies (Univ. of St. Andrews, Scotland)

Folklore (London)

Four Quarters

Foxfire

Gambit

GaR / *Georgia Review*
Genre
HAB / *Humanities Association Bulletin* (Univ. of New Brunswick, Canada)
Hasifrut (Tel-Aviv Univ.)
HEQ / *History of Education Quarterly*
HL / *Humanistica Lovaniensia*
HLB /*Harvard Library Bulletin*
Hochland (Munich)
Horizon
HSE / *Hungarian Studies in English*
HSL / *Hartford Studies in Literature*
HudR / *Hudson Review*
Hunters & Healers / Wilson M. Hudson, ed. *Hunters & Healers* (Austin, Tex., Encino Press)
HussR / *Husson Review*
IF / *Indiana Folklore*
IllQ / *Illinois Quarterly*
IMH / *Indiana Magazine of History*
IowaR / *Iowa Review*
IJAS / *Indian Journal of American Studies* (Hyderabad)
IPQ / *International Philosophical Quarterly*
IQ / *Italian Quarterly*
IY / *Idaho Yesterdays*
JA / *Jahrbuch für Amerikastudien*
JAAC / *Journal of Aesthetics and Art Criticism*
JAF / *Journal of American Folklore*
JAmS / *Journal of American Studies*
JFI / *Journal of the Folklore Institute* (Ind. Univ.)
JHI / *Journal of the History of Ideas*
JISHS / *Journal of the Illinois State Historical Society*
JL / *Journal of Linguistics* (Linguistic Assn. of Great Britain)
JML / *Journal of Modern Literature*
JNH / *Journal of Negro History*
JNT / *Journal of Narrative Technique* (Ypsilanti, Eastern Mich. Univ. Press)
JoIP / *Journal of Individual Psychology*
JPC / *Journal of Popular Culture*
JPH / *Journal of Presbyterian History*
JQ / *Journalism Quarterly*
JRUL / *Journal of the Rutgers University Library*

KanQ / *Kansas Quarterly*
KFQ / *Keystone Folklore Quarterly*
KFR / *Kentucky Folklore Record*
KN / *Kwartalnik Neofilologiczny* (Warsaw)
KuL / *Kunst und Literatur*
L&I / *Language and Ideology* (Montreal)
L&P / *Literature and Psychology* (Univ. of Hartford)
LaHist / *Louisiana History*
Lang&S / *Language and Style*
LaS / *Louisiana Studies*
LC / *Library Chronicle* (Univ. of Pa.)
LCrit / *Literary Criterion* (Univ. of Mysore, India)
LE&W / *Literature East and West*
LHY / *Literary Half-Yearly*
Lituanus: Lithuanian Quarterly (Chicago)
LJ / *Library Journal*
LWU / *Literatur in Wissenshaft und Unterricht* (Kiel)
M-A / *Mid-America*
MarkhamR / *Markham Review*
MD / *Modern Drama*
Meanjin / *Meanjin Quarterly* (Univ. of Melbourne)
MFR / *Mississippi Folklore Register*
MFS / *Modern Fiction Studies*
MichA / *Michigan Academician*
Minor American Novelists / Charles A. Hoyt, *Minor American Novelists* (Carbondale, So. Ill. Univ. Press)
MissQ / *Mississippi Quarterly*
MLQ / *Modern Language Quarterly*
MLR / *Modern Language Review*
Mosaic: A Journal for the Comparative Study of Literature and Ideas
MP / *Modern Philology*
MPS / *Modern Poetry Studies*
MQ / *Midwest Quarterly*
MQR / *Michigan Quarterly Review*
MR / *Massachusetts Review*
MSE / *Massachusetts Studies in English*
MTJ / *Mark Twain Journal*
MVHR / *Mississippi Valley Historical Review*
NALF / *Negro American Literature Forum*
NaS / *Nature Study*

NCarF / *North Carolina Folklore*
NCF / *Nineteenth-Century Fiction*
NCHR / *North Carolina Historical Review*
NConL / *Notes on Contemporary Literature* (Carrollton, West Ga. College)
NEQ / *New England Quarterly*
NewL / *New Letters* (formerly *University Review*)
New Yorker
NH / *Nebraska History*
NHJ / *Nathaniel Hawthorne Journal*
NLH / *New Literary History*
NMW / *Notes on Mississippi Writers*
Northeast Folklore
Northwest Review
Novel: A Forum on Fiction
NS / *Die neueren Sprachen*
NYFQ / *New York Folklore Quarterly*
OH / *Ohio History*
OHQ / *Oregon Historical Quarterly*
PADS / *Publication of the American Dialect Society*
PBSA / *Papers of the Bibliographical Society of America*
PCP / *Pacific Coast Philology*
PF / *Pennsylvania Folklife*
Phylon
Players
PLL / *Papers on Language and Literature*
PMHB / *Pennsylvania Magazine of History and Biography*
PMLA / *PMLA, Publications of the Modern Language Association*
PoeS / *Poe Studies* (formerly *Poe Newsletter*)
PQ / *Philological Quarterly*
PR / *Partisan Review*
Private Dealings / David J. Burrows et al., *Private Dealings: Eight Modern American Writers* (Stockholm, Almqvist and Wiksell, 1970)
Prologue, the Journal of the National Archives (Washington, D.C.)
Proof / *Proof: The Yearbook of American Bibliographical and Textual Studies* (Univ. of S.C.)
PrS / *Prairie Schooner*
PULC / *Princeton University Library Chronicle*

PURB / *Punjab Univ. Research Bulletin* (Arts)
QH / *Quaker History: Bulletin of the Friends Historical Association*
QJLC / *Quarterly Journal of the Library of Congress*
QJS / *Quarterly Journal of Speech*
RALS / *Resources for American Literary Study*
RANAM / *Recherches Anglaises et Américaines* (Strasbourg)
Reality and Idea / David H. Hirsch, *Reality and Idea in the Early American Novel* (The Hague, Mouton)
Rediscoveries / David Madden, ed. *Rediscoveries: Informal Essays in which Well-known Novelists Rediscover Neglected Works of Fiction by one of their Favorite Authors* (New York, Crown)
REF / *Revista de Etnografie si Folclor*
Renascence
Rendezvous: Journal of Arts and Letters
RES / *Review of English Studies*
Review / *The Review, A Magazine of Poetry and Criticism* (London)
RLC / *Revue de littérature comparée*
RLM / *La revue des lettres modernes*
RLV / *Revue des langues vivantes*
RomN / *Romance Notes*
Roots (New York)
RQ / *Riverside Quarterly* (Univ. of Saskatchewan)
RS / *Research Studies* (Wash. State Univ.)
SA / *Studi americani*
SAB / *South Atlantic Bulletin*
SALCS / *Studies in American Literature* (Chu-Shikoku American Literature Society)
SAmL / *Studies in American Literature* (The Hague, Mouton)
SAQ / *South Atlantic Quarterly*
SatR / *Saturday Review*
SB / *Studies in Bibliography: Papers of the Bibliographical Society of the University of Virginia*
SBL / *Studies in Black Literature*
SCHM / *South Carolina Historical Magazine*
SCR / *South Carolina Review*

SELit / *Studies in English Literature* (English Literary Society of Japan, Univ. of Tokyo)

Semiotica: Revue Publiée par l'Association Internationale de Sémiotique

Sense and Sensibility / Brom Weber, ed., *Sense and Sensibility in Twentieth-Century Writing: A Gathering in Memory of William Van O'Connor* (Carbondale, So. Ill. Univ. Press, 1970)

SF&R / *Scholars' Facsimiles and Reprints*

SFQ / *Southern Folklore Quarterly*

Shaken Realist / Melvin J. Friedman and John B. Vickery, eds., *The Shaken Realist: Essays in Modern Literature in Honor of Frederick J. Hoffman* (Baton Rouge, La. State Univ. Press, 1970)

SHR / *Southern Humanities Review*

SIR / *Studies in Romanticism*

SLib / *Southeastern Librarian*

SLJ / *Southern Literary Journal*

SLN / *Sinclair Lewis Newsletter*

SNL / *Satire Newsletter*

SNNTS / *Studies in the Novel*

SoR / *Southern Review*

SR / *Sewanee Review*

SS / *Scandinavian Studies*

SSCJ / *Southern Speech Communication Journal*

SSF / *Studies in Short Fiction*

StH / *Studies in the Humanities* (Indiana Univ. of Pa.)

StQ / *Steinbeck Quarterly*

StTC / *Studies in the Twentieth Century* (Russell Sage Coll.)

Studies in Medieval, Renaissance, American Literature / Betsy F. Colquit, ed. *Studies in Medieval, Renaissance, American Literature: A Festschrift Honoring Troy C. Crenshaw, Lorrain Sherley, and Ruth Speer Angell* (Fort Worth, Tex. Christian Univ. Press)

Style

SWR / *Southwest Review*

Symposium

TCL / *Twentieth Century Literature*

TD / *Theatre Documentation*

TFSB / *Tennessee Folklore Society Bulletin*

The American Novel / Malcolm Bradbury and David Palmer, eds. *The American Novel and the Nineteen Twenties* (London, Edward Arnold)

The Fifties / Warren French, ed. *The Fifties: Fiction, Poetry, Drama* (Deland, Fla., Everett/Edwards, 1970)

The Politics / George A. Panichas, ed. *The Politics of Twentieth-Century Novelists* (New York, Hawthorn)

The Sounder Few / R. H. W. Dillard, George Garrett, and George Rees Moore, eds. *The Sounder Few: Essays from the "Hollins Critic"* (Athens, Univ. of Ga. Press)

Thought

ThQ / *Theatre Quarterly* (London)

THQ / *Tennessee Historical Quarterly*

ThR / *Theatre Research*

TJQ / *Thoreau Journal Quarterly*

TLS / *Times Literary Supplement* (London)

TPJ / *Tennessee Poetry Journal*

TQ / *Texas Quarterly*

TriQ / *Tri-Quarterly*

TS / *Theatre Survey*

TSB / *Thoreau Society Bulletin*

TSL / *Tennessee Studies in Literature*

TSLL / *Texas Studies in Literature and Language*

TUSAS / *Twayne United States Authors series* (New York, Twayne Publishers)

UCQ / *University College Quarterly*

UDR / *University of Dayton Review*

UES / *Unisa English Studies*

UMPAW / *University of Minnesota Pamphlets on American Writers*

UMSE / *University of Mississippi Studies in English*

UPR / *University of Portland Review*

UR / *University Review* (Kansas City, Mo.)

VLit / *Voprosy literatury* (Moscow)

VLU / *Vestnik Leningradskogo U. Ser. Istorii, Jazyka i Literatury*

VMHB / *Virginia Magazine of History and Biography*

VQR / *Virginia Quarterly Review*
WAL / *Western American Literature*
WCR / *West Coast Review*
WF / *Western Folklore*
WHR / *Western Humanities Review*
WMQ / *William and Mary Quarterly*
WR / *Western Review*
WWR / *Walt Whitman Review*

XUS / *Xavier University Studies*
YCGL / *Yearbook of Comparative and General Literature*
YLM / *Yale Literary Magazine*
YR / *Yale Review*
ZAA / *Zeitschrift für Anglistik und Amerikanistik* (East Berlin)

Part I

1. Emerson, Thoreau, and Transcendentalism

John C. Broderick

Fifteen books, more than thirty dissertations, and a never-ending stream of critical and biographical articles on Emerson, Thoreau, and the Transcendentalists appeared in 1971 or otherwise fell within the scope of this report. The books included some long-awaited basic publications for study of Emerson and Thoreau as well as others more or less adventitiously put together. All in all, the scholarly output for the year was notable for texts, editions, and bibliographical work more than for critical, though two books on Orestes Brownson will find their places in the working libraries of specialists.

Like other fields of American literary study, the literature of New England Transcendentalism has lately been beset by "symposia." Such gatherings, although invariably the occasion of some memorable individual essays, rarely cohere. There is a need for synthesis, to be sure, especially in Thoreau studies, but it is unlikely to come about through an editor's happy thought and facility in attracting the right contributors. Dissertations on important topics are emerging from many universities (not all from departments of language and literature, by the way). One must hope that the state of the world and the state of the profession will permit their authors patiently to cultivate them properly rather than dissipate their energies in two- and three-page notes and studies.

i. Texts, Editions, Bibliographies

New, definitive editions of both *Walden* and *Nature, Addresses, and Lectures* were published in 1971, the first volumes, respectively, in complete editions of the "writings" of Thoreau and the "collected works" of Emerson, the former published by Princeton University

Press, the latter by Harvard's Belknap Press. Both editions are receiving long-range support from the National Endowment for the Humanities and are subject to the editorial review of the Center for Editions of American Authors.

Both *Walden* and *Nature, Addresses, and Lectures,* of course, carry the CEAA seal and contain some of the usual apparatus of CEAA editions. There are, however, some differences. All apparatus, textual and otherwise, follows the text of *Walden* whereas Robert E. Spiller's introduction and Alfred R. Ferguson's discussion of the text precede writings by Emerson in the Harvard volume. Moreover, J. Lyndon Shanley is responsible for the entire *Walden* volume, whereas for the Emerson edition, like those of Crane and Melville, for example, among other CEAA editions, the text has been established by one man (Ferguson) and the historical introduction supplied by another (Spiller). The Emerson volume includes more than twenty pages of "informational notes" (supplied by Spiller), a feature lacking in the *Walden.* There is also a ten-page list of "parallel passages," keying parts of the Emerson texts to appropriate passages in the *Journals and Miscellaneous Notebooks.* Both volumes are handsomely styled, with aptly chosen illustrations and facsimile reproductions. The compact format of the Thoreau volume, however, is unique among CEAA editions, making Thoreau's writings seem less intended for the shelves of an institutional library than for the pocket of an all-weather coat.

These two books contain a very large portion of the permanent literature of New England Transcendentalism. Their textual problems vary considerably in complexity, however, as do the editors' solutions. For copy text Shanley has used the page proofs of *Walden* as Thoreau corrected them, with some modifications from his corrected copy of the first edition and others from the only "authorized" printings, in 1854 and 1862. For his copy text Ferguson selects first printings of *Nature,* "The American Scholar," "The Divinity School Address," etc. There were significant substantive revisions of these texts in the 1849 volume which collected them under the title *Nature, Addresses, and Lectures.* Ferguson regards most of these as Emerson's retouching of his image, and he therefore rejects them. The edition of Emerson's collected works, therefore, no less than those of the *Early Lectures* and the *Journals and Miscellaneous Notebooks,* restores the "radical" or "infidel" Emerson of the 1830s. The textual apparatus, of course, makes possible each reader's consideration of the evidence on his own.

Meanwhile, the edition of Emerson's *Journals and Miscellaneous Notebooks* (Cambridge, Harvard Univ. Press) continues inexorably. Volume 9, edited by Ralph H. Orth and Alfred R. Ferguson, covers five "regular" journals (U, V, W, Y, and O), variously dated 1843–1847. These journals contain evidence of Emerson's reading to acquaint himself with his chosen "representative men," especially Napoleon and Plato. Bronson Alcott also figures prominently, and journal O contains several pages occasioned by Thoreau's arrest in July 1846. Volume 9 does not cohere around a few concerns, though "reform," its requirements, and apparent demands on Emerson himself are recurrent. The vignette of Edward Everett's inauguration as president of Harvard College (pp. 379–81) is worthy of inclusion in any future volume of "miniatures" from Emerson journals (see below).

A persuasive vindication of the editorial approach taken in the edition of the *Journals and Miscellaneous Notebooks* is provided by the chief editor, William H. Gilman, in "How Should Journals Be Edited?" (*EAL* 6:73–83), a review essay occasioned by publication of the first volume of Washington Irving's *Journals and Notebooks*. According to Gilman, there are three options open to the editor of "private manuscripts": facsimile text, clear text with full report of changes, and inclusive text. Both the Irving and Emerson editors, rightly, Gilman thinks, choose inclusive text, but by eschewing the editorial intervention practiced by the Emerson editors, the Irving edition does not satisfy the need for "a quotable text at the minimal level." The Gilman article and the introduction to the Irving volume will become basic texts for editors of private journals.

For nearly 100 years, editors have sought to convey the character of Thoreau's voluminous journals in one-volume selections. The most recent is *Thoreau's World: Miniatures from His Journal*, edited by Charles R. Anderson (Englewood Cliffs, N.J., Prentice-Hall). Anderson's volume competes for attention with *The Best of Thoreau's Journals*, edited by Carl Bode (Carbondale, So. Ill. Univ. Press), a reissue of a volume first published in 1967 under the title *The Selected Journals of Henry David Thoreau*. Whereas early editors such as H. G. O. Blake and Francis H. Allen sought a thematic unity in their selections (*Early Spring in Massachusetts, Men of Concord*, etc.), Bode, like

Odell Shepard before him, has provided a varied sampling, arranged in the chronological sequence established for the entire published *Journal*. Anderson, however, adopts a new approach. In his belief, Thoreau's journals are filled with "miniatures," "finished creations, unified wholes intended to stand alone." Under seven general headings ("People," "Places," "Wildlife," etc.), Anderson prints about 250 of these miniatures. Symptomatic of the difference in their approach, Bode prefaces his selection with a foreword, "Diary of a Private Man," whereas in addition to a conventional introduction Anderson adds an afterword entitled "The Writer's Art," a discussion of Thoreau's aesthetic and his literary technique. *Thoreau's World*, in short, attempts to add another literary masterpiece to the Thoreau canon, not merely to provide a convenient introduction to a formidable body of private commentary. Despite apparent differences in approach, many of the same passages appear in both volumes.

In one respect only is the welcome due these volumes less than totally enthusiastic. The pending publication of a new edition of Thoreau's journals (Volume 1 expected in 1973) will make obsolete the texts used for the selections and may challenge some of Anderson's inferences about "the writer's art."

Three "Unpublished Emerson Letters to Louis Prang and Whittier" are printed by Roger W. Cummins (*AL* 43:257–59). In "Emerson and Humboldt" (*AL* 42:546–48), Robert E. Spiller prints a letter which invalidates the abstract of his lecture on Alexander von Humboldt of September 13, 1869, apparently a reconstruction by Robert C. Waterston.

In two important bibliographical articles ("The Early Printing Records of Thoreau's Books," *ATQ* 11:44–59; "The First Year's Sales of Thoreau's *Walden*," *TSB* 117:1–3) Walter Harding has drawn upon the editorial records of Ticknor and Fields in Harvard's Houghton Library to provide new information about sales of Thoreau's books, including the first purchaser of *Walden*. (He was W. R. Alger, who later wrote a damning essay about Thoreau.) Harding's articles supplement Tryon and Charvat, *The Cost Books of Ticknor and Fields* (1949), which reproduced only the first two of fourteen volumes of cost books.

The identification of contributors to *The Dial* has been based upon several marked sets, the most detailed being Emerson's personal set. Unknown to George Willis Cooke was a second set of *The Dial* belonging to Alexander Ireland, which Emerson annotated on his second visit to Great Britain. Collation of the various lists is provided in Burton R. Pollin, "Emerson's Annotations in the British Museum Copy of *The Dial*" (*SB* 24:187–95). Two attributions seem clarified by the new evidence: sonnets by B. F. Presbury and Caroline Sturgis.

Before his death, Leo Stoller had completed much of the editorial work on a segment of Thoreau's "Notes on Fruits," an unpublished manuscript in the Berg Collection, New York Public Library. In anticipation of its inclusion in the CEAA edition of Thoreau's *Writings*, this segment has been published in a limited edition: *Huckleberries* (Iowa City and New York, Windhover Press and New York Public Library [1970]), with an introduction by Stoller and a preface by Alexander C. Kern. Though incomplete, *Huckleberries* is on the pattern of "Autumnal Tints" and "Wild Apples."

Two articles by Wendell Glick also seem to grow out of preparation of Thoreau's *Reform Papers* for the CEAA edition of the *Writings*. In the first, "An Early Encounter with Joe Polis" (*TJQ* 3,i:12–15), he has discovered an apparent reference to Polis, Thoreau's Indian guide on his third trip to Maine in 1857, in *Herald of Freedom*, April 5, 1844. Since Thoreau is known to have read *Herald of Freedom*, he may have had the advantage of knowing about Polis more than ten years before meeting him. In a second article, "Thoreau's Use of His Sources" (*NEQ* 44:101–09), Glick points out Thoreau's carelessness or disregard in transcribing quotations from other writers in several of his essays, a disregard Glick finds "baffling," especially in view of Thoreau's objections to James Russell Lowell's editorial tampering with his own writing. Douglas A. Noverr, "A Note on Wendell Glick's 'Thoreau's Use of His Sources'" (*NEQ* 44:475–77), successfully defends Thoreau within the context of his own times.

The quarterly checklists in *TSB* have been cumulated in *A Bibliography of the Thoreau Society Bulletin Bibliographies, 1941–1969: A Cumulation and Index* (Troy, N.Y., Whitson Publishing Co.). The volume was compiled by Jean Cameron Advena with an introduction by Walter Harding. The subtitle is only half correct: the volume, alas, lacks an index, and its usefulness is seriously impaired by the lack. Nevertheless, the all-inclusiveness of *TSB* checklists makes the cumulation an indispensable, if defective, tool.

Emerson and Thoreau, of course, are two members of the nineteenth-century pantheon discussed in *Eight American Authors*, edited by James Woodress. The bibliographical essays on Emerson and Thoreau are the work of contributors to the original edition (1956), Floyd Stovall and Lewis Leary, respectively. The revised chapters add discussions of books and articles of the past fifteen years to the patterns established in the 1956 publication.

A bibliography which has been overlooked by *ALS* and the *MLA International Bibliography* since its publication in 1967 is Christopher A. Hildenbrand, *A Bibliography of Scholarship About Henry David Thoreau, 1940–1967* (*FHS* 3). Some of its shortcomings have now been pointed out by Douglas Noverr in *TJQ* 3,i:7–11. Issued as a Thoreau Society booklet was *Thoreau in the Spanish Language: A Bibliography* by Justo Barate (Geneseo, N.Y., 1970).

Additional bibliographical information is available in T. D. Seymour Bassett and John J. Duffy, "The Library of James Marsh" (*ESQ* 63:2–10), which lists titles once owned by Marsh now in Bailey Library at the University of Vermont.

Checklists of current commentary about Emerson and Thoreau are provided in *ESQ* 63:50–57 and in *TSB*, all issues.

ii. Biography, Literary History, Sources and Influence

The special place which Elizabeth S. Hoar held in the Emerson family following the death of Charles Emerson in 1836 is summarized by Elizabeth Maxfield-Miller, "Emerson and Elizabeth of Concord" (*HLB* 19:290–306), as a preliminary to printing Emerson's sixteen pages of references to her in his journals, which Emerson copied out for E. R. Hoar shortly after Elizabeth's death in 1878. (The manuscript itself is among the George F. Hoar papers in the Massachusetts Historical Society.) Sophia Foord ("Thoreau's feminine foe") died April 1, 1885, aged 83, as discovery of the Foord family headstone in Dedham Cemetery, Massachusetts, demonstrates. See Anton Kovar, "Sophia Foord" (*TJQ* 3,i:22–23).

A new letter from James Russell Lowell to Nathan Hale, Jr., written during Lowell's rustication in Concord in 1838, is printed by Joel Myerson in "Lowell on Emerson: A New Letter from Concord in 1838" (*NEQ* 44:649–52). Its juvenile asides on "The Divinity School Address" confirm other evidence that Lowell played the *enfant terrible* during his rustication. (The letter is in the New York State Library. Other letters from the same group were published in *TSLL* 3[1962]:557–82.)

Two articles based chiefly on research in local newspapers contribute new, if slight, evidence on Emerson's reception in the West and Midwest. See Donald F. Tingley, "Ralph Waldo Emerson on the Illinois Lecture Circuit" (*JISHS* 64:192–205) and Richard Tuerk, "Los Angeles' Reaction to Emerson's Visit to San Francisco" (*NEQ* 44:477–82).

In "Emerson and John Brown" (*NEQ* 44:377–96) John J. McDonald reviews the extent to which Emerson was acquainted with Brown, his public and private utterances about him, and his capacity to understand Brown. In doing so, he substantiates in a detailed way the thesis first advanced by Gilman Ostrander (*MVHR* 39[1953]: 713–26), namely, "whatever Brown's ultimate place in history, Emerson was in no position to determine it," since everything he knew about Brown came directly from Brown himself or from his fervid disciples.

Two new books on Orestes Brownson are complementary studies, since one concerns the pre-Catholic career in detail and the other, though comprehensive, is especially full on the later career. In *Orestes A. Brownson's Road to Catholicism* (Oslo, Universitetsforlaget; New York, Humanities Press [1970]), Per Sveino admits that the road was "long and winding." Nevertheless, he has sought to rationalize it, chiefly in terms of Brownson's "synthetic philosophy," following Pierre Leroux, the sacramental tendencies of Christianity in contemporary England and the United States, Transcendental correspondences, and the psychological need for a "father," which was both particular to Brownson and characteristic of thoughtful Americans generally. Sveino's analysis is detailed and documented but also repetitive and unduly hospitable to all secondary comment on Brownson, which, no less than the latter's road to Catholicism, the author seeks to rationalize. For these and other reasons Sveino's study does not replace *Charles Elwood* and *The Convert* as basic sources of understanding, but it is a welcome adjunct.

Orestes Brownson and the American Republic: An Historical Perspective, by Hugh Marshall, S.T. (Washington, Catholic Univ. Press), is a revision of the author's 1962 dissertation in history. Although it shows evidence of good use of the voluminous Brownson papers at the University of Notre Dame (now widely available on microfilm), the study nevertheless carries analysis of Brownson's political thinking little beyond that of Arthur M. Schlesinger, Jr.,'s honors essay at Harvard more than thirty years ago. (The exception is the Catholic dimension of Brownson's thought after 1844.) Constrained by its organization to be repetitive ("The Patriot," "The Anti-Abolitionist," "The Free-Soiler," etc.), Marshall's book is nevertheless valuable, if only for its seven-page review of previous Brownson scholarship. Despite the title, Marshall is not primarily concerned with Brownson's *The American Republic* (New York, 1865), a work which even George Ripley found a "psychological curiosity," but with making intelligible the shifts and turns in Brownson's thought under the impact of events in mid-nineteenth-century America, as revealed in his magazine articles.

If Brownson was a "weathercock," he emerges from both books a pathetic one, always slightly north-by-northwest, or belatedly adopting popular positions for reasons which struck his contemporaries as discreditable or strained. A case in point is provided by Vincent A. Lapomarda, "Orestes Augustus Brownson: A 19th Century View of the Blacks in American Society" (*M-A* 53:160–69), who points out Brownson's antebellum view that slavery was morally wrong but more tolerable than destruction of the Union, his endorsement of emancipation as a war measure, and his postwar repudiation of the Fourteenth and Fifteenth Amendments.

Among early admirers of Thoreau was Horace Greeley, who not only sought to further his career as an author but also referred to Thoreau on the lecture platform. In "Horace Greeley on Thoreau: A Forgotten Portrait" (*TSB* 116:5–7) Walter Harding reprints "The Bases of Character," an extract from Greeley's widely delivered lecture, "Self Culture," in which Thoreau's Walden experiment is described and praised. The extract was published in *The Rose of Sharon: A Religious Souvenir*, edited by Mrs. C. M. Sawyer (Boston, 1856). Reviews of *Walden, A Week*, and *The Maine Woods* appeared in *The Circular*, the weekly newspaper of the Oneida Community, March 28, April 25, and June 27, 1864, respectively. The reviews, which may have been the work of Alfred Barron, are reprinted in "Thoreau at the Oneida Community" (*TSB* 115:3–5). The Boston muckraker, B. O. Flower, should also be known for early recognition of Thoreau in his monthly *Arena;* see Paul P. Reuben, "Thoreau in

B. O. Flower's *Arena*" (*TSB* 117:5–6). Two articles, one by Flower and one by Walter Leighton, appeared in *The Arena* 30:497 (Nov. 1903) and 32:151 (Aug. 1904).

An overlooked study of influences upon Emerson's thought is Yukio Irie, *Emerson and Quakerism* (Tokyo, Kenkyusha [1967]). In it the author reexamines evidence first systematically presented by Frederick B. Tolles in "Emerson and Quakerism," *AL* 10:142–65 (May 1938). He finds the Quaker influence especially marked in Emerson's resignation from the ministry, his religious philosophy, his practice of religion (Irie finds Emerson an active reformer in the Quaker signification), his theory of poetry, and his ultimate philosophical stance, which is a monism compatible with Quakerism. Irie is unnecessarily contentious toward earlier students of this subject, especially Tolles and Mary Turpie. In fact, he takes Emerson himself to task for some sharp hits against the Quakers in his lecture on George Fox.

It is a commonplace that the Transcendentalists did not care much for fiction (Thoreau: "I never read a novel," etc.). How little the commonplace fits the facts with respect to Emerson's reading is explored by Paul Hourihan, "Ambiguities in the Emerson Sage-Image: The Facts of his Novel Reading" (*HAB* 22,ii:44–55). Emerson is shown to have read more of the work of his notorious antipathies (Jane Austen, Thackeray, Dickens, and Hawthorne) than one would suppose. Beyond these, the evidence indicates that Emerson read fiction pretty widely. Hourihan's second purpose is to discredit Emerson on the basis of the evidence. "He read *fiction*, and in considerable quantity—that is the point; and lied, hedged, or deceived about it," deceptions which Hourihan is disposed to regard as evidence of "other, larger deceptions." The facts come from the reading lists of Kenneth W. Cameron, Walter Harding's *Emerson's Library*, and the various volumes of *Journals and Miscellaneous Notebooks*.

There were five brief notes concerning possible echoes in Thoreau of earlier writers or specific sources (see George Monteiro, "Thoreau's Defense of Man, The 'Reading Animal,'" *ATQ* 11:13–14; George W. Smith, Jr., "Thoreau and Bacon: The Idols of the Theatre," *ATQ* 11:6–12; David G. Hoch, "Thoreau's Use of *The Hindoos*," *TSB* 114:1–2; Richard Tuerk, "An Echo of Virgil in *Walden*," *TSB* 117:4–5; Raymond Benoit, "Walden as God's Drop," *AL* 43:122–24).

A number of studies take up the impact of Emerson and Thoreau on the twentieth century, their kinship with recent writers, the extent of their "relevance" today, etc. Several such articles are gathered in *Emerson's Relevance Today: A Symposium*, edited by Eric W. Carlson and J. Lasley Dameron (Hartford, Conn., Transcendental Books). In brief, the contributors find Emerson's relevance in his anticipation of the protest movement of the 1960s, his anticipation of modern literary themes, such as alienation, and his anticipation of modern psychological themes and concerns. A number of the individual essays are discussed in sections iii and iv below, s.v. Barton, Buell, Redding, and Hopkins. An essay, also entitled "Emerson's Relevance Today" (*BYUS* 11:241–48), challenges the approach to relevance taken by many contributors to the symposium. Its author, Ray S. Williams (replying specifically to James E. Miller, Jr., "The 'Classic' American Writers and the Radicalized Curriculum," *CE* 31[1970]:565–70), argues that to present Emerson merely as a rebel against conformity without recognition of his "strong positive voice" is a distortion which robs him of his true relevance.

Henry Miller's extensive acquaintance with the work of Emerson is analyzed by Paul R. Jackson in "Henry Miller, Emerson, and the Divided Self" (*AL* 43:231–41). Miller has frequently acknowledged Emerson's influence, but his relationship to Whitman and even to Thoreau has received more scholarly attention. One of the most interesting parallels is Miller's character Osmanli in *Sexus*, a fantasized self-image of Miller himself. Jackson believes that Osmanli is Miller's version of Emerson's alter ego, Osman. (The change in the name may mean that Osmanli is more "manly" than Osman.) Herein is the most important indebtedness of Miller to Emerson: "the artistic necessity of using autobiographical fact . . . and the difficulty of understanding the mystery of selfhood basic to autobiographical fiction." Emerson's Osman suggested the possibilities for dramatizing "the simultaneous levels of being" which Miller felt "in his own divided self."

Somewhat akin to Jackson's commentary on Emerson and Miller is Morton L. Ross, "Thoreau and Mailer: The Mission of the Rooster" (*WHR* 25:47–56), in which the two are said to share three concerns: (1) a prophetic demand for life awakened into the immediate present, (2) a preoccupation with self as a symbol of that awakened life, and (3) a prose protean enough to record the awakened self. The article does not argue influence, merely comparable literary strategies for comparable purposes. The exhibits for comparison are Mailer's "The Man Who Studied Yoga" and *Walden.*

In "Katahdin, Wachusett, and Kilimanjaro: The Symbolic Mountains of Thoreau and Hemingway" (*TJQ* 3,ii:1–10) Charles W. Bassett also avoids claiming direct influence, though he does observe that Hemingway's hero was originally named "Henry Walden." His interest is more in the use of mountains by the two authors (Katahdin "a symbol of absolute negation"; Wachusett, "symbol of transcendental unity"; Kilimanjaro, also a scene of beatific vision, "ambiguous, ironic, lethal").

Thoreau Abroad: Twelve Bibliographical Essays, edited by Eugene F. Timpe (Hamden, Conn., Archon Books), takes up the extent of Thoreau's international influence, a subject, it develops, which should be muted, not bruited. Few of the essays—eight on European countries, and one each on Israel, India, Japan, and Australia—are really "bibliographical," and throughout there is an inconsistency of approach common in such enterprises. By the usual measures (translations, scholarly studies, etc.) Thoreau lags well behind his major American contemporaries except in India, where his writings are available "on a scale unmatched by the works of any other major American author." Despite growing general interest, his impact still seems more impressively felt by the chosen few, as in the familiar examples of Yeats, Tolstoy, and Gandhi. For that reason the essays which explore such individual influence (on Frederik van Eeden or Australians such as Edmund James Banfield) seem more substantial than the straightforward national survey. Of the latter, "Thoreau in France" by Maurice J. Gonnaud and Micheline Flak is carefully done. The book contains much useful and intriguing information, but the omission of any essays on Spain, Latin America, Africa, or Scandinavia makes it introductory rather than definitive.

Thoreau's own poetry has found few champions, but, like Falstaff, he has been the cause of poetry in other men. In "Twentieth Century Poetry About Thoreau" (*TSB* 116:1–2) Robert F. Stowell briefly reviews some of the more memorable evidences of this form of influence. The poets include Adin Ballou, Philip Booth, Irwin Edman, Paul Engle, Adrienne Rich, and others. For concentrated awareness, few of these match Helen Bevington's quatrain in *19 Million Elephants:*

Mr. Thoreau: so odd and frank
Found *Leaves of Grass* a little rank
But wondered, when it came to this,
Whose thoughts he blushed at, Walt's or his?

In "Charles Ives: Music, Transcendentalism, and Politics" (*NEQ* 44:433–43) Alfred F. Rosa contends that the Concord group was not only the subject of Ives's "Concord Sonata" but that Ives was, in effect, a twentieth-century Transcendentalist. Through analysis of the sonata and his *Essays Before a Sonata*, Rosa concludes that Ives carried Emerson's organicism into music, which was also influenced by Hawthorne's local color, Alcott's benevolence, and Thoreau's love of nature and reform. Ives seems particularly close to Thoreau, and in the *Essays* he roundly excoriated Thoreau's critics such as James Russell Lowell, Robert Louis Stevenson, and Mark Van Doren.

iii. Criticism: Poetry and Prose

Specifically literary criticism was more abundant for Thoreau than for Emerson, but two articles on aspects of literary form in Emerson deserve close attention. In "Emerson's Search for Literary Form: The Early Journals" (*MP* 69:25–35) Ralph C. LaRosa believes that the habit of collecting *sententiae* in his early journals directed Emerson's attention to questions of art, morality, and originality. He espoused originality, not eccentricity; the former quality was achieved through discovery of the appropriate proverbial sentence. He thus came to regard the proverbial sayings of prudential men as the origin of all morality; hence, since the ends of art are moral, "the sentence was an essential means to expressing that morality and . . . the essay was the proper vehicle for moral art." (See *ALS 1970*, p. 11, for companion studies by LaRosa.)

In "First Person Superlative: The Speaker in Emerson's Essays" (*Emerson's Relevance Today*, pp. 28–35) Lawrence Buell believes that insufficient attention has been paid to Emerson's autobiographical style, "the sense of a persona as opposed to a mere editorial voice," as well as local color to familiarize the context. He finds the personal element a composite of private voice and exemplary or representative voice, the latter Emerson's equivalent of the speaker in Whitman's "Song of Myself." Surprisingly, the private voice becomes increasingly prominent in Emerson's later writings, but, equally surprisingly, the later essays do not therefore have increased appeal. One reason is that the uncompromising exemplary persona, although generalized, has an appealing personality of its own. In the early writings the exemplary voice pronounces universal laws, which are in turn validated by effective intrusions of the private voice. When the private voice takes over, the style becomes anecdotal. Whereas the early writings are "far more vigorous, fresh, and exciting," the later ones are "comparatively tame and vapid."

The ingredients of Thoreau's style continue to invite scholarly attention. In 1959 David Skwire compiled "A Check List of Wordplays in *Walden*" (*AL* 31:282–89), admittedly a preliminary effort only. Over the years, many other wordplays have been the subject of comment in critical articles with less specialized concerns. Recently however, three scholars turned their attention to this very subject. Mario L. D'Avanzo in *Expl* 29[1970]:item 41 analyzed the aptness of the punning comparison of the pickerel of Walden and the Waldenses. Lauriat Lane, Jr., also in *Expl* 29[1970]:item 35 found sixteen wordplays in the first three paragraphs of *Walden* whereas Skwire had listed none. One of these, "sojourner," is extensively analyzed. The most systematic approach, however, was by Donald Ross, Jr., "Verbal Wit and *Walden*" (*ATQ* 11:38–44). Ross, whose linguistic analysis of Emerson's and Thoreau's style was noticed in *ALS 1970* (p. 12), classifies Thoreau's wordplays into six categories. After defining each one and illustrating it with examples from *Walden*, Ross rearranges Skwire's checklist into his categories. See also Robert R. Hodges, "The Functional Satire of Thoreau's Hermit and Poet" (*SNL* 16:105–08).

The "two-handed engine" of *Walden* is the passage on the hound, the bay horse, and the turtle dove in "Economy." Like Thoreau himself, many scholars are still on their trail, even though most return with only glimpses to report. Kenneth G. Johnston's "Thoreau's Star-Spangled Losses: The Hound, Bay Horse and Turtle Dove" (*TJQ* 3,iv:10–20), is the latest. Johnston, however, has something original to say, though he adopts a method applied to this crux by Frank Davidson. Johnston finds the meaning of the famous crux in the constellations Canis Major, Pegasus, and the Pleiades. Hence, the hound stands for pure instinctive response to life; the horse for poetic imagination; and the dove, youthful love (associated with Ellen Sewall). "In the hound-horse-dove passage, Thoreau is taking a nostalgic, backward glance over his lost but cherished enterprises and poetically entering his losses that had prevented a flourishing commerce with the Celestial Empire." The weakness of Johnston's presentation, it seems to me, is that it makes the passage more elegiac than its tone warrants.

A more general discussion of Thoreau's symbols is found in Richard Colyer, "Thoreau's Color Symbols" (*PMLA* 86:999–1008). Colyer discusses the equivalences for five colors: green (organic life activity), white (spirituality), blue (meditation), yellow (spiritual cause and material effect), and red (heroism, strength, and spiritual fruition). Colyer buttresses his analysis by some effective readings, especially a passage from "Spring" in *Walden* where phrases like "green spear" and "green blade" combine the sense of heroism and renewal and "Autumnal Tints," the basic text for Thoreau's most personally significant color, red.

Thoreau's "scornful, abrasive, corrosive, acidic, and sardonic" style is the subject of John J. McAleer's "The Therapeutic Vituperations of Thoreau" (*ATQ* 11:81–87). McAleer believes that Thoreau relished the role of reformer, his disclaimers notwithstanding. Only in 1843 did he make a momentary effort to please audiences. The result was his dullest essays: "A Walk to Wachusett," "A Winter Walk," and "The Landlord." In a related study, "The Absurd in Thoreau's *Walden*" (*TJQ* 3,iv:1–9), Harold F. Mosher, Jr., calls attention to the wordplays, exaggerations, oversimplifications, and other aspects of the absurd as a technique, a technical characteristic which has been overlooked by scholars. (Less *au courant* in terminology but penetrating in its examination of some of the same literary characteristics is Raymond Adams's anticipatory study, "Thoreau's Mock-Heroics," *SP* 52[1955]:86–97.)

The compositional history of *Walden* is approached from a new point of view by Leonard Neufeldt in "'Extravagance' Through Economy: Thoreau's *Walden*" (*ATQ* 11:63–69). "Extravagance" is defined thus: "raising his expression beyond a recording of facts and creating and confirming 'faith' through symbolic action." But "extravagance" and "economy" are interrelated. Both become prominent in version six of *Walden*. Several examples support the analysis, in particular the artist of Kouroo, who exemplifies achievement through economy of means and concentration of aim.

Some lesser works of Thoreau were the subject of three brief arti-

cles in the *American Transcendental Quarterly*, with a fourth on
Walden. Kenneth E. Harris, "Thoreau's 'The Service'—A Review
of the Scholarship" (11:60–63), argues that the early and important
essay has received little attention because of the unavailability of the
text, the superficiality of existing commentary, and the paradoxical
and forbidding style which Thoreau employs. More penetrating criticism will explore the essay's relationship with peace discourses of the
1840s, its style, and its possibilities in the study of Thoreau and music, and the personality of the author. Richard Tuerk, "Thoreau's
Early Versions of a Myth" (10:32–38), finds that Thoreau's writings
were mythopoeic almost from the beginning. Both "Natural History
of Massachusetts" and "A Walk to Wachusett" are susceptible to
analysis in terms of "the archetypal monomyth of the hero's retreat
from society, his initiation, and final return." Joseph Campbell, *The
Hero with a Thousand Faces*, provides the theoretical framework.
See also Reginald L. Cook, "An Encounter with Myth at Walden"
(10:39–42). Lauriat Lane, Jr., "*Cape Cod*—Thoreau's Sandy Pastoral"
(11:69–74), finds the pastoral tradition crucial to understanding
Thoreau's travel book, heretofore regarded as merely a descriptive
narrative. It is "a sandy pastoral" because it is not sentimental but
ironic and complex (the senility of the Oysterman, the disagreeable-
ness of the Fool, the presentation of "a fallen, reptilian, anti-pastoral
world" like that of Melville's *The Encantadas*). The book presents a
parody of values associated with living with nature, and its conclusion
is the opposite of a ringing utterance of a pastoral prospect.

There was little criticism of Transcendental poetry. Melvin G.
Storm, Jr., in "The Riddle of 'The Sphinx': Another Approach" (*ESQ*
62:44–48), contends, among other things, that Thoreau made a more
satisfactory statement about the poem than did Emerson himself.
Richard Tuerk has incidental commentary on "The Sphinx" in "Emerson as Translator—'The Phoenix'" (*ESQ* 63:24–26), which is primarily a comment on Emerson's translation of a Persian poem from
the German version. Tuerk finds in it evidence of Emerson's critical
skill and possible influences on his own poetry.

iv. Criticism: Ideas

John Q. Anderson's monograph, *The Liberating Gods: Emerson on
Poets and Poetry* (Coral Gables, Fla., Univ. of Miami Press), as-

sembles Emerson's comments under headings suggested by the organization of "The Poet" (the nature of the poet, his function, his use of subject matter and form, and the ideal poet), with two final chapters: "Emerson on His Contemporaries" and "Emerson's Contribution to Poetic Theory." Throughout Anderson's essay, there is citation of Platonic and Neoplatonic origins of concepts and phraseology, especially as derived through the translations of Thomas Taylor, a dimension which should probably be regarded as the chief contribution of the study. Anderson places Emerson as theorizer midway between Wordsworth and Whitman.

A strong vindication of Emerson the philosopher is offered by William B. Barton in "Emerson's Method as a Philosopher" (*Emerson's Relevance Today*, pp. 20–28). According to Barton, Emerson is "among the first modern philosophers to set forth the outlines of a thoroughgoing process philosophy of organism founded on evolutionary principles." In this he is "at least as imposing as Bergson or Whitehead." In this achievement lies his modern relevance, along with his ideas on the identity of natural and moral ideas relevant to bridging the two cultures. As if to validate Barton's codification of Emerson's process philosophy, Leonard Neufeldt provides a detailed and sophisticated analysis of Emerson's most explicit epistemological treatise, "Intellect," in "The Vital Mind: Emerson's Epistemology" (*PQ* 50:253–70). The action of thinking, according to Neufeldt's analysis, is a natural ascension from a sensuous reciprocity with one's world to the level of the symbolic and abstract, an ascent for which Emerson's favorite metaphors are the plant, the expanding circle, and the ladder. "Emerson's epistemology ends as an argument for 'the vital mind.'"

Two other essays from the symposium, *Emerson's Relevance Today*, take up Emerson's anticipation of twentieth-century positions and concerns. Vivian C. Hopkins, "Emerson and the World of Dreams" (pp. 56–69) discusses the record of Emerson's own dreams and those of others in his journals, letters, etc., and the lecture on "Demonology," which Erich Fromm has called "one of the most beautiful and concise statements on the superior rational character of our mental processes in sleep." Whereas in Emerson's writings negative moods are occasional, not habitual, the opposite is true of his subconscious life. Of seventeen dreams which Emerson records, only one is truly pleasant. Although Emerson's record of his dreams is more impressive than their interpretation, he clearly anticipates present-day theories and methods. (Hopkins's analysis supports that of William E. Bridges; see *ALS 1969*, p. 6.)

A picture decidedly more mixed is presented by Mary Edrich Redding, "Emerson's 'Instant Eternity': An Existential Approach" (pp. 43–52). According to Redding, Emerson, unable to reconcile mind and matter philosophically, sought to do so through "pictures" or metaphorically. He did not, however, escape the pitfalls inherent in mistaking metaphors for reliable structures. Thus he gradually "drew away from the passionate inwardness of his reaction to the existence of death and . . . developed what became an increasingly structured definition of immortality." Two polar approaches of nineteenth-century thought meet in Emerson, the cognitive and the existential. But it was his existential approach which was inspirational for Thoreau and Whitman, not the cognitive. Although his structures strike us as "pasteboard and filigree," his existential utterances are haunting. (Throughout, Mrs. Redding glosses Emerson by means of quotations from Martin Buber, especially *I and Thou*.)

There were fewer commentaries of note on Thoreau's ideas. Jonathan Fairbanks, "Thoreau: Speaker for Wildness" (*SAQ* 70:487–506), has little new to say about the principal theme but some very provocative asides. For example, he discounts the now-standard argument that Thoreau was dramatically changed by his experience on Mount Katahdin. Perhaps Thoreau *should* have been deeply affected, but he was not. The reason, according to Fairbanks, is that Thoreau is a fluctuating and resilient thinker, not an evolving one.

William Bysshe Stein, "Thoreau's *A Week* and *Om* Cosmography" (*ATQ* 11:15–37) argues that Thoreau's first book "traces in consecutive stages the ascent of the true Self (loosely, the soul) to the sun where it is absorbed into the inevitable silence of the soundless *Brahman*." The "mythic scenario" of the "Hindu itinerary of the divine journey" is in four stages: (1) "waking dream" (Saturday, Sunday, Monday), (2) "waking sleep" (Tuesday, Wednesday), (3) "in dreams awake" (Wednesday, Thursday), and (4) awakening of the true Self (Friday). The book yields a number of illuminating parallels to Hindu thought and symbols, which Stein presses skillfully. For the past several years Stein has presented a number of studies designed to counter the widespread impression that Thoreau's Orientalism is mere window-dressing or, as Thoreau acknowledges, texts supplied after the sermon has been written. He has undoubtedly opened Thoreau's writings to new levels of insight, though at the cost of reductive readings to highlight the Oriental dimension. This body of commentary must be accommodated in any future synthesis of Thoreau's intellectual and aesthetic obligations. Stein also discusses "The Yoga of Reading in *Walden*" (*TSLL* 13:481–95).

v. Dissertations

More than thirty dissertations pertaining to Emerson, Thoreau, and the Transcendentalists were abstracted in *Dissertation Abstracts International* in 1971. This number makes individual commentary, even on the abstracts, impracticable. On the other hand, coverage of this body of material in standard listings is so spotty and difficulties of retrieving titles from *DAI* so great that, without some notice in *ALS*, many studies will be overlooked.

Among dissertations primarily concerned with Emerson, two focus on his literary techniques: David Whitten Hill, "Emerson's Search for the Universal Symbol" (32:2689A), and Elinore Hughes Partridge, "Emerson: A Stylistic Analysis of His Prose" (31:6564A). Three others take up his ideas: Constantine Santas, "Emerson's Theory of the Hero" (32:3329A); Donald Louis Gelpi, S.J., "Emerson's Philosophy of Religious Experience" (31:5461A); and Godefroy Midy, "Ralph Waldo Emerson's Philosophy of the Person" (32:2140A). The last two named both come from the Department of Philosophy at Fordham University. Two others are Erik Ingvar Thurin, "Love and Friendship: Emerson and the Platonic Tradition" (31:5429A), and James E. Mulqueen, "Emerson and Stevens: Transcendentalism and Radical Transcendentalism" (31:5418A). Wallace Stevens is said to have adopted his radical transcendentalism from George Santayana at Harvard. A related study is Marguerite LaVoy Kaiyala, "The Poetic Development of Theodore Roethke in Relation to the Emersonian-Thoreauvian Tradition of Nature" (31:3507A–08A), in which Roethke's early interest in the Concord writers is demonstrated through a study of manuscript evidence in the Roethke papers at the University of Washington.

Among dissertations dealing chiefly with Thoreau, there was a gratifying diversification of interest. Two dissertations focused on *A Week*: Gail Baker, "The Organic Unity of Henry David Thoreau's

A Week on the Concord and Merrimack Rivers" (31:5349A–50A), and James Karabatsos, "A Concordance to Henry David Thoreau's *A Week on the Concord and Merrimack Rivers*" (31:6012A). John F. Jaques, "The Discovery of 'Ktaadn': A Study of Thoreau's *The Maine Woods*" (32:3309A), was the other dissertation on a single work. The political essays are analyzed by Michael Glenn Erlich in "Selected Anti-Slavery Speeches of Henry David Thoreau, 1848–1859: A Rhetorical Analysis" (31:4929A–30A), a speech dissertation at Ohio State University. The mythic and conceptual, in various degrees, figure in four dissertations, the first another product of the philosophy department at Fordham: Gerald Joseph Galgan, "The Self and Society in the Thought of Henry David Thoreau" (32:2131A–32A); John Fulton Taylor, "A Search for Eden: Thoreau's Heroic Quest" (32:3334A); Philip Walter Eaton, "The Middle Landscape: Thoreau's Development in Style and Content" (32:1467A); and Louise C. Kertesz, "A Study of Thoreau as Myth Theorist and Myth Maker" (31:6615A). Literary relationships are the subject of Laraine Rita Fergenson, "Wordsworth and Thoreau: A Study of the Relationship Between Man and Nature" (32:1468A), in which both writers are found to have inherent instability in their views of nature; Miriam Alice Jeswine, "Henry David Thoreau: Apprentice to the Hindu Sages" (32:3254A–55A); and Edward C. Peple, Jr., "The Personal and Literary Relationship of Hawthorne and Thoreau" (31:4730A), of which *The Marble Faun* is said to be the "culminating expression."

Four dissertations were reported on Transcendentalists other than Emerson and Thoreau: Daniel R. Barnes, "An Edition of the Early Letters of Orestes Brownson" (32:906A); William George Heath, Jr., "Cyrus Bartol, Transcendentalist: An Early Critic of Emerson," (32:1474A–75A); Henry Lawrence Golemba, "The Balanced View in Margaret Fuller's Literary Criticism" (32:2641A); and Louis B. Weeks III, "Theodore Parker: The Minister as Revolutionary" (31:5515A–16A), a religion dissertation from Duke University.

There were also numerous general studies abstracted. Of these several were historically oriented: Robert D. Lewis, "Individualism and Associationism in American Literature, 1830–1850" (32:924A); Alfred R. Ferguson, "Reflections on Transcendental Abolitionist Perfectionism in American Life, 1830–1860: Biography of a Fantasy" (32:1420A–21A); and William C. Jones, "The New England Transcendentalists and the Mexican War" (32:360A). The last two cited both are products of the University of Minnesota history department. The course of Transcendental thought in later generations occupies three dissertations: Peter Herbert Barnett, "Retreat from Idealism: Emersonian Themes in American Religious Philosophy," (32:481A–82A), a philosophy dissertation at Columbia; Patrick G. Gerster, "Aesthetic Individualism: Key to the Alienation of the American Intellectual—Studies in Ralph Waldo Emerson, Henry David Thoreau and Walt Whitman" (31:4673A), another history dissertation from Minnesota; and Paul P. Reuben, "Dynamics of New England Transcendentalism in Benjamin Orange Flower's *Arena* (1889–1909)" (31:4731A–32A). Another attempt to relate Hawthorne to the Transcendentalists is Alfred F. Rosa, "A Study of Transcendentalism in Salem, with Special Reference to Nathaniel Hawthorne" (32:1485A). Finally, the Transcendentalists figure prominently in two studies of American interest in ancient literature: Lee Robert Newcomer, "Classical Mythology in the American Renaissance" (31:4730A), and Jacob P. R. Rayapati, "Early American Interest in Vedic Literature and Vedantic Philosophy" (32:397A).

This is a formidable output for a single year (nearly 10,000 pages). Whether or not these studies reach print (as some already have), their availability in their present form can enrich thin and impressionistic essays. It is of some significance that fully one-quarter of the number of dissertations reported were prepared outside departments of language and literature.

vi. Miscellaneous

Articles appearing in *ATQ* 11 and discussed separately above (Harding, Ross, Neufeldt, Harris, Lane, etc.) have been gathered and issued as *Artist and Citizen Thoreau,* edited by John J. McAleer (Hartford, Conn., Transcendental Books), with an introduction by the editor, "Thoreau's Reputation—Past and Present," and a "Verse Foreword" by Indira Gandhi.

Another publication of Transcendental Books (Hartford, Conn.) is Kenneth Walter Cameron's *Young Emerson's Transcendental Vision: An Exposition of His World View, with an Analysis of the Structure, Background, and Meaning of Nature* (*1836*). This is an abridgement and photoreprint of Cameron's *Emerson the Essayist*. Most of Volume 1 of the earlier work is intact, but some of the readings from

Volume 2 have been omitted. A few chapters are added, all of which seem to have been published earlier.

At the end of the year *ESQ* passed from the hand of its founder, editor, and most substantial contributor, Kenneth Cameron, to the Washington State University. Its emergence in a new format, from another coast, will no doubt be a principal feature of 1972.

Library of Congress

2. Hawthorne

Nina Baym

Although there were no major books on Hawthorne, the year's work comprised more than 75 published items and seventeen dissertations covering a wide range of topics. Quantitatively speaking, then, interest in Hawthorne continues and clearly will continue for some time to come. Too much of the published material, however, is disturbingly insubstantial—unoriginal, slight in scope, rarified in argument, and distressingly amateurish in learning, style, and critical method. It would seem that most of the people writing about Hawthorne at present subscribe to the interpretations and approaches laid down in the fifties, and doing so, have very little to say. The criticism is like puttering, or even fumbling, in a well-tended garden: here a weed is removed, there a drooping plant propped up, but the overall intention is to preserve, by iteration of the agreed-upon. If indeed the important work on Hawthorne has largely been done, then scholars ought to turn their attention elsewhere, no matter how much they admire the author and how central or great a writer he is. If previous criticism is incomplete or in error, then more of what is being done today ought to be vigorous, imaginative, and informed.

In the review that follows I will try to cover all published material except that appearing in foreign-language journals, and I will omit considering the dissertations, assuming that in due time they will appear in print. The major event of the Hawthorne year was the appearance of *The Nathaniel Hawthorne Journal*, a handsome, illustrated, hardbound annual of 308 pages. The journal is edited by C. E. Frazer Clark, Jr., and published in Washington, D.C. by NCR Microcard Editions. The journal focuses largely on textual and bibliographical matters, though it contains critical and appreciative articles as well. Most of its twenty-nine items are primary documents, suitably introduced by various Hawthorne scholars, from Clark's excellent collection. Much of the material in this group derives ultimately from the researches of George W. Holden, an early and accomplished Hawthorne collector and scholar. Some of these items, as well as the critical articles, will be noted further on in this review. Every Hawthorne scholar ought to examine the journal and consider how it adds to and alters the shape of Hawthorne studies.

i. Texts, Life, Reputation, Bibliography, Miscellaneous Editions

Although there was no new volume added to the Centenary Edition in 1971 (three are expected in 1972), the debate over its merits continued in reviews of the 1970 *Our Old Home* and in general estimates. Among these, Joseph Katz, "The Centenary Edition of the Works of Nathaniel Hawthorne: *Our Old Home*" (*NHJ* 1:287–89), deserves note as the most illiberal of the group, and deserves quotation as an example of an all but defunct style of critical polemic. "An edition of this kind," Katz declares, "has two side benefits, one positive, one negative. Positively, it provides a vast amount of information that can be mined by other students in many fields. This is good. Negatively, it provokes the amateur masquerading as a professional man into expressing his dismay that this stuff has nothing to do with literature. That is good too. At a time when evaluation of teachers and scholars is both important and difficult, self-exposure in a recognizable form ought to be particularly welcomed by anyone concerned with his own world." In contrast to this apocalyptic approach is O. M. Brack, Jr.,'s historical assessment of the edition, "The Centenary Hawthorne Eight Years Later: A Review Article" (*Proof* 1:358–67). This succinct piece makes two points. First, within the span of years that the edition has been underway its editorial principles have changed to cope with different editorial situations. Briefly, from a decision to follow a chosen copy-text faithfully, the editors have moved to a decision to mediate between surviving manuscripts and first editions on largely conjectural grounds. The Centenary is thus now printing texts which contain individual readings for which no existing source supplies authority. Second, modern popular-priced editions claiming to reprint the Centenary text turn out to have as many errors, or deviations from copy text as do the various editions which the Centenary was designed to rectify and supercede. Extrapolating from his collation of chapters 16, 21, and 23 of the Viking,

Harpers, and Bobbs-Merrill *Scarlet Letter*, Brack calculates that each
of these editions must contain some fifty errors; while the Riverside
Edition of 1883, supposedly the most corrupt edition, had sixty-two.
One would conclude from this that the Centenary may well have no
effect on the accuracy of the texts most people will read.

As an aid to biographical knowledge C. E. Frazer Clark, Jr., has
published a valuable "Census of Nathaniel Hawthorne Letters, 1813–
1849" (*NHJ* 1:257–82). The census lists 407 letters, giving date and
inscription for each, as well as present location. Manuscript materials
in *The Nathaniel Hawthorne Journal* include (1) two Hawthorne letters pertaining to a never-realized collaboration between himself and
Longfellow in starting a newspaper in Boston (pp. 3–11); (2) brief
materials relating to "Susan," Hawthorne's first love (pp. 12–17);
(3) a biographical sketch by James T. Fields (pp. 19–26); (4) an
account by Hawthorne's English friend Francis Bennoch of an outing
he and Hawthorne took together (pp. 29–45); (5) records of reminiscences by Elizabeth Hawthorne (pp. 67–69), Elizabeth Peabody (p.
70), James Upton (pp. 113–15), John L. O'Sullivan (pp. 117–21);
(6) a letter to Horace Conolly from Hawthorne (pp. 72–76); (7) a
contemporary genealogy (pp. 77–82); (8) a contemporary appreciation (pp. 213–27). Among primary materials published elsewhere is
a reprinting of F. B. Sanborn's 1908 *Hawthorne and his Friends* (*ATQ*
9sup.:3–24). Benjamin Lease in "Salem Vs. Hawthorne: An Early
Review of *The Scarlet Letter*" (*NEQ* 44:110–17) reprints an antago-
nistic review from the Salem *Register*, and recounts in part the local
furor when Hawthorne published "The Custom-House." C. E. Frazer
Clark, Jr., in "Hawthorne and the Pirates" (*Proof* 1:90–121), surveys
the English piracies preceding Chapman and Hall's edition of *The
Blithedale Romance*—the first English edition for which Hawthorne
was paid, but hardly the first English edition. Clark suggests that the
many piracies gave Hawthorne a visibility and popularity which
paved the way for his later, official English success. The article is
accompanied by seventeen beautiful plates and a 46-item checklist of
"Hawthorne title pages bearing English publishers' imprints, 1837–
1856."

In "Hawthorne, Park Benjamin, S. G. Goodrich: A Three-Cornered
Imbroglio" (*NHJ* 1:83–112), Lillian B. Gilkes studies the literary attitudes and policies of Benjamin (editor of the *New-England Magazine*) and Goodrich (editor of the *Token*), especially as they attacked

each other and published or encouraged Hawthorne. Gilkes finds
Goodrich a mercenary who preferred N. P. Willis to Hawthorne, while
Benjamin, devoted to the idea of a national literature, estimated Hawthorne highly. Edward C. Peple, Jr.,'s "The Background of the
Hawthorne-Thoreau Relationship" (*RALS* 1:104–12) doesn't dispute
that the actual acquaintanceship began in 1842 when Hawthorne
moved to Concord, but points out that because of mutual friends, especially Elizabeth Peabody and Emerson, "in all probability the men
knew about each other before they actually met." No doubt, but this
obvious inference scarcely warrants an article. B. Bernard Cohen's
"Hawthorne's Library: An Approach to the Man and His Mind"
(*NHJ* 1:125–39) studies the approximately 270 volumes either in
Hawthorne's private library or connected with him through members
of his family, "to consider the man in the context of the books which
he collected over many years." Cohen's basic interest is in marginalia;
his contention, which seems a non sequitur, is that Hawthorne was a
"normal" person, not an "eccentric," neither Hoeltje's plaster saint
nor Crews's "case."

Jennifer E. Atkinson's "Recent Hawthorne Scholarship, 1967–
1970: A Checklist" (*NHJ* 1:295–305) is unannotated and incomplete,
but two substantial bibliographical reviews did appear in 1971. Theodore L. Gross wrote a chapter on Hawthorne in a book by him and
Stanley Wertheim entitled *Hawthorne, Melville, Stephen Crane: A
Critical Bibliography* (New York, Free Press), pp. 1–100. The chapter is a numbered and indexed list of 196 entries, each providing summary and evaluation. The best-known books and articles through 1968
appear, though there is a heavy bias toward fifties criticism. Among
purely interpretive criticism, I counted fifty-seven items dating before 1950, forty-one dated 1960 and after, and ninety-four from 1950
to 1959. This may be an accurate reflection of the actual contours of
Hawthorne criticism, or it may simply represent the compiler's personal history. I found his summaries fine, but the evaluations have an
oddly elementary hortatory quality, betraying the fact that the book
is designed for beginners in criticism.

That indispensable work of bibliographical scholarship, *Eight
American Authors*, edited by James Woodress (New York: W. W.
Norton) has been completely and successfully revised. Walter Blair's
Hawthorne chapter (pp. 85–128) is a triumph. It follows the same
format as in the first edition, but conforms to the changed style of the

whole work, a brisk, concentrated style necessitated by the vastly increased quantity of scholarship covered. Materials reviewed run through 1969, and full as the chapter is, it is necessarily selective. Blair's own reaction to the material surveyed is that "a suggestion that four-fifths of the books and articles on Hawthorne now in the works be strangled and eaten seems no more than a modest proposal." Reporting on Hawthorne scholarship for 1970 and 1971, I note that the modest proposal has been disregarded.

Richard H. Rupp edited *The Marble Faun* for Bobbs-Merrill this year, and David B. Kesterson edited *Studies in "The Marble Faun,"* a collection of reprinted criticism, for Charles E. Merrill. J. Donald Crowley contributed *Nathaniel Hawthorne* to a series of introductions to authors published in England by Routledge and Kegan Paul, and in this country by Humanities Press in New York. It is a short book largely comprised of extracts from Hawthorne's writing which, together with commentary and analysis, are supposed to delineate the chief concerns and methods of the author. The extracts are well-chosen and skillfully interpreted.

ii. General Studies

The only study approaching book length is Michael Davitt Bell's *Hawthorne and the Historical Romance of New England* (Princeton, Princeton Univ. Press), a minor contribution which might more appropriately have been distilled into two or three articles. Historical romances of New England, Bell finds, waver between ideas of the Puritan as liberator and oppressor. Hawthorne reconciles this contradictory vision by portraying first-generation Puritans as liberators, second- and third-generation decadent Puritans as oppressors. Of course this sidesteps the basic question of the role of the Puritan community in *The Scarlet Letter*, or answers it by fiat. Hawthorne's main historical theme, Bell claims, is the decline in the American wilderness of the larger Old World personality into the narrow, tight New England character. A chapter on the treatment of the Hawthorne heroine seems to me especially weak, and the final chapter on the historical theme after *The Scarlet Letter* (the last three novels are considered to be "lesser" work) makes no reference to the historical romance of New England, and thus serves no identifiable purpose in the book.

History is also the concern of Leo B. Levy's " 'Time's Portraiture':
Hawthorne's Theory of History" (*NHJ* 1:192–200). Hawthorne sees
history as discontinuous; yet different epochs exhibit common dilemmas because "all are involved in the universal truths set forth in the
Providential vision." Levy's analysis, however, doesn't support his
thesis; it demonstrates rather that the theory of history is different
from work to work. Linear decline, linear progress, cyclical and providential structures all appear, so that Levy himself notes regarding
"My Kinsman, Major Molineaux" that "Hawthorne may have been
exercising the freedom to be inconsistent." Another focus of this article is patriotism, what Hawthorne thinks of it and how he depicts it.

Richard H. Fogle discusses "Hawthorne and Coleridge on Credibility" (*Criticism* 13:234–41), finding that both authors defend romance in terms of verisimilitude or truthfulness. "The sudden charm
. . . which moonlight or sunset diffuses over a known and familiar
landscape" is a true part of the landscape, which doesn't exist to an
observer apart from the light by which he sees it. In their similar defenses of romance, however, Hawthorne is more cautious and self-
deprecatory than Coleridge. Nina Baym's "Hawthorne's Women: The
Tyranny of Social Myths" (*CentR* 15:250–72) brings to bear ideas
and approaches from the field of women's studies on a topic which has
heretofore been purely descriptive (catalogues of females and their
traits) or male-centered Freudian and Christian analysis (woman as
fall and temptation to man, woman as male neurosis). The article sees
a difference in the depiction of women in the stories and in the long
romances, although women always offer the male protagonists release and fulfillment which, in their own personalities, they cannot
achieve. The stories embody a relatively simple primitivism, wherein
women represent a warm, loving domesticity to which is contrasted
the involuted, isolated rationalism of the male heroes. The male is
unable to accept the woman's natural and saving warmth, however,
for he sees it as threatening to the male rationality and rectitude
which he values. In the long romances the women are symbols of passion, imagination, and intellectual boldness in contrast to the social-
ized, conforming timidity of the men. The novels, however, go beyond their own female stereotyping to an awareness of the condition
of actual women in actual society, and even suggest a sense of the
connection between real conditions and sex stereotyping. This is most
obvious in *The Blithedale Romance* where feminist themes appear on

the novel's surface, but in *The Scarlet Letter*, where Hester broods over the lot of woman and the relationship between the sexes, as well as in *The Marble Faun*, such awareness sharpens and deepens his feminine portraits.

iii. Long Romances

In recent years "The Custom-House" has been increasingly examined as an integral part of *The Scarlet Letter* and as a significant essay-fiction in its own right. David Stouck, in "The Surveyer of the Custom-House: A Narrator for *The Scarlet Letter*" (*CentR* 15:309–29), takes the former position, while Paul John Eakin, "Hawthorne's Imagination and the Structure of 'The Custom-House'" (*AL* 43:346–58), argues the latter. Stouck argues that the voice of the narrator of *The Scarlet Letter* is identifiably the "I," the surveyer, in "The Custom-House." The protagonist of "The Custom-House" experiences a three-part drama: he returns to Salem to face his guilt-inspiring ancestors; he masters these ancestors symbolically through his power over the elderly customs officers; and he writes his romance, through which his guilt is released. Chillingworth, Dimmesdale, and Hester are all seen as projections of the narrator, and the root experience of all is his sense of isolation from the community. Eakin believes that the design of "The Custom-House" as a whole dramatizes Hawthorne's experience of the creative process. Its theme is the working, and the failure to work, of the imagination. "Hawthorne," or the character in the essay who represents him, finds that his subject is the living past, and that without distance from his topic he cannot write. "As soon as the life of the custom-house is a dream behind him, he can write about it." Though an interesting article, Eakin's piece does not fully cohere.

On *The Scarlet Letter* itself, Alex M. Baumgartner and Michael J. Hoffman produced a confused article entitled "Illusion and Role in *The Scarlet Letter*" (*PLL* 7:168–84), which says that Hawthorne believes man must escape from society's crippling roles and illusions while remaining in society, but at the same time believes that man's right perceptions will enable him to adjust socially. The point, of course, is that if society is comprised entirely of roles and illusions, then right perception must necessarily produce maladjustment. In any event, the moral argument in the article is conducted at some distance from the text. Clifford M. Caruthers, "The 'Povera Picciola' and *The Scarlet Letter*" (*PLL* 7:90–94) attempts, not very convincingly, to establish a popular novel called *Picciola* (1836) as a source for Hawthorne's work. Walter Shear, in "Characterization in *The Scarlet Letter*" (*MQ* 12:437–54) calls attention to Hawthorne's use of sentimental and melodramatic characterizations and devices. The novel is both a seduction tale and a triangle situation; it stresses the beneficent influence of a child; Dimmesdale is a man of feeling, and so forth. Hawthorne used such devices because he shared the nontheological morality of the sentimental melodramatists, but he used them ironically because he lacked their hope. The limits of this interesting approach are clearly seen in the fact that Hester cannot be contained within it, and Shear concludes that "there is a void in the middle of [her] character."

Terence Martin, in a fascinating article, discusses "Dimmesdale's Ultimate Sermon" (*ArQ* 27:230–40). Martin argues that although Dimmesdale's desire to terminate his public career by giving the Election Day sermon—to leave the stage, so to speak, with a great gesture —is an expression of his delusion and weakness, the sermon ironically is so powerful and persuasive that it converts and saves him. "God works in mysterious ways" one must conclude. Despite its unorthodox deployment of the sermon, Martin's reading takes for granted the existence in *The Scarlet Letter* of an orthodox theological frame where salvation and damnation are thematic realities; and clearly he believes that Dimmesdale does make a triumphant exit from the scene after all. An attack on *The Scarlet Letter* in particular and Hawthorne in general from a Marxist-Maoist point of view is the substance of "Bourgeois Social Relations in Nathaniel Hawthorne" by Caroline Borden (*L&I* 10:21–28). As an accepted classic author in a bourgeois society, Hawthorne serves the interests of his class by presenting an ideology in which social change is not possible. He broods over the mysteries of evil and human nature in such a way as to make the brooding itself the only possible action to take in regard to these mysteries; and he encourages, by romanticizing, a subjective individualism which gratifies the ego but avoids social problems. Hawthorne should realize that people do not have innate, nonsocial essences, but are essentially social beings formed by class circumstances. Ironically, Hawthorne is much more aware of the shaping power of society, and that power figures much more in his work, than Borden realizes. The romantic individualism that his characters display is often shown to be undermined precisely because it has a social dimension to it.

William L. Vance's "Tragedy and 'The Tragic Power of Laughter': *The Scarlet Letter* and *The House of the Seven Gables*" (*NHJ* 1:232–54) assumes that *The Scarlet Letter* is a true tragedy, *The House of the Seven Gables* a true tragicomedy, and that both rely on humor as part of their tonal texture. The assumption that the two works exemplify pure genres is not—and I think cannot be—demonstrated. The discussion of humor is hampered on the one hand by the inadequacy of a critical vocabulary for variations of humorous tone, and on the other by Hawthorne's own frequent lapses of humorous taste and control. Another article which attempts to make a genre interpretation of Hawthorne's second romance is James W. Mathews's "The House of Atreus and *The House of the Seven Gables*" (*ESQ* 63:31–36). The romance is likened to Greek tragedy in its structures and preoccupations, and particularly to the Oresteia. Clifford and Hepzibah are compared to Orestes and Electra, but neither Holgrave nor Phoebe in the one work, nor Clytemnestra in the other, have counterparts. Since, above all, the strong sexual and intrafamilial passions of the Oresteia are missing from *The House of the Seven Gables*, Mathews's article seems to me unconvincing. Sargent Bush, Jr., in " 'Peter Goldthwaite's Treasure' and *The House of the Seven Gables*" (*ESQ* 62:35–38) has produced a neat paper that points out many similarities in the works and argues effectively for the genesis, or trial run, of many of the romance's elements in the story. Jerome F. Klinkowitz, "In Defense of Holgrave," (*ESQ* 62:4–8) asserts that since Holgrave is a free spirit from the beginning he can change at any time; therefore his alleged conversion does not spoil the novel's logic.

Rex S. Burns, in "Hawthorne's Romance of Traditional Success" (*TSLL* 12 [1970]:443–54) interprets *The House of the Seven Gables* as a defense of the traditional idea of success: competence, independence, and morality, as finally realized by the surviving characters—against a new idea of success as purely material. The most interesting article of the year on this book is Edgar A. Dryden's "Hawthorne's Castle in the Air: Form and Theme in *The House of the Seven Gables*" (*ELH* 38:294–317), a phenomenological examination, à la Bachelard, of the house symbolism of the romance. The book, Dryden says, is an extended meditation on "the meaning of the house's situation in the world." Hawthorne wished both to live immersed in the world and withdrawn from it: the house is an attempt to mediate between these desires, and also between the self and the world. But it is successful neither as withdrawal nor as a mastery of social forms, and "the house of fiction" is not a solution either. Moving thus between the romance and the author, Dryden concludes that Hawthorne was never at home anywhere.

Gustaaf Van Cromphout, in "Emerson, Hawthorne, and *The Blithedale Romance*" (*GaR* 25:471–80), compares Emerson's views on reform in his "Lecture on the Times" with Hawthorne's in *The Blithedale Romance*, finding Emerson to be perhaps uncharacteristically Hawthornian in his essay. Both men opposed group reforms and found individual reformers to be narrow and amateurish in goals and procedures. An important source study on this romance is John C. Hirsch, "Zenobia as Queen: The Background Sources to Hawthorne's *The Blithedale Romance*" (*NHJ* 1:182–91). Hirsch discusses the "Zenobia tradition," which derived from Gibbon and had wide currency. He finds Hawthorne indebted specifically to William Ware's *Zenobia, or the Fall of Palmyra*, published in America in 1937. Hirsch's discussion of how Hawthorne interpreted the material he found—in the tradition Zenobia is destroyed by external repression, and therefore treated sympathetically, whereas Hirsch believes that Hawthorne shows Zenobia destroyed by internal fears and passions—does not depend on sources, but on internal evidence, and constitutes a second focus of the article. "*The Blithedale Romance*: The Holy War in Hawthorne's Mansoul" by Robert Emmet Whelan, Jr. (*TSLL* 13:91–110) is a fiercely Christian and allegorical interpretation of the book which treats Hawthorne as though he were John Bunyan. *The Blithedale Romance* is read as an allegorical description of the holy war between flesh or the selfish principle, in the person of Zenobia, and the spirit or love, in Priscilla. The Will is Hollingsworth, and his act of casting off Zenobia for Priscilla equals regeneration. This act is accomplished under the guidance of Intellect which is represented in all its functions by Coverdale. Whelan agrees with Hollingsworth that he has in effect murdered Zenobia, but since that act means inflicting death on the unregenerate self, finds it praiseworthy.

Two articles on the Coverdale-Zenobia relationship are by Donald Ross ("Dreams and Sexual Repression in *The Blithedale Romance*," *PMLA* 86:1014–17) and Ellen E. Morgan ("The Veiled Lady: The Secret Love of Miles Coverdale," *NHJ* 1:169–81). Ross sees the major conflict of the novel to be Coverdale's effort to suppress his sexual desire for Zenobia, or to translate related emotions into acceptable conduct, the ultimate example of which is his avowal of love for Priscilla. While dealing with these emotions Coverdale "stumbles on the fringes of his unknown mind" and "discovers mental phenomena beyond the influence and control of conscious thought." Morgan's article agrees with Ross at many points but has more a social than a psychological orientation. Morgan says that Coverdale loves Zenobia but turns away from her for fear of a rebuff. "Perhaps, feeling that Zenobia is a hopeless and humiliating and sexually awesome goal for which to strive, Coverdale keeps his desire for her concealed, possibly even from himself, and pretends that his real interests are the fathoming of her secrets and the winning of Priscilla." Morgan concludes astutely that neither Coverdale nor Zenobia is comfortable erotically outside the cultural stereotype of male dominance. For this reason Coverdale selects as his conscious love object the submissive Priscilla while Zenobia turns to the masterful Hollingsworth.

A note by William E. Graddy, "Another Error in *The Marble Faun*" (*ESQ* 63:26–27), points out a curious discrepancy between chapters 15 and 20 of the book. In the first conversation about the resemblance of Guido's demon to the model, Miriam denies the likeness; but in the later chapter the characters recall that it was Hilda who could not see the similarity. This is a nontrivial error in terms of the characterization of Miriam, and Graddy cannot understand (nor can I) how Hawthorne came to make it. There was only one article on *The Marble Faun*, Nina Baym's "*The Marble Faun*: Hawthorne's Elegy for Art" (*NEQ* 44:355–76). This continues Baym's series of articles reinterpreting the novels as tragic romances rather than as conservative-humanist documents. *The Marble Faun* coheres around Kenyon, whose story is—like Dimmesdale's, Holgrave's, and Coverdale's—that of the failed or destroyed artist. As an American innocent, Kenyon equates great art with inhibiting Victorian ideas of purity and denial of evil. His exposure to classic art as well as to the turbulent history of Miriam and Donatello teaches him that great art is built on confrontation, acceptance, and transcendence rather than on evasive idealism. Yet he is not a strong enough character to follow through: the demands of art are too great for him. He turns back to Hilda, the bowdlerizing copyist who personifies inhibition and refusal to acknowledge the truth of things. Turning to her, he saves his sanity but renounces art. Baym develops this thesis with attention to the use of art and the images of woman.

iv. Shorter Works

Donald A. Ringe, in "Hawthorne's Night Journeys" (*ATQ* 10:27–32), discusses the night journey structures of "My Kinsman, Major Molineux," "Young Goodman Brown," and "Ethan Brand." He says of the three protagonists that each "confronts a personal vision of evil and reacts in a manner that reveals his kinship to the demonic world he has created." Much the same point is made about "Young Goodman Brown" by Robert Emmet Whelan, Jr., whose article "Hawthorne Interprets 'Young Goodman Brown'" (*ESQ* 62:2–4) closely resembles Allison Ensor's piece (see *ALS 1970*, p. 31) in using the "whispers of the bad angel" passage from *The Scarlet Letter* as a gloss on Goodman Brown. When contrasted to Hester, who resists the demonic urge to believe evil of those about her, Brown's giving in to the temptation "reveals no one's depravity but his own." These two articles, like many others published this year, are competent but their theories are so shopworn that one is surprised to find them presented as fresh merchandise.

Two articles on "My Kinsman, Major Molineux" argue against the generally prevailing view that Robin, in casting off his kinsman, achieves identity and moral maturity. Sheldon W. Liebman offers a conventional but efficient analysis of character, action and imagery in "Robin's Conversion: The Design of 'My Kinsman, Major Molineux'" (*SSF* 8:443–57), showing that Robin has sunk into the ethic of the townspeople and become a victim of doubt and cynicism. Carl Dennis's "How to Live in Hell: The Bleak Vision of Hawthorne's 'My Kinsman, Major Molineux'" (*UR* 37:250–58) makes the point more forcefully and originally: moral strength, he argues, would require Robin to reject the townspeople, not the major. Rejecting him, he repudiates the notion of human kinship. "If Robin were to show true wisdom he would see that his uncle's degradation is only an intensified form of the rejection which he himself has received. . . . When at the crucial moment he fails to see his uncle as himself, he shows that in a moral sense he has learned nothing at all from his own sufferings."

The bibliography of "Rappaccini's Daughter" was enriched, or at least lengthened, by five items this year. Jeannine Dobbs's "Haw-

thorne's Dr. Rappaccini and Father George Rapp" (*AL* 43:427–30)
attempts to establish a model for Hawthorne's character in the controversial commune builder whose Utopian establishments always
featured a symbolic garden and a beautiful girl to tend it. Isadore H.
Becker's "Tragic Irony in 'Rappaccini's Daughter (*HussR* 4:89–93)
is yet another article comparing Hawthorne to Sophocles. A note by
Eberhard Alsen, "The Ambitious Experiment of Dr. Rappaccini" (*AL*
43:430–31) asserts that Rappaccini's ambitions are not merely intellectual; he intends to send his poisonous couple out into the world to
dominate and destroy it. Robert Emmet Whelan, Jr., says in " 'Rappaccini's Daughter' and Zenobia's Legend" (*RS* 39:47–52) that
Beatrice personifies love attempting to find its rightful place in Giovanni's heart, and that "Giovanni will find salvation only if he, through
truth, courage, and holy faith, purges this love of those elements foreign to its true nature." The poison, like the lady's veil in Zenobia's
legend, can be overcome; had Giovanni's faith been sufficiently
strong, his antidote would have worked. All interpretations that
assume a profoundly theological cast to Hawthorne's mind are re-
futed, it seems to me, by Hawthorne's journal comments concerning
his friend Melville's penchant for such speculations: "It is strange
how he persists . . . in wandering to and fro over these deserts, as
dismal and monotonous as the sand hills amid which we were sitting."
It is the word *monotonous* that sounds the death-knell of orthodox
readings; but when Dr. Johnson kicked the stone he did not put an
end to idealistic philosophy, and I imagine that the sizable corpus of
doctrinal interpretations of Hawthorne will go on growing.

The most sophisticated piece of work on the story this year is
Morton L. Ross's "What Happens in 'Rappaccini's Daughter' " (*AL*
43:336–45). Ross says that all attempts to make the story cohere
around a single interpretation overlook a serious flaw in its technique.
Simply, the reader does not need to try to figure out if Beatrice is pure
or not, because the author has told him that she is; but poor Giovanni
has only his unaided senses to go by. We condemn Giovanni on the
basis of our unearned knowledge, and both our condemnation as
well as Hawthorne's means of achieving it are unjust to Giovanni.
Even though this article has almost nothing in common with Whelan's, both founder on what is certainly the story's trickiest point: the
poison. Whelan is wrong in imagining that any amount of faith might
separate Beatrice from her poison, Ross in his assertion that Beatrice

is "really" pure. The story is clear on this—Beatrice is poisonous, and to separate her from her poison is to kill her. The story seems similar to several others in the canon—e.g., "The Man of Adamant," or "The Birthmark." Carnality, sexuality, or mortality are an inescapable part of humanity, and unless the hero prefers his sweetheart dead, he must learn to accept it. Moreover, carnal attraction is an inescapable part of human love, and if the hero cannot accept that, he cannot love. The image of poison implies an ambivalent authorial view of carnality or sexuality; it is different from Georgiana's birthmark which is ugly only to the warped view of Aylmer. Because the poison is real, acceptance is more than a matter of right perception; it is a matter of heart as well as head—it demands a total change of heart. Thus the story evades the analysis of "modern" critics who find the equation of sex and evil unhealthy; but it just as surely escapes traditional critics who insist that, if Beatrice is indeed poisonous, Giovanni is right in trying to redeem her.

"Egotism; or the Bosom Serpent" received attention in three articles. Sargent Bush, Jr., wrote a workmanlike scholarly piece called "Bosom Serpents before Hawthorne: The Origins of a Symbol" (*AL* 43:181–99) in which he pulls together the many strands in the tradition of the bosom serpent. He shows that bosom serpents figure in *The Fairie Queene*, in Puritan theology, in contemporary newspaper accounts (he adds three of these to the two already turned up by other students), and in earlier medical works, so that Hawthorne had a multiplicity of sources for his figure. A similar point is made with different evidence by Daniel R. Barnes in " 'Physical Fact' and Folklore: Hawthorne's 'Egotism; or the Bosom Serpent' " (*AL* 43:117–21). His point is that the striking similarities in various newspaper accounts of bosom serpents strongly suggest that none of them is really factual, but all are "apocryphal belief tales." He hypothesizes a living oral tradition of the bosom serpent current as early as 1828. In an entirely different vein, Mildred J. Travis states that "Egotism" was probably the source of James's "The Jolly Corner." Her "Hawthorne's 'Egotism' and 'The Jolly Corner' " (*ESQ* 63:13–18) points out that both stories have solipsistic heroes, gnawing inner secrets, alter egos realized as beasts of prey. James tried to improve on the source by decreasing its mechanical and romantic elements and augmenting its realism.

Margaret V. Allen's "Imagination and History in Hawthorne's

'Legends of the Province House'" (*AL* 43:432–37) is a general discussion of the theme of the whole group: given the fact that our
knowledge of the past is of dubious validity, art as an imaginative
recreation is possibly more vital, more valid, and more moral than
history. The title of Lawrence Clayton's "'Lady Eleonore's Mantle':
A Metaphorical Key to Hawthorne's 'Legends of the Province House'"
(*ELN* 9:49–51) describes the note's thesis. There is a unity in the
sequence for which the mantle is the figure. In one of the best articles
I've read in a long time, Robert Regan's "Hawthorne's 'Plagiary';
Poe's Duplicity" (*NCF* 25[1970]:281–98), the author speaks mostly
about Poe, but demonstrates that "The Masque of the Red Death" is
almost certainly a deliberate distillation of elements from "Legends
of the Province House." This could be called plagiarism but might
also be a superb critical parody of Hawthorne's use of the mysterious
and menacing.

Jack Kligerman applies the methods of transformational grammar
in "A Stylistic Approach to Hawthorne's 'Roger Malvin's Burial'"
(*Lang&S* 4:188–94) to show that Reuben is always the object of
sentences whether the subjects are internal or external forces. Thus
Reuben is a character who is acted upon; not until he tells Dorcas
about the killing does he become a free agent. There are two serious
objections to the argument: first, a perusal of just about any Hawthorne work will reveal the same grammatical characteristic, so the
grammar in this respect does not disclose anything specific to Reuben
Bourne as opposed to other Hawthorne characters. And, concluding
with an active sentence to show that Reuben has become an active
character, Kligerman ignores the final sentence of the story, where
poor Reuben is once again the passive object: "a prayer . . . went up
to Heaven from the lips of Reuben Bourne." John Halligan's "Hawthorne and Democracy: 'Endicott and the Red Cross'" (*SSF* 8:301–
307) argues that Endicott is a power-obsessed demogogue, and that
the portrayal shows a strong skepticism regarding democratic processes on Hawthorne's part.

Among the year's very best articles is "Hawthorne's 'Haunted
Mind': A Subterranean Drama of the Self," by Barton Levi St. Armand (*Criticism* 13:1–25). St. Armand discusses Hawthorne's obvious interest in and use of the "hypnagogic state," that semiconscious
interval just before falling asleep when "the closed eye beholds a

continuous procession of vivid and constantly changing forms." Hawthorne sought in this state an "opportunity to examine his own burdened conscience and seek through meditation a reunification of his shattered self." But, afraid of the price of experiencing the full cathartic effect of this process—the approach of uncontrol and madness, he draws back. "The process," St. Armand says, "of conjuring up psychological demons who will not stay within the safe limits of a fantasy world, and their subsequent banishment and replacement by allowable stereotypes is one of the unifying themes of Hawthorne's entire work." Helen L. Elias, in "Alice Doane's Innocence: The Wizard Absolved" (*ESQ* 62:28–32), asserts that the mysterious evil wizard in the story is really just as innocent as Alice and her murdered lover; all the story's evil is in the mind of Leonard, the protagonist-murderer. The exonerated wizard is compared to the victims of the witchcraft trials at Salem. A surprising amount has been written on this minor and awkward piece; I've always been convinced that it is a clumsy parody of contemporary Gothic, wherein Hawthorne tries to contrast the absurdities of manufactured melodrama to the real tragedies of history—but I have yet to see that idea advanced in print.

James G. Janssen's "Hawthorne's Seventh Vagabond: 'The Outsetting Bard'" (*ESQ* 62:22–28) studies "The Seven Vagabonds" in terms of its recognizable Hawthorne qualities as well as its view of the artist in society. Janssen shows that even at this early point in his career the alienation of the artist is part of Hawthorne's view of the vocation. What he does not note, however, is that the idea of the artist's alienation is different in the early and later parts of his career. Finally, there was some attention paid to Hawthorne apocrypha. Gerald R. Griffin in "Hawthorne and 'The New-England Village': Internal Evidence and a New Genesis of *The Scarlet Letter*" (*EIHC* 107:268–79) advances an admittedly circular but still effective argument. The story is by Hawthorne, he says, because it resembles *The Scarlet Letter*, especially in the Dimmesdale-like character of Mr. Forester. Moreover, if we assume that Hawthorne wrote it, we have an interesting genesis for *The Scarlet Letter*. And C. E. Frazer Clark, Jr., in "'The Interrupted Nuptials': A Question of Attribution" (*NHJ* 1:49–66), reprints the story and opts for including it in the canon. He provides a convincing chart comparing its motifs to motifs in nine other early Hawthorne stories. If the attribution is accepted, this would be the earliest published Hawthorne fiction (1827). The article is readable not only for its scholarship but for the excitement it conveys as Clark embarks on "the archeology of Nathaniel Hawthorne."

University of Illinois

3. Melville

Merton M. Sealts, Jr.

There were few striking developments in Melville study during 1971. The major scholarly work was the Northwestern-Newberry edition of *Pierre*; half of the other books are for class or reference use, and many of the articles and notes are gleanings rather than original harvesting. Fifteen items deal chiefly with *Moby-Dick*, clearly the favorite subject for critical interpretation. The total number of publications, seventy-one in all, stands well below the totals for 1969 and 1970, which were both in the mid-nineties; the number of dissertations on Melville remains high, however, with eighteen reported in *Dissertation Abstracts International* for 1971 (there were twenty-three in 1970) plus another from the University of Copenhagen in *Extracta* (1971).

i. Books

Most of the book-length publications of 1971 concerning Melville, since they deal with individual works, are covered in sections ii-vii below. In addition, four reference works devoted wholly or in part to Melville are examined in section viii.

Melville and His World, a volume in the Studio Book series (New York, Viking Press), reproduces over a hundred engravings, photographs, and miscellaneous manuscripts related to Melville's career. There is an accompanying narrative by Gay Wilson Allen (based chiefly on Anderson's *Melville in the South Seas* and Leyda's *The Melville Log*) that emphasizes Melville's years at sea; a brief bibliography, a chronology, notes on the pictures, and an index complete the volume. Melville's *Journal up the Straits*, edited by Raymond Weaver (New York, Cooper Square), is a reissue of the Colophon edition of 1935—the text of which was long since superseded by that established by Howard C. Horsford in *Journal of a Visit to Europe and the Levant* (1955).

One study of Melville published two years ago in Japan I have
not yet seen: *Kami no Chinmoku—Herman Melville no Honshitsu to
Sakuhin* by Takehiko Terada (Tokyo, Chikumashobo [1969]), treating "God's Silence—Melville's Character and Works." Two American
interpretations of 1971, *Melville's Drive to Humanism* by Ray B.
Browne (Lafayette, Ind., Purdue Univ. Studies) and a long chapter
in *A Cheerful Nihilism: Confidence and "The Absurd" in American
Humorous Fiction* by Richard Boyd Hauck (Bloomington, Ind.
Univ. Press), approach Melville from such divergent points of view
that they seem to be discussing two entirely different authors and
their works.

Ray Browne thinks other critics have made entirely too much of
Melville's supposed skepticism and despair. *Melville's Drive to Humanism*, by contrast, presents Melville as "an earthy, common, 'popular' person" who detested snobs and aristocrats, thought nonwhite
people superior to whites, espoused the political philosophy of
Thomas Paine but pulled back from "extremism in political organizations and deeds," mistrusted Emerson and the Transcendentalists,
doubted the sincerity of all ministers of the gospel, but favored wine,
sex, bawdy humor, popular art forms, and the tenets of humanism as
Browne defines it: "recognition of the innate value and dignity of
man" and belief that "the solution of man's problems lies not with any
supreme power but with man himself." Browne's no-nonsense readings of the various works draw on his previously published studies of
Moby-Dick, "Bartleby," *Israel Potter*, and *Billy Budd* (see *ALS 1966*,
p. 30; *ALS 1967*, p. 38; *ALS 1968*, pp. 42–43), always with an eye to
elements he can characterize as humanistic. His discussion mingles
shrewd observations, factual and typographical errors, and controversial pronouncements in fairly constant proportions throughout.
Melville's views, especially in the works after *Pierre* that get special
attention, seem much "less bleak" and less problematic to Browne
than to most critics; in the conclusion of *The Confidence-Man*, for
example, "there is a hint of hope," and the seeming ambiguity of *Billy
Budd* is really "only seeming." The story of the Handsome Sailor
demonstrates to Browne that

> Melville ended life with the same attitude he had held all of his
> mature years. He realized that in this man-of-war world in
> which Christ cannot exist, or has been extracted by God or ex-

pelled by man, the only hope of and for man is mankind itself.
. . . The feeling may be one of quiet acceptance but not at all
one of resignation. There is no sniveling, no regret, no remorse.
If life is that way, he seems to say, so be it. One must walk with
dignity and with hope. [p. 371]

Melville's persistent "hope," according to Browne, lies "with the
common man, the people, with democracy"; it is an affirmation of his
"basic humanism."

Hauck, by contrast, says less of Melville the man than of his
major writings. Though it ranges over American literature from the
colonial period to the present, *A Cheerful Nihilism* concentrates on
the work of Melville, Mark Twain, William Faulkner, and John
Barth, giving a long chapter to each; Melville is "the American author
who defined confidence and the absurd most completely and accurately." Hauck's supporting analysis is easier to sample than to sum-
marize; the following key passage illustrates his epistemological emphasis, his indebtedness to Camus, and his own "absurdist" reading
of *Moby-Dick*:

> The ambiguities of Melville's techniques reflect directly the
> theme in all his books that the meaning of the universe is not
> available to men because all evidence contradicts itself. This
> theme is the source of the tragedy of *Moby-Dick, Billy Budd,*
> and the last half of *Pierre.* It is also the source of the absurd
> humor in all of his books. This means that Melville's comedy
> always yields that laughter in the face of ambivalence which
> must be strictly arbitrary. Camus was probably not thinking
> of Melville's humor when he called *Moby-Dick* a truly absurd
> work. In context, Camus was apparently referring to *Moby-
> Dick* as one example of a book whose central point was the im-
> possibility of discovering abstract meaning. In this view, Ahab
> is the imaginative man, striking through the mask in the tradi-
> tionally heroic attempt to discover essential truth. Ahab ap-
> pears at first to be the absurd creator because he assigns
> meaning to the whale and shapes the quest for himself and the
> crew. On the other hand, Ahab does not re-create reality, solv-
> ing the problem of how to live in the world. In Camus's view,
> Ahab is the suicide. The creators in the book who "live doubly"
> —Camus's phrase—are Ishmael and Queequeg, and these two

are comic characters. And they have an affirmative sense of humor. [pp. 78–79]

Since Melville "displayed his sense of the absurd best in *The Confidence-Man*," according to Hauck, "and there showed most clearly how the comic response to the absurd is a matter of purely arbitrary confidence," I will return to Hauck's views in section v below, where his reading stands in contrast to other interpretations of the book as sharply as his general position on Melville differs from Browne's.

In *Olson / Melville: A Study in Affinity* (Berkeley, Calif., Oyez) Ann Charters surveys the late Charles Olson's long interest in Melville, perceptively analyzes his *Call Me Ishmael* (1947), and glances both at Olson's other pronouncements on Melville and his sometimes sulphurous comments on members of "the Melville lobby." There are accompanying photographs of Olson and of his house and neighborhood in Gloucester, Massachusetts.

ii. From *Typee* to *Moby-Dick*

Except for the incidental discussion in Hauck and Browne, relatively little of the work of 1971 concentrates on the works before *Moby-Dick*, though *Redburn* is something of an exception. Merlin Bowen, contributing a skillfully written introduction to a classroom edition of *Redburn* (New York, Holt, Rinehart and Winston) that uses the Northwestern-Newberry text of 1969, stresses "the approach of Melville's artistic maturity" in the book: as Melville dealt with the problems of composing *Redburn*, Bowen writes, he "found his way to the edge of a consistently symbolic vision of reality and to the possession of a style simple and strong enough to express it." Two articles also consider *Redburn*: a note on "Melville's Jackson: Redburn's Heroic 'Double'" by Charles N. Watson, Jr. (*ESQ* 62:8–10) and a longer discussion of "Melville's *Redburn* and the City" by Harold T. McCarthy (*MQ* 12:395–410). McCarthy holds that the sights of Liverpool, the example of Jackson, and the sufferings of the Irish emigrant passengers aboard the *Highlander* awaken in Redburn "the understanding, compassion, and inclusive love" characteristic of Ishmael in *Moby-Dick*.

"Melville and the Deformation of Being: From Typee to Leviathan" by James L. Babin (*SoR* 7:89–114) is an analysis of Melville's early work with reference to the thought of Eric Voegelin. Babin's article, concentrating on *Typee, Mardi,* and *Moby-Dick,* takes *Typee* and *Mardi* as illustrating, respectively, the principal ways in which Americans have attempted to escape the conditions of man's existence in time: either through "return to an intimate relationship with primal nature," from which man's self-consciousness has separated him, or through some attempted realization in the actual world of "the yearnings of that self-consciousness." But "the mystery of human existence" is not so easily resolved; "both the return to the natural world and the visionary quest" are shown in the two books to be "paths to self-destruction." In *Moby-Dick,* by contrast, Babin sees the Melvillean protagonist for the first time directly facing the condition of his existence by actually going whaling. Ishmael thus "confronts Leviathan, which he expects, but he also discovers Ahab, whom consciously he does not expect." Ahab's hatred for the source of being itself constitutes a "wilful deformity," exemplifying that failure of transcendence that Voegelin refers to as "closure."[1] Ishmael's crucial choice, says Babin, is "whether to persist in his oath to destroy Leviathan, or whether to accept Leviathan's mystery and might and the dependent condition of his own existence. Ishmael survives because Ahab, the impulse toward closure, does not."

Babin's analysis of *Moby-Dick* is likely to please those interpreters who find Ishmael's vision of existence more congenial than Ahab's, who speak of Ishmael's "salvation" as well as his physical survival, and who tend with Babin to identify the Ishmaelian outlook as Melville's own—for example, Ray Browne or Benjamin L. Reid, who sees a "saved" Ishmael as "the embodiment and the spokesman of Melville's own superb courage and intelligence" (Reid, "Leviathan Is the Text," *Tragic Occasions: Essays on Several Forms,* Port Washington, N.Y., Kennikat Press, pp. 95–135). But Richard Blau, in "Melville in the Valley of the Bones" (*ATQ* 10:11–16), maintains that it is Ahab rather than Ishmael who pushes to the limits—external and in-

1. Such "deformation of personal and social reality," Voegelin himself observes elsewhere, comes with "the fateful shift in Western society from existence in openness toward the cosmos to existence in the mode of closure against, and denial of, its reality. As the process gains momentum, the symbols of open existence—God, man, the divine origin of the cosmos, and the divine logos permeating its order—lose the vitality of their truth and are eclipsed by the imagery of a self-creative, self-realizing, self-expressing, self-ordering, and self-saving ego that is thrown into, and confronted with, an immanently closed world." See his "Postscript: On Paradise and Revolution" (*SoR* 7:27).

ternal—of man's being. Ahab acts as surrogate both for Ishmael and
for Ishmael's readers in projecting "our darkest desires"; in him there
is "something abhorrent as well as exemplary." Ishmael, who en-
deavors "to safeguard himself and his reader from the direct consequences" of Ahab's "extremism of being," is not Melville's protagonist
but "a prime witness" of Ahab's action, one who survives what he has
seen "in much the same way that we survive his book." Like Blau,
Grant McMillan also regards Ishmael as the retrospective narrator
rather than as an actor. In "Ishmael's Dilemma—The Significance of
the Fiery Hunt" (*CentR* 15:204–17) McMillan describes Ishmael the
narrator as seeking "a conversion factor for translating material objects and experience into spiritual significance" without following
Ahab into madness and self-destruction. As he oscillates between a
materialistic and an allegorical interpretation of the voyage, according to McMillan, Ishmael's ambivalence "reveals itself in the evasive-
ness, the circumlocutory structure of his narrative"; what he finally
achieves is not reconciliation or salvation but only a retreat from "the
painful examination of his experiences."

    A differing contrast of Ahab and Ishmael is drawn by Daniel C.
Noel in "Figures of Transition: *Moby-Dick* as Radical Theology"
(*CC* 20[1970]:201–20): Ahab, he contends, is not "Melville's norma-
tive figure" as the "Death-of-God" school of radical theologians sup-
poses. Noel, author of a dissertation on the religious and psychological
implications of Melville's imagery (see *ALS 1967*, p. 47), charges
that Gabriel Vahanian and Thomas J. J. Altizer "have missed much of
what *Moby-Dick* has to say theologically," largely because "they
have missed the way Melville has of saying it." At the center of Melville's vision Noel finds such "transfigured" characters as Queequeg,
Bulkington, and Ishmael and such dynamic images as that of the
spiral, which not only signifies change but also reconciles "what
throughout the early Melville was a conflict between circle images
of regression and linear images of aggression."

    How the circle imagery of *Moby-Dick* functions in "The Grand
Armada," "The Castaway," "The Chase," and the "Epilogue" is explored in "Circles and Orphans" by Darrell E. Griffiths (*BBr* 24:68–
81), who observes that the recurrent pattern involves a transient
interlude both preceded and followed by chaos, and that, upon its
passing, a waif, an orphan, or a castaway frequently appears. The vision in the circle, according to Griffiths, "is not only 'ungraspable' and

fatal, but there seems no way of knowing how trustworthy the vision is or to what extent it reflects the viewer." In general, he concludes, the circle symbolizes an experience that Melville conceived as repetitive rather than progressive: "Man is on the circle's circumference, forever tracing the 'eternal round' and occasionally making brief forays into the 'calm' of its center." Another circular device in *Moby-Dick* is examined by Daniel H. Garrison in "Melville's Doubloon and the Shield of Achilles" (*NCF* 26:171–84), who persuasively demonstrates "how Melville has shaped a technique of the earliest European epic," the *Iliad*, to his own contrasting views and purposes. For Ahab, "the doubloon is as much a symbol of contracted vision as the shield is of Achilles' expanded vision," Garrison writes; for Ishmael, it is representative of "ambiguous double vision," a talisman of both "withdrawal and redemption," since in Spanish *Quito* means "withdraw,' but it also means 'redeem, set free.'" Where Homer is "primarily affirmative," *Moby-Dick* "contains a strong element of the everlasting nay," for Melville "hints that the coin means nothing at all, and he implies that a balanced view of things leaves open only one course of action: withdrawal (*Quito*)." Along with Blau, McMillan, and Griffiths, Garrison thus takes a less sanguine view of Ishmael's role than do Babin, Reid, and Noel.

That both Ishmael and Ahab achieve "God-realization" through contrasting paths of death and resurrection is among the observations of H. B. Kulkarni in *Moby-Dick: A Hindu Avatar, A Study of Hindu Myth and Thought in "Moby-Dick"* (Logan, Utah State Univ. Monograph Series 18,ii[1970]). The core of Kulkarni's provocative seventy-page essay is an examination of various forms of sacrifice in *Moby-Dick*, as in his earlier article on the same subject (see *ALS 1969*, p. 40). Among the principal additions in this longer study are a critique of previous scholarship dealing with Melville's knowledge of Hindu myth, such as the work of James Baird, H. Bruce Franklin, and John Seelye; an explication in mythological terms of "The Sphynx," "The Doubloon," the "Epilogue," and other key passages; and a consideration of the White Whale as representing both the creative and the destructive forces of life, like the Hindu Vishnu and Siva. In the Hindu perspective, Kulkarni writes, "the appearance of opposites is fused into the oneness of reality. This is the ultimate vision of *Moby-Dick*." The intention of his study is to bring out every possible reflection of specifically Hindu myth and thought; at the same time, holding that

Melville "presents a supreme example of mythological synthesis," he recognizes the "subtle interaction" of Hindu elements with Christian, Islamic, and Egyptian symbolism. Though some of Kulkarni's specific interpretations seem tenuous, his case for reading *Moby-Dick* in other than exclusively Western terms is truly impressive.

Several studies of possible sources and analogues of *Moby-Dick* also refer to a variety of mythological, religious, and literary traditions. Mario D'Avanzo in "Ahab, The Grecian Pantheon and Shelley's *Prometheus Unbound:* The Dynamics of Myth in *Moby Dick*" (*BBr* 24:19–44) cites those Greek myths and their romantic adaptations that in his view bring out the design, the artistry, and the meaning of Melville's book. David H. Hirsch in "Verbal Reverberations and the Problem of Reality in *Moby Dick*" (*BBr* 24:45–67) suggests that "Yojo," the name of Queequeg's idol-god, is a pun on the Hebrew name of Jehovah ("YHWH") and learnedly explores the pun in conjunction with another Hebrew word that transliterates into "Leviathan." He sees both aesthetic and thematic implications of the juxtaposition of "Yojo's diminutiveness as opposed to Moby-Dick's magnificence," his "limited presence as opposed to the White Whale's ubiquity." In a further generalization Hirsch suggests that Melville's "multivalent 'reality'" grows out of "a belief in the ultimate potency and generative capacity of language itself." Janez Stanonik, examining "The Sermon to the Sharks in *Moby Dick*" (*AN* 4:53–60), finds "a clear-cut parody" of such medieval sermons as St. Francis of Assisi preaching to the birds and St. Anthony of Padua addressing the fishes. As for Melville's literary indebtedness, Edward Stone proposes the schoolmaster in Thomas Hood's poem "The Dream of Eugene Aram" (1829) as the original of "Melville's Late Pale Usher" (*ELN* 9:51–53); Keith Huntress thinks "The Lee Shore" chapter may derive in part from Cheever's *The Whale and His Captors* ("Melville, Henry Cheever, and 'The Lee Shore,'" *NEQ* 44:468–75); and Helen P. Trimpi points again to the analogous theory and practice of Sir Walter Scott (see *ALS 1967*, p. 46, and *ALS 1969*, pp. 40–41) in distinguishing five "Conventions of Romance in *Moby-Dick*" (*SoR* 7:115–29).

iii. Pierre

The sixth volume of the Northwestern-Newberry Edition of Melville to be published is *Pierre; or, The Ambiguities*, edited by Harrison

Hayford, Hershel Parker, and G. Thomas Tanselle (Evanston, Ill., Northwestern Univ. Press). Along with the customary textual apparatus assembled by the editors, this volume includes an unusually detailed Historical Note in which Leon Howard discusses the composition and first publication of *Pierre* and Hershel Parker traces its reception and later critical history. Howard is particularly concerned with Melville's shifting attitudes toward the book as it took form in 1851 and 1852; Parker has turned up new evidence to show that *Pierre* was indeed "a disaster for Melville," both financially and critically. Attempts of a few contemporary reviewers to comprehend the book "were submerged in the foul wash of publishing gossip, old literary feuds, new personal attacks, and morally and aesthetically outraged diatribes." As for its standing today, in Parker's well-chosen words, "Critics are still confused by the extent and the function of autobiographical elements, by Melville's intentions and actual accomplishments in plot and style, by the book's precise relationships to its literary ancestors, and—most conspicuously—by the meaning of the set-piece which constitutes the philosophical crux of the novel," Plinlimmon's pamphlet.

The range of critical discussion over the years is well represented in Ralph Willett's compilation of twenty-four selections, *The Merrill Studies in "Pierre"* (Columbus, Ohio, Charles E. Merrill), which opens with extracts from Evert Duyckinck and Fitz-James O'Brien and closes with a complete essay of 1970: Raymond J. Nelson on Pierre as author of his own story.

iv. The Tales

Of nine articles on the shorter fiction of 1853–1856, four deal with "Bartleby." James K. Bowen quotes *The Myth of Sisyphus* to counter those critics who assess "Bartleby" "in absurd terms" and thus do "a disservice to both Melville and Camus" ("Alienation and Withdrawal Are Not the Absurd: Renunciation and Preference in 'Bartleby the Scrivener,'" *SSF* 8:633–35). Leo F. McNamara, comparing "Subject, Style, and Narrative Technique in 'Bartleby' and 'Wakefield'" (*MichA* 3,i:41–46), distinguishes "what Melville and Hawthorne share and how they differ, as artists and as men, in face of the problem of the isolated individual, the isolated person," discerning "in 'Bartleby' Melville's troubled, restless putting questions to the world

at large (and to Hawthorne in particular?), and in 'Wakefield' the
tones of response: apologetic, self-deprecatory, not without compassion, but in effect cool and unyielding." Liane Norman, considering
"Bartleby and the Reader" (*NEQ* 44:22–39), emphasizes "the reader's implication in a puzzling, disturbing, and even accusing experience": "As a consequence of recognizing that he shares the Lawyer's
assumptions and attitudes to a large extent, the reader is made to find
the Lawyer ultimately wanting in humanity and to recognize Bartleby, who disrupts the functioning of what the Lawyer represents, as an
extreme example of one who is protected and even celebrated by the
laissez-faire, democratic, and Christian code of value."

In "Hautboy and Plinlimmon: A Reinterpretation of Melville's
'The Fiddler'" (*AL* 43:437–42) R. K. Gupta takes issue with critics
who see Hautboy as embodying "Melville's concept of ideal human
qualities," arguing that like Plinlimmon in *Pierre*, Hautboy negates
"the heroic ideal"; Gupta traces the difficulty in interpreting "The
Fiddler" to Melville's ironical treatment of Helmstone, his unreliable
narrator. Frederick Asals also stresses Melville's narrator in discussing
"Satire and Skepticism in *The Two Temples*" (*BBr* 24:7–18); noting
the increasing skepticism the narrator displays in acting out his successive roles, Asals relates this element in the diptych to Melville's
own epistemological preoccupations.

Carolyn L. Karcher, considering "The 'Spiritual Lesson' of Melville's 'The Apple-Tree Table'" (*AQ* 23:101–09), calls it both a topical
satire on the spiritualist cult of the 1850s and an indictment of the
orthodox Christian belief in a bodily resurrection. Marvin Fisher, in
"Bug and Humbug in Melville's 'Apple-Tree Table'" (*SSF* 8:459–
66), thinks the story an elaboration of controversy about "the existence of the soul and the hope of immortality." Seeing "Thoreau's bug"
in the conclusion of *Walden* becoming "Melville's humbug," Fisher
writes that "to force a correspondence between the birth of an insect
and the emergence of the soul" appears in Melville's story only as
"sentimental at best and silly at worst." In another article, "Melville's
'Tartarus': The Deflowering of New England" (*AQ* 23:79–100), Fisher argues that through the allegory of "The Tartarus of Maids" Melville is explicitly and implicitly denouncing industrialism, "setting the
factory and its machines in opposition to the warmth and fertility of
both nature and women." The sketch illustrates "Melville's method of
artistic concealment," according to Fisher, who advances the "overall

thesis" that "the fifteen short stories which Melville wrote between 1853 and 1856 constitute important examples of advanced experimental narrative and symbolic technique as well as some penetrating attempts to define and evaluate American manners, morals, and institutions."

v. Israel Potter and The Confidence-Man

Recent critical interest in *Israel Potter* has tapered off but *The Confidence-Man* continues to draw attention. Melville's transformations of Franklin and Emerson in the two books are compared by Martha Banta in "The Man of History and the Mythy Man in Melville" (*ATQ* 10:3–11), which examines how Franklin and Winsome-Emerson function in their respective contexts and considers their implications for Melville's myth-making. Other studies emphasize the title character of *The Confidence-Man*. In 1969 Johannes D. Bergmann identified "The Original Confidence Man" as William Thompson, a real life criminal of Melville's day (see *ALS 1969*, p. 48); Michael S. Reynolds covers essentially the same ground in "The Prototype for Melville's Confidence-Man" (*PMLA* 86:1009–13). That the Confidence-Man is "a (literal) devil" has been a commonplace among such critics as Elizabeth Foster, John W. Shroeder, and Hershel Parker; Shroeder reaffirms the point in "Indian-Hating: An Ultimate Note on *The Confidence Man*" (*BBr* 24:1–5), which reviews the conclusions of his influential article of 1951 on Melville's sources and symbols. The devil's antagonist in *The Confidence-Man*, according to Shroeder, is the Indian-hater, whom he still regards as "the one sound man and the one sane hope" in the book. But now, acknowledging that there is no full-fledged Indian-hater aboard the *Fidèle*, Shroeder has come to think that the absence of such a figure is "a disastrous lack. The sway of the confidence-man is unopposed. We have legends of a hero who knows just what the Devil is, and who can handle him— *and the legends are all we have*." This "quite bleak, hopeless, desperate" situation characterizes for Shroeder the "final statement" of "the thoroughly Timonized Melville."

The Confidence-Man as devil is a guiding idea of Hershel Parker's annotated edition of *The Confidence-Man* (New York, Norton), which brings together much useful material: a textual appendix that includes "The River"; a compilation of "Backgrounds and Sources" featuring a chronological survey of Melville's relations to the Transcendentalist movement; selections from contemporary reviews and subsequent criticism; and a fourteen-page annotated bibliography compiled by Watson G. Branch (one item listed under "1971" will not be found elsewhere). In the section of criticism are four previously unpublished notes. Branch argues that the mute of chapter 1 is indeed "an avatar of the Confidence Man" ("The Mute as 'Metaphysical Scamp,'" pp. 316–19), and Brian Higgins shows how "an awareness of the pervasive Christian references" in the Winsome-Egbert episode "is essential to an understanding of its satiric intention, while a knowledge of Plinlimmon's Pamphlet in *Pierre* makes all the clearer the nature of Winsome's and Egbert's offenses" ("Mark Winsome and Egbert: 'In the Friendly Spirit,'" pp. 339–43). In "'The Story of China Aster': A Tentative Explanation" (pp. 355–56) Parker speculates about the story's possible autobiographical and satirical elements; in "Private Allegory and Public Allegory in Melville" (pp. 285–86), under the pseudonym of "Samuel Willis"—an alias of "the Original Confidence-Man," he draws a distinction between "the 'Devil-in-disguise' allegory" of the book as a whole, which he calls "public and conventional" in the manner of Hawthorne's "Celestial Railroad," and the deliberate concealment that he thinks Melville practiced in several of his own short stories.

That the Confidence-Man is wholly diabolic, as Parker and Shroeder believe, is by no means a unanimous critical verdict, however. Warner Berthoff, Paul Brodtkorb, and Frank Jaster have recently offered other interpretations (see *ALS 1969*, pp. 48–49, and *ALS 1970*, pp. 47–48); now Richard Boyd Hauck in *A Cheerful Nihilism* (pp. 112–30) writes of him not only as "a multiple mythical figure, appearing to be Christlike and Satanic at the same time," but as a "lightbringer" whose operations, though admittedly ambiguous, "are not destructive but educative." Melville's real subject, he thinks, "is not the character of the Confidence-Man but the confidence of the Confidence-Man," and what "confidence" means "is both the great joke and the moral of the book." Hauck puts it this way:

> The center of the circle of truth is not ours to know. If we are to have any truth, we must create it. An act of faith is required, yet at the same time an act of faith is irrational and foolish. The question the book asks is why do men not accept the ab-

surd act of confidence as the only creative act open to them. All the reasons that all of the potential victims give for not doing so are under satirical attack. . . . The joke, finally, is on the reader. He must accept the Confidence-Man's message, yet he does not dare accept it. . . . The Confidence-Man and *The Confidence-Man* admonish us to recognize that we, too, are men dependent on confidence in our confidence and thus must be Confidence-Men or nothing. [pp. 128–29, 130]

vi. The Poetry

On the Slain Collegians: Selections from the Poems of Herman Melville, edited by Antonio Frasconi (New York, Farrar, Straus and Giroux), contains all or parts of eleven poems (ten from *Battle-Pieces* plus "Billy in the Darbies") illustrated by Frasconi's striking woodcuts. " 'Drum Taps' and *Battle Pieces*: The Blossom of War" by John P. McWilliams, Jr. (*AQ* 23:181–201) is a comparative study of the war poetry of Whitman and Melville, examining "the unfolding of the war in the terms in which the poets themselves saw it." Melville, sharing "the puritan impulse to view history typologically," employs themes and characters from *Paradise Lost* and the Bible both "to assert a providential view of history" and "to impart an heroic and cosmic grandeur" to the tragic events of the war, according to McWilliams, but certain of the poems and the prose Supplement reveal his disillusionment and express his characteristic inconclusiveness and inconsistency. "One leaves Melville with a feeling of having witnessed universal struggle and historical tragedy, but a doubt as to their resolution. 'Drum Taps' offers a limitless love for suffering humanity and implies that nothing else matters."

Totally contrasting interpretations of *Clarel* are given by Joseph G. Knapp in *Tortured Synthesis: The Meaning of Melville's "Clarel"* (New York, Philosophical Library) and Stanley Brodwin, "Herman Melville's *Clarel*: An Existential Gospel" (*PMLA* 86:375–87). Father Knapp's monograph sets forth the position he developed in his doctoral dissertation and outlined in an earlier article (see *ALS 1970,* p. 48): the thought and art of *Clarel* move toward a "dynamic synthesis" of the conflicts in post-Civil War America and in Melville himself. Like Clarel in the poem, Melville avoided identification with either those "Yea-Sayers" such as Derwent "who do not question their times" or their opposites, the existentially alienated "Nay-Sayers," Celio, Mortmain, and Ungar. On the evidence of *Clarel*—especially its "Epilogue"—Knapp holds that by the mid-1870s Melville had freed himself from "the despair of *The Confidence-Man*" and achieved an "ultimate wisdom" of endurance that has religious implications but stopped somewhat short of conventional religious allegiance. But Brodwin, characterizing *Clarel* as "an anti-gospel," contends that its "overwhelming thrust of existential despair" belies the "forced and unconvincing affirmation of immortality" in the "Epilogue": "The most that can be said is that Melville does not take a totally nihilistic view," since the action of the poem ends with Clarel still pursuing his quest for faith. Though the narrative is structured by "the Magi-search for the star of God," with Derwent, Vine, and Rolfe as its three Magi, the dominant themes in Brodwin's reading are predominantly negative: "isolation and alienation, the failure of reason, the agonized freedom to choose from among a welter of conflicting and paradoxical faiths, the death of God, and, above all, death's stamp of limitation on man."

vii. Billy Budd, Sailor

A brief note on "Melville's *Billy Budd*" by Blair G. Kenney (*AN&Q* 9:151–52) links "'Starry' Vere" and the legal principle *stare decisis*, "to stand by past decisions," a principle to which the captain as judge assents, though "against his will." Citing Vere's "names and titles," Kenney regards him as both "a 'strict constructionist'" and "a just man." "But Laugh or Die: A Comparison of *The Mysterious Stranger* and *Billy Budd*" by Ruth Miller (*LHY* 11,i[1970]:25–29) postulates that "Mark Twain never conceded, never gave in to total despair," but in *Billy Budd* "Melville was totally unable to renew his belief in goodness as a possible mode of existence in this world." Detecting an absense of humor and "a growing sense of compression" in his story, the author remarks that "The vital, the uncontained, the expansive Melville who wrote *Moby Dick* is gone."

That the tone of *Billy Budd* differs significantly from that of Melville's earlier writing is also the position of Bernard Rosenthal in "Elegy for Jack Chase" (*SIR* 10:213–29). Rosenthal interprets the book as "a deliberate farewell to that quest for a spiritually ordered world which first received artistic form in *Typee*." Jack Chase had emerged in *White-Jacket*, according to this ingenious argument, as Melville's recurrent symbol for such a world, which Rosenthal finds recapitulated once more in *Billy Budd* aboard Billy's first ship, the *Rights-of-Man.* Contrasting with this "dream world of innocence" is the real world of the *Bellipotent*, where Billy, like his predecessors among Melville's questing heroes, "learns the painfulness of experience"; it is on the second ship that he confronts John Claggart. As both Redburn and White Jacket are antecedents of Billy, Rosenthal reasons, so both Jackson and Jack Chase must anticipate the complex figure of Claggart, who is also a double of Billy himself; behind all of these interrelated characters stands another seaman, Schriften in Marryat's novel *The Phantom Ship* (1839), whom Rosenthal had previously nominated as Jackson's prototype ("Melville, Marryat, and the Evil-Eyed Villain," *NCF* 25[1970]:221–24). In the *Bellipotent*'s nightmare world of experience there is no redeemer—no Jack Chase or Jesus Christ. Billy, Claggart, and the "pathetic" Vere, as Rosenthal calls him, are all lost and helpless victims, and it is a "world weariness" akin to Melville's own that, in Rosenthal's words, "leads Billy to will his own death on the scaffold"—a controversial inference.

Howard P. Vincent, in *Twentieth Century Interpretations of "Billy Budd"* (Englewood Cliffs, N.J., Prentice-Hall), has edited the third recent collection of critical essays on the book; his volume and those compiled by William T. Stafford and Haskell S. Springer (see *ALS 1968*, p. 31, and *ALS 1970*, p. 35) differ less in their coverage of the critical spectrum than in size, organization, and associated apparatus. Vincent provides a ten-page introduction that suggests "a possible semibiographical, symbolic interpretation of the composition of *Billy Budd*"; along with twelve varied "Interpretations" there are eleven briefer selections, a chronology, and a short bibliography.

viii. Miscellaneous

Melville's relationship with the Young America group between 1847 and 1852 is the subject of two essays: "Melville and the Young America Movement" by Leonard Engel (*ConnR* 4,ii:91–101), which derives largely from Perry Miller's *The Raven and the Whale*, and "German Melvill i 'Molodaja Amerika'" by Ju. V. Kovalev (*VLU* 2:39–48). Kovalev, author of a recent monograph on Young America, charges that American scholars have underrated Melville's affiliations with the group and "the influence of 'loco-foco' literary ideas upon his work."

A reproduction in full color of Melville's copy of the contract with Harper and Brothers for *The Whale* (*Moby-Dick*) and a black-and-white reproduction of his contract with Richard Bentley for an untitled work (*The Whale*) are features of the initial volume of *Proof* (1:iii–vi,4–5); an accompanying note by Harrison Hayford considers the bearing of information derived from the contracts on certain differences between the English and American editions of *Moby-Dick* ("Contract: *Moby-Dick*, by Herman Melville," 1:1–7). In the same issue Hershel Parker cites examples from the Northwestern-Newberry edition of Melville in discussing "Melville and the Concept of 'Author's Final Intentions'"; an accompanying illustration reproduces p. 358 of the first American *Omoo* (*Proof* 1:156–68). G. Thomas Tanselle, the third of the Northwestern-Newberry editorial team, also draws examples from Melville in his "Textual Study and Literary Judgment" (*PBSA* 65:109–22).

In "A Melville Letter and Stray Books from His Library" (*ESQ* 63:47–49) Kenneth Walter Cameron reproduces from an auction catalogue the facsimile of a previously unknown letter of November 16, 1857, to an unnamed correspondent concerning the possibility of Melville's lecturing in or near Rockford, Illinois. Cameron's five "stray books" are items listed in other dealers' catalogues. One of these is an unidentified volume given Melville in 1846 by his Aunt Priscilla Melville, as indicated by the inscription apparently cut from its flyleaf; four others are works said to contain his autograph, though the reproduction on p. 49 of one of the inscriptions does not persuade me that the writing is indeed Melville's. Only the unidentified volume, not the four other titles, is included in "A Supplementary Note to *Melville's Reading* (1966)" by Merton M. Sealts, Jr. (*HLB* 19:280–84), among twenty-nine additions and changes to the check-list of books that Melville once owned and borrowed (see *ALS 1966*, pp. 25–26). The number of titles he owned stands at 384 as of 1971; of the 251 books that apparently survive, 223 have now been located.

Paul McCarthy, examining "City and Town in Melville's Fiction" (*RS* 38[1970]:214–29), observes that as microcosms of society Melville's urban settings "can be as challenging, mysterious, and dangerous as the great Pacific or the Marquesas Islands"; their truths do not differ fundamentally from those of the sea, "and they may be as significant." Luther Stearns Mansfield's " 'Very like a Whale': Herman Melville and Shakespeare" (*Studies in Medieval, Renaissance, American Literature,* pp. 143–56) is a general survey of Melville's acquaintance with Shakespeare, including a few specific illustrations and comparisons drawn from *Moby-Dick* and the plays. Henry J. Yeager, studying "Melville's Literary Debut in France" during the decade 1846–1856 (*MQ* 11[1970]:413–25), notes that his works, unlike those of his major contemporaries, were not translated into French, being familiar to French readers only through extracts in reviews; his popularity suffered when the new regime of Napoleon III brought about a change in the intellectual climate of France. Merton M. Sealts, Jr., in "Melville and Richard Henry Stoddard" (*AL* 43:359–70), brings together what is known concerning the relations between Melville and Stoddard, particularly Stoddard's three reviews of Melville's poetry (including a hitherto unidentified notice of *Battle-Pieces*) and a retrospective essay of 1891. George Monteiro, in "Elizabeth Shaw Melville as Censor" (*ESQ* 62:32–33), cites evidence that Melville's widow tried unsuccessfully to have certain words omitted from her husband's letters to Hawthorne as printed in Rose Hawthorne Lathrop's *Memories of Hawthorne* (1897).

A variety of bibliographical aids for students and scholars also appeared in 1971. For student use, there is a selective list of Melville bibliographies, texts, biographies, and critical studies in one of the Goldentree Bibliographies, *American Literature: Poe Through Garland* by the late Harry Hayden Clark (New York, Appleton-Century-Crofts; pp. 65–73). James K. Bowen and Richard Vanderbeets, in *A Critical Guide to Herman Melville: Abstracts of Forty Years of Criticism* (Glenview, Ill., Scott, Foresman), have brought together abstracts of over a hundred critical essays on Melville's prose and poetry. The number of abstracts for each work covered is governed by what the editors consider the relative importance of that work and the amount and kind of critical attention it has received; the arrangement of abstracts under each title follows the order of publication of the original articles. As a selective overview of the course of critical discussion dealing with Melville's various works the collection has obvious advantages but one major limitation: it covers articles only and not book-length studies (e.g., Gilman's "Melville's Liverpool Trip" but not his *Melville's Early Life and "Redburn"*).

A summary and evaluation of books as well as articles is provided by Theodore L. Gross in *Hawthorne, Melville, Stephen Crane: A Critical Bibliography* (New York, Free Press), compiled by Gross and Stanley Wertheim. The section on Melville (pp. 101–201) includes an introduction and chronology; three annotated listings surveying primary materials and bibliographies, biographies, and selected criticism; and a concluding bibliographical index. The several listings are relatively inclusive if not exhaustive, though there are troublesome inaccuracies in some of the entries and commentaries and also in the index. The alphabetical arrangement under each heading is convenient, but it precludes demonstrating the chronological development of scholarship and criticism concerning a given topic. For some entries Gross has written his own digests and assessments; for others he has drawn on published reviews or cited contrasting interpretations by other authors. His summaries are useful, though his evaluations do not carry the authority that Nathalia Wright brings to her chapter on Melville in the revised edition of *Eight American Authors*. Miss Wright's essay (pp. 173–224) points out successive trends in both research and interpretation from the beginnings of Melville scholarship through the 1960s as it surveys in turn bibliographies, editions, biographies, and criticism, concluding with a brief glance at dissertations and periodicals. (For fuller consideration of critical articles appearing before 1956 she refers the reader to the original edition of *Eight American Authors*, to which the late Stanley T. Williams contributed the chapter on Melville.) Her discussion, though tightly packed by necessity, is at once inclusive, incisive, and judicious; there is no other survey which so well represents and evaluates the present state of Melville studies.

University of Wisconsin–Madison

4. Whitman and Dickinson

Bernice Slote

The volume of work on Whitman has been somewhat reduced from its peak in 1969, with no new critical books appearing in 1971. However, the publication of the new illustrated edition of *Specimen Days* (Boston, Godine) gave a shine to the year. The numerous reviews agree with Charles W. Mann, Jr.,'s judgment—"one of the loveliest books of its kind" (*LJ* 96:3761). And although there have been many general and biographical accounts of Whitman, including sections in two books, the most impressive critical collection was the Whitman issue of *American Transcendental Quarterly* (no. 12, Fall 1971), which included a group of photographs. The most promising new field being explored in Whitman is the journalism. The most suggestive new techniques recently applied to the works of both Whitman and Dickinson are those of linguistic analysis. In Dickinson studies, general critical articles rather than explications of the poems have predominated; three books on Dickinson were published during 1971, all strikingly different and some controversial.

i. Whitman

a. **Bibliography, collections.** One of the more interesting bibliographical problems in Whitman scholarship might by now be called "The Case of the Whitman Notebooks." Of six manuscript notebooks originally listed in the Harned Collection in the Library of Congress, three (items 80, 84, and 86) are missing and exist now only on microfilms once obtained by Floyd Stovall. One of them, No. 80, along with its entries, has been given the early date of 1847, first by Emory Holloway and later by Edward F. Grier (see *ALS 1969*, p. 58). Now, after a close examination of the microfilm, Professor Stovall concludes that the entries and the poems in No. 80 were, like those of the other notebooks, inscribed at about 1854 ("Dating Whitman's Early Notebooks," *SB* 24:197–204). He therefore agrees substantially with Esther Shephard, who has added another clue in "A Fact Which Should Have Been Included in 'Whitman's Earliest Known Notebook: A Clarification' by John C. Broderick" (*PMLA* 86:266). She was told in 1939 that the notebooks were not available for public use until the material was organized and examined by Dr. Auslander, then the Consultant in English Poetry; she was told in 1946 that the notebook could not be located.

Unpublished Whitman material comes now only in occasional letters or manuscript fragments. Two of those fragments in the Huntington Library are presented in a commentary by Karl Adalbert Preuschen in "Walt Whitman's Undelivered Oration, 'The Dead in This War'" (*EA* 24:147–51). Whitman's notes on the manuscript indicate that the passages are for a lecture planned in the spring of 1863, and some additions were made in late 1864. Although the oration was not finished, material in the fragments went into "When Lilacs Last in the Dooryard Bloom'd." William White presents and annotates two unpublished Whitman letters to Dr. John H. Johnston in 1887 and 1891 ("Two More Unpublished Whitman Letters," *AN&Q* 10:3–4). Facsimiles of a note from Whitman to A. R. Spofford on editions of *Leaves of Grass*, and of Spofford's query to Whitman, are reproduced in John Y. Cole's "Of Copyright, Men & a National Library" (*QJLC* 28:114–36).

b. **Biography.** Partly bibliographical, partly biographical, are recent studies of Whitman's journalism. Three important articles this year by Herbert Bergman give as full an account as we have had of Whitman's journalistic career ("Whitman on Editing, Newspapers and Journalism," *JQ* 48:345–48; "Walt Whitman as a Journalist, 1831–January, 1848," *JQ* 48:195–204; "Walt Whitman as a Journalist, March, 1848–1892," *JQ* 48:431–37). Based on his work with William White for the five-volume edition of *The Journalism*, volumes forthcoming in *The Collected Writings of Walt Whitman* (New York Univ. Press), Professor Bergman's summary accounts in these articles are literally packed with detailed information and illustration, revealing of Whitman's self and time. Bergman calls Whitman's sixty years of journalism a "substantial achievement," and Whitman "a hardworking professional, not a loafer, whose name would live for his journalistic accomplishment alone, even had he not written *Leaves* *of Grass.*" This is a strong statement, and one which only the completed volumes of *The Journalism* can support. In any case, the Whitman journalism is of formidable scope and well worth the scholarly attention it has received.

Whitman's relationship with the firm of Lorenzo and Orson Fowler and Robert Wells—phrenologists, publishers, and booksellers—is the subject of several new studies. James K. Wallace contributes an unrecorded review of *Leaves of Grass* in the Fowler and Wells publication, *Life Illustrated*, on July 28, 1855, less than a month after the firm had put the volume on sale, and notes that two additional announcements of the book appeared in August and October ("Whitman and *Life Illustrated*: A Forgotten 1855 Review of *Leaves*," *WWR* 17:135–38). It is generally known that on July 16, 1849, Whitman submitted his head to the phrenological survey of Lorenzo Fowler, and that the results in slightly differing forms were several times printed, by Whitman and others. In "A Poet's Self-Esteem: Whitman Alters His 'Bumps'" (*WWR* 17:129–35) Arthur Wrobel suggests that there may have been two, or even three, separate examinations and reports. After examining Bucke's copy of the analysis (Trent Collection), Wrobel notes that Bucke's figures vary somewhat from the printed versions. A longer account of Whitman's phrenological interest is given in "Walt Whitman, Care of Fowler and Wells," a chapter of Madeleine B. Stern's *Heads & Headlines: The Phrenological Fowlers* (Norman, Univ. of Okla. Press, pp. 99–123). The account by Stern is sound and very readable, with full references, though it does not include the material in the articles by Wallace and Wrobel discussed above. In the book, the passages from the phrenological report of Lorenzo Fowler differ slightly from those quoted by Wrobel; it is not clear whether Stern consulted the manuscripts directly. As a result, scholars interested in the report might better go directly to the Trent Collection themselves for final decisions. In context, the account of Whitman and the Fowlers gains greatly, and any student of Whitman and his period will find *Heads & Headlines* illuminating.

A gathering of information on a group of Whitman's friends and acquaintances—many of whom he met on a visit to William Francis Channing in Providence, R.I., in the fall of 1868—as well as a focused view of Whitman's life in relation to these friends, is in Alvin H. Rosenfeld's "Whitman and the Providence Literati" (*BBr* 24:82–106). Some unpublished letters from the Feinberg Collection are used and

other letters reprinted to give this view of Whitman and literati such
as Nora Perry, Sarah Helen Whitman, Mr. and Mrs. Thomas Davis,
and William Douglas O'Connor. The long section on Whitman's
friend John Hay is especially valuable.

Two biographical notes by William White include "Billy Duckett: Whitman Rogue" (*ABC* 21,v:20–23) and "Walter Whitman:
Kings County Democratic Party Secretary" (*WWR* 17:92–98). The
Billy Duckett story includes the text of an unpublished manuscript
in Whitman's handwriting, presumably the poet's account of himself
prepared for use by the young neighbor boy in Camden who was both
a help and a nuisance in Whitman's last years. Duckett's own less
literate "notes" on Whitman are also printed in the article. The second item reprints from the *Brooklyn Daily Eagle* the account of a
colorful political meeting on October 30, 1846, signed by both the
party's president and its secretary, Walter Whitman.

c. Criticism: general.   The attempt to find the "voice" of Whitman
—to define its quality and to realize fully the force of the poet as
speaker—is not new in Whitman studies, but it has recently gained
impetus. Two substantial articles this year turn to some redefinitions.
In "Whitman and Modern Literary Criticism" (*ATQ* 12:4–11) John
Lee Jellicorse takes the strong position that Whitman must be read
for what he says rather than for how he says it; that is, as a teacher
rather than as an artist. It is the rhetorical function that is uppermost,
he says, supporting his case by Whitman statements such as, "I don't
value the poetry in what I have written so much as the teaching; the
poetry is only a horse for the other to ride." Few will quarrel with the
argument that Whitman has often been misjudged because an inappropriate critical orientation has been applied, or with at least three
of the six ways of reading Whitman advocated by Jellicorse: that
the writings, not explications or criticism of the writings, should be
read; that *Leaves of Grass* should be read as a whole; and that the
reader should not expect a single meaning from the book. The other
three—to avoid modern stereotypes of Whitman, to read only editions
prepared by Whitman, and to avoid group reading—seem less imperative. One difficulty in accepting the thesis of the article whole-
heartedly, however, is that categories are made overly rigid. It is one
thing to say that a writer's intention is to "move men and women,"

but another to say that the way by which a writer achieves his end is unimportant. In the four major orientations to literature defined in the article (mimetic, rhetorical, expressive, and objective), "the expressive theory of the Romantic movement" is defined as "self-expression in isolation from an audience"; this is not true, however, of most of the great romantics—Shelley, Keats, and Wordsworth, especially, were concerned about the function of poetry in reaching others—and it is likewise doubtful that Whitman could be contained completely in one mode.

A similar view of Whitman and Whitman criticism is held by Quentin Anderson in *The Imperial Self: An Essay in American Literary and Cultural History* (New York, Knopf, pp. 88–165). Whitman is discussed principally in two chapters, "Consciousness and Form in Whitman" and "The World in the Body," in which Anderson first distinguishes "the prophetic office of Emerson and Whitman" from its "unacknowledged successor," the religion of art, and discusses at length the personal, prophetic force of Whitman's self-involvement; in the following chapter he applies his definitions in a reading of "Crossing Brooklyn Ferry." There are good ideas in Anderson's book, some interesting alignments with contemporary poets, and some very murky writing.

In his "Personae in Whitman (1855–1860)" (*ATQ* 12:25–32), Bruce R. McElderry, Jr., defines several voices in *Leaves of Grass*—principally those of the orator and the bard, with fewer uses of the "personal, autobiographical Walt Whitman" in the 1855 edition. The 1860 edition is also "dominated by the bardic Whitman" but the "truly lyric persona, quieter than the bard, more controlled than the uncertain personal Walt Whitman," begins to be more evident, culminating in the two poems McElderry considers the finest achievements up to 1860—"Crossing Brooklyn Ferry" and "Out of the Cradle Endlessly Rocking." These, he thinks, are greater poems than "Song of Myself."

Another attempt to see the book whole is the evaluation of Whitman's epic impulse and achievement by Richard Gid Powers ("*Leaves of Grass*: The Evolution of an Epic," *BBr* 24:107–18), who notes that Whitman gradually reduced his American or epic emphasis in *Leaves of Grass*; that being the national poet seemed to mean less to him as he developed the book; and that it was eventually the federal shape, or the "many in one" that seemed most significant to him. The later prefaces "introduce a universal poem created from American materials." Steven Earl Kagle in "Temporal Structure in *Leaves of Grass*" (*IllQ* 33,ii:42–49) traces throughout the book "increasing levels of experience and insight," going "spatially from Paumanok of Whitman's birth to the edge of the universe, spiritually from the personal to the universal." In another article, "Time as a Dimension in Whitman" (*ATQ* 12:55–60), Kagle elaborates and illustrates Whitman's view of time as a continuum, seeing this "divine perspective external to time" as essential in Whitman's philosophic convictions. Time as a dimension rather than a process makes immortality possible.

Articles on particular aspects or on groups of poems are slighter. Two short pieces have good points on the contradictions in Whitman's attitudes, Edward Butscher noting the double view of death as both beauty and horror ("Whitman's Attitudes Toward Death: The Essential Paradox," *WWR* 17:16–19), and B. Christian Megna seeing in "Whispers of Heavenly Death" and other poems "the polarity of the 'one and the many' " as fundamental in the structure of his work ("Sociality and Seclusion in the Poetry of Walt Whitman," *WWR* 17:55–57). A similar doubleness is discussed by Lenny Emmanuel in "Whitman's Fusion of Science and Poetry" (*WWR* 17:73–82). In "Walt Whitman in League with Women" (*WWR* 17:62–63) Thomas L. Brasher points to some strongly supportive passages in *Democratic Vistas* for those of the organized New Women who are, according to Whitman, willing to "launch forth, as men do, amid real, independent, stormy life." Less helpful is an article by Arvind K. Mehrotra, "The Bard and the Foundry: A Reaction to Whitman's *Black Poems*" (*RS* 39:33–39), several pages of bombast that say mainly that the author does not like Whitman. The term *black poems* (misleadingly italicized in the title) refers to the phrase in Whitman's open letter to Emerson in the 1856 *Leaves of Grass*—"those splendid resistless black poems"—which the writer extends to all mechanical aspects of American life. Mehrotra quotes with a freewheeling inaccuracy. He quotes Malcolm Cowley as saying that Whitman's poems read "like the names of parts and organs in an anatomical chart"; what Cowley says in his introduction to his edition of the 1855 *Leaves of Grass* (New York, 1959) is that "the interminable bald inventories" (not poems) read thus. And Mehrotra quotes seriously as a description of Whitman

Bernice Slote's phrase, "the wild-eyed gusty busy formless citizen poet" (*Start with the Sun,* 1960), which in context is a parody of the wrong view of Whitman. These adjustments of text and meaning may either dismay or amuse, but in any case the article seems out of place in a scholarly journal.

There have been a number of articles on Whitman's style, notably V. K. Chari's "The Limits of Whitman's Symbolism" (*JAmS* 5:173–84). Although he does not deal with new material, Chari effectively defines and discusses the like and unlike qualities of Whitman's poems and those of the symbolists. Whitman was prevented from becoming "a full-blown Symbolist" by two things—his realism and his "concern about avoiding an opaque style that would obscure the lineaments of his vision" (to Whitman "there was no conflict between simplicity and suggestive delicacy"). Chari's summary is that "Whitman's claim for being considered a modern Symbolist must rest on a few isolated passages," but not on his language or the organization of his major poems. Some of Whitman's most beautiful indirections are not of the symbolists: instead of "turning nature into a metaphor of the mind" his verse captures nature's "spirit of freedom and largeness, its rhythms and harmonies"; and by panoramic imagery objects themselves are incorporated into the language.

In "Water Imagery in *Leaves of Grass*" (*WWR* 17:82–92) A. Helen Smith illustrates five predominant images: swimming or bathing, ocean or sea as a fearsome life-death force, river or stream as journey through life, ocean or sea as unifying force, and ocean or sea as journey to death. She notes that Whitman's fear of death diminished in his later poems. An informative article by Kenneth G. Johnston and John O. Rees, Jr., is "Whitman and the Foo-Foos: An Experiment in Language" (*WWR* 17:3–10), in which the term *foo-foos,* used by Whitman in section 22 of "Song of Myself," is traced to contemporary usage in the play *A Glance at New York* (1848). Whitman's use is an example of his "great interest in the living English language, in the popularity of the plays which made current this slang word from the New York stage, and in Whitman's shifting image of the poet." What are foo-foos? An outsider, says a character in the play—"a chap wot can't come de big figure." One evidence of the growing interest in applying modern linguistic principles to the analysis of poetry is a study by Edmund Reiss, "Whitman's Poetic Grammar: Style and

Meaning in 'Children of Adam' " (*ATQ* 12:32–41). The technique used by Reiss to discover Whitman's meaning is not universal, by any means, but his analysis of Whitman's "grammatical ordering of language" shows links between form and meaning.

d. **Criticism: individual works.** As in other years, the enticement of defining once and for all the divisible structure of "Song of Myself" has drawn forth some excellent plans. In "The Partitive Studies of 'Song of Myself' " (*ATQ* 12:11–17) F. DeWolfe Miller offers his own analysis, which though not too different from some others, does use a unifying theme: the preparation, the announcement, the sermon, and the call to redemption of the Poet-Messiah. Most helpfully, Miller includes, in addition to his own, a review and comparison of eight previous analyses. A departure from the usual structure is J. Albert Robbins's three-part division, outlined with convincing clarity in "The Narrative Form of 'Song of Myself' " (*ATQ* 12:17–20). The three principal units of "Song of Myself," he says, are framed by a preface (1–5) and an epilogue (51–52); they include (1) (6–32), "a search for certitude and identity"; (2) (33–38), "a visionary journey of the self to encompass and possess all time and all life"; and (3) (39–50), the "true vision" or "the ministry of the Poet Savior." Key lines which mark the divisions are also noted. The narrative movement of the poem within this structure, suggests Robbins, is from the self in its "passive testifying," through identification with others, to the giving of the self to others, or "bestowal." The theme of the poem, then, is "the rebirth of the flawed poet into poet-savior."

Although he does not suggest divisions in the poem, B. Bernard Cohen in " 'Song of Myself': Enticement to Faith as Knowledge" (*ATQ* 12:49–54) offers a plan of progression in which Whitman by various strategies leads "his readers on the long poetic journey to faith and hence to knowledge." These strategies include "a posture of mystery and elusiveness," "the use of questions and answers," the reconciliation of opposites, and "the depiction of transcendental or mystical experience." These are all fully discussed and illustrated. In another analysis of movement in the "Song" Donald D. Kummings sees a change in Whitman's role from private to public, or a shift from poetry to eloquence or persuasion ("Whitman's Voice in 'Song of Myself': From Private to Public," *WWR* 17:10–15). Ida Fasel sees the poem as a picturing "by voice and scene, the proud man in prayer, celebrating the sources of his joy in private meditation and public credo" ("'Song of Myself' as Prayer," *WWR* 17:19–22). She divides the poem into four parts: adoration, thanksgiving, confession, and petition; but adds sensibly: "Of course there is an overlapping of parts. . . . 'Song of Myself,' like *Leaves of Grass*, is cumulative, and echoes become the structural unity of the poem."

A. Helen Smith in "Origin and Interpretation of the Hero of 'Song of Myself'" (*WWR* 17:45–54) traces Whitman's changing ideas between 1842 and 1855 "from the hero as political-military leader to the hero as literary artist," and makes some use of Whitman's journalistic statements and his early notebook (discussed above under Bibliography). As poet-hero, however, Whitman chooses to be both the democratic representative poet and the bardic-hero, combining different ideologies. Another evaluation by Peter Wolfe ("'Song of Myself'—The Indirect Figure in the Word-Mosaic," *ATQ* 12:20–25) points up the immediacy of Whitman's poet, and the direct involvement of the reader, though with the strategy of "roundaboutness." Joel Jay Belson adds a note defining "fraction" (section 38) as "fragment" but also as "the rite of breaking the bread in the celebration of the Eucharist" ("Whitman's 'Overstaid Fraction,'" *WWR* 17:63–65).

One pleasure in reading Whitman criticism this year was to come upon a monograph by Daniel M. McKeithan, *Whitman's "Song of Myself" 34 and Its Background* (*ESALL*, 1969). In section 34 Whitman writes of a Texas battle and "the murder of the four hundred and twelve young men." The monograph is a detailed and moving account of this episode, identified as "the Battle of Coleto, March 19 and 20, 1836, in the Texas Revolution and the massacre of the Texas prisoners a week later, on Palm Sunday, March 27, at Goliad." In a careful study of Whitman's possible sources, Mr. McKeithan concludes that some material, but not all, was gathered from an article in *Blackwood's Magazine* for January 1846. And knowing the facts, he says, we can appreciate Whitman's "superb economy of words, vividness of detail, and restraint of emotion." It is "the most artistic description of the events ever written."

Among the studies of "When Lilacs Last in the Dooryard Bloom'd" one by Ellen S. Goodman deserves special mention ("'Lilacs' and the Pastoral Elegy Reconsidered," *BBr* 24:119–33). In a care-

ful examination of the correspondences and variations in the poem
when viewed as a traditional pastoral elegy, the writer shows particularly that Whitman rejected the mythological and allegorical elements
of past elegies, emphasized the real, and worked often by analogy; yet
he used the tradition enough to make its recognition in "Lilacs" essential. Robert Emerson Carlile examines the leitmotif of lilac, star, and
bird in the poem, supplying interesting relationships with Wagner and
showing charts of the musical progression in the poem ("Leitmotif
and Whitman's 'When Lilacs Last in the Dooryard Bloom'd,' " *Criticism* 13:329–39). Among other studies of particular poems are " 'Ei-
dōlons': An Entrance-Song" (*WWR* 17:35–45) by Phillipa P. Harrison, an analysis of the poem as a medley of Whitman's major themes;
Douglas A. Noverr's " 'Aboard at a Ship's Helm': A Minor Sea Drama,
the Poet, and the Soul" (*WWR* 17:23–25); and an appreciative account by Robert B. Sweet, "A Writer Looks at Whitman's 'A Sight in
Camp in the Daybreak Gray and Dim' " (*WWR* 17:58–62).

One work which is not a poem has been given some understand-
ing attention. In *"Franklin Evans*: A Sportive Temperance Novel"
(*BBr* 24:134–47) Barton L. St. Armand does a fine job of placing
Whitman's early novel in its genre. It largely avoids the standard attitudes of the temperance novel, the writer observes; he concludes that
"Franklin Evans might be considered as the first full-fledged anti-
hero in American literature." And Whitman has, in fact, "written a
Temperance Novel which is not a temperance novel, he has written a
Franklinian success story which is not a Franklinian success story,
and he has written a *bildungs-roman* in which no one really grows up
or learns anything of lasting value."

e. **Relationships, influence.** A comparison of Melville and Whitman by John P. McWilliams, Jr., in " 'Drum Taps' and *Battle-Pieces*:
The Blossom of War" (*AQ* 23:181–201) concentrates on observing
"the unfolding of the war in the terms in which the poets themselves
saw it." The conclusion, well-demonstrated and discussed, is that
Whitman ended in triumph, Melville in disillusion. "One leaves Melville with a feeling of having witnessed universal struggle and historical tragedy, but a doubt as to their resolution. 'Drum Taps' offers a
limitless love for suffering humanity and implies that nothing else
matters." In the form, Melville's "consciously ordered history with

overtones of an epic" is Whitman's "succession of dramatic lyrics." Another comparison is D. M. McKeithan's note on the "am'rous birds of prey" in Marvell's "To His Coy Mistress" and in Whitman's "The Dalliance of the Eagles" ("Two Avian Images in Marvell and Whitman," *WWR* 17:101–03).

Sources are not often suggested, but Thomas LeClair observes some striking parallels with Whitman in T. S. Eliot's "The Love Song of J. Alfred Prufrock" ("Prufrock and the Open Road," *WWR* 17:123–26). Other spiritual rather than formal likenesses are suggested in Arnold Mersch's "Teilhard de Chardin and Whitman's 'A Noiseless Patient Spider'" (*WWR* 17:99–100) and in Alfred S. Wang's "Walt Whitman and Lao-Chuang" (*WWR* 17:109–22), which shows Whitman as a precursor of "the Renaissance of Orientalism in philosophy and literature" in America. One of the best of these articles on relationships is James Hazen's "Whitman and Hopkins" (*ATQ* 12:41–48), a judicious evaluation of the very "diffuse and generalized kind" of influence Whitman had on Hopkins, who was torn by a feeling of affinity and a moral judgment of dislike for Whitman. Yet, suggests Hazen, that Whitman altered the "tradition" made an earlier acceptance of Hopkins possible. Charles E. Burgess has a note on what is shown about Edgar Lee Masters in his bad biography of Whitman ("Masters and *Whitman*: A Second Look," *WWR* 17:25–27). And in "Henry Miller's Democratic Vistas" (*AQ* 23:221–35) Harold T. McCarthy draws a number of parallels. As Whitman in his *Democratic Vistas* had tried to formulate "the motivating ideals of America," so Miller's work turned to similar redefinitions. There are occasional references to Whitman throughout the article, with a deliberate comparison of the two writers in the last two pages. Another interesting account of Whitman's strangely repelling-attracting effect on some writers who came after him is in a twenty-five-page monograph by Ronald Hayman, *Arguing with Walt Whitman* (London, Covent Garden Press). Hayman considers principally Ezra Pound, T. S. Eliot, William Carlos Williams, Hart Crane, and—though further removed—Wallace Stevens. The connections are well-documented, though in such a brief study only samplings can be given. The *Long-Islander*'s Walt Whitman Page in the issue of May 27, 1971, edited by Roger Asselineau, presented various accounts of Whitman's world position, including Asselineau's "Scholars Discuss Walt Whitman's

Reputation in Western Europe," with Mariolina Meliado Freeth on Italy, Hans Joachim Lang on Germany, Guillaume Toebosch on Belgium, and Concha Zardoya on Spain.

ii. Dickinson

a. **Bibliography, manuscripts.** The chief bibliographical contribution to Dickinson studies this year is the essay, "Emily Dickinson," by James Woodress in *Fifteen American Authors* (pp. 139–68). Woodress gives a wealth of information, summaries, figures, and a series of firm reviews. Certainly Dickinson is "America's number one woman poet," and she is now securely with "the handful of major nineteenth-century figures who long have dominated our literary history." Interest in Emily Dickinson in Spanish-speaking countries is illustrated by a series of bibliographical items by George Monteiro, adding to current bibliographies with "Hispanic Additions to Woodbridge" (*EDB* 18:72–73) and in "Brazil's Emily Dickinson: An Annotated Check List of Translations, Criticism, and Reviews," with an appendix of criticism on the subject of Emily Dickinson and Brazil (*EDB* 18:73–78). In "The Mind Alone, Part II: Distortion of the Letters, 1914–1930" (*EDB* 17:34–44), Robert R. Lawrence continues a chronology of publications by and about Dickinson (see *ALS 1970*, p. 71).

One of three books on Dickinson published this year is Edith Wylder's *The Last Face: Emily Dickinson's Manuscripts* (Albuquerque, Univ. of N. Mex. Press), which presents the theory that what look like dashes scattered through the poems in manuscript are actually a variety of nineteenth-century elocutionary symbols that mark "inflection, pause, and stress." In an extensive introduction, the author clarifies and expands her theory, first introduced (under the name of Edith Perry Stamm) in a brief 1963 article which received some adverse criticism (see *ALS 1963*, p. 127; *ALS 1966*, p. 142). Sample poems are analyzed, and thirty-five are reprinted from the manuscripts with type symbols that represent the notations. The chief strength of Mrs. Wylder's response to her earlier critics is to establish the symbols as rhetorical signs rather than guides to oral reading—for "the mind's ear," or for "*impressions* of voice"—and to associate the system with the efforts of modern linguists to relate spoken and written language. Perhaps her statement that Dickinson used the notations as substitute punctuation—for a "grammatical as well as rhetorical purpose"—may not completely satisfy those who found similar marks in manuscripts of the prose. As far as they are shown in the samplings of poems reprinted in the text, the notations as translated here from the manuscripts seem to work as reasonable rhetorical guides. For a full acceptance of Mrs. Wylder's interpretation, however, there will need to be a close scrutiny of all the manuscripts, both poetry and prose.

b. **Biography.** After all of the conjectures about the personal life of the retiring poet of Amherst, it is inevitable that psychiatrists as well as scholars and ordinary readers would attempt to understand Emily Dickinson and show her to us plain. An important book this year is John Cody's *After Great Pain: The Inner Life of Emily Dickinson* (Cambridge, Mass., Harvard Univ. Press), a psychoanalytical biography which, from poems, letters, and the evidence of those who knew Dickinson, traces and defines the emotional and mental states of its subject. Two of the chief elements in Dr. Cody's analysis are that much of the disturbance in Emily Dickinson's personality came from an early psychological division from her mother, and that she suffered a mental breakdown sometime in her late twenties, a state of mind operating in some of her most brilliant poetry. As a whole, the book is more satisfying than the sections which were first published separately (see *ALS 1970*, pp. 71–72); in isolation the scalpel gleams too sharply for its own sake. In a reasonable introduction, Dr. Cody disclaims the role of literary critic, but defends the usefulness of psychological knowledge in those works which are closely tied to their authors. However, he views creativity with a colder eye than do most of us, concluding that Emily Dickinson's "psychological calamities, decades of frustration, isolation, and loneliness all created a void" that her talent rushed in to fill: "Without this void there might well have been no poet." However, even if one does not wish to accept all of the conclusions, there is much in the book to fascinate and convince. The sections analyzing the relationships of Emily, her brother Austin, and her sister-in-law Sue, for example, seem convincing, as does the suggestion that the love poems are more "the airy embodiments of unfulfilled longing." Yet one is likely to balk at some overly literal readings of the poems. "Me from Myself—to banish—" is used to illustrate a "disturbed person"; yet haven't many others, sane as well as insane, recognized and written of a self within the self?

Another biographical study by John Evangelist Walsh, *The Hidden Life of Emily Dickinson* (New York, Simon and Schuster) is readable but erratic. Walsh's strong candidate for Emily Dickinson's love interest in the "Master" letters is the same Otis Lord whom she did love in later years. Again, not every one will be convinced, but the arguments are worth considering. The book shows evidence of useful research, but on the point of Dickinson's intensive use of material and language from Elizabeth Barrett Browning's *Aurora Leigh* the conclusions are almost hopelessly naive. Without question Dickinson loved Browning's book, and many of her poems reflect her liking for passages or images in it, but not even a pot-boiling poet (which Emily was not) writes by hunting up words and phrases to make into a poem, as Walsh implies was done with *Aurora Leigh* as muse and material. A close look at the examples of correspondences given in Walsh's text will show them to be vague enough, but if one follows through with all of the parallels listed in four pages of the notes he will find that only a fraction of them have any real connection; most are the slightest possible likenesses—the use of the same word or the same proper name, or a subject like "darkness." Walsh's term is "borrowings" from *Aurora Leigh*. As has been said before of Keats and Mrs. Tighe—they both used the English language.

c. **Criticism: general.**   Critical articles on Dickinson have turned more to general considerations rather than the explication of individual poems. For example, Frederick L. Morey submits a classification in "Eleven Major Themes in 356 Important Poems (*EDB* 17:28–33) and argues for a new organizing principle for collections on the basis of type or excellence rather than the traditional grouping under headings such as nature, love, life, and death (*MarkhamR* 2[1970]: 74–78). He divides the poems into two general groups, the rococo (poignant, beautiful, humorous, small, delicate, colorful) and the sublime (deep, profound, powerful, tragic, painful, awful, obscure, ambiguous), both with a range of excellence. The most complete general article is Eleanor Wilner's "The Poetics of Emily Dickinson" (*ELH* 38:126–54), surveying elements of the life, themes, psychology, and language. She disagrees with critics who call Dickinson modern. In spite of her innovations, "the two characteristics which are most typically modern—the tendency to take the physical world on its own terms and to see the world as a place of process, of endless metamorphosis and becoming, are tendencies entirely antithetical to Emily Dickinson." The poet's concern for things as emblems was medieval rather than modern. A full analysis of "A Bird came down the Walk—" shows the poem as an allegory of poetic creation. In another general article Zacharias Thundyil suggests that Dickinson's theory of poetics and her religious thinking are linked in meaning ("Circumstance, Circumference, and Center: Immanence and Transcendence in Emily Dickinson's Poems of Extreme Situations," *HSL* 3:73–92). "Her poems of extreme situation are a medium and expression of her poetic and religious life." In these poems there is a double movement of immanence and transcendence, but after 1865 "center" rather than "circumference" was dominant. Less ambitious but well presented with examples and analysis are two other articles: David Luisi's "Some Aspects of Emily Dickinson's Food and Liquor Poems" (*ES* 52:32–40), which concludes that such imagery is the most pervasive in her poetry, used to describe even immaterial things such as love and knowledge, and giving an elemental or primitive quality to her poems; and Marlene Springer's "Emily Dickinson's Humorous Road to Heaven" (*Renascence* 23:129–36), showing the sprightly effect of child-imagery and persona used in the religious poems. A good article not previously noted in *ALS* is John Emerson Todd's "The Persona in Emily Dickinson's Love Poems" (*MichA* 1,i–ii[1969]:197–207), in which a strong case is made for an element of dramatizing in the love poems. This Todd sees as a mark of excellence, a kind of Shakespearean quality. The device of the persona enables the poet to project herself into a created world, with a "centrifugal movement outward that sometimes enables her to gain an artistic control rare in the poetry of her time."

Using "When Etna Basks and purrs" and "After great Pain," Samuel R. Levin makes an intensive linguistic analysis of the "nonrecoverable deletions" in the two poems, concluding that "it is precisely the effect of these deletions to induce a sense of and hence a response of compression" ("The Analysis of Compression in Poetry," *FLang* 7:38–55). This, says Levin, is a linguistic structure in some sense peculiar to poetry; it explains intuitive responses.

d. **Criticism: individual poems.** Fewer explications than usual have appeared recently. In "A Note on Dickinson's 'I cautious, scanned my little life—'" (*MarkhamR* 2[1970]:78–79) Gary D. Elliott sees that poem as illuminating Dickinson's withdrawal from society. Frederick Keefer and Deborah Vlahos suggest a relation between the phrase "Van Dieman's land" and the ritual of a children's game ("Dickinson's 'If you were coming in the Fall,'" *Expl* 29[1970]:item 23). In "Dickinson's 'Two Butterflies Went Out at Noon'" (*ESQ* 63:29–31), Frederick Asals, in a consideration of "the varied directions of Emily Dickinson's skepticism," compares two versions of the poem: the first is more ambiguous and "stands between Emerson's *Nature* and the masthead dreamer passage in *Moby-Dick*, gazing with a troubled eye on each, whereas the later version gives its allegiance unambiguously to the Melvillean view."

e. Relationships.   Michael West in "Shakespeare Allusion in Emily Dickinson" (*AN&Q* 10:51) identifies the phrase "There is a World elsewhere" as not biblical, as Thomas H. Johnson had thought in editing the *Letters* (1958, 2:613), but an echo from *Coriolanus* (3.3.134–136). Some interesting parallels between Henry James's "The Jolly Corner" and the poems (as they appeared in the 1891 edition) "Returning" and "Ghosts," are noted by Nan Sumner and Nathan Sumner, who also suggest that James might well have seen *Poems, Second Series*, 1891 ("A Dickinson-James Parallel," *RS* 39:144–47). A comparative note by the Brazilian scholar, Carlos Daghlian, points out many similarities between Dickinson and the South American poet Fernando Pessoa (1888–1935) in personality, themes, style, and publishing history ("ED and Fernando Pessoa: Two Poets for Posterity," *EDB* 18:66–72). The increasing interest in Emily Dickinson through Spanish-speaking countries supports the feeling that genius occupies one world, with no barriers.

University of Nebraska–Lincoln

5. Mark Twain

Hamlin Hill

It was a lean year for Mark Twain studies in 1971; excluding completed dissertations, fewer than three dozen articles and books appeared. Scholars may have been awaiting further volumes in the *Mark Twain Papers* from the University of California Press before venturing major appraisals. And John Tuckey's second volume of later materials, *Mark Twain's Fables of Man*, and Franklin R. Rogers's edition of *Roughing It* in the Iowa/California Edition of the works of Mark Twain were both scheduled for publication in 1972. Substantial work continued on the preparation of the complete notebooks, and there was some progress toward the appearance of additional volumes in the standard works. Meanwhile, it was slack times for both scholarly and critical studies.

i. Textual and Bibliographical

The revised edition of *Eight American Authors*, with the chapter on Mark Twain (pp. 273–320) begun by the late Harry Hayden Clark and completed by Howard Baetzhold, appeared at the end of 1971. The most obvious dilemma facing the editors of the updated bibliography was the conflict between the enormous proliferation of books and articles written on the subject since the first edition of *Eight American Authors* in 1956 and the lack of space in which to assess this more recent material. The section called "General Critiques" and the one on "Studies of *Huckleberry Finn*" have been greatly expanded, but a disappointingly large proportion of the essay is the barely-edited language of the earlier version. Consequently, while DeLancey Ferguson's *Mark Twain: Man and Legend* and many other vintage works receive extended analysis, more recent criticism is often checklisted without thorough evaluation. The revised *Eight American Authors* will provide students with a valuable introduction to Mark Twain scholarship and criticism in spite of its limitations and exclusions.

Joseph B. McCullough has made a detailed textual study of the files of the Buffalo *Express* during Mark Twain's tenure as an editor in "Mark Twain and the Hy Slocum-Carl Byng Controversy" (*AL* 43:42–59). Among the number of articles and anecdotes which appeared in the paper under the "Hy Slocum" or "Carl Byng" pseudonyms, McCullough points out that "Slocum" was used as a byline in March 1868, almost a year and a half before Clemens assumed his post—making it seem quite clear that "Slocum" was not an alternative for "Mark Twain." "Carl Byng," on the other hand, seems very probably to have been the new editor's name in items which bear striking topical similarities to comic paragraphs signed "Mark Twain." McCullough's article should convince anyone that the recent volume mistitled *The Forgotten Writings of Mark Twain* (see *ALS 1963*, p. 55) was substantially not the writings of Mark Twain at all and that much of the material was justifiably forgotten.

Clemens claimed that the poem "To Miss Katie of H–L," which appeared in the 6 May 1853 issue of the Hannibal *Journal* causing a furor among readers, was an inadvertent oversight. He said that the notorious dash he set up in the title was used because the entire word *Hannibal* was too long to fit the column width. Christene Zwahlen, in "Of Hell or of Hannibal?" (*AL* 42:562–63), has sensibly measured the column width and discovered that *Hannibal* could have been spelled out with "at least two picas of white space" at either side of the headline. The title was thus an intentionally ambiguous comic improvisation rather than a journalistic space-saver.

ii. Biographical

Lucian R. Smith has collected together in "Sam Clemens: Pilot" (*MTJ* 15,iv:1–5) a number of earlier critics' appraisals of the importance of his piloting career on Mark Twain's later life, intending to determine whether or not it was the most satisfying occupation in which the nascent humorist indulged. Smith concludes that Clemens was not a very impressive licensed pilot. And he suggests that Clemens might have returned to his "favorite" profession after the Civil War if he had wanted to. What prevented him were the two facts that (1) "he did not enjoy piloting nearly as much as he said he did," and (2) after the war, piloting "no longer offered the wealth and prestige Sam sought." "As long as piloting offered Sam the wealth and prestige he needed to compensate for a lack of self-esteem, Sam was a pilot," Smith argues. "But when it could no longer offer these rewards, piloting became no more valuable to Sam than printing or mining or newspaper writing had been, and so he let it go."

Arthur G. Pettit's "Mark Twain and the Negro, 1867–1869" (*JNH* 56:88–96) suggests that Mark Twain made raucous and tasteless fun at the expense of the black man during his Western days, but as he moved East he abandoned at least "some of his more extravagant forms of prejudice." He substituted *Negro* for *nigger* in public print, though not in private writings; he developed abiding concerns about slavery and violence against blacks which he was willing to express publicly; and he began experimenting, albeit awkwardly, with the accurate transcription of Negro dialect in his writing. Sources for the change in attitude were very likely the influence of liberal Eastern passengers on board the *Quaker City*, the even more liberal attitudes of his prospective in-laws the Langdons, and the maturing of his own private convictions.

Pettit carries his study of Mark Twain's attitude toward the Negro further in his "Mark Twain, the Blood-Feud, and the South" (*SLJ* 4,i:20–32). According to Pettit, by 1870 Mark Twain had focused his literary attentions on the Southern lust for violence—the blood feud and dueling. His earliest comments, in *Simon Wheeler, Detective*, for example, were low comedy; but after his return to the Mississippi River in 1882, his attitude became bitter and scornful, as an extended examination of the Grangerford-Shepherdson chapters of *Huckleberry Finn* shows. Both "Souths"—the "one of nostalgia, the other of nausea and nightmare"—continued throughout Clemens's life to conflict in his mind as one more of the interminable paradoxes of his personality.

Neal L. Goldstien tackles an immense question in "Mark Twain's Money Problems" (*BuR* 19,i:37–54). He discusses Mark Twain's concept of money and materialism as opposed to his idealistic instincts by examining, briefly in *Huckleberry Finn* and at length in *Roughing It* and *A Connecticut Yankee in King Arthur's Court*, the theme of the use of money. The pursuit of wealth in the early travel book is a morally complex issue, and Mark Twain includes both positive and negative arguments; but basically, according to Goldstien, *Roughing*

It is still dominantly optimistic. "It is a boyhood idyll, in a sense, and none of its railings can really mar the great adventure which lies at its core." By the time of the writing of *Connecticut Yankee*, Mark Twain "gives vent to all his mixed feelings about the dollar, attacking it for the easy path to brutality it builds, and at the same time revelling in it and needing it." Goldstien has barely scratched the surface of an important topic which needs to be expanded to include at the very least *The £1,000,000 Banknote, The Man That Corrupted Hadleyburg,* and *The $30,000 Bequest.*

And, finally, Frank Campbell and Ina Campbell have recounted their successful attempt to locate the villas Viviani and di Quarto in which Mark Twain lived in 1892–1893 and 1903–1904 in "Mark Twain's Florentine Villas in 1964–65" (*MTJ* 15,iv:12–14).

iii. General Criticism

Mark Twain, The Critical Heritage, edited by Frederick Anderson with the assistance of Kenneth M. Sanderson (New York, Barnes and Noble) reprints eighty-eight English and American reviews and critical appraisals of Mark Twain. The earliest selections are reviews from 1869 of *Innocents Abroad,* and the final pieces are the early posthumous evaluations by John Macy and H. L. Mencken in 1913. In between are contemporaneous evaluations of the major publications of Mark Twain's career. Anderson's introduction focuses upon the unusual relationship of a popular humorist who was publishing books by the subscription method with a genteel and cultivated standard of literary criticism. While recognizing the power of critical opinion, Mark Twain responded publicly only to "personal attacks and criticism which disparaged a book for not being what its author had never intended." By a series of literary and psychological strategies, Mark Twain managed to insulate himself from critical disapproval and perhaps to preserve the unique qualities which those critics and reviewers disparaged in his writings.

Mary E. Goad's *The Image and the Woman in the Life and Writings of Mark Twain* (*ESRS* 19,iii:5–70) is a monograph-length, fairly traditional study of its subject. There are chapters on Jane Clemens (Mark Twain's mother), Mary Mason Fairbanks (with a summary of those revisions of *Innocents Abroad* possibly attributable to her influence), and Olivia Clemens—three "censor figures." Only Olivia served as an effective reformer and literary arbiter, for which Miss Goad provides the standard and familiar editorial corrections and suggestions. The chapter on "Image into Art" questions why Mark Twain was never able "to create a female character, of whatever age, of whatever time and place, who is other than wooden and unrealistic." Probably, Miss Goad speculates, the cause lies in his use of his fiction to idealize those characteristics he invented in the three influential women in his life. His women characters were all of "one particular pattern, leaving no room for individualization." All his women are passionless, pure, forgettable. Roxy in *Pudd'nhead Wilson* is an exception because as a slave she is exempt from the idealization process Mark Twain imposed on his other female characters. According to Miss Goad, Mark Twain would have improved his art had he used "the real Livy, not the created one, as the model for the women of his novels." Left unanswered in Miss Goad's study is the essential question: what was it in Mark Twain's own psyche that prevented his use of the "real" Olivia in fiction?

A number of Lewis Leary's well-known essays have been collected in accessible form in *Southern Excursions, Essays on Mark Twain and Others* (Baton Rouge, La. State Univ. Press). In addition to "Tom and Huck: Innocence on Trial," "Mark Twain and the Comic Spirit," "Mark Twain's Wound," and "The Bankruptcy of Mark Twain," there is one previously unpublished essay, "The Lovingoods: Notes Toward a Genealogy" (pp. 111–30), which points out some similarities between the Lovingood and Finn families and meditates facetiously but felicitously on the possibility that Pap Finn was Sut Lovingood grown slightly older.

In "The Picaresque as a Flaw in Mark Twain's Novels" (*MTJ* 15,iv:10–12), Jeanne Bugliari makes some sweeping generalizations in a very brief space, concluding that the strict adherence to picaresque form produced failures in *The Prince and the Pauper, Roughing It, Tom Sawyer*, and *Life on the Mississippi* "because either their characters are more or less flat, static, and insufficiently drawn or because their themes are not purposefully directed." *Huckleberry Finn* almost escapes the limitations when Huck, in the middle sections, "is in control of the events now and no longer a wandering *picaro*." Such galloping syntheses and generalizations overlook the possibilities of growth and control over external circumstances in Tom, Prince Edward or the cub pilot and leave at least one reader befuddled at their meaning.

Joseph B. McCullough assesses "Mark Twain and Journalistic Humor Today" (*EJ* 60:591–95). He suggests that common links between nineteenth-century newspaper humorists and Thurber, Perelman, and Buchwald (among others) are philosophical pessimism and the use of "aspects of loneliness, melancholy, terror, violence, and death" for comic purposes.

iv. Earlier Works

Richard F. Fleck's "Mark Twain's Social Criticism in *The Innocents Abroad*" (*BRMMLA* 25:39–48) proposes that rather than measuring European countries by a purely chauvinistic American standard, Mark Twain developed in his first travel book a "standard of judgment—the welfare of the common man—as a criterion for all nations including his own."

In "The Gentle Blasphemer: Mark Twain, Holy Scripture, and the Book of Mormon" (*BYUS* 11:119–40), Richard H. Cracroft attempts to serve as apologist for Mark Twain's attitudes toward holy writings. The humorist used varying modes of comedy, depending upon his own "squeamishness." The more reverential the attitude of his audience, the more likely his humor was to be restrained and facetious. Sometimes, as with the Koran and Mary Baker Eddy's *Science and Health*, his method was more waspish and vitriolic. To create humor from the Book of Mormon in *Roughing It*, Mark Twain wrote "a non-vicious kind of hoax [which] should therefore be appreciated for what it is, and not dismissed, as it is by some, as a maliciously misguided attempt to write off the Mormons and their book." The humor achieved by distorting a passage from its context can amuse even a Mormon reader because Mark Twain was obviously unfamiliar with the text he was attempting to ridicule. Cracroft enumerates examples of this unfamiliarity and decides that the same methods pervade Mark Twain's discussion of the institutions of Mormonism in his descriptions of Salt Lake City in *Roughing It*. Richard F. Fleck compares Mark Twain's nature descriptions in *Roughing It* with Robert Louis Stevenson, Whitman, John Muir, and W. H. Hudson in "Mark Twain in the American Wilderness" (*NaS* 25,ii:12–14; 25,iii:10–11).

He argues that in such depictions of landscapes there is a "subtle barometer of his [Mark Twain's] varying emotional attitudes toward the land." The late Bryant M. French tabulated "James Hammond Trumbull's Alternative Chapter Mottoes for *The Gilded Age*" (*PQ* 50:271–80). Trumbull, who was commissioned to provide mottoes in foreign and exotic languages for the book by Twain and Warner, offered several choices to the two authors of the novel. Those rejected mottoes are printed here, together with their translations.

Judith Fetterley's "The Sanctioned Rebel" (*SNNTS* 3:293–304) suggests, as the title implies, that in *Tom Sawyer* Tom is a rebel whose actions are sanctioned by the adult society of St. Petersburg because he relieves the town of its habitual boredom without violating any of its true values. And in turn Tom requires the adults of the village as an audience to "prohibit" but secretly approve his pranks. Tom's "growth" throughout the novel is a growth to "adult" values—but values which are in many senses more negative than the child's because of their hypocrisy.

Harry Bergholz's "Strindberg's Anthologies of American Humorists, Bibliographically Identified" (*SS* 43:335–43) includes a brief discussion of the translation of "The Loves of Alonzo FitzClarence and Rosannah Ethelton" in the dramatist's 1879 collection, *Amerikanska humorister*.

v. Huckleberry Finn

Even Huckleberry aroused less than usual attention in 1971. Russell H. Goodyear noted in "Huck Finn's Anachronistic Double Eagles" (*AN&Q* 10:39) that although twenty-dollar gold pieces are mentioned twice in *Huck* (whose events occurred some time between 1835 and 1845), the first regular coinage of the double-eagle did not come from the mint until 1850. John R. Byers, Jr., "Miss Emmeline Grangerford's Hymn Book" (*AL* 43:259–63), nominates Isaac Watts's hymn "Alas! and Did my Savior bleed!" as the probable model for Emmeline's elegy, "Ode to Stephen Dowling Bots, Dec'd.," on the basis of similarities in stanza pattern and in its question-and-answer structure.

James L. Colwell explores Clemens's discovery of the huckleberry in New England in 1868 and its felicitous appropriation for a young

man who could never have known a huckleberry bush in the Mississippi Valley of the 1830s and '40s in "Huckleberries and Humans: On
the Naming of Huckleberry Finn" (*PMLA* 86:70–76). "The Spunk of
a Rabbit: An Allusion in *The Adventures of Huckleberry Finn*" (*MTJ*
15,iv:14–16), by William J. Scheick, argues that Huck's ironic request
for help in chapter 16—which persuades the slave hunters that a case
of smallpox exists on the raft and diverts them from a closer inspection—parallels Brer Rabbit's "Don't fling me in dat brier-patch" in
Uncle Remus, His Songs and Sayings. Although the chronology makes
the borrowing dubious (Mark Twain's chapter was written in 1876
and Joel Chandler Harris's tale first appeared in 1879), Scheick suggests that young Sam Clemens might well have heard the identical
story as a child.

Elizabeth E. McMahan has focused upon "The Money Motif: Economic Implications in *Huckleberry Finn*" (*MTJ* 15,iv:5–10), narrowing the concerns of Goldstien (above). She suggests that "a concern
for money permeates the novel and accentuates the major theme of
corruption in a materialistic society." After cataloging instances of
greed-motivated behavior in minor characters including Tom Sawyer
and relating such behavior to the economic theories of Thorstein
Veblen, Miss McMahan proposes that Huck himself is different.
"Huck never lets a desire for money come before sympathy for fellow
human beings," in spite of his "touch of parsimony."

Two articles by Neil Schmitz were the most important studies of
Huckleberry Finn in 1971. In "The Paradox of Liberation in *Huckleberry Finn*" (*TSLL* 13:125–36), Schmitz examines the paradoxical
and ambiguous implications of the word *freedom* in the novel. "The
freedom Huck strives to attain is his right to be a child," an aboriginal
savage; Jim's freedom, to the contrary, involves moving from a primitive state toward "purposeful social activity." Huck's and Jim's flights
are therefore contradictory: "The distance between the boy and the
man, between the black man desperate for a secure and honorable
place in society and the white youth in desperate flight from that
same society" cannot be closed. Mark Twain ultimately realized that
there was no solution to the problem and was content to allow Jim's
dilemma merely to serve Huck's growing awareness that "no one is
free unless all are free." The second article, "Twain, *Huckleberry
Finn*, and the Reconstruction" (*AmerS* 12:59–67), traces the ways in
which "Jim's situation at the end of *Huckleberry Finn* reflects that of

the Negro in the Reconstruction, free at last and thoroughly impotent, the object of devious schemes and a hapless victim of constant brutality." Perceptively, Schmitz views the antagonism and the ritual as resting squarely within the consciousness of Tom Sawyer, who makes Jim a "character in a fantasy" which frees but nevertheless demeans and torments him. But by verbalizing the search for liberation in terms of European romantic traditions, Tom effectively obscures the basic issue of black slavery. And further, by his benign acceptance of his role in Tom's farce, Jim succumbs to the white man's choice of a fate for him—shuffling, smiling, thankful, "a piece of statuary." Such a resolution represents the white man's logical solution, Mark Twain's own solution to the horror of Jim's plight.

vi. Later Works

Robert Rowlette announces at the beginning of *Mark Twain's "Pudd'nhead Wilson"* (Bowling Green, Ohio: Bowling Green Univ. Popular Press) that he "will examine what I consider to be Twain's structural achievement of integrating the novel's three apparently disparate themes and the plots that dramatize them: slavery, detection, and twinhood." Slavery, Rowlette argues, is a specific metaphor for the determinism that controls all men, black or white; and only two methods can resist the evil effects of training—reason, which should upset social institutions, and the changing of the oppressed-oppressor roles. An examination of Mark Twain's evolving depiction of slaves, in writings prior to *Pudd'nhead*, establishes a movement from traditional comic stereotyping to realistic individualizing in the characters of Jim (but only in *Huckleberry Finn*) and Roxy. Mark Twain's fascination with the detective story throughout his writing career is catalogued from his use of a fumbling, burlesque character in the 1870s to the transcendent liberator-detective who "applies his reason to the revelation of man's debased condition." Twinhood, in all its possible comic and serious variations as changlings and doubles, concern Rowlette in his next chapter. From the matrix of these themes and ideas came the design for *Pudd'nhead Wilson*: "So constrained is man by conditioning that neither the reason of the ordinary man nor the experience afforded by a change of identity can free him from his mental bondage." Three reversals in action use the three motifs of twinship, slavery, and detection: Roxy's exchange of the babies, Tom's discovery that he is a slave, and Tom's crimes, which are solved by Wilson's abilities as a detective. The explication of *Pudd'nhead* in chapter 5 examines these motifs with a number of minor variations, and discusses the use Mark Twain made of irony in establishing the tone of the novel.

Bertram Mott, Jr., examines *Joan of Arc* in the context of John Calvin's *Tenets* in 'Twain's Joan: A Divine Anomaly" (*EA* 23[1970]: 245–55). By Mott's reading, Joan represents absolute Good and Cauchon absolute Evil. Predestination is one of Joan's beliefs, as is Election. In addition, her Christlike qualities, both temperamental and biographical, fascinated Mark Twain. His narrative dilemma, residing in Le Conte's misanthropy, created an inconsistent voice for telling the romance. Ultimately, *Joan* is a "failure" as literature, but highly important "as a chapter in Mark Twain's moral-philosophical-religious history."

Elmo Howell's "Mark Twain's Indiantown" (*MTJ* 15,iv:16–19) examines the recently published fragment *Which Was It?* Howell nominates Napoleon, Arkansas, as the source and model for Indiantown and then undertakes to prove, somewhat gratuitously, that Indiantown was a Southern rather than a Midwestern village. Ultimately, according to Howell, Mark Twain "was always actually, even in moments of his greatest triumph, a simple-hearted Southern country boy a long way from home. And in moments of creation he went back there, to familiar country and to his own kind of people. Indiantown represents one of the last of these excursions and, in the intimacy of his description, one of the most satisfying."

Richard Lehan's "Recent Books: American Fiction" (*NCF* 25:502–08) begins as a review of William M. Gibson's edition of the *Mysterious Stranger* manuscripts, but expands to a discussion of the theme of duality in Mark Twain's writing, especially the dichotomy between idealistic dreamers and rigidly determined "man machines," which Lehan challenges Mark Twain critics to reconcile. John R. May also looks at *The Mysterious Stranger* in "The Gospel According to Philip Traum: Structural Unity in 'The Mysterious Stranger' " (*SSF* 8:411–22). May summarizes the plot-lines in the novel, all of which involve achieving salvation—by insanity, by laughter, and by negation. In spite of the solipsistic ending, Theodore is an old man reminiscing in his declining years, as May shows from scattered evidence which he argues is not lack of control of point-of-view or philosophical inconsistency.

Finally, Allison Ensor compares "The War Prayer" with Howells's short story "Editha" in "Mark Twain's 'The War Prayer': Its Ties to Howells and Hymnology" (*MFS* 16[1970]:535–39). He also notes that the hymn which precedes the stranger's sermon in the short story is "God the Omnipotent." Since the hymn is actually a request for Divine pity, perhaps Mark Twain chose it deliberately, aware of its irony in the mouths of a blood-lusting congregation.

University of Chicago

6. Henry James

William T. Stafford

The liveliest criticism on James to appear during the year was in, as is often the case, the letters column of *TLS*. However, the charges and counter-charges therein, between S. Gorley Putt and F. R. Leavis, on what James did or did not know at first hand about London "low-life" and on the possible influence of Dickens on *The Princess Casamassima* are by no means the most enlightening criticism. Four notable books appeared on James, two concerned with his relations with France (those by Jeanne Delbaere-Garant and Lyall H. Powers), and two raising some very basic questions about James's literary stature (those by Philip M. Weinstein and Charles Thomas Samuels). Also notable is Robert L. Gale's much expanded and now updated chapter on Jamesian criticism in James Woodress's revised edition of *Eight American Authors*. The *Arizona Quarterly* devoted all of its essay space in its summer issue to pieces on James. And individual articles of note appear to be in greater profusion than during most recent years.

i. Bibliography, Biography, Reputation

All Jamesians will be grateful for Robert L. Gale's greatly expanded survey of James scholarship in the revised edition of *Eight American Authors* (pp. 321–375). Pointing out in his introduction that if all James himself wrote "were to be assembled into one massive edition, it would come to . . . at least 10 million words," many, many more times that astronomical number of words must have been written about his work, 68 books devoted exclusively to James, for example, between 1950 and the early 1970s. His updating of Robert Spiller's original essay is a marvel of clarity and concision, following the same patterns already established: sections on bibliographical studies, editions, manuscripts (often with locations), biography, and criticism, all with variously convenient subdivisions. Necessarily selective, it is nonetheless surprisingly comprehensive—and thus certain to be a major scholarly tool for some years to come.

Much more highly specialized but also useful is R. E. Long's "Adaptations of Henry James's Fiction for Drama, Opera, and Films; With a Checklist of New York Theatre Critics' Reviews" (*ALR* 4:268–78), although it must only scratch the surface with its list of nineteen items. Even more specialized is George Monteiro's "Addendum to Edel and Laurence: Henry James in Portuguese" (*PBSA* 65:302–304), a "preliminary" list of James's work translated into that language.

A biographical item of note is Ben M. Vorpahl's "Henry James and Owen Wister" (*PMHB* 95:291–338), an almost monograph-length account of the James-Wister relationship, covering their long and surprisingly intimate friendship, and likely to be the definitive study of that friendship. Even if one discounts an opening statement that *The Virginian's* "focus and manner corresponded to those of *Roderick Hudson* and [that] its hero was Christopher Newman . . . gone to Wyoming for his health instead of to Europe for culture," one does see clearly in both an "intwisted . . . imagination" in their mutually revealed "assumption[s] about literature and history." Fanny Kemble Wister's note in the same issue, "Caroline Lewis and Henry James" (*PMHB* 95:339–50), reprints some sketches by and a letter from Miss Lewis explaining that the sketches, facetiously attributed to James, were in fact a domestic joke played upon him on the occasion of his visit with the Wisters on January 4 of 1881.

Pictures are much more important in Dean Flower's *Henry James in Northampton: Visions and Revisions* (Northampton, Mass., Friends of the Smith College Library), a beautifully printed little memoir in which are reproduced twelve fine photographs of James (eleven for the first time) taken by Katherine Elizabeth McClellan in her studio there when James gave his "The Lesson of Balzac" lecture at Smith College on 6 May 1905. Flower's accompanying essay recounts James's stay there, who entertained him and where, the newspaper reports, and so on; more importantly, he considers the artistic role the image of the small New England town plays in some of the major fiction (*Roderick Hudson*, for example, and *The Ambassadors*) and more generally in his creative imagination. The visit to Northampton itself is placed in the context of *The American Scene* and of all that Balzac meant to him, somehow seeing in such a town, Fowler concludes, an understanding of himself that had been made possible in part through an understanding of Balzac.

A footnote to James's American reputation among his contemporaries is provided in Charles E. Burgess's "The Master and the *Mirror*" (*PLL* 7:382–405), a long detailed history of the references to the writer in William Marion Reedy's St. Louis *Mirror*. The public taste therein revealed and reflected are pretty much the standard ones: "an emphasis on his obscure style and supposed snobbishness, plus jibes at his expatriation" with a steady contrasting respect for his literary stature. Daniel N. Roselli's "Max Beerbohm's Unpublished Parody of Henry James" (*RES* 22:61–63) is a brief discussion of a "pencilled in" parody of James at an unknown date in Beerbohm's copy of James's *Terminations*.

Finally, all good Jamesians will probably want to read Geoffrey T. Hellman's *New Yorker* profile of Leon Edel (13 March:43–86).

ii. Essays, Criticism, Drama

William F. Hall's "The Continuing Relevance of Henry James' *The American Scene*" (*Criticism* 13:151–65) is an important and elaborate analysis of James's greatest travel book in terms of its current significance. Aside from seeing many attitudes in it like those of F. Scott Fitzgerald, especially in *The Great Gatsby*, he describes it, at the beginning, as "the record of an individual quest for certainty, for identity, largely conceived in terms of a search for an object which will symbolize the America that *is* as distinct from that which was and that which may be." He concludes, however, by depicting James as "one of the best among the earliest examples of that peculiarly modern type . . . of the 'native,' now 'alien,' observing the 'alien,' the 'new native,' in a society whose survival depends on their somehow existing in it together with a minimum of destructive friction." This is the best essay on *The American Scene* I know since Wright Morris's in *The Territory Ahead*.

An entirely different sort of study is Scott Byrd's "Henry James's 'Two Old Houses and Three Young Women': A Problem in Dating and Assemblage" (*PBSA* 65:383–89), a neat little note that speculates that inclusion of the above in *Italian Hours* avoids apparent geographic and chronologic discontinuousness if we see the three-part essay as a "sort of literary triptych" paralleling a particular painting referred to in part 2. This is only for the James specialist, but deftly researched and presented for that specialist.

Attention to James's criticism as criticism during the year is quite limited, but Frederick S. Frank's "The Two Taines of Henry James" (*RLC* 45:350–65) and Paul Maixner's "James on D'Annunzio —'A High Example of Exclusive Estheticism' " (*Criticism* 13:291–311) are both solid studies. Frank's analysis of James's references to Taine is concerned with how, for James, the Frenchman was always "a great hero-villain of letters, an enviable intellect who was everything which the fine artist ought to be and everything as well which the responsible critic ought not to be." Maixner sees in James's curious attention to D'Annunzio "an important advance in his critical thought," for it first clearly reveals that for James an aesthetic that is "inclusive of and indeed identical to the moral is always" a higher aesthetic than one that excludes it. William Peterson, in "Henry James on *Jane Eyre*" (*TLS* 30 July:919–20), extracts material from a wide variety of sources in order to construct, all persuasively enough, an attitude he summarizes as Jamesian: "Charlotte Brontë's literary reputation depended more upon the picturesque and pathetic Brontë legend than upon the intrinsic merits of her book."

The only article I saw during the year on James's drama is an insignificant note covering ground already covered many, many times before (Joe B. Hatcher's "Shaw the Reviewer and James's *Guy Domville*," *MD* 14:331–34).

iii. Sources, Influences, Parallels

Jeanne Delbaere-Garant's *Henry James: The Vision of France* (Paris, Société d'Éditions [1970]) is anything but a conventional source study. The key word is *vision;* the key thrust of her thesis, the central positions the idea of France holds in the creative imagination of the various Henry Jameses who came in contact with and used it: James the student, the visitor, the tourist, the gossip, and, most importantly, the literary critic and writer. The result is a comprehensive, lucid, and original approach to this complex subject through placing James "against the French geographical, artistic, and moral background" in order "to provide a new focus for an explication of his mind and fiction."

This unfragmented approach to her subject results in some special virtues. And critics are not likely to quarrel, I think, with her views of James as tourist and critic. She catalogs with beautiful succinctness how as tourist, James's vision of France "oscillated between exasperation and adoration and never stopped at the dead centre of indifference." And her chapters on French critics, French poets, and the various ones on French novelists are also beautifully done. His changing attitudes toward French fiction, from that of Balzac to that of Proust, his struggles with the contrasting "pulls" of French "form" and English "life," and his ultimate assimilation of the two in his final commitment to the English tradition—all are as cleanly and clearly presented as they are ever likely to be.

Some of her views of the vision of France in the fiction (all of the fiction in which France is used as setting or background or theme) are somewhat more questionable—seeing *The American*, for example, as primarily "another variation of the theme of Art," reflecting his continuous involvement over "the French concern for plastic beauty" in conflict with "the Anglo-Saxon concern for moral beauty." The symbolic placement of Boulonge (in *What Maisie Knew*) halfway "between the moral angularity of England and the sexual solicitations of Paris" is, for me, another questionable view. But I quarrel not at all with her view of the uses of France in *The Ambassadors* where, in a great coalescing, "the concrete and the abstract, the literal and the figurative, the moral and the aesthetic all melt into each other."

Nor do I quarrel with one of her central, final views that France, for James, was "a country where life claimed its rights louder than elsewhere" and had thus "made him acutely aware of the tension between the expanding individual life and the contracting standards of society, between the powerful flow of life and the fixity of artistic forms, between the dynamism of his emotional needs and a static discipline imposed from outside." This tension in James is a primary source of his power, and the contribution of France and the French to its formulation is set forth here with persuasive authority.

Miss Delbaere-Garant's final view of James and his career as "a double spiral rooted at the one end in the American soil and in romanticism, contracting in its middle on contact with France and French naturalism and expanding again into the Anglo-Saxon world and into the twentieth century" provides a neat transition to Lyall H. Powers's quite different *Henry James and the Naturalist Movement*

(East Lansing, Mich. State Univ. Press). Powers's, for me, is a more limited book, a somewhat old fashioned one in its plodding thoroughness, and, of course, one with quite different goals from those of Miss Delbaere-Garant: the influence of the French naturalists on James's work. He provides detailed analyses of James's own three "naturalistic" novels—*The Bostonians, The Princess Casamassima,* and *The Tragic Muse*—and their surrounding short works, a quick survey of the 1890s, and a brief look at the achievement of *The Ambassadors,* all following two opening chapters devoted to James's early personal and critical views of these "grandsons" of Balzac.

His general method is to extract and detail the naturalistic techniques at work in these three novels of the late 1880s but without, at the same time, blinding himself to their ties to James's more pervasive thematic concerns. But one wonders at times whether the naturalistic elements he finds, say, in *The Bostonians* couldn't be found as well in *The Portrait of a Lady* or whether the many other traditions (the pastoral, say, or the romantic, see below) found in the American-set novel are not just as important. His insistence upon a "happy ending" for *The Bostonians* is for me totally unconvincing. His view of Hyacinth's tragedy as one of committing "himself before he has known himself" I find much more persuasive, as I do of his view of how the apparently differing resolutions of Miriam Rooth and of Nick Dormer (in *The Tragic Muse*) are at base really one "in their treatment of the problem of the conflict of 'art and the world.' "

His overview of James and his career in no basic way conflicts with Miss Delbaere-Garant's. And both books, within the confines of their quite differing schemata, are sufficiently comprehensive. They are thus neat complements, and both important. But for me *The Vision of France* is a vastly more original book—and a much more readable one.

Miss Delbaere-Garant is not so original, it seems to me, in her "Henry James's Divergences from his Russian Model in *The Princess Casamassima*" (*RLV* 37,v:535–44), another study of the ties and differences between James's novel and Turgenev's *Terre Vierges* with emphasis here on how he turned the Russian model into "a typically Jamesian novel with typically Jamesian preoccupations but . . . failed to free himself from the existing plot." P. R. Grover's "Two Modes of Possessing—Conquest and Appreciation: *The Princess Casamassima* and *L'Éducation Sentimentale*" (*MLR* 66:760–71) is still another

contrastive study of James and the French realistic tradition, especially as it is represented by Flaubert. He sees both novels reflecting
"the agglutinative imagination of man as he tries to subsume the
world to himself." James's, however, is a "receptive assimilation"
rather than an "exertion of the will and the acquisition of the power
to command or to own."

The controversy between F. R. Leavis and S. Gorley Putt, already
referred to above, is also, interestingly enough, on *The Princess Casamassima*, but in this case on an English influence, the role of Dickens
in James's pictures of London life in that novel. There is no need to
detail charge and counter-charge here. Suffice it to say that it began
with Putt's objection, under the title "Henry James and Dickens" in
the letter column of *TLS*, to the charge in Leavis's book, *Dickens the
Novelist*, that James "was dependent upon memories of Dickens for
his picture of London life" in *The Princess* on the grounds that there
was considerable biographical evidence to the contrary. It ends five
letters later just about where it began, with a cacophony of sharp
critical comment from both pens interspersed throughout. Interested
readers should see *TLS* as follows: Putt (19 Feb.:213; 12 Mar.:296;
26 Mar.:353); Leavis (5 Mar.:271; 19 Mar.:325). Thrown somewhere
in between is Arthur Freeman's letter (*TLS*, 12 Mar.:296) to the
effect that he couldn't care less about the Putt-Leavis contretemps
but that James demonstrably knew nothing at first hand about social
revolutionaries in London during the 1880s. Lionel Trilling's protes-
tations to the contrary, he adds, are "in fact utter nonsense." Fiction,
he concludes, is no place to get information about facts, anyway.

The remaining source studies are all on American writers. Paul
A. Newlin's "The Development of *Roderick Hudson*: An Evaluation"
(*ArQ* 27:101–23), in surveying the variety of sources identified as
contributing to this novel, focuses on Hawthorne's *The Marble Faun*
and its ties to the Rome of the American sculptor William Wetmore
Story as the major "indirect link between these two novels of Italian
settings." He concludes, however, that it is the diversity of literary
antecedents that is of major importance in this area of the novel's development. Scott Byrd, in "The Spoils of Venice: Henry James's 'Two
Old Houses and Three Young Women' and *The Golden Bowl*" (*AL*
43:371–84), sees attitudes toward Italy revealed in the travel sketch
also woven into *The Golden Bowl*, especially in James's picture of
Amerigo, which thereby enhances his symbolic weight in the novel

as "not simply a creature of a fallen world . . . [but] also a member of a fallen class and the citizen of a fallen nation." Two additional studies look at James's influence on others. Ashley Brown's "Landscape into Art: Henry James and John Crowe Ransom" (*SR* 79:206–12) finds the source for Ransom's *Old Mansion* (1924) in the Charleston chapter of *The American Scene*. And D. M. Murray, in "Candy Christian as a Pop-Art Daisy Miller" (*JPC* 5:340–48), sees Terry Southern's *Candy* as a work that "recalls Mark Twain in genre and Henry James in subject, the technique having been modernized in the key of Pop Art." "Daisy Miller," he concludes, "you've come a long way . . . and one wonders where and how you will appear next." One does, indeed.

iv. Criticism: General

The two books of general criticism devoted to James during the year both open, or reopen, some basic questions about the literary worth of the novelist. Philip M. Weinstein, in *Henry James and the Requirements of the Imagination* (Cambridge, Harvard Univ. Press) has as its central thesis James's continuous concern with the conflict between imagination and experience and his final inability successfully to accommodate experience to imagination in *The Golden Bowl*. Charles T. Samuels, in *The Ambiguity of Henry James* (Urbana, Univ. of Ill. Press), is equally explicit: James has been analyzed excessively. He has not been sufficiently evaluated. Samuels will correct the imbalance. The "heart of the matter," he writes, is James's "moral antinomies." And the central problem: "how to assert the essential difference between good and evil without oversimplifying their opposition, how to establish the validity of moral judgments without ignoring personal bias." His consequent method: James's ". . . greatness as a writer is partly measured by the magnitude of these challenges, and his books are successful by the extent to which each meets them effectively."

As I have pointed out elsewhere (see my longer review, *AL* 44:160–61), the conflicting pulls, the dread *and* fear of human experience, are "undeniably a central theme in James's works, perhaps even precisely the collective theme of the six novels Mr. Weinstein closely reads: *Roderick Hudson, The Portrait of a Lady, What Maisie Knew, The Sacred Fount, The Ambassadors,* and *The Golden Bowl.*"

The thread of this conflict is nicely and neatly traced, through some re-curring imagery, through parallel functions of characters in several novels, and through a unique if, for Weinstein, an unsatisfactory resolution of the conflict in *The Golden Bowl.*

My former and continuing quarrel with the book is not with what it demonstrates but with what it concludes from that demonstration: appearing to equate a deficient protagonist with the artistic vision of James himself, as if those limitations have to be perceived from some standards outside the book rather than refracted from implicit stan-dards within. And his tag for the world that *is* finally affirmed (in *The Golden Bowl*) as a "morally dubious" one—because, he claims, it is not essentially different from the fictional worlds which preceded it in James and there "rejected as uninhabitable"—still seems to me simply a rejection of James's view of the world because it is not Mr. Weinstein's view of the world. On this ground, of course, rejection is every reader's right.

Samuels's ultimate distinctions between what is good and bad in James may well be vulnerable to the same charge. He describes his organizational scheme as an "evaluative" one: "I begin with James's confused novels, move through his ambiguous ones, and end with his examples of achieved complexity." At the bottom of the scale is "The Turn of the Screw"; at the top, *The Ambassadors.* We work our way from one to the other. The ghostly tale is presented as "the paradig-matic case . . . an extreme version of James's basic plot: innocence fighting worldly knowledge." The result, however, is "perplexity"—a lower order even than confusion?—"because the tale's structure allows us to think that James might have mistaken the governess's moral op-portunism for righteousness and that worldliness isn't evil except in her overheated mind." *The Sacred Fount*, at the lowest order of his confused group, suffers from the same malady: "society is vampiristic and the narrator is crazy to say so." This is followed by a rejection of *The American* and *The Princess Casamassima*, on the one hand, and *The Wings of the Dove* and *The Spoils of Poynton*, on the other, be-cause in various ways "James makes us expect [in them] clear ad-vocacy or derogation and then either fails to validate or actually blurs his own distinction." The ambiguous books reflect such errors but do not succumb to them. *The Bostonians* and *The Portrait of a Lady*, a rung higher, possess a built-in doubleness, "a doubleness designedly apparent in plotting and characterization," but execution here is at times faulty, as with Isabel, because James "sometimes confused her responsibility with her victimization and thus perplexes us about the exact process of her downfall." He sees achieved complexity only in "The Europeans," *Washington Square, The Awkward Age, What Maisie Knew,* and *The Ambassadors* because "these books present innocence in a more authentic guise, not through renunciations that turn out to be self-serving but through energetic assertions of values and ideals." His conclusion is as explicit as his introduction: "when James tried to assert too complete a distinction between innocence and worldliness or virtue and vice, his intelligence pulls against the attempt, producing disorderly structure, dubious characterization, and equivocal themes. His best works are those in which all that can be said for the world and against innocence is built so firmly into his design that his fundamental dislike of the one and loyalty to the other are both clear and tenable." A brief final note on *The Golden Bowl* recognizes its healthy ambitions but sees its execution "dogged by old sentimentalities."

The dogmatic schematization here must be apparent enough, even from my necessarily over-simplified presentation of Samuels's argument. What perhaps is not apparent is my firm conviction that both Mr. Samuels and Mr. Weinstein are careful, sensitive, and knowledgeable readers of Henry James, honestly concerned about aspects of his moral vision that for them are ultimately if reluctantly found to be unpalatable.

The other general studies are on a variety of disparate subjects. Both Strother B. Purdy, in "Henry James's Abysses: A Semantic Note" (*ES* 51[1970]:424–33) and John Halverson, in "Late Manner, Major Phase" (*SR* 79:214–31), are concerned with James's style. Purdy's is another of those highly-specialized attempts "to plot the occurence" of a single word, here *abyss,* "and to characterize it semantically throughout James's work." Halverson's is a study of style at "the sentence level," seeing the late manner as "heavily adverbial" and employing "verbal tics" and "favorite adjectives." Nominals are abstract and vague, and "neuter pronouns and demonstratives carry a tremendous weight of indefinite and fluid reference." The more stylistically elegant early novels, however, lack "the superb moral vision" of the major phase. And the stylistic price for his late-manner "psychological and moral penetration" is seen as well worth that price.

Harold T. McCarthy, in "Henry James and the American Aristocracy" (*ALR* 4:61–71), in surveying James's comments in his autobiography and his early international novels about American "aristocrats," finds in some of James's major characters similar characteristics: "highly puritan standards, a dread of sex, a distrust of foreigners . . . and an assumed title to superiority and leadership." The "divisive branches in American life" that are represented by Isabel and Osmond (in *The Portrait of a Lady*) are said to be still "extending."

Two studies fit James into traditions. Irving Malin, in "The Authoritarian Family in American Fiction" (*Mosaic* 4,iii:153–73), presents James's concepts of family in a context of those depicted by Cooper, Poe, Hawthorne, Melville, and Faulkner, where the archetypes of the rigid father, the ineffectual son, and the terrifying shrew occur frequently. In James, however, "the father-son relationship, although significant," is said to be "less important than the portrayal of powerful or powerless women. Harsh will shadows both aspects of the family." James Gindin, in "Howells and James," in his *Harvest of the Quiet Eye: The Novel of Compassion* (Bloomington, Ind. Univ. Press, pp. 102–28), finds in James in particular that his "increasing complexity and . . . vast widening of the humanity involved in this definition of morality" are a movement toward "compassion" in American fiction not to be equaled before the examples of Faulkner and the later Fitzgerald.

James E. Mulqueen, in "Perfection of a Pattern: The Structure of *The Ambassadors, The Wings of the Dove*, and *The Golden Bowl*" (*ArQ* 27:133–42), is one of far too few critics who see these three last great novels as a kind of trilogy. His fine, if narrow, study discerns a similar pattern in all three: "a central character is deceived by an appearance which masks the truth of a social relationship; that character learns the truth; action follows which brings about a state of affairs in which appearance and reality coincide." The pattern is of course perfected only in *The Golden Bowl* where the reality is changed to fit the appearance. Very neat. Alfred Habegger's "Reciprocity and the Market Place in *The Wings of the Dove* and *What Maisie Knew*" (*NCF* 25:455–73) is another good article, questioning too simplistic or too isolated views of James's moral sense. The focus here in these two novels is on reciprocity, of "freely giving in return." It works with Milly and Densher in that her gift to him is his refusal of it for her, and with Maisie and Sir Claude, the demand for "a reciprocal sacrifice"—a giving up of Mrs. Beale for the giving up of Mrs. Wix. It was an appealing ethic for James, Habegger concludes, because it was "closely affiliated with James's feeling for symmetrical form."

v. Criticism: Individual Tales

E. Bruce Kirkham, in "A Study of Henry James' 'Mdme. de Mauves' " (*BSUF* 12,ii:63–69) is the only article of the year devoted to one of the early tales. This exhaustive study closely examines its symbolic names, its settings, the two cultures represented, the generations, and, in greatest detail, the characterization of Longmore, tracing his development from beginning to end where he is described as "a [now] wiser man who has achieved a degree of understanding but [still] lacks complete perception."

Two studies of "The Pupil" alternately attack and defend Pemberton. William Kenney, in "The Death of Morgan in James's 'The Pupil' " (*SSF* 8:317–22), defends the tutor by way of stressing the ties between Morgan and his family. Because Morgan "is the 'heart' of the family . . . his own diseased organ analogously gives out as the Moreens fall apart." He denies that Pemberton actually rejected Morgan. Elizabeth Cummins, in " 'The Playroom of Superstition': An Analysis of Henry James's *The Pupil*" (*MarkhamR* 2,iii[1970]: [13–16]), sees Pemberton, himself the pupil, "resisting Morgan's tutelage," and at the end, "while preparing himself for one final and . . . difficult evasion, he inadvertently smashes the one superstition which Morgan can no longer live without: belief in his tutor's absolute devotion."

Notwithstanding Mr. Samuels's denigration in *The Ambiguity of Henry James* (see above), "The Turn of the Screw" still provokes fervent reactions. Eloquently elaborate attention to the tale appeared in the *SoR* (7:1–48), with the publication of a letter Eric Voegelin wrote Robert Heilman in 1947 following Heilman's famous essay on the tale. Voegelin had read no James before, and his reaction to Heilman has to be understood in that context. Donald Stanford's prefatory note (1–3) explains that permission to print Voegelin's letter (9–24) was conditioned upon its also printing Voegelin's contemporary addendum, "Postscript: On Paradise and Revolution" (25–48), which modifies somewhat his earlier views in some instances and

extends them radically in others. Heilman's foreword explains his
relationship to Voegelin and reports that, after reading the story,
Voegelin had said to him, "It is a great book. It reveals an aspect of
American consciousness that I did not know about. If I had known
of it, my book about America [*Uber die Form des amerikanisches
Geistes*, 1928] would have been different."

Voegelin's earliest reading of the story is as an elaborate Christian
allegory, a study of the mystery of good and evil in relation to Puritan
complexes of consciousness, conscience, and virtue, with the em-
ployer, the governess, and the housekeeper symbolizing respectively
God, the soul, and ordinary existence, all with erotic and incestuous
connections. Voegelin himself describes those early-seen ties in his
later letter as follows: First, there is "the series of spectral identifications of the young man in Harley Street with Quint, of Quint with the
boy, of Miss Jessel with the governess and the girl; . . . second, the
sexual relationship between Quint and Miss Jessel; . . . third, the
relationship of brother and sister between boy and the girl; so that,
fourth . . . the *dramatis personae* are linked by an incestual relationship." All this, he continued, is linked "to a vision of the cosmic
drama of good and evil as an incestuous affair in the divinity." He
could not at the time, he concludes this passage, understand the connection between "a drama of the Puritan Soul and the motif of innocence."

The long postscript does not make clear that he still does, for he
now describes the ambiguity of the tale as an ambiguity inherent in
symbols which express deformed reality. And although Donald Stanford is surely right in seeing as noteworthy in this postscript Voegelin's analysis of the garden at Bly as a symbol of closed existence and
the failure of transcendence as a major contemporary theme, the other
posed connections Voegelin sees, "the Miltonian Paradise, the Swe-
denborgian perfect man, the God who is Satan, and the Jamesian
soul caught in self-pride," as "H.B." enumerates them in *Abstracts
of English Studies* (14:663), are tenuously seen connections indeed.
Still this whole Voegelin affair is a curious and important addendum
to the volumes of criticism devoted to this most troublesome tale.

Two additional studies of the tale strike me as less important. J. R.
Byers, Jr., in "*The Turn of the Screw*: A Hellish Point of View" (*MarkhamR*, 2:101–04), pretends to have resolved the conflict between the
apparitionist and non-apparitionist interpreters by posing instead a

view of the governess as herself an evil spirit with intercourse with the
dead and thus on a hellish mission and able to do with humans pretty
much as she liked. When Miles dies, he "becomes a companion for
our governess in hell until she goes on another mission to seduce
among others Douglas and his sister and . . . through a Jamesian
amusette, the public at large." More persuasive is Susan Crowl's
"Aesthetic Allegory in 'The Turn of the Screw'" (*Novel* 4:107–22),
which provides any number of ties between the story and James's
literary career at the time of its composition so that "perhaps farther-
est in of the nest of forms and coiled ironies of . . . [the tale] is James's
own confessed creed of the symbolic reach of style beyond the grip
of passion or of doubt, and his pity of the cost of that conversion."

In "James's 'Paste'" (*SSF* 8:468–69), Bernard Knieger maintains
that "the story centrally dramatizes Arthur's hypocrisy rather than
Charlotte's 'scrupulousness,'" as some critics have said. And in *The
Light of Common Day* (Bloomington, Ind. Univ. Press, pp. 39–43),
Edwin H. Cady presents a brief reading of "The Beast in the Jungle"
in a context which appears to contend that "perhaps the real secret
of the realist lay in the ambivalence of his sensibility with regard to
romance."

"The Birthplace" is the subject of Mildred Hartsock's "The Con-
ceivable Child: James and the Poet" (*SSF* 7:569–74), a good study
that carefully surveys other interpretations as preface to seeing it
herself as "about a fully realized human being whose imagination
enables him honestly to transcend a moral problem." Criticism,
biography, and the limits of knowing are all also subjects at play here.

vi. Criticism: Individual Novels

The preponderance of Jamesian studies continues to be devoted to
individual novels. And the numerous items which follow, moreover,
might well be supplemented by many of the studies already listed.

Attention to *Roderick Hudson* is steady, and the two articles here
examined have linked views about the role of Rowland Mallet. Peter
J. Conn, in "*Roderick Hudson*: The Role of the Observer" (*NCF*
26:65–82), rejects claims that Rowland is a "personified surrogate for
James's moral imagination." He is instead, says Conn, the "Observer,"
an observer, however, who finally "assumes control on all levels," and
although he considers himself very helpful, sees himself as "kind,"

his "kindness [in fact] is inevitably of the sort that James so often [later] anatomized to show how much outright mischief it can do." Paul S. Speck, in "A Structural Analysis of Henry James's *Roderick Hudson*" (*SNNTS* 2[1970]:292–304), is also critical of Rowland as one responsible for relegating "Roderick's plot to a position within his own" and as one whose shortcomings are directly responsible for Roderick's frustrations. In fact, Rowland's "blindness initiates the action; his self-frustration comprises the theme."

This writer's *Studies in "The American"* (Columbus, Ohio, Charles E. Merrill) reprints James's own comments on the novel, some early reviews, and a sampling of interpretive essays, from both books and periodicals.

Of two studies on *The Portrait of a Lady*, Sheldon W. Liebman's "Point of View in *The Portrait of a Lady*" (*ES* 52:136–47), strikes me as the much more original one via its attention to puns, positions, and points-of-view in the novel. In fact, the entire novel is here seen in terms of rendering Isabel's movements "in a literal as well as a figurative sense, from position to position, from 'point of view' to 'point of view.'" And what she discovers is "that points of view are as numerous as people who have them. . . . that [they] . . . are not one but multi-dimensional, and that any position has its advantages and disadvantages." Donald L. Mull, in "Freedom and Judgment: The Antinomy of Action in *The Portrait of a Lady*" (*ArQ* 27:124–32), focuses on Isabel's decision to marry Osmond, a decision he somewhat pretentiously describes as made "against choice . . . [in order] to make over to—or against—the man with the best taste in the world, the material agency of choice."

The Bostonians received better treatment, especially by Elizabeth Schultz, in "*The Bostonians*: The Contagion of Romantic Illusion" (*Genre* 4:45–59), who sees in this novel a "proving ground not only for the value of the romantic vision but also for the truth of romantic conventions." Both are used, she carefully demonstrates, in the unhappy ending because "Verena's tears suggest . . . that her involvement with suffering and with choice—conditions which the romantic conflict have introduced into her life— . . . is the inevitable condition of human life." Hence, "the romance, both as vision and form, can be the means to a significant end." In "*The Bostonians*: New England Pastoral" (*PLL* 7:374–81), Robert C. McLean sees the pastoral tradition at work, in its pictures of society, in its characterization, and in its settings. Hence, "basic pastoral metaphors" are exploited "to give structure to his novel, symbolic significance to its setting, and insight into his major characters."

Sam Bluefarb's "The 'Radicalism' of the Princess Casamassima" (*BaratR* 6,i:68–73) is a not very successful attempt to see in the "type" represented by the princess the modern dilettante radical, one who craves "bizarre adventure and a dash of sentimental philanthropy" and who, "should a contingency arise . . . , can always return to the comfort and safety" of her only temporarily-left security. In his *The Working Classes in Victorian Fiction* (New York, Barnes and Noble, pp. 46–52), P. J. Keating includes a brief account of this novel to illustrate that even when a good novelist attempts to depict the British working classes in fiction in this period he uses the same conventions to avoid depicting them directly as did such lesser novelists as William Barry or James Greenwood.

Two fine studies on Maisie are Paul Fahey's "*What Maisie Knew*: Learning Not to Mind" (*CR* 14:96–108) and A. E. Dyson's "On Knowing What Maisie Knew, Perhaps," in *On the Novel*, edited by B. S. Banedikz (London, J. M. Dent and Sons, pp. 128–39). Fahey accepts James's stated intention of maintaining " 'her essential human goodness,' her 'innocent wondering consciousness,' her 'pure unspotted soul.' " But what in fact happens is that although Maisie, as "the centre of consciousness" is " 'brought through' without disintegration," with it there is "a limiting of that intense life's potential for development in any fructifying *social* context." Thus, "the pressure of the book is towards acceptance of the view that, inescapably, human relationships are inadequate to the essential needs of the developing individual, even though such relationships are necessarily the means of discovering what those needs are." A. E. Dyson's is a witty and lucid recounting of the events of the novel, ending in the charge that Maisie's "last choice" is "between two evils, with adult demands having so effectively outpaced her 'knowledge' that she must renounce the one in life she really loves."

In "The Dramatist in His Drama: Theory vs. Effect in *The Awkward Age*" (*TSLL* 12:663–74), Francis Gillen utilizes this novel to assert that James "was ultimately a greater novelist than he was a theorist." His point here is that James's dramatic method is in fact something quite different from that "guarded objectivity" of which James boasted in his preface, for he controlled the reader's responses

frequently and variously through "direct comment." The result, however, is a virtue, not a fault.

Quite different aspects of the Victorian milieux are seen as the
real subject of *The Sacred Fount* by Elliot M. Schrero, in "The Narrator's Palace of Thought in *The Sacred Fount*" (*MP* 68:269–88), and
by William B. Stein, in "*The Sacred Fount* and British Aestheticism:
The Artist as Clown and Pornographer" (*ArQ* 27:161–73). For
Schrero, many affinities are seen between the activities of the narrator and "the psychical researches of the type William James admired,"
and many aspects of his method "approximate concepts of scientific
psychology as defined by Hugo Münsterberg." The narrator is thus
seen as fitting somewhere "between scientific materialism . . . and the
pragmatic humanism of William James . . . and other members of the
Society for Psychical Research." For Stein, the novel instead is "a
subtle parody of . . . British aestheticism and decadence of the *fin de
siècle*. It debunks the poses, pretenses, and predilections of the circle
of Oscar Wilde, Aubrey Beardsley, and Walter Pater, especially as
embodied in periodicals" with which they were associated. The off-
color pun and the double entendre are given a free rein here.

Aside from the interesting fact that *The Ambassadors* is examined as the major novel in all four of the books on James already
examined, it was also the subject during the year of five additional
studies, each representing a distinctly different critical approach.
For H. R. Wolfe, in "The Psychology and Aesthetics of Abandonment
in *The Ambassadors*" (*L&P* 21:133–47), the approach is psychological, seeing in Strether's quest "a search for psychic rebirth" and the
"quest for identity," giving to Strether a "'spectatorial' attitude"
which allows him both "to participate in experience (by seeking to
understand it) and to keep it at a safe distance." For William B.
Thomas, in "The Author's Voice in *The Ambassadors*" (*JNT* 1:108–
21), the approach is structural, seeing cavils about point of view
raised by various critics as mere "fetish[es]" of modern criticism. For
all practical purposes James was unequivocally successful in his intention to have us read the novel in its entirety "as Strether's experience,
registered by him, and relayed by him." For Franz Stanzel, in *Narrative Situations in the Novel*, translated by James P. Pusack (Bloomington, Ind. Univ. Press, pp. 92–120), the approach is illustrative,
the book being seen as an example of the "figural novel," a type defined as "linked on the one hand to the first-person novel (without

designation of the narrative act) and on the other . . . to the authorial novel." The approach in Richard Chartier's "The River and the Whirlpool: Water Imagery in *The Ambassadors*" (*BSUF* 12,ii:70–75) is imagistic, seeing the watery imagery "as the most lucid unifying element in the novel," operating "below the level of plot and character" and as "sublevel" perhaps "clearer than the surface level." Finally, we have, in C. M. Finn's "Commitment and Identity in *The Ambassadors*" (*MLR* 66:522–31), a historical approach, seeing in the novel's open-ended conclusion a protagonist "without a safe homecoming," which is as it should be, since "for the 'hero' of a modern novel there can be nothing so organized as an ending."

Three studies of *The Wings of the Dove* are more uneven. The best of the three is probably Tsugio Aoki's "Language of Love and Language of Things: Henry James's *The Wings of the Dove*" (*SELit* Eng. no.:55–71), an impressive reading of the novel in terms of the symbolic equations he makes between Milly and an idea of America, indicative as she is both of a dying civilization and a "nevertheless resurrected 'language of love.'" Sita P. Marks, in "The Sound and the Silence: Nonverbal Patterns in *The Wings of the Dove*" (*ArQ* 27:143–50), presents a brief, neat analysis of the various ways various concealments is a recurring and controlling pattern of the book's method and theme. And in Syndy M. Conger's "The Admirable Villains in Henry James's *The Wings of the Dove*" (*ArQ* 27:151–60), a potentially exciting subject, James's magnificent portrait of Kate is dissipated into stale clichés about the need for pity and understanding for individuals who occasionally make wrong turns.

Lee J. Richmond, in "Henry James and the Comedy of Love: *The Golden Bowl*" (*ErasmusR* 1,i:47–62), marshals an impressive list of parallels between the Commedia dell'arte tradition and the characterization, tone, and structure of this last great novel. "Sexual license . . . , scandalous intrigues, comic misunderstandings . . . are [all] echoed in James' narrative." Even the to-be, short-lived "happy ending" is in this tradition. The happy result is a refreshingly fresh view of the tone of that novel.

Purdue University

7. Faulkner

Michael Millgate

The quantity of writing about William Faulkner continues to increase year by year but, unhappily, it is impossible to speak of a corresponding rise in quality. The trouble with so many of the items is that we simply do not need them: they add little or nothing to our knowledge of Faulkner or to our prospects of appreciating him more fully, and they all too often appear to be written in total disregard of the last decade or so of Faulkner criticism and of all Faulkner scholarship. To ignore in this manner what others are saying, or have said in the past, is not merely to be redundant: it is to deny the very principles embodied in the terms *scholarship* and *criticism* and to undermine all possibility of rational discussion and interchange. The recent proliferation of new journals, some focused on particular areas of study, others in the nature of house organs devoted chiefly to publishing articles by local faculty, has obviously increased the opportunities for the publication of inferior work, but it would be unfair to suggest that such journals have necessarily been the worst offenders. Editors and their chosen advisors must bear most of the responsibility in such matters, and neglect of that responsibility is more serious in those journals—and university presses—whose scope is wide, whose reputation is high, and whose catchment area is correspondingly large. Some journals, indeed, deploy—or threaten to deploy—such batteries of readers that submitting an article to them seems as intimidating as taking an army medical. Yet sheer multiplication of inspectors is of little value if all of them are ready to stamp pieces as 1A on the basis of the most cursory inspection, and if none of them is prepared to give the kind of advice based on close and thoughtful reading from which the authors, and ultimately the academic community, could genuinely profit.

i. Bibliography, Editions, and Manuscripts

A major event in 1971 was the appearance (*Proof* 1:293–329) of James B. Meriwether's "The Short Fiction of William Faulkner: A Bibliography," which lists and describes, as Meriwether explains, "all textually significant forms known to me of all [Faulkner's] works of fiction shorter than full-length novels." The relationships between different forms have been established by collation, and the value of the bibliography is much enhanced by its inclusion of unpublished works and of a section on stories which once existed but which now seem to have disappeared. It is to be hoped that this authoritative piece of scholarship will give criticism of Faulkner's short stories the impetus it has long needed. Meriwether's "Two Unknown Faulkner Short Stories" (*RANAM* 4:23–30) corrects his own 1957 checklist by adding a story previously omitted, "Two Dollar Wife," and amending the description of "Sepulture South" from "essay" to "short story"; the bibliographical details are supplemented by important new information about two periods of Faulkner's career. Other items from James B. Meriwether in 1971 are "A Prefatory Note by Faulkner for the Compson Appendix" (*AL* 43:281–84)—the first publication of a brief note apparently intended to preface the reprinting of the Compson Appendix in the 1946 Modern Library double volume of *The Sound and the Fury* and *As I Lay Dying*—and an offset reissue, with a new preface and a brief errata list, of *The Literary Career of William Faulkner: A Bibliographical Study* (Columbia, Univ. of S.C. Press), first published by Princeton University Library in 1961 and long unavailable except in a shoddy pirated version.

A few surveys of Faulkner criticism have recently appeared. In "Contemporary American Literature in Spain" (*TSL* 16:155–67) M. Thomas Inge reports that, of major American writers, Faulkner's reputation in Spain stands second only to Hemingway's. The article lists a long series of translations published in Spain and in South America and gives special praise to a 1940 translation of *The Wild Palms* by Jorge Luis Borges. Mario Materassi's "Faulkner Criticism in Italy" (*IQ* 15,i:47–85) is an English version of the survey originally appended to the same author's *I romanzi di Faulkner* (see *ALS 1970*, pp. 117–18). Two dissertations in this area of Faulkner studies are John E. Bassett, "Faulkner's Readers: Crosscurrents in American

Reviews and Criticism, 1926–1962" (*DAI* 32:1502A), and Peter L. Makuck, "Faulkner Studies in France: 1953–1969" (*DAI* 32:3314A).

ii. Biography

O. B. Emerson's "Faulkner and His Friend: An Interview with Emily W. Stone" (*Comment* 10:31–37) adds little to what Phil Stone's widow has already said or written elsewhere, and the other three items under this heading do not pretend to do more than briefly annotate minor aspects of Faulkner's use of local topography. Calvin S. Brown points out, in "Faulkner's Three-in-One Bridge in *The Reivers*" (*NConL* 1,ii:8–10), that Faulkner seems to have combined details of three actual bridges across the Tallahatchie River in creating the one bridge which Boon and his companions cross on their way to Memphis, while Beverley E. Smith, in "A Note on Faulkner's 'Greenbury Hotel' " (*MissQ* 24:297–98), identifies the references in *Knight's Gambit* and "Mississippi" as being to the Hotel Peabody in Memphis. Allen Cabaniss, in "To Scotch a Monumental Mystery" (*NMW* 3[1970]:79–80), says only that the Confederate monument in the Oxford town square was erected in 1907.

iii. Criticism: General

a. **Books.**   The only full-length study devoted wholly to Faulkner is Hans Bungert's *William Faulkner und die humoristische Tradition des amerikanischen Südens* (Heidelberg, Carl Winter), an examination of the varieties of the comic mode to be found in Faulkner's work and especially of its relationship to the tradition of Southwestern humor. There is an English summary and, of particular interest, an appendix which prints both sides of the Faulkner-Anderson "correspondence" about Al Jackson; Faulkner's second letter appears here for the first time. Among the books partly concerned with Faulkner a special welcome must be given to Maurice Edgar Coindreau's *The Time of William Faulkner: A French View of Modern American Fiction*, edited and chiefly translated by George M. Reeves (Columbia, Univ. of S.C. Press). Coindreau has long been well-known as a translator; this collection of essays is a reminder of his distinction as a critic.

Faulkner items take up rather more than half the book, and while they are not all of equal quality it is certainly valuable to have so readily accessible, in English, the important prefaces to *The Sound and the Fury*, *Light in August*, and *The Wild Palms*. The chapter on Faulkner (pp. 182–210) in Morris Beja's *Epiphany in the Modern Novel* (Seattle, Univ. of Wash. Press) explores the occurrence in several Faulkner novels of those moments of sudden unanticipated revelation or recognition that Joyce has taught us to call epiphanies. Faulkner's "frozen moments" are of course familiar ground, but Beja approaches these and related phenomena from a fresh angle, suggesting, for example, how they can sometimes operate as structural pivots, serving to move the narrative in and out of flashback passages. The considerably longer section on Faulkner in Floyd C. Watkins's *The Flesh and the Word: Eliot, Hemingway, Faulkner* (Nashville, Vanderbilt Univ. Press, pp. 169–273) offers to analyze and chart in his work a gradual shift and decline—seen as paralleled in the careers of Eliot and Hemingway—from "the hardness of fact and flesh . . . toward abstract, moralistic, didactic discursiveness." There are interesting comments on Faulkner's tendency to admire the silent doers among his characters rather than the ineffective verbalisers, and on the verbal ironies to be encountered in novels like *Light in August* and *Absalom, Absalom!*, but the discussion as a whole breaks little new ground and rather dismayingly peters out in what is virtually a blanket dismissal of the last twenty years or so of Faulkner's career.

It was not a good year for introductory studies of Faulkner. The chapter in Will and Ariel Durant, *Interpretations of Life: A Survey of Contemporary Literature* (New York, Simon and Schuster, 1970, pp. 11–27) is wholly superficial; the attempt in Joachim Seyppel's *William Faulkner* (New York, Frederick Ungar) to combine a general introduction to Faulkner with a more particular study of the "hermaphrodite" in his work proves doubly disastrous; Eric Mottram's compilation, *William Faulkner* (London, Routledge and Kegan Paul)—which contains in its 110 pages an introduction, extracts from the English texts of six novels, and a somewhat erratic bibliography—has nothing to offer North American readers. I record the existence in Polish of Franciszek Lyra's *William Faulkner* (Warsaw, Wiedza Powszechna, 1969). I might also add that no one should be misled by the publisher's advertising into thinking that Michael Millgate's

William Faulkner (New York, Capricorn Books) is anything other than an unrevised reissue of the volume first published in 1961.

b. **Articles and Dissertations.** Arnold Goldman's "Faulkner and the Revision of Yoknapatawpha History," in *The American Novel and the Nineteen Twenties*, edited by Malcolm Bradbury and David Palmer (Stratford-upon-Avon Studies, 13; London, Edward Arnold, pp. 164–95), is concerned with Faulkner's gradually elaborated conception of Yoknapatawpha County and with the difficulties presented by the coexistence of different versions, and different valuations, of the same events. Goldman suggests that Faulkner is simultaneously committed to "a single history of his chosen county and to successive reconstitutions of that history," and that a novel like *Absalom, Absalom!* with its contrasted viewpoints, "displays in the highest degree of tension the impulses towards the 'linear' elaboration of Yoknapatawpha history and a thrust of intense revision." Though certainly not without interest, Linda Welshimer Wagner's discussion of the formal aspects of several novels in "Faulkner's Fiction: Studies in Organic Form" (*JNT* 1:1–14) remains disappointingly unfocused, while Sorin Alexandrescu's attempt, in "A Project in the Semantic Analysis of the Characters in William Faulkner's Work" (*Semiotica* 4:37–51), to provide "a typological analysis of Faulkner's universe"—including both characters and "civilizations," or value-systems—founders on what seem to me the limitations of its methodology and on its unqualified acceptance of once-fashionable generalizations (e.g., "the Snopses, whom Faulkner hates . . . the Sartorises, whom Faulkner admires"). N. Anastasjew's "Faulkners Weg zum Roman 'Das Dorf'" (*KuL* 19: 956–74), a rather unoriginal and occasionally inaccurate survey of the realistic elements in Faulkner's fiction prior to *The Hamlet*, is apparently a translation from the same author's "Folkner: Put' k'Derevuvške" (*VLit* 14,xi[1970]:122–41). On the evidence of Michiko Yoshida's "The Voices and Legends in Yoknapatawpha County" (*SELit* Eng. no.:174–76) the article in Japanese of which this is an English abstract can reasonably be left untranslated.

There are also a number of dissertations on general topics: Bill K. Addison, "The Past in the Works of William Faulkner" (*DAI* 32: 2669A–70A); Joe C. Buice, "The Rise and Decline of Aristocratic Families in Yoknapatawpha County" (*DAI* 31[1970]:2375A–76A);

Samuel C. Coale V, "The Role of the South in the Fiction of William Faulkner, Carson McCullers, Flannery O'Connor, and William Styron" (*DAI* 31[1970]:6596A–97A); Albert J. Devlin, "Parent-Child Relationships in the Works of William Faulkner" (*DAI* 31 [1970]:2910A); Robert C. Ferguson, "The Grotesque in the Fiction of William Faulkner" (*DAI* 32:1508A); Jewell H. Gresham, "The Fatal Illusions: Self, Sex, Race, and Religion in William Faulkner's World" (*DAI* 31[1970]:5402A); Gladys W. Milliner, "Faulkner's Young Protagonists: The Innocent and the Damned" (*DAI* 31[1970]: 2928A); Robert K. Musil, "The Visual Imagination of William Faulkner" (*DAI* 31[1970]:3558A); Sally R. Page, "Women in the Works of William Faulkner" (*DAI* 31[1970]:2396A); Richard P. Pindell, "The Ritual of Survival: Landscape in Conrad and Faulkner" (*DAI* 32: 3324A); Richard A. Reed, "A Chronology of William Faulkner's Yoknapatawpha County" (*DAI* 32:2101A); Andrew J. Westbrook, "The Commitment of Self in the Works of William Faulkner" (*DAI* 31 [1970]:3568A–69A).

iv. Criticism: Special Studies

a. **Ideas, influences, intellectual background.** Mick Gidley's "Another Psychologist, a Physiologist and William Faulkner" (*ArielE* 2,iv:78–86) discusses the possible influence on Faulkner of Havelock Ellis's *Little Essays of Love and Virtue* (1922) and Louis Berman's *The Glands Regulating Personality* (1921), both ordered by Phil Stone in 1922 from the Brick Row Bookshop and presumably available to Faulkner. There are two comments on possible echoes in the Nobel Prize speech: James B. Meriwether, in "A. E. Housman and Faulkner's Nobel Prize Speech: A Note" (*JAmS* 4:247–48), identifies poem ix of Housman's *Last Poems* as the probable source of Faulkner's image of the false artist as one whose "griefs grieve upon no universal bones"; C. H. Edwards, in "A Hawthorne Echo in Faulkner's Nobel Prize Acceptance Speech" (*NConL* 1,ii:4–5), suggests that the phrase about the "truths of the heart" might owe something to Hawthorne's reference to "the truth of the human heart" in the preface to *The House of the Seven Gables*. A medieval source for the titles of *Light in August* and *The Reivers* is rather unconvincingly offered by Benjamin W. Griffith in "Faulkner's Archaic Titles and the *Second*

Shepherds' Play" (*NMW* 4:62–63), and there are five unremarkable pages devoted to Dostoevski and Faulkner in T. Motyljowa's "Dostojewski und die ausländischen Schriftsteller des 20. Jahrhunderts" (*KuL* 19:938–55), a translation of the second part of an article originally published in Russian as "Dostoevskij i zarubežnye pisateli xx veka" (*VLit* 15,v:96–128).

Rather different in kind is W. M. Frohock's "Faulkner in France: The Final Phase" (*Mosaic* 4,iii:125–34), which argues that Faulkner's influence upon French writers in recent years has been so pervasive that it has passed beyond the stage at which specific instances of "indebtedness" can be positively identified. He cites several modern French novels with a "detective" element in which he believes a Faulknerian presence to be unmistakable but nonetheless unprovable. Also to be mentioned here are William H. Nolte's "Mencken, Faulkner, and Southern Moralism" (*SCR* 4:45–61)—a not very convincing demonstration of a distant parallelism between H. L. Mencken's criticism of Southern varieties of religious and moral intolerance and Faulkner's handling of kindred themes in a novel like *Light in August*—and a small group of dissertations: Roxandra I. Antoniadis, "The Human Comedies of Honoré de Balzac and William Faulkner: Similarities and Differences" (*DAI* 31[1970]:4753A); Joseph E. Brogunier, "The Jefferson Urn: Faulkner's Literary Sources and Influences" (*DAI* 31[1970]:2375A); Winifred Clark, "The Religious Symbolism in Faulkner's Novels" (*DAI* 32:1506A); Jessie A. Coffee, "Faulkner's Un-Christlike Christians: Biblical Allusions in the Novels" (*DAI* 32:1506A).

b. **Language and style.**   Though several items on particular works, and especially on *Absalom, Absalom!*, might well have been cross-listed here, the only items specifically to be recorded at this point are a minor note on Faulkner's use of the cumulative sentence, Herbert R. Eschliman's "Francis Christensen in Yoknapatawpha County" (*UR* 37:232–39), and a dissertation, Paul R. Lilly, Jr.,'s "Silence and the Impeccable Language: A Study of William Faulkner's Philosophy of Language" (*DAI* 32:973A).

c. **Race.**   There is a dissertation: Evalyne C. Robinson, "The Role of the Negro in William Faulkner's Public and Private Worlds" (*DAI* 32:2704A).

v. Individual Works to 1929

Soldiers' Pay was the subject only of a dissertation by Margaret J. Yonce, "*Soldiers' Pay*: A Critical Study of William Faulkner's First Novel" (*DAI* 32:991A).

In "Faulkner's *Mosquitoes*: A Poetic Turning Point" (*TCL* 17: 19–28), Kenneth W. Hepburn argues that the three artist-figures—Gordon, Fairchild, and Julius—move in section 9 of the novel toward a position of "tacit convergence" focused on the asserted values of "form solidity color." He refers to links with the unpublished "Elmer" in suggesting that complex levels of authorial self-irony are at work in *Mosquitoes* and insists, most interestingly, that the combination of artistic assertion and ironic undercutting helped to make this novel, rather than *Sartoris*, the crucial turning point in Faulkner's early career.

Sartoris itself comes in for more—and more serious—discussion than we have seen in the recent past. John W. Corrington's "Escape into Myth: The Long Dying of Bayard Sartoris" (*RANAM* 4:31–47) is a thoughtful article which speaks of Miss Jenny as the quasi-narrator of the novel and sees Bayard, trapped in a world made meaningless by his brother's death, his own terrors, and the corrosion of the old Southern value system, as eventually taking refuge in the Sartoris myth—which may be obsolete but which has not yet been satisfactorily replaced. Albert J. Devlin, in "*Sartoris*: Rereading the MacCallum Episode" (*TCL* 17:83–90), very cogently demonstrates that the MacCallums, five of whom have no prospect of marriage or children, scarcely justify the claims sometimes made for them as ideal representatives of normality and familial harmony; he also explores psychological aspects of the relationship between the various brothers and their dominating father. Less important but still noteworthy is E. A. Muir's "A Footnote on *Sartoris* and Some Speculation" (*JML* 1:389–93), which quite persuasively identifies the "original" of the experimental aircraft in which Bayard is killed but much less persuasively suggests that Faulkner drew upon its name, the Christmas "Bullet" (after W. W. Christmas, its designer), in evolving "a Christ-figure allegory" in the novel as a whole. Also worth mentioning here for the contribution it makes to our knowledge of Faulkner's working methods in both *Sartoris* and *The Hamlet* is James E. Kibler's review

(*MissQ* 24:315–19) of Stephen N. Dennis's dissertation, "The Making of *Sartoris*" (cited *ALS 1970*, p. 121).

John E. Bassett's "William Faulkner's *The Sound and the Fury*: An Annotated Checklist of Criticism" (*RALS* 1:217–46) usefully lists, with brief summaries, contemporary reviews (both American and English) and subsequent criticism of the novel up to early 1971; an index of authors is included. Among new contributions, Donald M. Kartiganer's "*The Sound and the Fury* and Faulkner's Quest for Form" (*ELH* 37[1970]:613–39) is an intelligent but not, in the end, especially innovative study of *The Sound and the Fury* as Faulkner's "diagnostic" novel, one which probes contemporary reality, mirroring its "wasteland" fragmentation, but fails to arrive at any satisfactory solution to the problem of finding a comprehensive form. In a crisply written article, "*The Sound and the Fury*: The Emotional Center" (*MQ* 11[1970]:371–87), Carey Wall sees the emotional movement of the novel section by section—"relative peace, growing tenseness, frenzy, and finally emotional exhaustion"—as reflected in the way each of the monologues is so structured as to bring out "the same drama of spiritual pain." In these terms, Benjy's section is not random in its organization but precisely self-justificatory, while Jason's evident suffering wins him sympathy which his equally evident villainy does not entirely dissipate. A more elaborate case for a sympathetic view of Jason, as the ignored and unloved child and exploited adult breadwinner, is made out by Linda Welshimer Wagner in "Jason Compson: The Demands of Honor" (*SR* 79:554–75). Her advocacy seems over-zealous and her arguments occasionally extravagant, but the exercise of seeing Jason in this more kindly light is very much worthwhile. A more traditional valuation lies behind James M. Mellard's "Type and Archetype: Jason Compson as 'Satirist'" (*Genre* 4:173–88), an overextended and somewhat arbitrary analysis of Jason both as a paranoid personality and as "a typical satiric *persona* in the narrative archetype of satire." Two other articles can safely be passed over—Jackson J. Benson's "Quentin Compson: Self-Portrait of a Young Artist's Emotions" (*TCL* 17:143–59) because its attempt to project Quentin as a Faulknerian self-portrait is based on highly tenuous and largely unsubstantiated biographical "evidence," and Carol L. Luedtke's "*The Sound and the Fury* and *Lie Down in Darkness*: Some Comparisons" (*LWU* 4:45–51) because the comparisons offered are of a quite simplistic kind. There is also a dissertation: Diane L. Hinkle, "The Mystery of Significance and the Enigma of Time: An Analysis of the Thematic Structures of Faulkner's *The Sound and the Fury* and Claude Simon's *L'Herbe*" (*DAI* 32:2689A–90A).

vi. Individual Works, 1930–1939

The brief article on *As I Lay Dying* by Potter Woodbery—"Faulkner's Numismatics: A Note on *As I Lay Dying*" (*RS* 39:150–52)—posits as an error on Faulkner's part what could equally have been a conscious avoidance of anachronism, and an earlier item in the same journal, Delma E. Presley's "Is Reverend Whitfield a Hypocrite?" (*RS* 36-[1968]:57–61), mounts a gallant defence of Addie's pastoral lover that seems to me only to damn him further. The one dissertation is John B. Rosenman's "*As I Lay Dying*: A Study of the Poor White in Faulkner" (*DAI* 31[1970]:6069A–70A).

"*Sanctuary* and Frazer's Slain Kings," by Thomas L. McHaney (*MissQ* 24:223–45), is the most important essay on the novel to appear in some years. It demonstrates convincingly that Faulkner not only derived the title of *Sanctuary* from Sir James Frazer's evocation of the sanctuary of Diana at Nemi in the opening pages of *The Golden Bough* but incorporated into his novel a substantial number of specific and identifiable allusions to Frazer's work. Some of McHaney's more speculative suggestions are unlikely to find universal acceptance, but the approach he has taken seems bound to prove extremely significant in terms both of *Sanctuary* itself and of similar investigations of other Faulkner works.

M. Thomas Inge's "William Faulkner's *Light in August*: An Annotated Checklist of Criticism" (*RALS* 1:30–57) lists and briefly summarises contemporary American reviews of the novel as well as essays in books or journals up to the middle of 1970. The survey is evidently a useful by-product of Inge's compilation, *The Merrill Studies in "Light in August"* (Columbus, Ohio, Charles E. Merrill), which includes some comments from *Faulkner in the University*, the Nelse Patton material from *Old Times in the Faulkner Country*, five early reviews and seven critical essays, among them a revised version of Robert M. Slabey's very interesting "Myth and Ritual in *Light in August*." The liveliest of the new essays is Stephen E. Meats's "Who

Killed Joanna Burden?" (*MissQ* 24:271–77), which disturbingly
questions the universal assumption that Joe Christmas was Miss Burden's murderer and skillfully demonstrates the thinness of the evidence on the basis of which "all of us—the sheriff, Gavin Stevens,
Percy Grimm, the community, the reader—are more than ready to
pass judgment." T. M. Adamowski's "Joe Christmas: The Tyranny of
Childhood" (*Novel* 4:240–51) draws frequently upon Sartre in the
course of an extended review of those elements in Christmas's childhood (e.g., the episode with the dietician, the watching presence of
Doc Hines, the stern moralism of McEachern) which shape him
into an adult permanently dominated by his own past. A particular
aspect of the same general topic is briefly discussed in Richard F.
Peterson's "Faulkner's *Light in August*" (*Expl* 30: item 35), while in
"The Pattern of Thought in *Light in August*" (*BRMMLA* 24[1970]:
155–61) Robert R. Wilson offers minor but suggestive comments
about the relationship between conscious and preconscious levels of
mind in the novel and especially about the way in which characters
such as Christmas and Hightower reach an end to their search for the
certainty of knowledge by discovering "that what they can know is
merely that which they already know without conscious awareness."

The interconnections between Christmas and Lena Grove are
quite interestingly touched upon in Leonard Neufeldt's "Time and
Man's Possibilities in *Light in August*" (*GaR* 25:27–40), though the
essay contains little else that is new, and from the English summary
(pp. 884–85) I gather that Tsfira Porat's "Sawdust Dolls: Tragic Fate
and Comic Freedom in Faulkner's *Light in August*" (*Hasifrut* 2:767–
82) deals with the contrast between Byron Bunch's escape through
self-knowledge from enslavement to Calvinistic values and Joe
Christmas's failure through self-ignorance to make a corresponding
escape from domination by the spirit of McEachern, his Calvinistic
foster-father. Three dissertations should be noted here: Regina K.
Fadiman, "Faulkner's *Light in August*: Sources and Revisions" (*DAI*
32:427A); Don N. Smith, "The Design of Faulkner's *Light in August*:
A Comprehensive Study" (*DAI* 31[1970]:2402A); Mary T. Strauss,
"The Fourteenth View: A Study of Ambiguity in William Faulkner's
Light in August" (*DAI* 31[1970]:6074A).

Richard Pearce's "*Pylon, Awake and Sing!* and the Apocalyptic
Imagination of the 30's" (*Criticism* 13:131–41) points to the contra-

dictions, the sexual frenzy, and the perpetual meaningless motion of *Pylon* in linking it with Odets's play and with such novels as *The Day of the Locust* as an expression of an irrational apocalyptic vision characteristic of the 1930s. *Twentieth Century Interpretations of "Absalom, Absalom!": A Collection of Critical Essays* (Englewood Cliffs, N.J., Prentice-Hall) contains an introduction by the editor, Arnold Goldman, and seven previously published items, including the extensive notes to the relevant chapter of Cleanth Brooks's *William Faulkner: The Yoknapatawpha Country*. There are also some new contributions of more than usual interest, notably Max Putzel's "What is Gothic about *Absalom, Absalom!*" (*SLJ* 4,i:3–19). Putzel seems to me rather to dodge the issues raised by his title, except insofar as he touches upon the importance of medieval chivalry in the novel's imagery, but this is nonetheless an extremely intelligent, wide-ranging, and perceptive study both of the Sutpen tragedy itself and of the tragic experience compelled upon the reader. C. Hugh Holman's "*Absalom, Absalom!*: The Historian as Detective" (*SR* 79:542–53) moves from an opening insistence on the novel's closeness to "the standard detective story" to a general discussion of its handling of history; Shreve is seen in the role of scientific historian—to whose viewpoint Faulkner "does not give a place of highest honor"—and the novel as a whole is praised for its demonstration of the artist's capacity to "transmute the data of history into the enlarged reality of art." In "Meaning Called to Life: Alogical Structure in *Absalom, Absalom!*" (*SHR* 5:9–23) J. R. Raper explores the possibility that the frozen tableaux, crowding images, and varied rhythms of the novel may owe something to Faulkner's knowledge of the cinema; though interesting in itself, the idea is not developed very persuasively in terms of analyses of specific passages.

The techniques of *Absalom, Absalom!* have received study from several quarters, most ambitiously from Gerald Langford's *Faulkner's Revision of "Absalom, Absalom!": A Collation of the Manuscript and the Published Book* (Austin, Univ. of Tex. Press). Despite the length and large format of this book, its usefulness is sadly limited. It is of course interesting to have substantial quotations from the Texas manuscript available in print, but the proferred collation of that manuscript with "the published book" (a 1951 printing is for some reason selected, in apparent disregard of the possibility that the plates might have undergone change or deterioration *after* first publication) is rendered largely pointless by the failure to consider, or even mention, the many changes made at an intervening stage of the text—the typesetting copy, which is complete, accessible at the University of Virginia, and described in James B. Meriwether's *The Literary Career of William Faulkner* (1961). Parts of the argument of John A. Hodgson's "'Logical Sequence and Continuity': Some Observations on the Typographical and Structural Consistency of *Absalom, Absalom!*" (*AL* 43:97–107) seem very much open to question (e.g., the suggestion that chapter 3 is spoken by Mr. Compson not at the same time as chapters 2 and 4 but after Quentin's return from Sutpen's Hundred), but the article warrants attention as a serious attempt to come to grips with some of the devices which Faulkner employs with such obvious care but often to somewhat puzzling effect. The failure of Fred V. Randel's "Parentheses in Faulkner's *Absalom, Absalom!*" (*Style* 5:70–87) to make any very marked progress toward a solution of these difficulties derives largely from its concentration on a single feature of Faulkner's technique in isolation from the others. The article makes clear, as do the two preceding contributions, the urgent need for a scholarly edition of the novel based on *all* relevant forms of the text.

There are two other articles of quite minor significance—Stewart Rodnon's "*The House of the Seven Gables* and *Absalom, Absalom!*: Time, Tradition, and Guilt" (*StH* 1, ii[1970]:42–46) and Hisao Tanaka's "Quentin Doomed as a Southerner: A Study of *Absalom, Absalom!*" (*Studies in American Literature* [Hiroshima Univ.] 7:1–14)— and two dissertations: Oliver L. Billingslea, "The Monument and the Plain: The Art of Mythic Consciousness in William Faulkners' *Absalom, Absalom!*" (*DAI* 32:3293A), and Sister Mary D. Pires, "Plot Manipulation and Kaleidoscoping of Time as Sources of Tragic Perception in Faulkner's *Absalom, Absalom!*" (*DAI* 31[1970]:4176A).

The Unvanquished attracted no attention apart from Hilton Anderson's brief "Two Possible Sources for Faulkner's Drusilla Hawk" (*NMW* 3:108–10), which suggests that the presentation of Drusilla may owe something to the martial heroines of Col. W. C. Falkner's *The Spanish Heroine* and *The Siege of Monterey*.

Apart from the reprinting of Coindreau's essay (section iii above), *The Wild Palms* was also neglected in 1971.

vii. Individual Works, 1940–1949

The only items specifically on *The Hamlet* are a dissertation—James E. Kibler, Jr.,'s "A Study of the Text of William Faulkner's *The Hamlet*" (*DAI* 31:5407A)—and an article by Robert C. Pierle, "Snopesism in Faulkner's *The Hamlet*" (*ES* 52:246–52), which is distinguished chiefly by the fact that its opening survey of criticism includes nothing published since 1962.

There are, however, several items on the Snopes trilogy as a whole. "William Faulkner's Snopes Trilogy: The South Evolves," by Mark Leaf (*The Fifties*, pp. 51–62) could be challenged as an approach to Faulkner's work of the 1950s on the grounds of its avoidance of the problems posed by *Requiem for a Nun* and *A Fable*; but as a study specifically of the Snopes novels the essay is for the most part cogent and sympathetic, especially in its treatment of the trilogy's economic aspects. The review of past criticism which opens Glenn O. Carey's "William Faulkner: The Rise of the Snopeses" (*StTC* 8:37–64) stops short at 1959; the remainder of the article offers little more than narrative summary. Nor is there anything new in Duane Edwards's "Flem Snopes and Thomas Sutpen: Two Versions of Respectability" (*DR* 51:559–70) or Patricia Kane's "Adaptable and Free: Faulkner's Ratliff" (*NConL* 1,iii:9–11). There are two dissertations: Roger L. Davis, "William Faulkner, V. K. Ratliff, and the Snopes Saga (1925–1940)" (*DAI* 32:3300A), and John O. White, "The Existential Absurd in Faulkner's Snopes Trilogy" (*DAI* 32:3336A).

Go Down, Moses was the subject of several articles, none of them of major significance. Even Gary D. Hamilton's "The Past in the Present: A Reading of *Go Down, Moses*" (*SHR* 5:171–81), though its approach seems promising, does not ultimately achieve any real depth or originality; again, a lack of familiarity with the relevant criticism may be partly responsible. Ralph Maud's "Faulkner, Mailer, and Yogi Bear" (*CRAS* 2:69–75) links the novel with Mailer's *Why Are We in Vietnam?* in the course of developing what is essentially an argument about ecology. Audrey L. Vinson's "Miscegenation and Its Meaning in *Go Down, Moses*" (*CLAJ* 14[1970]:143–55) scampers rather breathlessly among the references to racial mixing. Less ambitious but more useful are the definitions of local technical terms in an article which has only now come to my attention, Gerald W. Walton's "Some Southern Farm Terms in Faulkner's *Go Down, Moses*"

(*PADS* 47[1967]:23–29). Three articles tackle particular sections of the book: Raymond G. Malbone, in "Promissory Poker in Faulkner's 'Was'" (*EngR* 22,i:23–25), makes a valiant but only partially successful attempt to unravel the complexities of the betting in the contest between Hubert Beauchamp and Uncle Buddy; Rosemary Stephens, in "Mythical Elements of 'Pantaloon in Black'" (*UMSE* 11:45–51), makes a number of interesting suggestions but considers only one strand of what is most satisfactorily seen as an integral part of the novel as a whole; Malcolm A. Nelson, in "'Yr Stars Fell' in *The Bear*" (*AN&Q* 9:102–03), supplies what must now be a superfluous reminder that Faulkner's allusion is to the extraordinary meteor shower of 1833. The one dissertation is Carol A. C. Harter's "The Diaphoric Structure and Unity of William Faulkner's *Go Down, Moses*" (*DAI* 31[1970]:6057A–58A).

Mary M. Dunlap has a dissertation on "The Achievement of Gavin Stevens" (*DAI* 31:3544A), which is relevant to both *Intruder in the Dust* and *Knight's Gambit*.

viii. Individual Works, 1950–1962

Requiem for a Nun is the subject of a dissertation by Noel Polk—"A Textual and Critical Study of William Faulkner's *Requiem for a Nun*" (*DAI* 32:980A)—and of two articles by the same author. In his valuable analysis of the prologue to act 1, "Alec Holston's Lock and the Founding of Jefferson" (*MissQ* 24:247–69), Polk makes it clear that the novel as a whole has so far been very incompletely understood, that its complexities and ironies are more intricate and more interesting than has generally been perceived, and that its essential thrust is toward a mature acceptance of the sad but inescapable facts of "change and alteration"—in nature, in society, and in the individual human experience. Polk's review-essay, "The Staging of *Requiem for a Nun*" (*MissQ* 24:299–314), not only demonstrates the grave shortcomings of the work under review—"*Requiem for a Nun*": *Onstage and Off* (see *ALS 1970*, p. 128)—but adds substantially to our knowledge of the genesis of the stage version of *Requiem*.

The only item on *A Fable* is a dissertation, Abner K. Butterworth's "A Critical and Textual Study of William Faulkner's *A Fable*" (*DAI* 31[1970]:5390A). Discussions of *The Town* and *The Mansion* can be found in the items dealing with the Snopes trilogy which are listed above (section vii), but on *The Reivers* there is nothing to report apart from the background note by Calvin S. Brown (see section ii).

ix. The Stories

In " '*Being Pulled Two Ways*': The Nature of Sarty's Choice in 'Barn Burning' " (*MissQ* 24:279–88), Gayle E. Wilson uses terms from Ruth Benedict's *Patterns of Culture* in presenting the story as a dramatized conflict between two opposed life-styles—the lawless "Paranoid," based on blood ties and embodied in the figure of Ab Snopes, and the law-abiding, community-centred "Apollonian," which Sarty's naming after Colonel Sartoris invokes and which the boy himself eventually chooses. In another study of the same story, "Colonel Sartoris Snopes and Gabriel Marcel: Allegiance and Commitment" (*NMW* 3:101–07), James K. Bowen and James A. Hamby find in the ideas of Marcel a parallel for the boy's choice between his inherited "blood" and his own independent self-awareness. "A Rose for Emily" has also attracted two articles: Helen E. Nebeker's "Chronology Revised" (*SSF* 8:471–73) worries some more at the story's elusive chronology, while Ruth Sullivan's "The Narrator in 'A Rose for Emily' " (*JNT* 1:159–78) is a piece of extravagant psychologising which side-steps Faulkner's use of the communal "we" in order to indict the narrator of voyeurism, sadism, symbolic rape, and would-be cannibalism. Donald E. Houghton's "Whores and Horses in Faulkner's 'Spotted Horses' " (*MQ* 11 [1970]:361–69) comments perceptively on the quasi-sexual attraction the gaudily coloured horses exert upon their purchasers, whose drab wives are meanwhile reduced to the role of work-animals; its value, however, is severely undercut by the implausibility of some of the detailed arguments (e.g., the identification of "circus posters" as "advertisements or lures to a profane show in a bawdy house") and by the dubious contention that the extract from *The Hamlet* included in *The Portable Faulkner* qualifies as an independent short story. Frank Cantrell's "Faulkner's 'A Courtship' " (*MissQ* 24:289–95) is a straightforward analysis, sympathetic and careful but not especially revealing. There is also a dissertation by Cantrell, "Faulkner's Late Short Fiction" (*DAI* 31:5391A), and another by James B. Carothers, "William Faulkner's Short Stories" (*DAI* 31:4757A).

University College, University of Toronto

8. Fitzgerald and Hemingway

Jackson R. Bryer

Although, quantitatively, Fitzgerald and Hemingway studies in 1971 seem about the same as in 1970 and although the year did not produce any single piece of scholarship or research of seminal importance, a number of significant items appeared. As has been the case for several years, there were many more entries for Hemingway in the *1971 MLA International Bibliography* (eighty, including twenty in the 1971 *Fitzgerald/Hemingway Annual*) than for Fitzgerald (forty-seven, including twenty-two in the *Annual*). And the number of dissertations on Hemingway, nine, is almost double the number of those on Fitzgerald, five. But these kinds of statistics are, for 1971 at least, very misleading. Among the twenty-five Fitzgerald publications exclusive of those in the *Annual*, eight are full-length books wholly devoted to the author; and, of these, at least four fill real gaps in Fitzgerald studies. On the other hand, there are only three full-length books among the Hemingway listings and all are rather specialized in their concerns. Further, the thirty-nine shorter pieces on Fitzgerald probably contain more examples of worthwhile criticism and research than do the seventy-seven Hemingway items. In the end, however, one must return to the statistics and note the continuing and steady flow of material on these two writers. This can perhaps best be exemplified by remarking that the third volume of the *Annual*, which began in 1969 as a 146-page publication and grew in 1970 to 276 pages, was 380 pages in length. This growth also is reflected in the quality of the contributions. It is in the pages of the *Annual* this year that one finds a disproportionately large share of the significant articles and notes on Fitzgerald and Hemingway. Perhaps this is because many of the contributors are acknowledged experts on the two authors and thus are in an excellent position to know where the research needs are. But whatever the reasons, the editors of the *Annual*, Matthew J. Bruccoli and C. E. Frazer Clark, Jr., deserve praise and appreciation for encouraging and publishing so much valuable material on two such seemingly exhaustively studied writers.

i. Bibliographical Work and Texts

Jennifer McCabe Atkinson's "Lost and Unpublished Stories By F. Scott Fitzgerald" (*FHA 1971*:32–63) is one of the year's most substantial contributions on either Fitzgerald or Hemingway. Miss Atkinson does far more than simply list the nineteen stories which have never appeared in print; she gives long plot summaries and analyses of each item, often relating it stylistically or thematically to other work; and, when applicable, she traces Fitzgerald's unsuccessful effort to market the story. Her piece is a gold-mine of information, all the more valuable because none of it has previously been available and because, based on Miss Atkinson's summaries, several of Fitzgerald's unpublished stories are as interesting as many that did appear in print.

With three exceptions, all the other recent bibliographical and textual work on Fitzgerald and Hemingway also appeared in the *Annual*. To deal with the exceptions first, Jean Muir Rogers and Gordon Stein contribute some detailed and helpful "Bibliographical Notes on Hemingway's *Men Without Women* (*PBSA* 64[1970]:210–13); while Joan Crane gives descriptions of three Hemingway items in "Rare or Seldom-Seen Dust Jackets of American First Editions: VI" (*Serif* 8,iii:29–31); and George Monteiro adds several rather exotic foreign items to Hanneman in "Hemingway: Contribution Toward a Definitive Bibliography" (*PBSA* 65:411–14).

Bibliographical work in the *Annual* can be roughly divided into textual and descriptive essays and enumerative listings. Among the former, we get Matthew J. Bruccoli's description of "Fitzgerald's Marked Copy of *This Side of Paradise*" (pp. 64–69), which includes a list of the author's often humorous and sometimes self-critical marginal comments and corrections; and briefer notes by Daniel G. Siegel on "T. S. Eliot's Copy of *Gatsby*" (pp. 290–93), which indicates that Eliot's copy contains several marginal comments of interest; and by C. E. Frazer Clark, Jr., on "The Crosby Copy of *In Our Time*" (pp. 236–38), which includes Harry Crosby's pencilled-in ranking of Hemingway's stories. All three of these items are aimed primarily at the book collector, as is Archibald S. Alexander's brief but entertaining "Collecting Hemingway" (pp. 298–301), describing how Alexander acquired his collection and touching on one of the highlights therein, an exchange of correspondence between Fitzgerald and Boni and Liveright regarding *The Torrents of Spring*. Fitzgerald called it "about the best comic book ever written by an American" but the publisher rejected it, not as previously assumed because of its satirical portrait of Boni and Liveright author Sherwood Anderson, but because they disagreed with Fitzgerald's judgment as to the quality of the book.

Audre Hanneman's second list of addenda to her definitive bibliography (pp. 343–46) and an extensive checklist of the year's work in Fitzgerald studies (pp. 366–74) are the most valuable of the *Annual*'s enumerative contributions.

Briefer but also valuable is Matthew J. Bruccoli and Jennifer M. Atkinson's listing of "F. Scott Fitzgerald's Hollywood Assignments, 1937–1940" (pp. 307–08), which provides precise documentation for an area of Fitzgerald research which received a great deal of attention in the past year, as will be seen below. Also the recipient of considerable recent attention was Hemingway's posthumous novel, *Islands in the Stream*; and William R. Anderson, Jr. (pp. 326–32) helpfully digests thirty of the most significant reviews. Thirteen are described as "basically favorable," nine as "favorable," and eight "express ambivalent or neutral judgments." A checklist with full publication data about each review is appended.

Enterprising scholars and editors continue to uncover unpublished or at least uncollected Fitzgerald and Hemingway pieces; and while the quality of the material often seems dubious, in most instances it is at least convenient to have it so readily available. The first half of Matthew J. Bruccoli and Jackson R. Bryer's collection, *F. Scott Fitzgerald in His Own Time: A Miscellany* (Kent, Ohio, Kent State Univ. Press) presents Bruccoli's selection of previously uncollected work from the entire range of Fitzgerald's career. There are generous samples of the verse, Triangle Club lyrics, and *Nassau Lit* and *Princeton Tiger* humor of his undergraduate days; the reviews of books by Hemingway, Anderson, Huxley, Mencken, Tarkington, and others which he did at Princeton and during the early 1920s; and the humorous articles on love, marriage, and sex which he wrote to order for mass circulation magazines and newspaper syndicates in 1924 (a sample title: "Why Blame It on the Poor Kiss if the Girl Veteran of

Many Petting Parties Is Prone to Affairs After Marriage?"). Though much of this material, as editor Bruccoli admits, is of dubious value taken by itself, we are helped to understand Fitzgerald's reputation in his own time and we have "glimpses of Fitzgerald's talent during its formative stages."

Bruccoli provides an even earlier glimpse of Hemingway's talents in embryo in *Ernest Hemingway's Apprenticeship: Oak Park, 1916–1917* (Washington, D.C., NCR Microcard Eds.). Beginning with the premise that "everything Ernest Hemingway wrote is important because he wrote it," Bruccoli brings together the thirty-nine articles Hemingway wrote for his high school newspaper, *The Trapeze*, and his eight contributions to the literary magazine, *The Tabula* (three stories, four poems, and a humorous "Class Prophecy"). As Bruccoli points out in his introduction, the *Trapeze* material indicates little distinction as journalism but is of importance in showing that the young Hemingway was "an active joiner, a big man in the school"; whereas the *Tabula* pieces "show promise and anticipate the material —though not the style—of the later Hemingway."

The September 1971 issue of *Esquire* included what purported to be the text of Fitzgerald's previously unpublished story, "Lo, the Poor Peacock" (pp. 154–58). A comparison of the *Esquire* text with Jennifer M. Atkinson's summary and analysis (*FHA* 1971:41) of the story, however, reveals that *Esquire* silently cut the original story, omitting long and important sections including the passage which gives the story its title. The fact that such a corrupt text was presented without explanation or justification represents one of the most irresponsible exploitations of Fitzgerald's popularity within recent memory. That it should appear in *Esquire*, a magazine which literally sustained Fitzgerald during some of his darkest days and whose editor, Arnold Gingrich, then as now was his close friend, simply adds to the irony and puzzlement.

The 1971 *Annual* includes three new Fitzgerald items of uneven value. The most worthwhile is "Fitzgerald's Ledger" (pp. 3–31), the first printing of Fitzgerald's detailed yearly accounting of his earnings through 1936. This actually is only one-third of the full ledger; but it is an interesting document of Fitzgerald's finances. A facsimile of the typescript of Fitzgerald's unused "Preface to 'This Side of Paradise'" (pp. 1–2) presents the author's self-assured autobiographical account of the novel's composition, initial refusal by Scribner's, revision, and final acceptance. Far more slight is " 'Oh Sister, Can You Spare Your Heart,' A Fitzgerald Lyric" (pp. 114–15) which was found attached to a Fitzgerald letter of June 12, 1933. A novelty item tipped into each copy of the 1971 *Annual* is a plastic phonograph recording of Fitzgerald reading Masefield's "On Growing Old," Keats' "Ode to a Nightingale," and Othello's address to the Venetian Senate. This is the only known recording of Fitzgerald's voice.

Two obscure Hemingway pieces also surfaced in the 1971 *Annual*: a review of plays by Shaw and Hans Sachs, which originally appeared in German in the January 13, 1926, issue of *Vorarlberger Landes-Zeitung*, is translated by James Franklin (pp. 195–96); and C. E. Frazer Clark, Jr., presents a facsimile of a previously unattributed Hemingway contribution to the Toronto *Daily Star* (April 20, 1920): "Buying Commission Would Cut Out Waste" (pp. 209–11).

ii. Letters and Biography

When Andrew Turnbull's edition of Fitzgerald's letters appeared in 1961, the editor admitted that it included less than half of the letters available, thus leaving reviewers free to speculate about those omitted and also to complain, in a few instances, about the one-sidedness of Turnbull's volume, i.e., the fact that he included no letters to Fitzgerald. John Kuehl and Jackson R. Bryer's edition, *Dear Scott/Dear Max: The Fitzgerald-Perkins Correspondence* (New York, Scribner's), attempts to answer the second of these criticisms of Turnbull by providing a selection from both sides of Fitzgerald's twenty-one-year correspondence with his only editor. It also brings into print fifty-nine new Fitzgerald letters. The collection shows little that is new about Fitzgerald; but it does draw the most complete portrait available of Perkins, perhaps this country's greatest literary editor, and of his relationship with one of his three most famous authors (Wolfe and Hemingway were the others). It also contains a great deal of gossip about the literary milieu of the 1920s and 1930s, and abundant proof of how Perkins's confidence and encouragement were major factors in sustaining Fitzgerald when his personal and creative lives were at their lowest ebb.

Material for a similarly interesting two-sided volume is implied in

Robert Emmet Long's brief discussion of "The Fitzgerald-Mencken Correspondence" (*FHA 1971*:319–21) which is available at the New York Public Library, having been opened to scholars for the first time on January 29, 1971. Long notes that there are fifty-seven separate items in the Fitzgerald-Mencken file and that the most interesting are letters Fitzgerald wrote to Mencken (Turnbull included only two Fitzgerald-to-Mencken letters). He quotes from two of these and clearly the publication of the entire correspondence would be welcome.

"Letters of Ernest Hemingway to Soviet Writers" by Ivan Kashkeen (*FHA 1971*:197–208) reprints from the November 1962 issue of *Soviet Literature* the abridged texts of two letters Hemingway wrote to Kashkeen (1935 and 1939) and one addressed to Konstantin Simonov in 1946. In them we find Hemingway's animosity towards critics; his views on Communism ("I cannot be a communist now because I believe in only one thing: liberty"); on writing (". . . writing is something that you can never do as well as it can be done. It is a perpetual challenge and it is more difficult than anything else that I have ever done—so I do it. And it makes me happy when I do it well."); and on Russia; and his sarcastic autobiographical comments.

Biographical material on both Fitzgerald and Hemingway continues to appear regularly despite a lingering suspicion that virtually all of substance in that area must already be in print. Two recent books on Fitzgerald afford little reason to doubt this suspicion. Sara Mayfield's *Exiles from Paradise: Zelda and Scott Fitzgerald* (New York, Delacorte) is a highly slanted biography which deliberately attempts to exonerate Zelda from most of the blame for what befell the Fitzgeralds and to place a good deal of it on Scott. This approach leads Miss Mayfield to absurd assertions: Zelda married Scott not because she was in love with him "in a romantic way" but because "she felt it was her mission in life to help him realize his potential as a writer." She was admirably qualified for this task because she was the "natural" and "original" writer that neither Scott nor Ernest Hemingway was—"The effects that Fitzgerald and Hemingway struggled to wring from themselves flowed from her as easily and naturally as water from an open tap." Such attempts at literary judgment are fortunately infrequent in the book; but it is full of Miss Mayfield's biased and selective use of biographical information. This is the more regrettable because Miss Mayfield knew Zelda for forty years and Scott for half that time and obviously could have drawn on those friendships with profit. But she does not do so. There are a few memorable personal recollections—of an utterly wild evening in 1926 spent careening through the streets of Paris in a rented hearse with Scott, accompanied by two French prostitutes and some Princeton undergraduates; and her touching memory of a final view of Zelda, in 1945, taking the spastic child of a neighbor for a walk. But such moments are buried beneath Miss Mayfield's conscientious efforts to dismiss all the derogatory stories about Zelda as myths and to show how ill-bred, lazy, jealous, callous, and cruel Scott was. In contrast to Nancy Milford's very balanced appraisal of their marriage, Miss Mayfield presents a totally distorted picture.

Aaron Latham's *Crazy Sundays: F. Scott Fitzgerald in Hollywood* (New York, Viking) is ostensibly both biography and criticism, but it is so much the former and so little the latter that it properly belongs only in this section. On the positive side, using published sources and interviews with Fitzgerald's Hollywood friends and associates, Latham gives us a lively anecdote-filled account of Fitzgerald's day-to-day existence in the movie capital. But this is not enough material to fill a book; and Latham's attempts to discuss the scripts Fitzgerald worked on are hampered by several studios' refusal to allow direct quotations and by Latham's own apparent reluctance to evaluate or analyze the texts. To compensate for this, he pads his work in two unfortunate ways: he too frequently uses passages from Fitzgerald's fiction, especially *The Last Tycoon*, to fill in missing biographical information; and he devotes long sections to the rather irrelevant discussion and documentation of Fitzgerald's interest in and use of the movies and drama in his works. When we add to these factors the numerous factual lapses which Alan Margolies (*FHA* 1971:362–65) has pointed out in his perceptive review, *Crazy Sundays* emerges as one of the poorer pieces of Fitzgerald research done in the last few years.

In contrast to Latham's somewhat pretentious volume, 1971 also saw the reprinting in a slim volume of Calvin Tomkins's charmingly written 1962 *New Yorker* profile of Gerald and Sara Murphy, *Living Well Is the Best Revenge* (New York, Viking), which contained much information on the Fitzgeralds on the Riviera while Scott was working on *Tender Is the Night*, whose central character was modelled on Gerald Murphy. The text of the book is almost identical to

the original in the magazine but a large collection of photographs has
been added, along with an illustrated section on Gerald Murphy's
paintings.

Among the shorter biographical pieces, the best are Anthony
Powell's reminiscence of Fitzgerald in Hollywood in 1937, which
originally appeared in 1970 in the London *Times* (*FHA 1971*:71–
80); Benjamin Lease's "An Evening at the Scott Fitzgeralds: An Unpublished Letter of Ring Lardner" (*ELN* 8:40–42), in which a turbulent evening is described during which Scott broke his hand throwing
a punch at a hard-headed Texan; and Donald Ogden Stewart's "Recollections of Fitzgerald and Hemingway" (*FHA 1971*:177–88), reminiscences which extend from his first meeting with Fitzgerald in St.
Paul in 1919 through riotous times with Hemingway in Paris, on the
Riviera, and in Pamplona at fiesta time, down to working with Scott
on the screenplay of *The Women* in the late thirties. Of less value but
interesting nonetheless are Morrill Cody's memories of Hemingway
and the real-life characters of *The Sun Also Rises* (*ConnR* 4,ii:5–8);
R. L. Samsell's meticulously researched account of the circumstances
and time of Fitzgerald's death (*FHA 1971*:173–76); the Reverend
R. C. Nevius's note on Fitzgerald's early mentor, Monsignor Sigour-
ney Fay, who, Nevius shows, was an Episcopalian before his conversion to Catholicism (*FHA 1971*:105–13); and Fraser Drew's recollections of the role Hemingway played in turning Drew into "a serious
Hemingway collector" (*FHA 1971*:294–97).

iii. Criticism

a. **Collections.** The second half of Bruccoli and Bryer's *F. Scott
Fitzgerald in His Own Time: A Miscellany* (Kent, Ohio, Kent State
Univ. Press) collects Bryer's selection of fifteen interviews; forty-six
reviews of Fitzgerald's books, by Mencken, Cowley, Aiken, Bishop,
Seldes, Van Vechten, and others; essays and editorials by, among
others, Heywood Broun, Frances Newman, and Edmund Wilson;
parodies by Dorothy Parker, Donald Ogden Stewart, and Christopher
Ward; and a range of obituary editorials by James Gray, Westbrook
Pegler, Arnold Gingrich, Amy Loveman, and others. Most of this material has never been collected previously; and, as with the first half
of the *Miscellany*, the intention is to give a sampling of the reception
which Fitzgerald and his work received during his lifetime in order

to suggest "a more realistic and balanced overall view of his total critical reputation than is generally given."

There are three other recent collections. Matthew J. Bruccoli's *Profile of F. Scott Fitzgerald* (Columbus, Ohio, Charles E. Merrill) is noteworthy principally because its reprinted selections include some unorthodox pieces such as novelist Vance Bourjaily's wonderful humorous fantasy about the afternoon when Fitzgerald attended his Fitzgerald seminar; Fitzgerald's own recently discovered essay, "My Generation," first published in the October 1968 *Esquire*; and John Kuehl's two very valuable but little-known essays on Fitzgerald's reading and critical opinions. The title of Henry Dan Piper's *Fitzgerald's "The Great Gatsby": The Novel, The Critics, The Background* (New York, Scribner's) suggests its scope and concerns. One of Scribner's research anthologies, it brings together the text of the novel and a variety of materials which are useful in understanding it, i.e., some of Fitzgerald's letters to and from Perkins, contemporary reviews, recent critical articles, and background items on the Jazz Age and the American Dream concept. While there are some new selections added, Piper's collection does not really go far enough beyond Frederick J. Hoffman's 1962 volume to warrant its publication. Sheldon N. Grebstein's *Merrill Studies in "For Whom the Bell Tolls"* (Columbus, Ohio, Charles E. Merrill) reprints some of the best material available on the novel, including contemporary reviews by Howard Mumford Jones, Gilbert Highet, Graham Greene, and others; and later pieces by Warren French, Allen Guttmann, Robert P. Weeks, Earl Rovit, and Thornton H. Parsons, among others. Significantly, Grebstein's selections from recent studies emphasize work done within the last decade and thus not often reprinted.

b. **Full-length Studies.** As in recent years, the critical articles on Hemingway range widely over his novels and stories, while the pieces on Fitzgerald are, with very few exceptions, concerned not only with the novels, but even more specifically primarily with *The Great Gatsby* and *Tender Is the Night.* But the one full-length critical study of Fitzgerald published in 1971 is focused solely on his short stories. John A. Higgins's *F. Scott Fitzgerald: A Study of the Stories* (Jamaica, N.Y., St. John's Univ. Press) may not be the definitive work on the subject but it is the first and is, in many respects, extremely useful. Higgins has two purposes in mind—to evaluate the art of the stories and to relate them to the novels. In pursuit of these goals, he goes through Fitzgerald's entire canon of short fiction chronologically, with both good and bad results. On the positive side, he writes well about many stories which have never before been studied and often shows in plausible fashion how a little-known piece was important apprentice work for a novel or a better story. Higgins is also effective at indicating how often Fitzgerald utilized the same themes and plot patterns, tailoring his work to what would sell. Further, this is a very well-researched study, with the voluminous footnotes representing a reference work in themselves for all the scholarship available on the stories. But these footnotes are, as well, representative of one of the book's faults. Probably because it was originally a dissertation, Higgins's work relies far too heavily on secondary sources and is much too indulgent of the previous research on the stories. The generally poor quality of that research is, after all, the reason for his project. More significantly, he often depends on a previous critic for his final evaluation of a story; and he very seldom quotes directly from the stories themselves, using plot summaries in all but a very few instances. This in turn directs his attention away from style and towards theme and structure, a direction lamentably all too evident in most Fitzgerald criticism. But these are perhaps unduly harsh judgments for a book which does make a significant contribution to Fitzgerald studies. In a field which is over-populated with redundancy and trivia, Higgins has broken new ground. For this fact alone his work deserves attention.

The single full-length critical study of Hemingway, Emily Stipes Watts's *Ernest Hemingway and the Arts* (Urbana, Univ. of Ill. Press), also breaks new ground; but it is no doubt an indication of a major difference between Fitzgerald studies and Hemingway studies that new ground here is a far more limited and esoteric area than with Fitzgerald. Full-length books on Hemingway have obviously covered much more of his work from many more points of view than have those on Fitzgerald. Thus, Emily Watts chooses what at best would seem to be the subject for a good long article and writes a 234-page book. To be sure, there are many suggestive sections in her study: Cezanne's influence on Hemingway's depiction of landscape; Hemingway's affinities with Goya, Bosch, and Brueghel in his fictional portraits of despair, violence, war, and death; parallels between Cezanne's creation of form by color with Hemingway's similar use of color and between Hemingway's use of black and white and Goya's chiaroscuro technique; and good discussions of the roles art and artists play in his novels, especially *Islands in the Stream* and *To Have and Have Not*. In the end, Emily Watt's study does relatively little to enhance our understanding of Hemingway's fiction. Mary Hemingway probably had the last word about the book when she wrote its author, "A number of people are beginning to attribute to Ernest interests and activities in which they themselves are interested and I find it shameful."

c. **General Essays.** In an age where specialization extends throughout all areas of activity, we should not be surprised to find that very few scholars and critics write general articles on Hemingway or Fitzgerald. We have seven such studies of Hemingway and only one of Fitzgerald. Further, only one of the Hemingway pieces deals exclusively with him; significantly, it is the best of the group. In "The Silence of Ernest Hemingway" (*Shaken Realist*, pp. 5–20), Ihab Hassan begins with the premise that Hemingway's "style, morality, and vision derive from silence and enlarge its definition," and discusses his use of language, his distrust of language, and his desire to purify it. Specifically, he points to Hemingway's small vocabulary, his use of slang ("a colorful form of reticence") and his understatement which "stems from a private conviction that good things deserve to remain unexpressed." Succeeding sections of the essay study silence as a metaphor in *In Our Time*, *The Sun Also Rises*, and *A Farewell to Arms*. This is an original and provocative piece of criticism.

Of the other general articles, Edward T. Jones's "Hemingway and Cezanne: A Speculative Affinity" (*UES* 8,ii[1970]:26–28) anticipates Emily Watts's book in examining the similarities between the two artists; D. R. Sharma's "Moral Frontiers of Ernest Hemingway" (*PURB* 2,ii:49–59) is a far-ranging series of commonplaces about the social and moral virtues in Hemingway's characters; and Donald J. Greiner's "Emerson, Thoreau, and Hemingway: Some Suggestions About Literary Heritage" (*FHA* 1971:247–61) works very tenuously with broad concepts in claiming that "Hemingway's ideas about literature owe as much to certain artistic principles which were first worked out in American literature by Emerson and Thoreau as they do to the literary principles which he learned in Paris."

Two general essays connect Hemingway with Eliot. Marion Montgomery, in "Emotion Recollected in Tranquility: Wordsworth's Legacy to Eliot, Joyce, and Hemingway" (*SoR* 6[1970]:710–21), examines *A Moveable Feast* as "Hemingway's version of 'Tintern Abbey'" and tries to point out parallels between the two works as well as differences between Wordsworth's "honest openness" and Hemingway's "self-delusion" about the past. In what may well be the most forced essay of the year, Reginald Fitz examines "The Meaning of Impotence in Hemingway and Eliot" (*ConnR* 4,ii:16–22), with emphasis on the motifs of sexual wounding and castration as they appear in the two writers. A far more sensible article is Ben Merchant Vorpahl's "Ernest Hemingway and Owen Wister: Finding the Lost Generation" (*LC* 36[1970]:126–37). Vorpahl uses passages from the Hemingway-Wister correspondence to trace the friendship which developed and later deteriorated between the two men. He sensibly understates the extent of Wister's influence, asserting only that he interested Hemingway in the Rockies; that he gave Hemingway the most direct contact he ever had with Kipling—whom Hemingway admired and Wister knew personally; he provided encouragement; and he helped Hemingway achieve an awareness of his own abilities.

The one general essay on Fitzgerald, Anne R. Gere's study of "Color in Fitzgerald's Novels" (*FHA* 1971:333–39), adds to earlier work on this subject by suggesting that Fitzgerald uses color imagery to emphasize his view of a corrupted moral code. She points out that Fitzgerald employs colors in contexts opposite from their usual associations: green, "instead of appearing in association with fertility, naturalness, and immortality, . . . highlights sterility, contrivance and death"; and yellow, "instead of being associated with the life-giving qualities of the sun, . . . appears strongly in scenes of death and disaster." Similar conclusions are reached about pink, white, and gray; and the illustrative passages are drawn from all the novels, not just *Gatsby*, which has usually been the sole subject in earlier studies of Fitzgerald's use of color.

d. **Essays on Specific Works: Fitzgerald.** As usual and not surprisingly, *The Great Gatsby* is still the most popular specific Fitzgerald work for scholar-critics. Good general essays on the novel are those by Richard Foster (*Sense and Sensibility*, pp. 94–108) and Richard Lehan (*American Dreams*, pp. 106–14). Lehan identifies the novel and its characters with the materialism versus idealism duality pattern which he traces through James, Adams, and Twain down to Fitzgerald, pointing out that, for Nick, Gatsby is the embodiment of this duality. He is not quite the "dynamo" that Tom is, but rather a "grotesque distortion" of Tom; while at the same time he is faithful to his romantic dreams. Lehan also relates the action and milieu of the novel to Spengler's Faustian and Apollonian cultural periods, noting that it fits Spengler's definition of the Faustian period which is characterized by "flux and disruption with man generally dissatisfied and longing for the unattainable."

Foster's essay is one of several recent pieces which have focused on Nick. Like several other recent critics, Foster comes not to praise Fitzgerald's narrator but to expose him as "one of life's voyeurs," "subtly corrupt and potentially corrupting," and "a flawed narrator." In doing this, he links Nick to Tom (while Tom has been born to riches, Nick has been born to "moral certainty"); and sees him as identifying as much with the Buchanans and Jordan as with Gatsby. Thus, we must see that Nick's "moral vision is at best of an uncertain purity and that his harsh poignant, gross, beautiful . . . recreation of it in words is a kind of siren song . . . to be resisted." This is a relatively original approach and Foster presents it convincingly. Oliver Evans's essay (*FHA* 1971:117–29) is much less harsh but still takes Nick to task for what Evans sees as his inadequate understanding of Gatsby and of his motives for not betraying Daisy: "Gatsby becomes for Nick what Daisy was for Gatsby, an embodiment of an ideal, and Gatsby is as far removed in reality from the ideal Nick imagines him to be as Daisy was far removed from what Gatsby imagined her to be." Nick's approval of Gatsby, Evans claims, is based upon his belief that he and Gatsby alone possess "fundamental decencies"; when, in fact, Gatsby's decision has nothing to do with "fundamental decencies" but is rather based on his remaining faithful to his dream. The novel then becomes as much an account of what Nick has failed to learn as of what he has learned.

A. E. Elmore's article (*FHA* 1971:130–47) is not as provocative as Foster's or Evans's and concentrates heavily on the novel's first chapter and on Nick's introduction of himself. In general, Elmore defends

Nick against previous criticisms of his morality and sees him as the perfect narrator. John J. McNally, in "Prefiguration of Incidents in *The Great Gatsby*" (*UDR* 7,ii:39–49), also focuses on the first chapter and on Nick, concerning himself with demonstrating that Nick's character is consistent throughout the novel and that certain images and language patterns which are introduced in the opening chapter are echoed through the remainder of the novel.

A second article by McNally, "Boats and Automobiles in *The Great Gatsby*: Symbols of Drift and Death" (*HussR* 5:11–17), presents an excellent consideration of two significant leitmotifs in the novel. McNally suggests that Fitzgerald uses boats and water imagery "to emphasize the lack of stability of most of the novel's characters and to symbolize the anachronism inherent in the American Dream as typified by Jay Gatsby." Gatsby's disintegration is symbolized by the kinds of water in which he finds himself: he moves from Dan Cody's yacht on the largest of the Great Lakes to an air mattress in an artificial body of water, a swimming pool. In the automobile, McNally claims plausibly, Fitzgerald found "a workable symbol, not only to illustrate the rampant carelessness so typical of the corrupt easterners in the novel, but also to forbode injury as well as accidental and natural death." Richard Cohen traces another symbolic pattern in the novel less convincingly in an earlier essay not previously examined, "The Inessential Houses of *The Great Gatsby*" (*HussR* 2[1968]:48–57). Cohen's thesis is that the houses in the novel not only provide settings for the action but also each is "representative of the personality, beliefs, character, and social status of the particular individual or individuals who occupy the dwellings." He then examines Gatsby's, Nick's, and the Buchanans' houses in detail; but, when he comes to the Wilsons' garage, the flat in New York, and the parlor suite, his article becomes sketchy and his claims weaken considerably.

There is the usual quota of essays linking *Gatsby* with works of other authors. Perhaps the most original is Nancy Y. Hoffman's "*The Great Gatsby: Troilus and Criseyde* Revisited?" (*FHA 1971*:148–58), where she compares the two works in terms of structure, themes (artificial values, falsity of standards), the crucial rainstorm scenes in both, and the concepts of gentilesse which bring both heroes down. She stresses the theme of the man from the outer moral provinces moving into society and the progress from innocence to experience.

Daisy and Criseyde are compared, as are Tom and Calchas and
Diomede, and Nick and Pandarus. While some of these parallels
seem strained, as is the notion that Fitzgerald had Chaucer's story in
mind when writing *Gatsby*, Hoffman's article performs a useful service in moving critical comment on this novel from its usual concentration on the American Dream-American Experience theme to a
more universal area of concern.

Keats's influence on Fitzgerald has often been examined, but almost always with application to *Tender Is the Night*; so Dan McCall's
" 'The Self-Same Song That Found a Path': Keats and *The Great
Gatsby*" (*AL* 42:521–30) is a welcome contribution. Focusing primarily on "The Eve of St. Agnes," "Ode to a Nightingale," and "Ode
on a Grecian Urn," McCall compares Keats's imagery, technique,
language, and themes to Fitzgerald's. Thematically, *Gatsby*'s desire
to reach into the past, to buy back a moment of pleasure and beauty,
and his feeling that "no present pleasure, realized and consummated,
can fulfill the yearning for 'the orgiastic future,' " show that Fitzgerald's truth is the truth of the Grecian Urn.

Two briefer pieces also suggest sources for *Gatsby*. Lewis A. Tur-
lish's "*The Rising Tide of Color*: A Note on the Historicism of *The
Great Gatsby*" (*AL* 43:442–44) links Tom Buchanan's reference to
The Rise of the Colored Empires by "a man named Goddard" to
Theodore Lothrop Stoddard's *The Rising Tide of Color* and claims
that the "historical framework" of Stoddard's book is a source for
the "decline and decay historicism" of *Gatsby*. Dalton Gross's "F.
Scott Fitzgerald's *The Great Gatsby* and Oswald Spengler's *The Decline of the West*" (*N&Q* 17[1970]:467) rehashes a by now familiar
claim of influence.

Four recent essays on *Tender Is the Night* show that novel to be
holding strongly in second place among Fitzgerald's works. Frank
Kinahan (*American Dreams*, pp. 115–28) ranges widely over the
novel in a well-written and carefully-constructed piece. His central
concern is with the development of the dream and reality tension
which he sees as existing primarily in Dick Diver; but he also discusses a variety of motifs in the novel—the "two worlds" motif, exemplified most clearly in Nicole's schizophrenia; the stage motif in
which Dick is the creator-director; and the motif of Dick as ultimately coming to stand for America. While Kinahan's essay lacks a
thesis, it is filled with helpful and suggestive readings. Such is not

the case with E. Nageswara Rao's confusing and fragmented article on "The Structure of *Tender Is the Night*" (*LCrit* 8,iv[1969]:54–62), a mixture of old theories and a thoroughly unconvincing idea that the novel is ultimately a drama which fits the five-act structure of classical tragedy.

The two other essays deal with the Divers. Mary E. Burton's "The Counter-Transference of Dr. Diver" (*ELH* 38:459–71) argues rather ingeniously that Dick, like other Fitzgerald male protagonists, is a victim of the American Dream, but, unlike them, he effects "a counter-transference and becomes morally infected with the dream he sought to break and cure." At the end of the novel, however, he is freed from his neurosis; he has been "released forever into the liberty of the lost." Tom C. Coleman III, in "Nicole Warren Diver and Scott Fitzgerald: The Girl and the Egotist" (*SNNTS* 3:34–43), examines Nicole from a variety of vantages, concluding that "to understand Nicole Warren Diver adequately, the reader should regard her as a work of art, a creation of Dick's romantic imagination, rather than as an actual American girl." It is "as a work of art, an ideal, that she fails Dick, not as a human being."

The only article of any substance which deals exclusively with one of Fitzgerald's other novels, Peter Rodda's "*The Last Tycoon*" (*ESA* 14:49–71), is as vague and unfocused as its title. Rodda glances briefly and inconclusively at the characterizations of Stahr and Cecilia Brady; but most of his rambling essay is an outline of the novel's action. Far more valuable are Alan Margolies's remarks on Fitzgerald's last novel in his "The Dramatic Novel, *The Great Gatsby*, and *The Last Tycoon*" (*FHA* 1971:159–71). Concerned primarily with demonstrating Fitzgerald's use of dramatic structure in *Gatsby*, Margolies does have some interesting things to say about how this same structure underlay Fitzgerald's plans for *The Last Tycoon*. In making these claims, Margolies makes good use of unpublished notes and diagrams in the Fitzgerald Collection at Princeton; and his essay is a model of scholarly research combined with critical insight.

Aside from a brief note pointing out errors in logic and chronology in " 'Babylon Revisited' Revisited" by Kenneth McCollum (*FHA* 1971: 314–16), there are no essays on Fitzgerald's short stories; but 1971 did see two very good and very different articles on his film scripts. Taken together, they supply the sort of analysis and evaluation

lacking in Latham's *Crazy Sundays*. Alan Margolies's "F. Scott Fitzgerald's Work in the Film Studios" (*PULC* 32:81–110) draws on
unpublished notes and correspondence in the Fitzgerald Collection
at Princeton in examining the scripts Fitzgerald wrote and contributed to, principally "Three Comrades," "Cosmopolitan," and "A
Yank at Oxford." Concluding that, while Fitzgerald "was not an
exceptional scriptwriter," he "worked seriously at his new craft,"
Margolies points out that an examination of his film work can provide "insight into his methods, showing not only how he applied the
newly learned film techniques, but also how he employed many of
the procedures—the use of the dramatic curve, the awareness of the
necessity to develop character dramatically, as well as others—that
he used as a writer of novels and short stories." Lawrence D. Stewart's "Fitzgerald's Film Scripts of 'Babylon Revisited'" (*FHA*
1971:81–104) is, as its title suggests, narrower in its focus than
Margolies's article; but Stewart is just as detailed in his analysis of
the two film versions of the story Fitzgerald wrote. His work, like
Margolies's, is based primarily on unpublished sources and hence
is of even more value. But both Margolies and Stewart are most noteworthy in that they deal directly and specifically with the texts of
Fitzgerald's scripts and do not get bogged down, as Latham does, in
irrelevant gossip and background.

e. **Essays on Specific Works: Hemingway.**   As noted earlier, Hemingway criticism in 1971 is quite evenly spread over the corpus of his
work. Thus, we have four pieces each on *The Sun Also Rises* and
A Farewell to Arms, two each on *For Whom the Bell Tolls* and *The
Old Man and the Sea*, one on *A Moveable Feast*, and nineteen articles
on eleven different short stories.

The essays on Hemingway's first novel fall into two groups. There
are two excellent ones and two that are merely competent readings.
The best is Scott Donaldson's careful and highly original "Hemingway's Morality of Compensation" (*AL* 43:399–420). Donaldson defines Hemingway's morality of compensation as his belief that you
get what you pay for—and only with money that you yourself have
earned—and then traces the various financial transactions which run
through the novel. He points out that money as an indication of a
character's worth can be applied to Jake, Romero, and Bill, all of
whom have earned their money and realize the proper way of using

it, in contrast to Mike, Brett, and Robert, who have not earned it and do not know how to use it. Hemingway heroes, Donaldson concludes, "pay their bills in full, sometimes at the cost of their lives." Very different but almost as good as Donaldson's article is Harold F. Mosher, Jr.,'s fascinating study of "The Two Styles of Hemingway's *The Sun Also Rises*" (*FHA* 1971:262–73): one composed of simple and complex sentences (staccato style) and one composed of compound and compound-complex sentences (rhythmical style). He then notes that staccato passages usually deal with lifelessness, chaos, emptiness, violations of the Hemingway code, and failure of communication; while rhythmical passages are usually associated with nature, order, sensuous comfort, and comradeship. Because the novel ends in the staccato style, Mosher sees it concluding in emptiness. While there may be a certain mechanical aspect to this approach, Mosher presents his thesis carefully and convincingly.

Bruce L. Grenberg's "The Design of Heroism in *The Sun Also Rises*" (*FHA* 1971:274–89) is a sensible but not very striking study of Jake as "the essence of Hemingway's conception of the hero." Earl Wilcox's "Jake and Bob and Huck and Tom: Hemingway's Use of *Huck Finn*" (*FHA* 1971:322–24) is not as labored as its title might make one think it is; but its conclusion—that, like Huck and Tom, Jake and Cohn are radically different in that Cohn is a romantic who relies on books while Jake is a realist who tries to come to grips with life—hardly seems very revealing or new.

The major essay of the year on *A Farewell to Arms* is Dewey Ganzel's "*A Farewell to Arms*: The Danger of Imagination" (*SR* 79: 576–97). Ganzel sees the central theme of the novel to be Frederic Henry's discovery of death and his progressive loss of his "suspended imagination." At the outset, he is free, unattached, uncommitted; but, step by step, "he discovers the circumstances which the biological trap forces on all men: the unavoidable emotional commitments one must honor and the way progressive death finally shapes man to the cycle of living and dying." Frederic's discovery of death is paralleled with his increasing love for Catherine. That love in turn forces him "into life," awakens his imagination to the possibility of a viable future, allows him to find value in living, but also forces the tragic loss of that value. This is a very tightly organized and focused piece of criticism which presents a challenging reading. Robert Murray Davis's " 'If You Did Not Go Forward': Process and Stasis in *A Fare-*

well to Arms" (*SNNTS* 2[1970]:305–11) is somewhat less seminal in its concerns, but is helpful nonetheless. Davis feels that the novel is about "process and about the necessary illusion that stasis is possible, about not only the natural inevitability but the human necessity of process, and about the central importance of 'realization' in the sense defined by the novel." In support of this interpretation, Davis discusses symbolic contrasts such as mountain-plain, rain-snow, and night-day; and Hemingway's notion in the novel that one must necessarily "experience" before he can "realize," although experience itself is not sufficient for realization. Davis's argument is more abstract than Ganzel's and his article is somewhat more difficult to follow.

Two briefer pieces offer rather tenuous sources for parts of the novel. Robert M. McIlvaine suggests, in "A Literary Source for the Caesarean Section in *A Farewell to Arms*" (*AL* 43:444–47), that the death of Angela Witla in Dreiser's *The "Genius"* might have furnished a "partial model" for the death of Catherine. Richard Allan Davison (*Expl* 29:Item 46) makes a connection between the poem "Western Wind," Charles Anderson's comment that its poet "surely knew of the traditional medieval symbol of Christ as the gentle rain falling on earth in spring to make it green and fertile," and Hemingway's use of Christian overtones in *A Farewell to Arms*. The symbolic equation of Catherine and Christ and rain is cited as support.

Both essays on *For Whom the Bell Tolls* see the novel in a framework imposed from the outside. Gerry Brenner's modus operandi is made clear in his title, "Epic Machinery in Hemingway's *For Whom the Bell Tolls*" (*MFS* 16[1970]:491–504). Relying heavily on Thrall and Hibbard's definition of epic, Brenner makes a good, if occasionally forced, case for the presence in the novel of "numerous epic traits." Comparing Hemingway's novel to *The Iliad*, he demonstrates how the former's use of epic machinery causes its "several esthetic weaknesses." Hemingway, Brenner claims, spent too much energy concealing his use of the epic mode; and, as a consequence, the novel "lacks an organic pulse, that pulse having been subdued by the rigorously superimposed grids of epic formulae and mechanical structure." John Ditsky's approach, in "Hemingway, Plato, and *The Hidden God*" (*SHR* 5:145–47), is through Donne's "Devotions, xvii," the poem from which the novel derives its title. Ditsky contends that the Neoplatonic concepts of Donne's poem and indeed the concepts of sensuality and spirituality which permeate most of Donne's poetry have a greater influence on the novel than the concepts of Christianity with which Cleanth Brooks views it in *The Hidden God.*

Sheldon Norman Grebstein's "Hemingway's Craft in *The Old Man and the Sea*" (*The Fifties*, pp. 41–50) is another important essay. Grebstein begins with the assertion that literature "will owe more to [Hemingway's] technique than to his vision of life," and then examines three symbolic patterns in the novel. The first is "the movement from inside to outside, or, conversely, from outside to inside," which, in this novel, is represented by the movement from shore to sea to shore. Each of these is ambivalent: the shore represents "home, safety, comradeship, . . . peace, rest," but it is also where "Santiago lives in total poverty and is mocked by other fishermen"; the sea is "beneficent, the source of peace and nourishment, and of inexpressible grandeur," but it is also "a trap, . . . the element populated by deceptively beautiful yet poisonous creatures such as the Portuguese Man-of-War, and by the vicious sharks." The second pattern is "together-alone-together" and it is not ambivalent: "from his aloneness on the sea Santiago is restored to human love on shore." But there is a great deal of ambivalence in the third pattern, "darkness-light-darkness," just as there is in Hemingway's portrait of his hero: he "commends Santiago to our affection and admiration; at the same time, he carefully foreshadows the story's tragic or ironic outcome and demonstrates the protagonist's frailties as a man." Grebstein's reading is a skillful one, extremely sensitive to the complexities of what is undoubtedly Hemingway's most deceptively simple novel. Far more limited in scope is Yukio Fujimoto's piece on "The Relationship Between Santiago and Manolin" (*SALCS* 7:26–33). Fujimoto sees Manolin's function as not simply to heighten our sympathy for Santiago, but also to heighten "the aesthetic effect of this story; since at the close as well as at the beginning . . . the boy proves himself to be the only one that understands how the old man is different from ordinary fishermen and also the only one that makes it known to us."

Walter A. Bunnell, in "Who Wrote the Paris Idyll? The Place and Function of *A Moveable Feast* in the Writing of Ernest Hemingway" (*ArQ* 26[1970]:334–46), tries to show that "*A Moveable Feast* is, in fact, closely related to and consistent with the main body of Hemingway's *fictional* work, although that relationship involves a recognition of certain purposeful inversions of the author's fictional precepts." Bunnell finds the major inversion in the book's depiction of the hero: "If the old hero could be said to win by losing, this one would seem to lose by winning." But this hero, "the new, always right, perfectly healthy Papa" (in the words of Wilfrid Sheed), can win only through a technique of "both fictional and factual dishonesty and deception." One often gets the feeling in reading Bunnell that he has set up his own vocabulary and critical apparatus with which to analyze the work of literature. Hence he is unassailable in his claims, once one assumes his basic premises, an assumption not necessarily easy to make here. His view of *A Moveable Feast* as autobiographical fiction is immediately open to dispute and, if it is disputed, his entire essay is obviously much weakened.

All of the essays on the short fiction are close explications of one or two individual stories, except for Carl Ficken's "Point of View in the Nick Adams Stories" (*FHA 1971*:212–35). Ficken's basic contention is that "Hemingway matched his narrative perspective with his hero's mental state." The narrative is more objective in the earlier stories when Nick's understanding is limited; it becomes more complex and probing in the stories around the wound. Defining the various points of view used in the stories—the effaced narrator, the author-observer, the central consciousness, the narrator-agent—Ficken argues convincingly that variation in point of view adds dimension to Nick's character. This is another closely argued essay with valuable insights.

All four of the year's essays on "A Clean, Well-Lighted Place" are concerned with the state of the text and two are in complete disagreement over John Hagopian's emended version ("Tidying Up Hemingway's Clean, Well-Lighted Place," *SSF* 1[1964]:140–46). Charles E. May, in "Is Hemingway's 'Well-Lighted Place' Really Clean Now?" (*SSF* 8:326–30), claims that Hagopian's alteration "changes the meaning of the story in a major way" in that it puts the knowledge of the old man's attempted suicide in the old waiter from the beginning and thus the old waiter never changes, depriving the story of one of its major dramatic elements—the gradual realization by the old waiter of his affinity with the old man. In a much longer essay, "Hemingway's Clean, Well-Lighted, Puzzling Place" (*EIC* 21:33–56), David Lodge begins by approving Hagopian's version for providing the story with consistency, and then examines the text in detail, especially the dialogue between the two waiters and how the distinction between the two becomes apparent to the reader. Lodge concludes with a discussion of Hemingway's "artful use of repetition . . . to generate a kind of verbal intensity of the kind we associate with lyric poetry."

In two briefer notes on the story in the 1971 *Fitzgerald/Hemingway Annual*, Nathaniel M. Ewell III (pp. 305–06) and George Monteiro (pp. 309–11) also deal with textual matters. Ewell adds to Warren Bennett's suggestion (see *ALS 1970*, p. 142) that the confusing dialogue between the two waiters is due to a missing slug of type by claiming that, in fact, two slugs must have been misplaced. Monteiro notes that recent (1957 and 1965) Spanish editions of the story omit the final 334 words, including the two prayers, probably because the "blasphemies which the author assigns to the older, disillusioned waiter were more than Hemingway's Castilian translator or publisher or both would (or could) risk in Franco's Catholic Spain."

Of the three essays on "The Short Happy Life of Francis Macomber," only one, Clifford Lewis's "The Short Happy Life of Francis Scott Macomber" (*EA* 23[1970]:256–61), is worthy of more than passing mention. Using Hemingway's description of the marital failures of the Fitzgeralds in *A Moveable Feast* as a point of departure, Lewis convincingly suggests that Scott and Zelda were the models for Francis and Margot. Both T. G. Vaidyanathan's "Did Margot Kill Francis Macomber?" (*IJAS* 1,iii[1970]:1–13) and Masao Nakamura's "E. Hemingway's 'The Short Happy Life of Francis Macomber'" (*SALCS* 7:34–42) are superficial and inconclusive.

Three studies of "Hills Like White Elephants" cover various aspects of the story. W. Keith Kraus, in "Ernest Hemingway's 'Hills Like White Elephants': A Note on a 'Reasonable' Source" (*EngR* 21, ii[1970]:23–26), suggests that the source might be the situation in *The Sun Also Rises* between Robert Cohn and Frances Clyne. He bases this on general similarities between the two situations but also on the use of the word *reasonably* which he finds used strangely at the end of the story but in exactly the same manner as it is employed in the novel. Reid Maynard's "Leitmotif and Irony in Hemingway's 'Hills Like White Elephants'" (*UR* 37:273–75) considers the repetition of the word *two* as an ironic leitmotif in the story. All but one of the *two* images suggest unity and thus "operate ironically . . . , for they suggest a kind of life (symbolized by the river, mountains, and fields) which is the direct opposite of the life now being experienced by the couple." In " 'Hills Like White Elephants': A Study" (*IJAS* 1,iii[1970]:33–38), S. P. Jain deals with several critical problems. Disputing earlier views that the heroine is "dependent and weak," Jain feels that she is not weak but exhibits "vain and hopeless evasions, utter gloom, deep anguish." He also disagrees with Frank O'Connor's accusation that the story shows the "preponderance of technique over subject matter" by claiming that Hemingway uses "a different and distinct technique [which] . . . lies in exploiting more the advantages of dramatic means than those of narrative means." The treatment and the material "form a mixture that can't be unmixed."

Lawrence A. Walz's " 'The Snows of Kilimanjaro': A New Reading" (*FHA* 1971:239–45) traces the three contrasts which are set up in the story: Harry's past life versus his present state; the character contrast between Harry and Helen; and the differences between what Harry is and what he finally becomes at the end. After exploring these in detail, Walz concludes that the theme of the story is that "a person who, even though virtually destroyed, tries to act as he should and does not allow himself to be defeated can find some kind of fulfillment or victory." John M. Howell, in "Hemingway's Riddle and Kilimanjaro's Reusch" (*SSF* 8:469–70), prints a letter he received from Richard Reusch, who actually found a leopard on the snow-covered higher peak of Kilimanjaro. Critics to the contrary, the leopard was not, like Harry, trying to work "the fat off his soul," but, as Reusch suggests, "trying to keep it on."

In "Hemingway's 'Fifty Grand': The Other Fight(s)" (*JML* 2: 123–27), James J. Martine rejects all previous suggestions that the fictional Jack Brennan-Jimmy Walcott fight is based on any one real-life bout and sees it as a combination of the Jack Britton-Mickey Walker and Battling Siki-Georges Carpentier fights, the latter of which Hemingway attended. Edward Stone, in "Hemingway's Mr. Frazer: From Revolution to Radio" (*JML* 1:375–88), compares the first two printings of "The Gambler, The Nun, and the Radio," in *Scribner's Magazine* for May 1933 and in *Winner Take Nothing* (published in October 1933). This shows us Hemingway reshaping "a merely puzzling (and occasionally amusing) story into a respectable work of art." The major change was the addition of the last paragraph, an indication that the author realized that "resignation, not defiance—radio, not revolution—was its theme."

Howard Livingston's "Religious Intrusion in Hemingway's 'The

Killers' " (*EngR* 21,iii:42–44) considers the question of why Hemingway finds it necessary to reveal that Al is Jewish and Max Catholic, concluding that, from this incident, Nick "has learned an historical truth—the sterility of religion as a force in combatting evil in the world." And the killers' own sensitivity regarding the religious labels they wear shows that "their behavior precludes any commitment to the moral and ethical precepts of religion." Julian Smith also delves into Hemingway's theological views, this time in "A Man of the World," in "Eyeless in Wyoming, Blind in Venice: Hemingway's Last Stories" (*ConnR* 4,ii:9–15). Smith sees the character Blindy in the story as in some respects a Christ figure and feels that the bar setting "can be a kind of theological microcosm, a twentieth century church." Smith also discusses another late story, "Get a Seeing-Eyed Dog," suggesting that it is to a great extent autobiographical—Hemingway bemoaning his own failing powers as an artist, his own blindness to the world around him, and his desire to remember the past.

Hemingway's "much deeper understanding of the nature of homosexuality than his public reputation as a fist-in-the-face hater of it seems to indicate" is the subject of J. F. Kobler's "Hemingway's 'The Sea Change': A Sympathetic View of Homosexuality" (*ArQ* 26[1970]:318–24). Kobler concedes that Hemingway still thinks of homosexuality as a vice but with far greater forbearance. Finally, in "Hemingway's 'Out of Season' and the Psychology of Errors" (*L&P* 21:41–46), Kenneth G. Johnston brings to bear on the story a variety of psychological interpretations, contending that the wife's mishearing of "doctor" for "daughter" is a Freudian error called a "compromise formation" in which is expressed "part success and part failure for each of the two intentions." The wife wants to have her baby; her husband wants her to have an abortion. In either case, a doctor would be involved; and Johnston sees this quarrel as the center of the story. Further, the husband's desire to fish illegally, out of season, in a muddy discolored river (the waters of life), parallels his desire for the abortion—to prevent the inopportune, out-of-season arrival of a child; but he cannot defy the law in either instance.

f. **Foreign Criticism.**   As in the past, there is far more foreign criticism of Hemingway listed this year than of Fitzgerald. Two Japanese books are included, Ichiro Ishi's *Hemingway no Sekai* (Tokyo, Kochi Shuppansha) and Motoo Takigawa's *Hemingway Saiko* (Tokyo,

Nan-un-do, 1967), and a Russian title, B. Gribanov's *Xeminguèj* (Moscow, Molodaja gvardija, 1970). Shorter Japanese studies of Hemingway are Katsuji Takamura's "Hemingway no Rojin to Sho-nen" (*EigoS* 114[1970]:300–01), on Hemingway's old men and small boys; Motoo Takigawa's "*The Short Happy Life of Francis Ma-comber* no Shusei" (*EigoS* 115[1969]:98–100), on revisions in the story; Seijiro Hamada's "Kilimanjaro e no Hisho" (*EigoS* 115[1969]: 699–701); Toshihiko Kawasaki's "Hemingway to futatsu no Bunseki Hihyo" (*EigoS* 114[1968]:498–500); and Fumio Ano's "Hemingway and Politics" (*Bull. Coll. of Gen. Educ. Tohoku U.* [Sendai, Japan] 12,ii:105–20). A Spanish-language piece is Germán Vargas' "Un libro de cronicas de Hemingway" (*BCB* 11,xii[1968]:55–56); and one in German is Horst Kruse's "Ernest Hemingways Kunst der Allegorie: Zeitgenössische und biblische Anspielungen in 'God Rest You Merry, Gentlemen'" (*JA* 16:128–50). The only foreign item on Fitzgerald is Peter Wang, "F. Scott Fitzgerald som engageret forfatter" (*Extracta* 3:315–21).

g. Dissertations. Of the five dissertations listed on Fitzgerald, one, John Aaron Latham's "The Motion Pictures of F. Scott Fitzgerald" (*DAI* 31:6617A–18A), was published in 1971 as a book and has been discussed above; while two others, Jennifer E. Atkinson's "Author and Agent: Appendices to *As Ever, Scott Fitz—*" (*DAI* 32:2671A–72A) and John F. Callahan's "When That Greater Dream Had Gone: His-tory and Self in *The Great Gatsby* and *Tender Is the Night*" (*DAI* 31[1970]:2376A), are scheduled to appear in book form in 1972. The remaining two Fitzgerald dissertations are Elaine P. Maimon's "The Biographical Myth of F. Scott Fitzgerald (1940–1970)" (*DAI* 32: 442A–43A) and Jere L. Williams's "The Cast of Glamour: A Study of Selected Short Stories of F. Scott Fitzgerald" (*DAI* 31[1970]:2945A). One dissertation deals with both Fitzgerald and Hemingway, Carole P. Gottlieb's "The Armored Self: A Study of Compassion and Con-trol in *The Great Gatsby* and *The Sun Also Rises*" (*DAI* 32:429A–30A).

The nine Hemingway dissertations is the largest number for a single year and may imply that several new books are in preparation: Anthony B. Dean, "Hemingway's Fiction: A Tragic Vision of Life" (*DAI* 32:961A); Frank M. Laurence, "The Film Adaptations of Hemingway: Hollywood and the Hemingway Myth" (*DAI* 31:

5411A); Reid N. Maynard, "The Writer and Experience: Ernest Hemingway's Views on the Craft of Fiction" (*DAI* 31:6620A); Richard M. O'Brien, "The Thematic Interrelation of the Concepts of Time and Thought in the Works of Ernest Hemingway" (*DAI* 31: 6066A–67A); Charles M. Oliver II, "Principles of 'True Felt Emotion' in Hemingway's Novels" (*DAI* 31:4787A); Roger L. Pearson, "The Play-Game Element in the Major Works of Ernest Hemingway" (*DAI* 31:6625A–26A); Michael S. Reynolds, "A Historical Study of Hemingway's *A Farewell to Arms*" (*DAI* 32:1525A–26A); Paul P. Somers, Jr., "Sherwood Anderson and Ernest Hemingway: Influences and Parallels" (*DAI* 32:985A); and Ronald G. Toop, "Technique and Vision in the Fiction of Ernest Hemingway: A Chronological Study" (*DAI* 31:4181A–82A).

University of Maryland

Part II

9. Literature to 1800

J. A. Leo Lemay

A welcome surprise of 1971 was the comparatively large number of writings about Southern colonial literature, due in part to Percy Adams's excellent work as guest editor of a special Southern issue of *EAL*, and in part to the publication of four books about Southern authors: Everett H. Emerson on Captain John Smith, Parke Rouse, Jr., on James Blair, Pierre Marambaud on William Byrd, and George William Pilcher on Samuel Davies. Two important editions appeared: Kenneth Silverman's readable selection of Cotton Mather's letters and Phillips P. Moulton's now standard edition of John Woolman. Essays of particular excellence or importance include Robert D. Arner on Ebenezer Cook(e), Dieter Schulz on Charles Brockden Brown, Roger E. Stoddard on the bibliography of early American plays, and two essays by William J. Scheick on Edward Taylor.

i. Edward Taylor

William J. Scheick, in "Tending the Lord in all Admiring Style: Edward Taylor's *Preparatory Meditations*" (*Lang&S* 4:163–87), concisely states his theses: "(1) how Taylor's view of the will and words informed the structure of the poems in the *Preparatory Meditations*; (2) how his concept of the Word led to the frequent images of mediation which he associated with language; (3) how this notion of words influenced and determined his poetic style and diction; and (4) how each of these points related to his use of metaphor, to the two primary sources of his imagery, and to circular imagery in particular." In a carefully reasoned argument, Scheick maintains that the structure of the poems in the *Preparatory Meditations* corresponds to Taylor's conception of the will and of words as reflected by the popular meditative traditions of the seventeenth century. Verbal piety was for Taylor an assertion of the "union of Godhead and manhood in the

Word" and should therefore reflect the disparate elements of the sublime and the colloquial, thus making the poem a microcosm of the
qualities of man, body and soul. Scheick's other essay on Taylor,
"Nonsense from a Lisping Child: Edward Taylor on the Word as
Piety" (*TSLL* 13:39–54), persuasively maintains that, in Taylor's
faculty psychology, "each of the will's modes of expression—those
of thought, word, and deed—[are] fundamentally verbal responses
to God." He documents Taylor's references to the functions of the
word, and contends that Taylor's quest for self-identity (but this
modern terminology has misleading implications) led him "to keep a
record of the verbal response of his heart." The title stresses the poet's
idea that his own words are but a shallow image of The Word, and
that man's words are necessarily imperfect until after his death and
glorification.

   An article well worth arguing with is Kathleen Blake's hypothesis
distinguishing the Protestant from the Catholic poetic in the seventeenth century: "Edward Taylor's Protestant Poetic: Nontransubstan-
tiating Metaphor" (*AL* 43:1–24). Blake contends that the Protestant
and the Catholic theological differences concerning the transubstantiation of the Lord's Supper have important implications for the
aesthetic of these writers; specifically, among the Protestant writers, the vehicle is not subsumed into the tenor, while among the
Catholic writers (who believe in transubstantiation) it is. Blake finds
Taylor an especially good illustration of her thesis because of the
centrality of the Lord's Supper in his poetry. The theory adumbrated
in the article is one that the Protestant and Catholic poets would have
found congenial, but we are reminded of other theories concerning
the Puritans' aesthetic which are based upon theological beliefs (e.g.,
that of Perry Miller et al. that Puritans are hostile to imagery) and
which, with more direct evidence to support them, are nevertheless
untrue for many genres and even for the sermons of some leading
Puritans. In order to be provisionally accepted, Blake's argument,
though an ingenious and appealing hypothesis, will need a fuller
presentation and many more, as well as more convincing, examples.

   An essay demonstrating the need for, and some of the uses of, a
concordance to Taylor is Gene Russell's "Dialectical and Phonetic
Features of Edward Taylor's Rhymes: A Brief Study Based upon a
Computer Concordance of His Poems" (*AL* 43:165–80), wherein
Russell shows that many of Taylor's seemingly imperfect rhymes are

true rhymes in his Leicestershire dialect, that Taylor "allowed as near rhymes or off-rhymes words which end in consonants that differ by only one phonetic feature," and that Taylor's poetic practice gradually changed, at least in so far as one can judge by his use of function words. In the last general essay on Taylor of the year, Franz H. Link, "Edward Taylors Dichtung als Lobpreis Gottes" (JA 16:77–101), reinforcing the arguments of Norman S. Grabo, sees a correlation between the art of religious meditation and the poetry of Taylor. Link points out where Taylor's praise of God echoes the Bible (especially Psalm 150), and compares Taylor's techniques of praise with the practice of the seventeenth-century English poets.

Using his exhaustive knowledge of the poet's biography and work, Donald E. Stanford shows that Taylor opposed the Presbyterian tendency of Benjamin Ruggles, a neighboring minister; and Stanford glosses three anti-Presbyterian passages in Taylor's elegy on Samuel Hooker: "Edward Taylor Versus the 'Young Cockerill' Benjamin Ruggles: A Hitherto Unpublished Episode from the Annals of Early New England Church History" (*NEQ* 44:459–68). Stanford elsewhere notes that Taylor's Meditation 1.33 was not, contrary to the usual supposition, written about the death of his wife; and, in another aspect of his "Two Notes on Edward Taylor" (*EAL* 6:89–90), points out that Thomas H. Johnson's list of the books in Taylor's library must be used with caution, for several of the identifications refer to complete sets, whereas the valuation placed on the books in the inventory suggests an odd volume. Thomas Davis and Virginia Davis respond ("Edward Taylor's Library: Another Note," *EAL* 6:271–73) that Taylor's library must have been larger than the inventory indicates, to judge from the exact references in his poetry, sermons, and notebooks. They further identify several of the editions of the works (including those of Augustine and Origen) that evidently were in Taylor's library. And Francis Murphy has reported that Taylor's own Bible has been located in the Westfield Athenaeum ("A Letter on Edward Taylor's Bible," *EAL* 6:91).

Control over the growing scholarship on Taylor has been well served by two publications. With great authority, Norman S. Grabo in *Fifteen American Authors* (pp. 333–56) has described the bibliography, editions, manuscripts, and letters (the most complete listing), biography and criticism (this last heading subdivided into poetic traditions, intellectual and theological traditions, and the poetry

itself) of Taylor. Perhaps some of the most recent criticism is neglected, but Grabo chronicles the history and continued existence of
the major cruxes in Taylor scholarship. I think, contra Grabo, that
Harold S. Jantz (by turning up John Fiske and a number of other
poets almost as good) proved both that Taylor is not a "rare poet in
a poetic desert" (given the comparative population, this would be a
truer description of Robert Frost's environment), and that colonial
New England was not a "culture absolutely inimical to real poetry."
This latter point is truer of the twentieth century than of the seventeenth or eighteenth, when poetry had perhaps as many practitioners,
proportionally, as today's popular folk-art, photography; and, of
course, with so many photographers, some—like Edward Taylor in
poetry—rise above the level of occasional snapshot excellence. But I
also recognize that the theory of American Puritan aesthetics has not
yet escaped the nineteenth-century attitudes and knowledge of early
American poetry and has not yet caught up with the ineluctable
facts that Jantz presented in 1943 but is instead still held spell-
bound by the theories of Perry Miller, who in this case did not escape
the influence of the Victorian stereotype of the Puritan. Less exciting
but more complete is Constance J. Gefvert's *Edward Taylor: An Annotated Bibliography, 1668–1970* (Kent, Ohio, Kent State Univ.
Press), with a twenty-page introduction tracing the history of Taylor
scholarship. Since there is an author index, I wish that all sections of
the bibliography were chronological. A subject index (by poem as
well as by topic) would have increased the usefulness of this useful
work.

ii. Puritanism, the Mathers, and their Contemporaries

In a fine appreciation of William Bradford's masterpiece, Alan B.
Howard, "Art and History in Bradford's *Of Plymouth Plantation*"
(*WMQ* 28:237–66), adumbrates Bradford's view of men and of
events, doing justice to Bradford's complex blending of charity with
forbearance, and to his recognition of human infirmity. Bradford
"knows full well that today's sinner may prove tomorrow's saint; even
good and just men may be led into evil or injurious courses through unwarranted fear or suspicion, because they are misled by others, or by
virtue of their own necessarily imperfect reason." Howard contends
that Bradford gives so much detail about Isaac Allerton, James Sher-

ley, and Robert Cushman partially because he is attempting to view their actions as charitably as possible, and partially because he sees that each incident is the result of a "welter of complicating factors." Much less rewarding is John J. Fritscher's "The Sensibility and Conscious Style of William Bradford" (*BuR* 17,iii[1969]:80–90), which points out a few similarities between Calvin's *Institutes* and Bradford's history, belabours Bradford's obvious Providential interpretations (omitting those times when Bradford is unwilling to hazard a Providential reading of events), and, betraying a lack of background in seventeenth-century culture outside America, superciliously refers to the "colonial American craze for almanacs."

A difficult poem by Bradford's contemporary, Thomas Morton, is the subject of a fascinating examination by Robert D. Arner: "Mythology and the Maypole of Merrymount: Some Notes on Thomas Morton's 'Rise Oedipus'" (*EAL* 6:156–64). With excursions into the use of mythology in Renaissance English literature, Arner persuasively speculates that Morton's poem "Rise Oedipus" portrays a fertility rite, and hypothesizes that there may have been a rudimentary play, written by Morton, acted out at the maypole of Merrymount. Another contemporary's delightful and complicated work is the subject of "Nathaniel Ward's Cobbler as 'Schoem-Aker'" (*ELN* 9:100–02), where William J. Scheick points out that "Schoem-Aker" is an English-Hebrew-Dutch pun, signifying "the harrower or wise speaker of little nothings" and argues that this concluding pun of *The Simple Cobler of Aggawam in America* is a microcosmic presentation of Ward's persona.

The more important of Cecelia Tichi's two articles on Puritan historians is "Spiritual Biography and the 'Lords Remembrancers'" (*WMQ* 28:64–85), which delineates the influence of the genre of spiritual autobiography upon the Puritan history, defending the historians from the common charge of repetitious copying from John Winthrop and William Bradford by claiming that the "common Rhetoric" of the historians is based on the "allusive shorthand" of key images and metaphors established by the genre of spiritual autobiography. Her other article, "The Puritan Historians and Their New Jerusalem" (*EAL* 6:143–55), examines the building imagery in Edward Johnson, William Hubbard, and Cotton Mather to show that the latter two historians felt that there was a falling-off in spirituality in the late seventeenth century.

The stereotypes and simplifications that characterize Norman Earl
Tanis's "Education in John Eliot's Indian Utopias, 1645–1675" (*HEQ*
10 [1970]:308–23) are fairly represented by the following: "Eliot was
typical of these fiery Puritans fresh from Laudian England; but unlike most of them, his warm love for his fellow men and his sincere
acts of charity shone brightly behind the harsh Calvinistic theology
he preached." Another article that may safely be ignored is Kline A.
Nall's "Love and Wrestling Brewster: A Study in the Puritan Ethos"
(*ArlQ* 3,i:80–97), which turns out to be a rambling essay on the obvious significance of Puritan names (William Brewster's sons were
named "Love" and "Wrestling"). The somewhat misleadingly entitled "The Philosophical Background of New England Puritanism"
(*IPQ* 10[1970]:570–97), by Robert J. Roth, examines the surviving
commencement sheets from Harvard (1642–1810) and Yale (1718–
1797) for what they reveal about such topics as "Philosophy of Man,"
"Freedom of the Will," "Natural Theology," and "Political Theory."

Anne Bradstreet: "The Tenth Muse" (New York, Oxford Univ.
Press) by Elizabeth Wade White presents the first full scholarly biography of our most charming colonial poet. Partially because the
materials for a biography of Bradstreet are so scanty, White has given
us more peripheral background material than even an interested student of Bradstreet may want to read. At the same time, the political
careers of Bradstreet's father, Thomas Dudley, and of her husband,
Simon Bradstreet—careers which the poet evidently avidly shared—
are comparatively neglected. The discussion of the poetry is, unfortunately, mainly quotation and summary; but all of the facts presently
known of the poet's life are to be found here.

In "Roger Williams Among the Narragansett Indians" (*NEQ*
43[1970]:593–604) Jack L. Davis argues that "Williams' intimate
acquaintance with Narragansett culture provided the catalyst for
both his powerful attack upon New England theocracy and his conception of an ideal commonwealth with which to supplant it." No
doubt the Indians influenced Williams, but, like nearly all other
seventeenth- and eighteenth-century commentators on the Indian,
Williams used them as props in order to criticize Western civilization
(even such earlier American writers as Captain John Smith and Andrew White—not to mention Montaigne—did so). To leap from such
criticisms to the assertion that Williams's experience with the Indians

provided the catalyst for his attack upon the Massachusetts Bay theocracy and for his conception of an ideal commonwealth slights more important aspects both of his biography (and even its chronology) and of his intellectual heritage. The manuscripts by or relating to a second important dissenter from the Massachusetts Bay theocracy are the subject of a note by Everett H. Emerson, "Thomas Hooker Materials at the Connecticut Historical Society" (*EAL* 6:187–88).

Robert Middlekauff's *The Mathers: Three Generations of Puritan Intellectuals, 1596–1728* (New York, Oxford Univ. Press) is a major new interpretation of American Puritanism, based upon an examination of the religious life and thought of Richard, Increase, and Cotton Mather. Whereas Perry Miller offered a single paradigm of American Puritanism, which was not in all particulars true of any Puritan, and which neglected the emotional aspect of Puritanism, Middlekauff has written a careful investigation of the intellectual life of three leading Puritans of successive generations, emphasizing the role that the emotions played in their religio-intellectual lives. Although it is not, strictly speaking, a history of American Puritanism; yet it is, by its truth to particular cases, more valid than a single paradigm of seventeenth-century American Puritanism could be, while it is also just that—a new paradigm of American Puritanism. It is of less value for literary students than Miller's work, and its consideration of such literary and religious intricacies as typology is unsatisfactory. Whereas Miller often broke new ground and always presented his evidence as an interested student hypothesizing to other interested students, Middlekauff often rehashes the work of others and presents his evidence as a teacher writing for students. But his appreciation of the significance of the intellectual and emotional careers of the three Mathers, if not of their literary qualities, is exemplary.

Increase Mather's anonymous biography of his father is the subject of William J. Scheick's "Anonymity and Art in *The Life and Death of That Reverend Man of God, Mr. Richard Mather*" (*AL* 42:457–67). The father image, which is synonymous with minister, teacher, and first settler, as well as with natural father, dominates the biography, according to Scheick. He explains that Increase Mather's anonymity helped him to assume the voice of the fathers and thus to continue the tradition of the (fore)fathers as well as to define its significance. Thus this interesting article is about the creation of the image of the first settlers, as well as a sensitive piece of literary criticism. Walter Lazenby comments on the style, timeliness, and sense of audience of Cotton Mather's trial and execution sermons in "Exhortation as Exorcism: Cotton Mather's Sermons to Murderers" (*QJS* 57:50–56). And Edward Cifelli follows up William Reid Manierre's *QJS* article of 1961, "Verbal Patterns in Cotton Mather's *Magnalia*," with "More of Cotton Mather's 'Verbal Patterns'" (*QJS* 57:94–97) by calling attention to a distinction between Mather's public (published) writings and private diaries.

Kenneth Silverman's *Selected Letters of Cotton Mather* (Baton Rouge, La. State Univ. Press) is a major resource for the study of Cotton Mather and of his time. It amounts to a life-and-letters biography of Mather. There are no notes, but groups of letters are introduced by long commentaries, explaining the place of the letters in Mather's life and identifying the correspondents and most of the subjects mentioned. In addition, a series of brief biographies at the end of the volume sketch all the correspondents and all others of any importance mentioned in the letters. As a book, this is more readable than a complete edition of all the letters, in their entirety, with full footnotes identifying all persons, events, and allusions, could have been—partially because of Silverman's own prose (comprising approximately one-fourth of the book and constituting at this time the best introduction to the life of Cotton Mather) and partially because he has selected fascinating letters to print. But this is not the scholarly and definitive edition that we hoped for. A contribution to the intellectual life of Cotton Mather is Kennerly M. Woody's monograph-length "Bibliographical Notes to Cotton Mather's *Manuductio Ad Ministerium*" (*EAL* 6sup:1–98), which identifies the references and allusions in Mather's heavily-documented work.

The leading authority on Latin in early America, Leo M. Kaiser, edited the text of Oakes's Latin commencement address of 1678, and, with 317 notes documenting the classical allusions, amply substantiates his claim that the evidence of Oakes's ability as a "pure and elegant Latinist" is "pretty overwhelming" ("The Oratorio Quinta of Urian Oakes, Harvard, 1678," *HL* 19[1970]:485–508). Kaiser also corrects, translates, or identifies a number of passages in Harrison T. Meserole's collection *Seventeenth-Century American Poetry* in "On the Latin in the Meserole Anthology" (*EAL* 6:165–66).

iii. The South

With an anachronistic thesis, Robert Detweiler, "Was Richard Hakluyt a Negative Influence in the Colonization of Virginia?" (*NCHR* 48:359–69), argues that Hakluyt's visionary schemes attracted aristocrats and get-rich-quick opportunists rather than the dirt farmers needed for a colony in North America. Philip L. Barbour, the eminent authority on Captain John Smith, puts together the known biographical and bibliographical information on "The Honorable George Percy, Premier Chronicler of the First Virginia Voyage" (*EAL* 6:7–17), incidentally documenting the successive embellishment of a travellers' tale told by this early explorer. And Barbour has also, in "The Earliest Reconnaissance of the Chesapeake Bay Area: Captain John Smith's Map and Indian Vocabulary" (*VMHB* 79:280–302), begun to clear the way for his forthcoming edition of the works of Captain John Smith. A valuable addition to the few literary studies of Smith is Everett H. Emerson's *Captain John Smith* (TUSAS 177). In addition to surveying the early writings about North America and sketching Smith's life, Emerson examines, chronologically, Smith's major writings. Emerson pays special attention to four topics: Smith's sources and the way that he adopted them; Smith's revisions and additions in later versions of the same adventure (I wish that Emerson had compared the revisions of the Pocohontas story and generalized about these revisions in comparison to Smith's practice elsewhere); an evaluation of the comparative excellence among Smith's writings (Emerson's favorites are books two and three of *The Generall Historie* and the final pamphlet, *Advertisements for the Unexperienced Planters*); and Smith's significance as a writer. Since much of the book deals with sources and revisions (valuable scholarly work but not the most fascinating reading), a brief explanation of the relationship among Smith's various writings would have been especially useful.

In *James Blair, King-Maker of Virginia* (Chapel Hill, Univ. of N.C. Press), Parke Rouse, Jr., has written a full biography of the founder and president of the College of William and Mary, author of a four-volume set of sermons, and joint-author of *The Present State of Virginia*. Rouse's scholarly biography chronicles Blair's many political fights and presents a realistic portrait of the proud, greedy, moral, self-sacrificing, dutiful, contradictory minister. And Robert A.

Bain has written an article and a note dealing with the writings of
Blair: "The Composition and Publication of *The Present State of
Virginia and the College*" (*EAL* 6:31–54) presents the complex and
elusive reasons for the publication of *The Present State* some thirty
years after its composition; and "A Note on James Blair and the Southern Plain Style" (*SLJ* 4,i:68–73) argues that Southerners such as
Blair, Robert Beverley, and Hugh Jones were, like the New England
Puritans, practicing and advocating a plain style in colonial America
and that this style has "persistently had its Southern practitioners."

Blair's younger and better-known contemporary, who succeeded
the octogenarian as President of the Council of Virginia, is also the
subject of a new study: Pierre Marambaud, *William Byrd of West-
over, 1674–1744* (Charlottesville, Univ. Press of Va.). The three divisions of Marambaud's book deal with Byrd's biography (excellent
though brief); his writings; and the culture of early eighteenth-
century Virginia (material found in numerous other places). The
treatment of Byrd's writings is disappointing. Byrd's polished writings
(histories, travel literature, and letters) are not evaluated in their
historical and generic contexts, and his diaries are judged to be
mainly valuable as history. One of the cruxes of Byrd's literary life is
investigated by Carl R. Dolmetsch, "William Byrd II: Comic Dramatist?" (*EAL* 6:18–30), who concludes, contrary to a colonial Virginia
anecdote recorded by Robert Bolling, that Byrd did not have a major
role in writing Colley Cibber's *The Careless Husband*, but that he
evidently did write a song used in the play.

The first good critical article ever written on the oft-anthologized
The Sot-Weed Factor is Robert D. Arner's "Ebenezer Cooke's *The
Sot-Weed Factor*: The Structure of Satire" (*SLJ* 4,i:33–47). Arner
defines the qualities of the persona of the sot-weed factor (pointing
out that the persona should not be confused with Cooke), and examines "a number of recurrent motifs, metaphors, and parallel episodes"
in the poem, particularly the curse. J. A. Leo Lemay's "Robert Bolling
and the Bailment of Colonel Chiswell" (*EAL* 6:99–142), introduces
an important literary figure, discusses the published arguments arising
from a notorious colonial murder case, and identifies the various
writers in the Virginia newspapers of 1766. Richard Beale Davis, following up his publication of Reid's long manuscript satire in *The
Colonial Virginia Satirist* (see *ALS 1967*, p. 117), comments on the
newspaper essays and poems of this Scotch tutor in "James Reid,

Colonial Virginia Poet and Moral and Religious Essayist" (*VMHB* 79:3–19).

The first full scholarly biography of the most important dissenting minister of the colonial South is George William Pilcher's *Samuel Davies: Apostle of Dissent in Colonial Virginia* (Knoxville, Univ. of Tenn. Press). Pilcher's account of Davies's relations with his brother-in-law, the patriot printer John Holt, is especially good, although his discussion of the hymns, poems, sermons, and literary quarrels of this important literary man is uncritical. But with this well documented biography and with the edition of Davies's poems brought out three years ago by Richard Beale Davis (see *ALS 1968*, p. 124), we are in a position to evaluate Davies's literary and intellectual achievements. Richard Walser calls attention to the fact that Governor Alexander Martin, of Princeton and North Carolina, was a poet and discusses three of his poems, in "Alexander Martin, Poet" (*EAL* 6:55–61). Julian Mason prints two poems and one prose description by that "literary diplomat," William Vans Murray (1760–1803), whose writings, though witty, hardly compare with the productions of his more prolific but nevertheless minor contemporaries ("William Vans Murray: The Fancy of a Poet," *EAL* 6:63–68). And Maurice Duke, in "John Taylor of Caroline, 1753–1824: Notes Toward a Bibliography" (*EAL* 6:69–72), gives locations for the books by Taylor, as well as notes on his manuscripts and letters.

iv. Franklin and the Enlightenment

In an essay presenting a "vision of American autobiography as American history," James M. Cox's "Autobiography and America" (*VQR* 47:252–77), anatomizes autobiography as a genre before dealing with Franklin, Thoreau, and Henry Adams, as well as, more briefly, with Whitman and Gertrude Stein. To simplify a rewarding essay, I may say that Cox sees Franklin's autobiography as a conscious paradigm of the American Revolution and as a key step toward the liberation of the modern self. More focused is John Griffith's "The Rhetoric of Franklin's 'Autobiography'" (*Criticism* 13:77–94), which validly distinguishes Franklin's point of view in the *Autobiography* from the young Franklin as character or subject. Griffith contends that the interplay between the persona and the subject is repeated, time and again, without any sense of progression or of organic connection, so that these interplays "are more properly to be seen as elements of

The Autobiography's rhetoric rather than of its plot or deep structure; for what they give to the book is the kind of imaginative unity which inevitably arises when similar dramatic situations are repeated in various forms."

Two other articles deal with Franklin's masterpiece. John J. McLaughlin and Rowena R. Ansbacher, "Sane Ben Franklin: An Adlerian View of his Autobiography" (*JoIP* 27:189–207), superfluously point out that Franklin healthily directed his energies, and maintain that modern readers are likely to find the *Autobiography* "significant because it is a prescription for mental health." And the *Autobiography* is examined by Campbell Tatham for evidence of Franklin's antipathy to the Puritan tradition: "Benjamin Franklin, Cotton Mather, and the Outward State" (*EAL* 6:223–33). While granting Tatham's conclusion, it seems to me that most scholars would prefer to view Puritanism in a wider framework (e.g., Franklin's attitude toward marriage and toward diet, as expressed in the *Autobiography*, perfectly dovetail with scholarly descriptions—which do not mention Franklin —of seventeenth-century Puritan attitudes toward these subjects); and even if one would accept a narrow definition of Puritanism, one might well argue that Franklin's antithetic values are a reaction to, and thereby an influence of, Puritanism.

Although every Franklinist recognized Cecil B. Currey's *Road to Revolution: Benjamin Franklin in England, 1765–1775* (New York, Doubleday Anchor Books, 1969) as a pack of distortions, misleading quotations, and unsubstantiated charges, it has nonetheless been incumbent upon others to reply to Currey's misrepresentations, and Paul H. Smith, in "Benjamin Franklin: Gunrunner" (*PMHB* 95:526–29), puts the quietus to Currey's statement that "It is indisputable that Franklin was involved in gunrunning." The enormous body of Franklin scholarship was the subject of an evaluative essay by Bruce I. Granger in *Fifteen American Authors* (pp. 185–206). All of the important books dealing with Franklin as a writer (including the best of them, Granger's own *Benjamin Franklin, An American Man of Letters*) are here, but the treatment of the numerous essays is necessarily highly selective.

Three articles in *The Ibero-American Enlightenment*, edited by Alfred O. Aldridge (Urbana, Univ. of Ill. Press) are relevant. Aldridge's general introduction to the volume, "The Concept of the Ibero-American Enlightenment" (pp. 3–30), deals with intellectual influences, the relationship between politics and the enlightenment, and the problems of defining and demarcating the enlightenment. Robert C. Black III, in "The Younger John Winthrop, Precursor of the Scientific Enlightenment" (pp. 309–16), summarizes the scientific interests of a Governor of Connecticut who lived over a century earlier than the group of Founding Fathers generally (and mistakenly) regarded as the earliest representatives of the American Enlightenment. And in an ambitious but brief essay, Lewis P. Simpson, "Literary Ecumenicalism of the American Enlightenment" (pp. 317–32), claims that the Third Realm or Republic of Letters had become a reality by the eighteenth century (nearly coequal in importance with the church and state), but that, paradoxically, the ideals of the cosmopolitan Republic of Letters in the United States were in part responsible for the literary provincialism of nineteenth-century American literature. Simpson believes that Jefferson's reply to "Query 19" in his *Notes on Virginia* (1785), where the future President turns from the ideals of the cosmopolitan city to those of Arcadia as embodied in the American farmer, set forth the dominant American version of literary ecumenicalism for such future writers as Thoreau.

I should also note a useful supplement to Gilbert Chinard's essays analyzing the key ideas in Samuel Miller's *Brief Retrospect of the Eighteenth Century*: Jacob L. Susskind's concise overview, which is especially good on the contemporary reception of the book ("Samuel Miller's Intellectual History of the Eighteenth Century," *JPH* 49: 15–31).

v. Edwards and the Great Awakening

Edward M. Griffin's *Jonathan Edwards* (UMPAW 97) is a masterful introduction to Edwards's life and writings. Using the distinctions of Lockean psychology, Griffin clearly explains the theory behind Edwards's discrimination of natural and reborn man. He also concisely elucidates the purposes and arguments of the major works, *Religious Affections, Freedom of the Will*, and *The Nature of True Virtue*. Griffin concludes with the debate of Vernon Parrington and Peter Gay versus Perry Miller and others whether Edwards is medieval or modern, calling the argument a stalemate. Instead he maintains that Edwards is an American artist who prefigures Thoreau, Melville, Hawthorne, Henry Adams, and others—all of whom were, according to

Griffin, fascinated "with the idea that man must locate himself in relation to God."

Edwards's juvenile notes on spiders are subjected to a searching analysis by David S. Wilson ("The Flying Spider," *JHI* 32:447–58), who describes the background of the essay, suggesting that Edwards knew earlier natural history essays on the phenomena, analyzes the distinguishing qualities of Edwards's two versions of the essay, and argues for an appreciation of the natural history writers. The only other article of interest to literary students on Edwards is Everett H. Emerson's evaluation of the scholarship, "Jonathan Edwards," in *Fifteen American Authors* (pp. 169–84). Sound in judgment, the article has an unexpected bonus in the appreciation of unpublished doctoral dissertations and generous praise for the excellent scholarship of the past and present.

Major work on John Woolman appeared in 1971. Phillips P. Moulton's *The Journal and Major Essays of John Woolman* (New York, Oxford Univ. Press) presents an excellent edition of the *Journal* as well as of "Some Considerations on the Keeping of Negroes," "Considerations on Keeping Negroes: Part Second," and "A Plea for the Poor." This definitive text includes hitherto suppressed passages, notes all substantive changes, and annotates all references and allusions. Helpful appendices (such as the "Major Extant Manuscripts," and an annotated bibliography) and a superb index add to the value of the edition. Some scholars may lament the fact that not all differences in accidentals are noted—but I do not. Moulton's full and comparatively inexpensive edition is now standard. In an article, Moulton has gathered together references to Woolman from a variety of later writers, including the English romantics, the American Transcendentalists, and Theodore Dreiser ("The Influence of the Writings of John Woolman," *QH* 60,i:3–13). And Henry J. Cadbury, in *John Woolman in England: A Documentary Supplement* (Supplement No. 31 to the *Journal* of the Friends Historical Society) prints a wealth of new information about Woolman's last months, as well as incidental new information about Woolman's contemporaries, including the American writer Sophia Hume.

Although no articles of literary interest appeared on the Great Awakening, there were two excellent essays on Samuel Johnson, President of King's College. Joseph J. Ellis III, in "The Puritan Mind in Transition: The Philosophy of Samuel Johnson" (*WMQ* 28:26–45), analyzes the clash between the "old Puritan metaphysic" and the "epistemological doctrines of the English Enlightenment" as they existed in Johnson's philosophy. Ellis also compares and contrasts the philosophies of Jonathan Edwards and Samuel Johnson. And in a wide-ranging essay, Norman S. Fiering, "President Samuel Johnson and the Circle of Knowledge" (*WMQ* 28:199–236), traces Johnson's successive schemes for organizing all of human knowledge, defines Johnson's importance as a thinker and educator, and, most valuably, assesses the important place of moral philosophy as a study and a concern from the eighteenth to the mid-nineteenth century.

vi. The Revolutionary and Early National Periods

The radical political propaganda of the pre-Revolutionary period and the men responsible for it constitute one aspect of a detailed essay by Alan and Katherine Day, "Another Look at the Boston 'Caucus' " (*JAmS* 5:19–42). William Ellery's poetic "A Farce" of 1780 is shown by William M. Fowler, Jr., "A Farce Re-examined" (*PMHB* 95:529–32), to satirize those members of Congress who wanted to build a group of expensive public buildings to house the fledging government. Another brief essay in explication is Charles E. Modlin's "Aristocracy in the Early Republic" (*EAL* 6:252–57), which shows that the anonymous poem *Aristocracy* (1795) satirizes Aaron Burr and Edmond Genet.

To judge by these two recent articles, the redoubtable Hugh Henry Brackenridge is gaining increased stature from his more recent readers. Wendy Martin, in "On the Road with the Philosopher and Profiteer: A Study of Hugh Henry Brackenridge's *Modern Chivalry*" (*ECS* 4:241–56), finds that the novel "foreshadows the themes of artistic isolation, subjectivity, and alienation which preoccupy many nineteenth- and twentieth-century American novelists," relates the relative formlessness of the work to eighteenth-century views of Lockean associationism, and plays up the weighty themes in the novel, particularly the reflections on learning, culture, style, law, and institutions of society. And in "*Modern Chivalry*: The Frontier as Crucible" (*EAL* 6:263–70), Amberys R. Whittle argues, without sufficient substantiating detail, that the novel "is fundamentally an examination of basic human nature in an ideal test situation, the American frontier."

Two short articles deal with the Connecticut Wits. Julian Mason prints one of the earliest poems praising Washington: "David Humphreys' Lost Ode to George Washington" (*QJLC* 28,i:28–37); and, in an insipid note, George E. Mize belabours the obvious: "Trumbull's Use of the Epic Formula in *The Progress of Dullness* and *M'Fingal*" (*ConnR* 4,ii:86–90). Following his earlier article (see *ALS 1970*, p. 170) on Elliott, Eugene L. Huddleston, "Indians and Literature of the Federalist Era: The Case of James Elliot" (*NEQ* 44:22–37), claims that Elliot's poetry consistently viewed the Indian through a borrowed literary lens and that his prose generally reflected his actual experience. New and reasonably conclusive evidence verifies the earlier opinion that William Hill Brown wrote *The Power of Sympathy* (John R. Byers, Jr., "Further Verification of the Authorship of *The Power of Sympathy*," *AL* 43:421–27). And William S. Kabel tracks down eight editions of a religious allegory written in South Carolina in 1784 by Edmund Botsford ("Addenda to Wright: Botsford's *The Spiritual Voyage*," *PBSA* 65:72–74).

Using both genre criticism and the insights of psychology, Dieter Schulz convincingly examines the psychological and generic unity of Charles Brockden Brown's novel in "*Edgar Huntley* as Quest Romance" (*AL* 43:323–35). Schulz believes that Clithero is a double of Huntly, that sleepwalking represents a descent into the dark self, that the Indian fight asserts "the truth of the aggressive self," that Huntly's failure to integrate his disparate experiences asserts his non-recognition of the dark self and the amoral aggressive self, and that this failure may be necessary to Huntly's spiritual survival. According to Joseph Katz, Brown was still writing *Wieland* while the first part of it was being printed; consequently he could not revise the first part and was forced, in composing the ending, to attempt to reconcile the earlier with the middle parts of the book: "Analytical Bibliography and Literary History: The Writing and Printing of *Wieland*" (*Proof* 1:8–34). And William S. Ward lists thirteen contemporary reviews of Brown's work, including five for *Wieland*, in "Charles Brockden Brown, His Contemporary British Reviewers, and Two Minor Bibliographical Problems" (*PBSA* 65:399–402).

The Early American Novel by Henri Petter (Columbus, Ohio State Univ. Press) is a worthy successor to Lillie D. Loshe's *The Early American Novel* (1907) and to Robert B. Heilman's *America in English Fiction, 1760–1800* (1937), for Petter both describes the novels (as Loshe did) and analyzes the themes (as Heilman did, although Heilman's field is somewhat different). Petter's organization is, happily, thematic, with more space being devoted to "Satirical and Polemical Fiction" than to any other single category. Major treatment is awarded Charles Brockden Brown, Washington Irving, James Kirke Paulding, and Susanna Rowson among others. Comparing Petter's treatment of *Modern Chivalry* with the articles characterized above, we may say that, while Petter makes few acute critical remarks, he is fundamentally sound—his comparative perspective makes him little inclined to claim that a loose, baggy, but interesting monster of a novel is a great masterpiece.

vii. Bibliography, Books, and Miscellaneous

Roger E. Stoddard, the foremost bibliographer of belletristic early Americana, in "Some Corrigenda and Addenda to Hill's *American Plays Printed 1714–1830*" (*PBSA* 65:278–95), lists eighteen additional plays, numerous corrections, and eighteen "unlocated titles and editions." Stoddard also follows up his *Catalogue of Books and Pamphlets Unrecorded in Oscar Wegelin's "Early American Poetry"* (see *ALS 1970*, pp. 172–73) with "Further Addenda to Wegelin's *Early American Poetry*," (*PBSA* 65:169–72), giving ten additional titles, plus notes (such as Sabin references) for a number of titles previously listed. A description of the Thomas W. Streeter copy of the first promotion tract of West New Jersey, *A Further Account of New Jersey* (1676), is given by Richard P. McCormick, "A Further Account" (*JRUL* 34:33–41). And Madeline Pecora demonstrates that a seventeenth-century American ballad (Evans 453) was written in 1689: "The Date of 'The Plain Case Stated'" (*EAL* 6:185–86).

Three articles deal with colonial Southern libraries. Walter B. Edgar, in "Noteable Libraries of Colonial South Carolina" (*SCHM* 72:105–10), finds 153 libraries in colonial South Carolina worth more than £50. John Mackenzie, a planter whose library was given to the Charleston Library Company, had the largest. And in "Some Popular Books in Colonial South Carolina," (*SCHM* 72:174–78), Edgar lists all titles appearing in at least five libraries, but comments neither on the contents of these books nor on their cultural significance. And Helen R. Watson itemizes some inventories in "The Books They Left: Some 'Liberies' in Edgecombe County, 1733–1783" (*NCHR* 48:245–57).

David Potter and Gordon L. Thomas, eds., in *The Colonial Idiom* (Carbondale, So. Ill. Univ. Press, [1970]), have gathered an extensive collection of colonial oratory, including legal and political speeches, sermons, academic addresses, and occasional speeches. The texts are selected from a variety of sources, including manuscripts; but the absence of any editorial apparatus (other than a brief bibliography and a skimpy introduction) reduces the usefulness of the anthology. A large collection of basic sources is *The Regulators in North Carolina: A Documentary History, 1759–1776* (Raleigh, N.C., State Dept. of Archives and History), edited by William S. Powell, James K. Huhta, and Thomas J. Farnham. There are few notes and no introductions to the various texts, but there is a brief general introduction, a bibliographical note, and a good index. Unfortunately, the reprintings are often from secondary sources rather than the originals; and except for the Virginia newspapers, the papers of other colonies were not examined for regulator materials: even the famous article from the *Massachusetts Spy* ("publicly burnt under the Gallows, by the common Hangman") is reprinted from a Virginia paper. Despite a host of other reservations, I welcome the book, for it is fascinating to browse in, containing the writings of Herman Husbands, the songs of Rednap Howell (some of which could have been sung to the tune of Yankee Doodle), and even an 1810 folkloristic recollection of the events.

John H. Kerr's meaty article, "The Bankruptcy of the Chestnut Street Theatre, Philadelphia, 1799" (*ThR* 11:154–72), traces the financial history of this theater in the decade before 1799, chronicling the plight of the managers, Thomas Wignell and Alexander Reinagle, who struggled against overwhelming odds to keep the theater going. And David Wilson, in "The Iconography of Mark Catesby" (*ECS* 4:169–83), praises the engravings in Catesby's *Natural History of Carolina* (1729–1747), contending that the "particular combinations of flora and fauna" in the plates are "esthetically inspired." Last, Richard Bauman's "Aspects of 17th Century Quaker Rhetoric" (*QJS* 56 [1970]: 67–74), discusses the radical democratic significance of the Quaker usage of *thee* and *thou*.

University of California, Los Angeles

10. Nineteenth-Century Fiction

M. Thomas Inge

Between 1969 and 1970, the amount of scholarship on nineteenth-century fiction exclusive of Hawthorne, Melville, Twain, and James increased nearly one hundred percent. In 1971, it appears to have leveled off with only a slight increase recorded in number of items published. The appearance of several important general critical volumes, two biographies of major figures, a multitude of new editions of fiction by major and minor writers, and a large number of dissertations make the year noteworthy, yet too few of the critical essays and articles truly advance our appreciation or understanding of the writings they examined. James Fenimore Cooper, William Dean Howells, Stephen Crane, and Sarah Orne Jewett were the most popular subjects this year, but a good many generally neglected writers were given fresh, modern appraisals by critics and students.

i. General Topics

Bringing to bear the results of a long and distinguished career in teaching and writing about nineteenth-century American literature, Edwin H. Cady provides one more attempt to define "realism" in *The Light of Common Day: Realism in American Fiction* (Bloomington, Ind. Univ. Press). No brief summary can do justice to Cady's theory, which rests finally upon his definition of what he calls a "common vision," and if what he says is not likely to resolve critical controversy over the matter, it will provide stimulating food for thought. The remainder of the volume, which does not grow integrally out of his theory, treats the work of James, Howells, Norris, Hawthorne, Twain, and Stephen Crane, and such matters as naturalism, the mock-heroic tradition in American fiction, the native sources of realism, and modern literary criticism. What it all adds up to is an immensely humane statement by a sensitive soul who greatly cares about American literature and critical practice.

Henri Petter's *The Early American Novel* (Columbus, Ohio State Univ. Press) is a comprehensive study in the European fashion: broad in general outline, eclectic in its synthesis of data and past scholarship, and detailed in its attention to such minutia as plot summary (appended in fact are plot synopses of over 80 novels discussed in the text). A descriptive survey of the American novel before 1820, its value will be as a reference work useful in understanding the backgrounds for and development of fiction after 1820, but not as a sound source of critical judgment about the novels it treats. There is material here to build upon aplenty, especially for serious research on writers shortly to be eclipsed by Irving and Cooper, but often Petter comes up with data of little use to anybody—for example, "If we assume the average size of the early American works of fiction to have been about 220 pages, one-sixth of these books are definitely subnormal in length, and as many have more than four hundred pages."

Two books which properly belong to the category of intellectual history, but both of which offer useful elucidation of the nineteenth-century cultural milieu, are *The Age of Energy: Varieties of American Experience, 1865–1915* by Howard Mumford Jones (New York, Viking Press) and *A Genteel Endeavor: American Culture and Politics in the Gilded Age* by John Tomsich (Stanford, Calif., Stanford Univ. Press). As he moves from popular culture to highbrow literature, Jones brilliantly outlines all the important literary and intellectual movements of the period, especially the period's devotion to the concept of "energy." Tomsich's study examines the genteel tradition as shaped by the writings of Richard Henry Stoddard, Thomas Bailey Aldrich, George Boker, Bayard Taylor, George William Curtis, Charles Eliot Norton, Edmund Clarence Stedman, and Richard Watson Gilder. Well-informed and clearly written, the book is especially welcome for its attention to these neglected but important writers.

A preliminary but useful research tool for the study of late nineteenth-century fiction is Clayton L. Eichelberger's *A Guide to Critical Reviews of United States Fiction, 1870–1910* (Metuchen, N.J., Scarecrow Press), an index to critical comment on major and minor fiction found in thirty selected periodicals of the period. Although published for nostalgic reasons in commemoration of the 125th anniversary of the founding of the publishing firm, *Scribner's Month-*

ly, 1871 (New York, Scribner's), a reprint of the complete 1871 issues, contains some surprisingly fascinating pieces of fiction by authors long forgotten, as well as essays, reviews, poems, and illustrations of the time.

General dissertations this year include: Judith M. Alter, "The Western Myth in American Literature and Painting of the Late Nineteenth and Early Twentieth Centuries" (*DAI* 31:5347A); Clarence E. Brown, "The American Gambler Story in the Sentimental Tradition, 1794–1870" (*DAI* 32:380A); Michael D. Butler, "The Literary Landscape of the Trans-Mississippi West: 1826–1902" (*DAI* 31:6542A), a bit ambiguous in title in that it deals with the depiction of landscape in far Western fiction; Mark F. Goldberg, "The Representation of Love and Romance in American Fiction About Eastern European Jews in New York City: 1894–1917" (*DAI*, 31:6055A–56A); Jean R. Kirkpatrick, "The Temperance Movement and Temperance Fiction, 1820–1860" (*DAI* 31:5365A); Thomas H. Pauly, "The Travel Sketch-Book and the American Author: A Study of the European Travelogues of Irving, Longfellow, Hawthorne, Howells, and James" (*DAI* 32:928A); Sylvia Saidlower, "Moral Relativism in American Fiction of the Eighteen Nineties" (*DAI* 31:6631A); Ruth A. Voth, "The Lyric Strain: A Study of the Heroine of the Old South" (*DAI* 31:3568A); and Dorothea C. Wright, "Visions and Revisions of the 'New Woman' in American Realistic Fiction from 1880–1920: A Study in Authorial Attitudes" (*DAI* 32:989A). By reputation Perry C. Lentz's dissertation, "Our Missing Epic: A Study in Novels About the American Civil War" (*DAI* 31:5412A), which ranges from Mary Johnston, Winston Churchill, and John Fox, Jr., to Warren, Faulkner, and Margaret Mitchell, may well prove the most significant of the lot.

ii. Irving, Cooper, and Their Contemporaries

As the literary historian or scholar reads *The Heart That Would Not Hold: A Biography of Washington Irving* by Johanna Johnston (New York, M. Evans and Company), he will find himself disturbed by the imagined thoughts of real people based purely on supposition, by the lack of documentation for quotations and facts, and by the tendency to arrange fact to suit romantic fancy. What he may discover afterwards, however, is that he has greatly enjoyed himself and come away with a rekindled interest in the subject. That is, after all, an intentionally popularized and romanticized version of Irving's life, though based on careful research, and if it accomplishes the feat of leading the reader back to the writer's work with aroused interest, this is more than can be said for most scholarly biographies. A highly readable and comprehensive view of scholarship on Irving by Henry A. Pochmann is found in *Fifteen American Authors* (pp. 245–61).

The year's essays on Irving have dealt with rather specialized and minor matters. In "Washington Irving and the Negro" (*NALF* 4 [1970]:43–44), Kenneth T. Reed notes the obvious, that Irving had no concern for the plight of the enslaved black and wrote of him in the stereotyped fashion, without attempting to deal with the thornier problem of how such a humane man could so easily adopt the racism of his age. Wayne R. Kime's "Washington Irving and *The Empire of the West*" (*WAL* 5:277–85) identifies and reprints an unknown review by Irving on the Westward movement and national destiny, and the same author analyzes a holograph journal by Alfred Seton which served as a reference to Irving while writing *Astoria*, especially the incident concerning the loss of the ship *Tonquin*, in "Alfred Seton's Journal: A Source for Irving's *Tonquin* Disaster Account" (*OHQ* 71: 309–24). "Alexander Robertson: Irving's Drawing Teacher" (*AN&Q* 9:148–50) by Burton Albert, Jr., asserts that the young author studied art and drawing under the livelier Alexander Robertson rather than his less inspiring brother Archibald as is generally believed. In "Washington Irving's 'Insuperable Diffidence'" (*AL* 43:114–15), David E. E. Sloane publishes an 1839 letter in which Irving declined an invitation to speak because of his diffidence to public speaking.

Three dissertations completed are Helen M. J. Loschky, "Washington Irving's *Knickerbocker History of New York*: Folk History as a Literary Form" (*DAI* 31:6559A); Robert C. Wess, "The Image and Use of the Dutch in the Literary Works of Washington Irving" (*DAI* 31:4799A–800A); and Barbara J. Martineau, "Dramatized Narration in the Short Fiction of Irving, Poe, and Melville" (*DAI* 31:4725A). This last dissertation examines Irving's use of point of view, as does an Italian article, "Il «corsivo vivente» di Washington Irving," by Guido Fink (*SA* 16[1970]:25–56). In the same publication appears Silvano Sabbadini's "La morte e le maschere: Note sullo *Sketch Book*" (*SA* 16[1970]:57–79).

The most interesting part of Robert Penn Warren's pleasant little essay on James Fenimore Cooper for *Atlantic Brief Lives* (pp. 180–

82) is his suggestion that through his treatment of "the problem of man's relation to nature and the other men in the great modern state" Cooper remains relevant to contemporary life. Warren also draws several interesting parallels between Cooper and Faulkner in a passage that concludes: "If neither believes in a gospel of progress, both see life as redeemed by human kindness, valor, and fidelity." In his chapter on Cooper in *Reality and Idea* (pp. 101–22) David H. Hirsch questions whether or not Cooper's lessons are still relevant and meaningful in the twentieth century because he feels that Cooper failed to make his ideas dramatized fictions rather than moral tracts: "The question . . . is not simply whether the ideas can be said to be alive, but whether they are alive because of or apart from Cooper's novels. Or putting the matter somewhat differently, we may ask whether Cooper enriches our understanding of these ideas." In this Warren-Hirsch disagreement lie some fruitful ideas for future critical debate. As one would expect, James Franklin Beard's review of research and criticism on Cooper for *Fifteen American Authors* (pp. 63–96) is discerning and comprehensive. Beard comments on the need for a definitive critical text of Cooper's works, which will apparently be a long time coming. In the meantime, James H. Pickering has provided for the Masterworks of Literature Series a modernized text of *The Spy* (New Haven, Conn., College and Univ. Press), although at least five editions are already available. In *James Fenimore Cooper: Short Stories from His Novels* (New York, International Publishers), Sidney Finkelstein excerpts so-called short stories embedded in his novels, a bold editorial act which finally does nothing for Cooper's reputation as a novelist or short story writer.

A formidable body of criticism confronts the Cooper student this season. The most distinguished critic to give Cooper his consideration is Henry Nash Smith, in "Consciousness and Social Order: The Theme of Transcendence in the Leatherstocking Tales" (*WAL* 5 [1970]:177–94), who applies Turner's frontier hypothesis to the adventures of Natty Bumppo. While modern historians have long ago abandoned Turner's imaginative theory as useful in historiography, Smith finds its metaphoric power still useful in understanding Cooper. In "Cooper's Later Fiction: The Theme of 'Becoming'" (*SAQ* 70:77–87), Paul Stein examines the period between 1833 and 1838, when Cooper ceased writing fiction, as a transitional period after which he emerged a significantly different novelist: "As artistic constructs, the novels written after 1838 bear the mark of a structural complexity of a quite higher order than distinguishes his work appearing between 1820 and 1838." Stein argues that the process of becoming, the movement of characters through choices toward their rightful places in a rationally organized society, becomes his major thematic concern. The influence of the past on the present in the fiction is the subject of "History and Progress: Some Implications of Form in Cooper's Littlepage Novels" by Edgar A. Dryden (*NCF* 26:49–64): "For Cooper, today stands fully revealed only when it is illuminated by the light of yesterday. The reality of his characters, therefore, is shaped not by their future possibilities but by the shadows of their pasts." Dryden analyzes the Littlepage trilogy as "an attempt to dramatize the progress of the American nation." In the wake of the women's liberation movement, we have had reason to expect an essay on "The Women in Cooper's Leatherstocking Tales" (*AQ* 33:696–709). Nina Baym finds that "women have an important place in his works even when they themselves seem like insignificant beings, or are very crudely drawn by the author."

In search of a formal sense of structure in Cooper's Leatherstocking novels, in "*The Prairie*: A Scenario of the Wise Old Man" (*BuR* 19,i:15–36) William Bysshe Stein finds a consistent pattern of ritualistic experience: "Each novel focuses on a different life cycle of Natty Bumppo, delineating his progressive initiation into higher forms of self-knowledge." Terence Martin's "From the Ruins of History: *The Last of the Mohicans*" (*Novel* 2[1969]:221–29) is a carefully detailed and fascinating study of what happens in one novel when Cooper comes "to focus the lens of history on his narrative in a way that will require his imagination to work within the contours of a specific historical event." In a thorough and equally interesting explication of the same novel, "*The Last of the Mohicans* and Sounds of Discord" (*AL* 43:25–41), which attempts to account for "its turbulent energy, its carnage and magic, its preposterousness and its power," Thomas Philbrick finds that Natty Bumppo "emerges as a principle of action rather than as a repository of value." Merrill Lewis's "Lost and Found—In the Wilderness: The Desert Metaphor in Cooper's *The Prairie*" (*WAL* 5[1970]:195–204) is an exhaustive explication of the use of the desert as a pervasive metaphor in that novel—"a part of a dramatic *situation* and a reflection of a moral *condition* rather than a stage or a painter's canvas." A careful political reading of Cooper's utopian novel *The Crater* is found in "*The Crater* and the Constitution" by John P. McWilliams, Jr. (*TSLL* 12:631–45). Two items of less interest are "Major Character Types in *Home As Found*: Cooper's Search for American Principles and Dignity" by Donald Kay (*CLAJ* 14:432–39), and "Cooper and the 'Semblance of Reality': A Source for *The Deerslayer*" by Richard Vanderbeets (*AL* 42:544–46).

Dissertations listed this year include Vincent E. Gillespie, "James Fenimore Cooper and the Concept of Civilization" (*DAI* 31:6009A); Jay S. Paul, "Actions and Agents: Cooper's Evolving Aesthetic" (*DAI* 32:3323A); Barbara L. Reed, "James Fenimore Cooper: Experiments Within Form" (*DAI* 31:6022A); and Glenn M. Reed, "Humor in the Early Novels of James Fenimore Cooper" (*DAI* 31:5373A).

The second published volume in the Centennial Edition of the Writings of William Gilmore Simms is Volume 3, containing *As Good As Comedy: or The Tennessean's Story* and *Paddy McGann; or The Demon of the Stump*, (Columbia, Univ. of S.C. Press) both interesting contributions on Simms's part to the tradition of Southern humor. The texts, as established by James B. Meriwether, maintain the usual high standards of the CEAA, and introductions and explanatory notes by Robert Bush are informed and competent. A fine appreciation of Simms's calculated use of figurative language is accomplished by L. Moffitt Cecil in his essay "Functional Imagery in Simms's *The Partisan*," in *Studies in Medieval, Renaissance, American Literature* (pp. 155–64). "The Literary Criticism of William Gilmore Simms," by John C. Guilds (*SCR* 2[1969]:49–56), ably argues that in the final estimate, "Simms will rank higher as a letter-writer, as a short-storyist, and as a critic than he will as poet and novelist . . . because Simms was at his natural best in these less pretentious fields." William E. Powell has made a brief study of "Motif and Tale-type of Simms's 'Grayling'" (*SFQ* 35:157–59); Robert A. Rees and Marjorie Griffin have edited and introduced eight recently discovered letters between the author and editor, Sarah Lawrence Griffin, in "William Gilmore Simms and *The Family Companion*" (*SB* 24:109–29), and Lillian B. Gilkes carefully outlines a very complicated misunderstanding in "Park Benjamin, Henry William Herbert, and William Gilmore Simms: A Case of Mistaken Identity" (*SCR* 3:66–77). Alan H. Rose, "The Image of the Negro in the Pre-Civil War novels of John Pendleton Kennedy and William Gilmore Simms" (*JAmS* 4[1970]:217–26), finds that both writers retreated from confronting the black and the reality of his situation as the Civil War approached, Kennedy by resort to fantasy and Simms by suppression of the demonic forces blacks symbolized to the white mind. Nell M. Woods completed a dissertation on "Gullah and Backwoods Dialect in Selected Works by William Gilmore Simms (*DAI* 32:2667A–68A).

Henry Nash Smith's essay on Harriet Beecher Stowe for *Atlantic Brief Lives* (pp. 746–47) is a fine appreciation of her work as a reflection of religious trends in New England, but he overstates the case for her literary gifts, as when he notes, "until the advent of William Faulkner, whom in some ways she oddly resembles, no one except Mark Twain had surpassed her as the interpreter of an American region." Whatever skill she had, which was considerably less than Smith would have it, is displayed at its best in John R. Adams's judicious selection of her journalistic pieces and stories for the Masterworks of Literature Series published under the title *Regional Sketches* (New Haven, Conn., College and Univ. Press). David Levin's "American Fiction as Historical Evidence: Reflections on *Uncle Tom's Cabin*" (*NALF* 5:132–36,154) makes out a strong case for finding considerable intellectual power in Mrs. Stowe's best known book as "an admirably complex statement of American social contradictions." Yet this reader comes away with the uneasy feeling that his argument is much more ingenious than Mrs. Stowe was. Eleanor A. Miller has completed a study of "The Christian Philosophy in the New England Novels of Harriet Beecher Stowe" (*DAI* 32:445A–446A) and two bibliographical items were published: Harry Opperman, "The Ghost Editions of *Uncle Tom's Cabin*" (*PBSA* 65:295–96); and E. Bruce Kirkham, "The First Editions of *Uncle Tom's Cabin*: A Bibliographical Study" (*PBSA* 65:365–82).

A perceptive, thorough, and well-written attempt to rescue a much-neglected writer is Ben Merchant Vorpahl's "The Eden Theme and Three Novels by Timothy Flint" (*SIR* 10:105–29)—easily one of the most rewarding articles published this year and especially worthwhile for its attention to Flint. Another attempt at resurrecting a less talented but interesting writer is the facsimile reprint of John Neal's novel *Seventy-Six* (1823) with a full biographical and critical introduction by Robert A. Bain (Bainbridge, N.Y., York Mail-Print).

iii. Local Color, Humor, and Popular Fiction

Among the local color writers, Sarah Orne Jewett appears to be the subject of the most extensive reassessment, largely through the efforts of Richard Cary. As editor of the *Colby Library Quarterly*, he assembled an entire issue devoted to her work, with three critical essays designed to enhance her reputation as an artist—"*The Country of the Pointed Firs*: A Novel by Sarah Orne Jewett," by Paul D. Voelker (*CLQ* 9[1970]:201–13); "*The Country of the Pointed Firs*: A Pastoral of Innocence," by David Stouck (213–20); and "*The Tory Lover, Oliver Wiswell*, and *Richard Carvel*," by Helen V. Parsons (220–31) —and several unpublished letters edited by Edward H. Cohen, Richard VanDerBeets, James K. Bowen, and Cary (231–43). Cary has edited further letters in the interesting correspondence between Miss Jewett and Whittier: "More Whittier Letters to Jewett" (*ESQ* 58[1970]:132–39) and " 'Yours Always Lovingly': Sarah Orne Jewett to John Greenleaf Whittier" (*EIHC* 107:412–50). Most significantly, he has edited a comprehensive collection of *The Uncollected Short Stories of Sarah Orne Jewett* (Waterville, Maine, Colby College Press), making available an extensive body of writing long hidden and in three cases until now unknown. Cary's informative introduction to this volume also appears as "The Uncollected Short Stories of Sarah Orne Jewett" (*CLQ* 9:385–408). Susan Allen Toth rightly discovers that unlike most other writers of her generation, Miss Jewett treated old age in her fiction with sensitivity and sympathy: "The Value of Age in the Fiction of Sarah Orne Jewett" (*SSF* 8:433–41). Partly devoted to Miss Jewett is Sister Sara McAlpin's "Enlightening the Commonplace: The Work of Sarah Orne Jewett, Willa Cather, and Ruth Suckow" (*DAI* 32:2061A).

A novel by Mary E. Wilkins Freeman which elicited high praise from Paul Elmer More, F. O. Matthiessen, and Edwin Arlington Robinson, among others, has been edited in a modernized text by Perry D. Westbrook for the Masterworks of Literature Series—*Pembroke* (New Haven, Conn., College and Univ. Press). Susan Allen Toth's "Mary Wilkins Freeman's Parable of Wasted Life" (*AL* 42: 564–67) is a perceptive explication of "The Three Old Sisters and the Old Beau" as a warning to accept and live a full life in the present or face the penalty of living in the past. James H. Quina, Jr., provides a brief summary of "Character Types in the Fiction of Mary Wilkins Freeman" (*CLQ* 9:432–39), and Claudette A. Diomedi has studied "Mary Wilkins Freeman and the Romance-Novel Tradition" (*DAI* 31: 4155A–56A). Relating to the work of Freeman, Jewett, Stowe, Rose Terry Cook, and Alice Brown is "New England Regionalism in the Context of Historical Change" by Sister Mary R. Coyne (*DAI* 31: 3498A–99A).

In "Kate Chopin's *The Awakening*: A Partial Dissent" (*Novel* 3[1970]:249–55) George M. Spangler disagrees with that novel's growing list of admirers by faulting Edna's characterization, which he finds inconsistent and diminished at the conclusion. Nevertheless, the Chopin revival moves ahead. Robert D. Arner draws on his dissertation—"Music From a Farther Room: A Study of the Fiction of Kate Chopin" (*DAI* 31:4753A–54A)—for two further studies: "Landscape Symbolism in Kate Chopin's *At Fault*" (*LaS* 9[1970]:142–53) and "Characterization and the Colloquial Style in Kate Chopin's 'Vagabonds'" (*MarkhamR* 2:110–12), both of which deepen our appreciation for the technical virtuosity of her work. Another brief study of interest is Kenneth M. Rosen's "Kate Chopin's *The Awakening*: Ambiguity as Art" (*JAmS* 5:197–99).

"Bret Harte and the Dickensian Mode in America" by Joseph H. Gardner (*JAmS* 2:89–101) examines in exhaustive detail the degree to which Harte was, as Twain phrased it, "the best imitation of Dickens in America." Elmo Howell's "Cable and the Creoles: A Note on 'Jean-Ah Poquelin'" (*XUS* 9[1970]:9–15) argues that Cable raises Jean Marie Poquelin above the level of burlesque to invest him with dignity and respect. Sister Eva M. Cox has examined "George Washington Cable's Handling of the Racial Problem in His Fiction" (*DAI* 31:4761A). Harriet R. Holman has continued her editing of unpublished Thomas Nelson Page materials with Page's *Mediterranean Winter—1906, Journal and Letters* (Miami, Fla., Field Research Projects) and contributed two minor notes on Page: "F. Marion Crawford and the Evil Eye" (*AN&Q* 9:103–04) and "U.S. Intervention in the Panamanian Constitution" (*AN&Q* 9:151). Donald Kay makes a good case for finding "Infant Realism in Eggleston's *The Hoosier Schoolmaster*" (*MarkhamR* 2:81–83), and John D. Roth has finished a study of "Down East and Southwestern Humor in the Western Novels of Edward Eggleston" (*DAI* 32:2652A). An informative essay on "Louisa May Alcott and the Racial Question" by Abigail

Ann Hamblen (*UR* 37:307–13) reveals that while she fiercely defended the rights and nobility of blacks, her class consciousness paradoxically led to racial condescension. Margaret Crompton's "*Little Women*: The Making of a Classic" (*ContempR* 218:99–104) is a superficial summary of what we already know about the Alcott family before Miss Alcott wrote the novel. Turning her attention to another minor nineteenth-century writer of a highly successful novel, in "Ramona: A Story of Passion" (*WR* 8,1:21–25), Abigail Ann Hamblen examines Helen Hunt Jackson's *Ramona* as "a poignant love story, a celebration of unabashed sexual passion" rather than local color or propaganda on the Indian question. A little studied Southern writer who was a transitional figure between the local colorists and the realists was Sherwood Bonner, whose diary of the year 1869 has been edited in three installments by William L. Frank: "Sherwood Bonner's Diary for the Year 1869" (*NMW* 3:111–30; 4:22–40,64–83). A modernized text of one of the earliest authentic Western novels, an extremely popular book in its day, has been prepared by H. Dean Propst for the Masterworks of Literature Series, *John Brent* by Theodore Winthrop (New Haven, Conn., College and Univ. Press), although he has inexplicably selected the thirteenth printing as the basis for his text rather than the first. A perceptive assessment of what motivated the numerous popular women authors of the nineteenth century to write is found in "The 'Scribbling Women' and Fanny Fern: Why Women Wrote" by Ann D. Wood (*AQ* 23:3–24). Numerous lady writers are mentioned, but Sara Payson Willis, or "Fanny Fern," is given the fullest attention in a most enlightening essay.

Richard Boyd Hauck puts the humorists of the Old Southwest to intriguing use in his provocative study *A Cheerful Nihilism* (pp. 40–76), wherein he considers their work the first major contribution to absurd fiction in this country. The application of his thesis to the work of Henry Clay Lewis, Augustus Baldwin Longstreet, Thomas Bangs Thorpe, William P. Hawes, Kittrell J. Warren, and Johnson Jones Hooper, among others, sheds fresh light on the complexity of their accomplishments. Unfortunately, however, the writer who might have contributed most to his theory—George Washington Harris—is badly misunderstood. Hauck states that "a reader's first reaction to George W. Harris's Sut Lovingood is usually incredulity—no one could be that repulsive." He also says, "Sut's laughter at his own vicious antics is grotesque. We do not laugh at them all, unless we laugh in derision of Sut himself." Perhaps it is a sign of incorrigibility and original sin, but the present writer and many of his friends find Sut's adventures hilariously funny. Those who can only laugh *at* Sut in derision seriously misapprehend their own natures as humans. As Lewis Leary so aptly puts it, "Read rightly, this 'natral born durn'd fool' reveals cousinship with us all." Leary says this in his essay "The Lovingoods: Notes Towards a Genealogy" in *Southern Excursions: Essays on Mark Twain and Others* (Baton Rouge, La. State Univ. Press), where he impishly twits all the Lovingood devotees for reading him too deeply and seriously, goes on to provide a delightful appreciation of the entire Lovingood family, and waggishly concludes, in terms of Sut's literary genealogy, that perhaps, "Sut, driven from the mountains, probably with a bounty on his head, found it advisable to feign death, flee the country, and change his name to Finn, to become, as deceit-filled as ever, Huck's deplorable Pap, whose first name is never revealed." Leary's essay is one of the few on Sut clearly invested with the kind of spirited humor Harris himself would have appreciated. Most Sutites, like M. Thomas Inge, with "a face as solemn as a tombstone" (as one critic once said of him), continue to produce dreary materials about Harris, as in his edition of "Early Appreciations of George W. Harris by George Frederick Mellen" (*THQ* 30:190–204).

Other materials of general interest to the student of American humor are two essays—"America's First Political Satirist: Seba Smith of Maine" by Alan R. Miller (*JQ* 47[1970]:488–92) and "The Durable Humor of Bill Nye" by Louis Hasley (*MTJ* 15,iii[1970]:7–10)—and five dissertations: Virginia L. Cox, "John Kendrick Bangs and the Transition from Nineteenth to Twentieth–Century American Humor" (*DAI* 31:4762A); Emory D. Estes, "Henry Cuyler Bunner: Editor and Author" (*DAI* 31:5359A) (Bunner was editor of *Puck* from 1878 to 1896); Robert L. Phillips, Jr., "The Novel and the Romance in Middle Georgia Humor and Local Color: A Study of Narrative Method in the Works of Augustus Baldwin Longstreet, William Tappan Thompson, Richard Malcolm Johnston, and Joel Chandler Harris" (*DAI* 32:2702A); Bette S. Weidman, "Charles Frederick Briggs: A Critical Biography" (*DAI* 32:3274A–75A); and Donald J. Yannella, Jr., "Cornelius Mathews: Knickerbocker Satirist" (*DAI* 32:990A).

In "The Real Alger Story" (*Horizon* 12,iii[1970]:62–65), reprinted in *A Many-Windowed House* Malcolm Cowley provides a pleasant survey of Horatio Alger's personal and artistic weaknesses and a summary of his message and meaning based on a careful reading of the novels, unlike the erroneous generalizations usually offered. Two handsome facsimile reprints of Alger novels—*Phil the Fiddler* (1872) and *Struggling Upward* (1890) (North Plainfield, N.J., Nautilus Books)—have been published with brief historical introductions by Rychard Fink. As surely as Alger captured the materialistic optimism of his age, Charles M. Sheldon captured the religious optimism in his novel *In His Steps* (1896); its cultural and sociological relevance in its time is explained by Paul S. Boyer, "*In His Steps*: A Reappraisal" (*AQ* 23:60–78).

iv. Howells, Realism, and Post-Civil War Fiction

Henry James predicted that William Dean Howells's "really beautiful time" would come, when the critical world would pay him universal homage. If this prophecy remains unfulfilled, certainly homage of a kind is being paid if only in terms of extensive publishing activity. Perhaps the best piece of homage yet paid him is Kenneth S. Lynn's biography, *William Dean Howells: An American Life* (New York, Harcourt Brace Jovanovich). Lynn underplays his role as a critic of Howells's fiction, devotes little space to his more illustrious literary acquaintances, and carefully designs a factual account of his life from which Howells the man emerges as a comprehensible human being—"a man of modern sensibility, whose awareness of life was rooted in radical doubt and anxiety." As John Seelye puts it in his review, "The Rise of William Dean Howells" (*New Republic* 165 [July 3, 1971]:23–26)—a fine appreciation of both Lynn's biography and Howells—"What Lynn has done is to abstract from the crowded whole of Howells's public and private life those aspects which emphasize the tensions—the Passion as it were—so as to counterbalance the popular impression left by the bludgeon attacks of Mencken and his literary boob-squad." Few can call Lynn's book the "definitive" biography—a foolish practice we should abandon, because every good biography is interpretive and therefore only one man's opinion—but Howells isn't likely to have a more judicious and fair-minded biographer.

Granville Hicks's brief essay on Howells for *Atlantic Brief Lives* (pp. 389–91) is kindly disposed but contributes no new insight.

James Gindin's chapter on Howells and James in his study of what he calls "the tradition of compassion" in the English and American novel, *Harvest of a Quiet Eye: The Novel of Compassion* (Bloomington, Ind. Univ. Press), contains some intelligent readings of the novels, yet one regrets the inevitable comparison which leads Gindin to consider James "more comprehensive, profound, and consciously artistic," and Howells "simpler, less artistically self-conscious and less consistent." This kind of comment is gratuitous, unfair, and finally not quite true. A brief but judicious survey of Howells research and criticism is George Fortenberry's contribution to *Fifteen American Authors* (pp. 229–44). *A Bibliography of William Dean Howells*, first assembled by William M. Gibson and George Arms in 1948, is now drastically outdated, but because of its inaccessibility, the New York Public Library has authorized a reprint (New York, Arno Press). As Gibson and Arms indicate, the comprehensive bibliography to stand at the end of *A Selected Edition of W. D. Howells* (Bloomington, Ind. Univ. Press) will be perhaps a decade in coming, so until then, this one still has its uses.

The *Selected Edition* made rapid headway with the publication of four titles: Vol. 6, *A Chance Acquaintance*, introduction and notes by Jonathan Thomas and David J. Nordloh, text established by Ronald Gottesman, Nordloh, and Thomas; Vol. 11, *Indian Summer*, introduction and notes by Scott Bennett, text established by Bennett and Nordloh; Vol. 12, *The Rise of Silas Lapham*, introduction and notes by Walter J. Meserve, text established by Meserve and Nordloh; and Vol. 25, *The Kentons*, introduction and notes by George C. Carrington, Jr., text established by Carrington and Gottesman. These uniformly attractive volumes, with brief but informative historical introductions, minimal textual apparatus, and CEAA-approved texts, accomplish the ideal editorial goal of producing clear, unencumbered, and wieldy primary texts. A useful edition for the classroom, until the Indiana text is freely available for reprinting, is Robert Lee Hough's paperback volume of *The Rise of Silas Lapham* (New York, Bantam Books), containing an introduction, a biographical sketch, and a critical supplement of five contemporary reviews and six essays or excerpts. Some hitherto inaccessible writings by Howells—his travel letters contributed to two Ohio newspapers during the summer of 1860 chronicling his tour of the industries of the eastern states—are admirably edited, annotated, and introduced by Robert Price in

"The Road to Boston: 1860 Travel Correspondence of William Dean Howells" (*OH* 80:85–154).

Although his results are likely to inspire a degree of incredulity among the anti-Freudians, George Spangler works out a carefully reasoned argument through limited use of Freudian psychology for reading one of Howells's novels as "a compelling exploration of the depths of the human mind"—*The Shadow of a Dream*: Howells' Homosexual Tragedy" (*AQ* 23:110–19). Joseph F. Trimmers's "American Dreams: A Comparative Study of the Utopian Novels of Bellamy and Howells" (*BSUF* 12:12–21) is a thorough analysis of the topic, and Clare R. Goldfarb reads *An Imperative Duty* as "a document of racist attitudes as well as a prescription for solving racial problems" in "The Question of William Dean Howells' Racism" (*BSUF* 12:22–30) and suggests that while in modern militant terms he was a racist, he was unusually liberal for his time. David L. Frazier's explication of "Howells' *An Open-Eyed Conspiracy*" (*Expl* 30:item 9) indicates the novel has to do with a paradox in his conception of romantic love, and James W. Mathews finds "Another Possible Origin of Howells's *The Shadow of a Dream*" (*AL* 42:558–62) in Shelley's poem "The Sensitive Plant." Paul A. Eschholz, "William Dean Howells: The Search for an American Identity, 1873–1897" (*DAI* 32:2638A), covers the novels from *A Modern Instance* to *The Landlord of Lion's Head*; Victoria S. Poulakis, "The Psychological Novels of William Dean Howells" (*DAI* 31:5420A) considers the novels of the 1890s; and Nancy C. Knox studies "The Realist as Short Story Writer" (*DAI* 31:6013A).

For over ten years now, the Monument Edition of the twelve novels of John W. DeForest has been underway with *Honest John Vane* published in 1960, *Playing the Mischief* in 1961, and *Kate Beaumont* in 1963, all three of which were edited and introduced by Joseph Jay Rubin. Begun before the CEAA was a reality, these handsome examples of design and binding contain regularized texts based on those last corrected by the author. The fourth volume to appear with an introduction by Chadwick Hansen and edited by Donna G. Fricke is *Witching Times* (State College, Pa., Bald Eagle Press), and future volumes are planned. DeForest was also the subject of one dissertation: Dock W. Adams, "John W. DeForest and the Search for a Rational Order: A Study in Ambiguity" (*DAI* 31:6041A–42A).

For some years, Mary E. Grenander has been producing informative essays and articles on the achievement of Ambrose Bierce. Now

she has capped her earlier work with an excellent study of the man
and the fiction in *Ambrose Bierce* (TUSAS 180) half of which accurately traces his life and the second half of which subjects his writings to a systematic critical appraisal by types. By no means the final
word on Bierce, it is perhaps the beginning of a period when the
much misunderstood writer will receive his proper due. Robert A.
Wiggins's subtitle reveals his thesis in "Ambrose Bierce: A Romantic
in an Age of Realism" (*ALR* 4:1–10), and Fred H. Marcus's "Film
and Fiction: 'An Occurrence at Owl Creek Bridge'" (*CEJ* 7:14–23)
contains an explication of the story paired with an explication of
Robert Enrico's celebrated film version. "Psychological Symbolism
in Three Early Tales of Invisibility" by Steven Dimes (*RQ* 5:20–27)
is an interesting comparison of Bierce's "The Damned Thing" with
Fitz-James O'Brien's "What Is It? A Mystery" and Guy de Maupas-
sant's "The Horla." "I racconti di Ambrose Bierce" by Carlo Pagetti
(*SA* 16:255–99) is a lengthy and what appears to be a sound general
assessment of his fiction. Useful bibliographical materials are "Ambrose Bierce: A Critical Bibliography of Secondary Comment" by
George E. Fortenberry" (*ALR* 4:11–56); "Ambrose Bierce's Contributions to *Cosmopolitan*: An Annotated Bibliography" by John C.
Stubbs (*ALR* 4:57–59); and Mary E. Grenander's "Ambrose Bierce
and *In the Midst of Life*" (*BC* 20:321–31), which offers evidence for
an 1892 publication date rather than 1891. Ernest J. Hopkins's one
volume edition of *The Complete Short Stories of Ambrose Bierce* has
been issued in a two-volume paperback format (New York, Ballan-
tine Books).

    In addition to these Bierce materials and the Norris articles cited
below, Volume 4 of *American Literary Realism* continues to make a
significant contribution to the study of the period 1870–1910, with
checklists on Hamlin Garland by Jackson R. Bryer and Eugene Harding (pp. 103–56), American Utopian literature by Kenneth M. Roe-
mer (227–54), Edgar Watson Howe and Joseph Kirkland by Clayton
L. Eichelberger (279–90), and Richard Harding Davis by Eichelberger and Ann M. McDonald (313–89); essay-reviews of scholarship
on George Ade by Harold H. Kolb (157–69), Rose Terry Cook by
Susan Allen Toth (170–76), Francis Marion Crawford by John Pilkington, Jr. (177–82), Susan Glaspell by Arthur E. Waterman (183–
91), and David Ross Locke by James C. Austin (192–200); and articles on R. W. Glider and John Hay by David E. E. Sloane (255–67),

and Richard Harding Davis by John Solensten (303–12); along with
the usual illustrations, photographs, poems, and miscellanea of the
age which go to make the journal such a pleasure to read. Three new
studies of the work of Harold Frederic are "Perspectives on Harold
Frederic's *Market-Place*" by Jean Frantz Blackall (*PMLA* 86:388–
405) an exhaustive analysis of the psychological, thematic, and auto-
biographic elements in that novel; "*The Damnation of Theron Ware*,
With a Backward Glance at Hawthorne" by Joan Zlotnick (*MarkhamR* 2:90–92), which finds *The Scarlet Letter* and several Hawthorne stories a major influence on Frederic's novel; and "Textural
Range in the Novels of Harold Frederic" by Nancy K. B. Siferd (*DAI*
31:4733A–34A), which finds his style, imagery, and symbolism highly complex. "Joseph Kirkland's Myth of Progress" by Gregory A.
Barnes (*DAI* 32:3291A) finds grounds for considering *Zury* (1887),
The McVeys (1888) and *The Captain of Company K* (1897) a trilogy. Calder M. Pickett, "Edgar Watson Howe and the Kansas Scene"
(*KanQ* 2[1970]:39–45), takes sensible issue with the belief that
Howe's *The Story of a Country Town* "offered the first harsh literary
criticism of the agrarian dream of Thomas Jefferson" by citing Howe's
general support of the rural, small-town life, but pays too little at-
tention to the novel to support the thesis. The Norwegian-born H.
H. Boyeson (1848–1895), one of Howells's staunchest allies in the
cause of realism, was the subject of two studies: Per Seyersted, "The
Drooping Lily: H. H. Boyesen as an Early American Misogynist"
(*Americana Norvegica* 3:74–87), and Robert S. Frederickson, "Hjal-
mar Hjorth Boyesen, Man of Letters" (*DAI* 32:918A).

v. Stephen Crane

Although its modest title suggests nothing of its complexity, *A Reading of Stephen Crane* by Marston LaFrance (Oxford, Clarendon
Press) is surely the most thorough, detailed analysis yet published of
the distinctive function of irony in his work. LaFrance defines and
traces Crane's ironic vision from the New York *Tribune* journalism
pieces through "The Upturned Face" and concludes, "Crane's world
is reality as he perceived it, externally amoral matter subject to
chance upheavals of purposeless violence and therefore ultimately
unknowable and forever beyond man's complete control; the mere
fact that human life has to be lived in such a world places full re-

sponsibility for all moral values upon man alone, and thus the separation between the physical world and man's moral world is absolute."
LaFrance earns his conclusions through a synthesis of past criticism
and his own independent judgment, yet his theories are applied so
dogmatically that one is left with the impression that he feels he has
solved all the critical problems of interpretation in Crane's writing.
This is hardly the case, yet one must admire the intelligence and
sensibility of his effort. One of the great problems of applying the
techniques of statistical analysis to style in literature is illustrated in
An Analysis of Prose Style to Determine Authorship by Bernard
O'Donnell (The Hague, Mouton). O'Donnell reflects only the most
rudimentary understanding of Crane as a writer or an artist, and it is
only accidental that he chose *The O'Ruddy* by Crane and Robert
Barr to try to determine who wrote what parts because it is so well
suited to his approach. He concludes that Crane wrote chapters 1–24
and Barr 25–33. While the present writer is not competent to judge
the validity of his approach and results, he is competent to judge the
following as the most irrelevant introduction to a study of Crane he
has ever read: "Tuberculosis has destroyed more human beings than
any other disease. Recent advances in medical research notwithstanding, it is still high on the list of death-causing illnesses. In 1900,
from this infection, over 80,000 people died—one of whom was
Stephen Crane, age 29." Never before has such a worthwhile individual been reduced to such a worthless statistic, which is exactly all
that Crane is for Mr. O'Donnell. Slightly larger than other volumes
in the series, Stanley Wertheim's *Studies in "Maggie" and "George's
Mother"* (Columbus, Ohio, Charles E. Merrill) is a well-selected
collection of contemporary reviews and critical essays on the novels.

   Fredson Bowers issued two further volumes in his CEAA-approved edition of The Works of Stephen Crane (Charlottesville,
Univ. Press of Va.): Volume 4, *The O'Ruddy*, with an introduction
by J. C. Levenson, and Volume 9, *Reports of War*, with an introduction by James B. Colvert. As usual, the editing and textual apparatus
are exhaustively thorough and impeccably precise. Levenson provides a fascinating account of the history of *The O'Ruddy* composition and complications, but Colvert's introduction is disappointing in
its brevity. (Incidentally, the discovery of *The O'Ruddy* manuscript
in time for Bowers's edition proves Bernard O'Donnell wrong by one
chapter: Crane wrote chapters 1–25.) In his essay on Crane research

and criticism in *Fifteen American Authors* (pp. 97–137) Donald Pizer takes issue with the Bowers edition and characterizes it as representative of "methodological absolutism" and "common sense be damned." He does make some telling points about the edition in its overscrupulousness and excessive virtues, yet surely this work will hasten and make possible the mean between the casual editing of the past and the careful critical editing of the present which Pizer wishes to see realized. His overview of Crane scholarship, in general, is sensible and discriminating. *Stephen Crane in the West and Mexico* by Joseph Katz (Kent, Ohio, Kent State Univ. Press) brings together seventeen newspaper articles written during a trip subsidized by a newspaper syndicate in 1895, a year after he completed *The Red Badge of Courage* and while he was negotiating for its publication. These writings are valuable for what they reveal about an artist in progress, and Katz has given them to us in a carefully edited, informatively introduced and attractively designed volume. Lewis H. Fine has edited "Two Unpublished Plays by Stephen Crane" (*RALS* 1: 200–16) with a useful introduction on Crane's interest in drama and playwriting, and James E. Kibler has assembled a helpful catalogue of "The Library of Stephen and Cora Crane" (*Proof* 1:199–246). Of bibliographic interest are Clayton L. Eichelberger, "Stephen Crane's 'Grand Opera for the People': A Bibliographic Identification and a Correction" (*PBSA* 69:70–72), and Thomas A. Gullason, "Stephen Crane and the *Arena*: Three 'Lost' Reviews" (*PBSA* 65:297–99), which concerns not reviews by Crane but three editorial notices about him. Gullason has also discovered and edited four examples of "The Fiction of the Reverend Jonathan Townley Crane, D.D." (*AL* 43: 263–73), which document that Crane's father believed fiction useful in his ministerial work.

Leverett T. Smith, in "Stephen Crane's Calvinism" (*CRAS* 2:13–25), argues that there are marked resemblances between Crane's central concerns and those of the Calvinists, and he creates his own pattern of conversion by modifying theirs, but perhaps the thesis is pushed a bit too far. "Stephen Crane and Death: A Moment Between Two Romanticisms" by Stanley R. Harrison (*MarkhamR* 2:117–20) seems partly to be concerned with Crane's manipulation of color and his blend of realism, naturalism, and impressionism, but the essay is so meandering and stylistically turgid that it is difficult to be certain. Carol B. Hafer's "The Red Badge of Absurdity: Irony in *The Red*

Badge of Courage" (*CLAJ* 14:440–43) is negligible and says the obvious. In "Murder by the Minute: Old and New in 'The Bride Comes to Yellow Sky'" (*NCF* 26:196–218), Ben M. Vorpahl contributes a very thorough explication of the story to support his contention that its final sentence is the most remarkable Crane ever wrote: "It illuminated the story's setting, mirrored its structure, and precisely designated its theme." The essay is an admirably accomplished piece of criticism. Two other interesting explications are "The Open Boat: Additional Perspective" by Donna Gerstenberger (*MFS* 17:557–61), and "Society and Nature in Stephen Crane's 'The Men in the Storm'" by George Monteiro (*PrS* 45:13–17). Katherine R. Simoneaux has catalogued and interpreted the "Color Imagery in Crane's *George's Mother"* (*CLAJ* 14:410–19) to find that "red and black are related to anger, violence, and death; yellow to age and decay." In line with recent studies of treatments of ethnic groups in American literature, Raymund A. Paredes examined "Stephen Crane and the Mexican" (*WAL* 6:31–38) and discovered that unfortunately "there are few characterizations of the Mexican in serious American literature less flattering than Crane's. His Mexicans perpetuate a traditional Yankee stereotype; they are wicked, drunken, and cowardly." Of course, as long as such studies merely stop at the point of name-calling and fail to probe into the complicated cultural-psychological reasons behind cultural stereotyping, we are not really making any progress in racial understanding.

Four Crane dissertations were announced for the year: Lewis H. Fine, "The Plays of Stephen Crane" (*DAI* 31:5398A); Philip L. Krauth, "The Necessary Coxcomb: The Theme of Egotism in the Works of Stephen Crane" (*DAI* 31:6014A); James M. Reynolds, Jr., "Man and the Universe in the Fiction of Stephen Crane" (*DAI* 32:982A); and Alan R. Slotkin, "A Study of the Use of Dialect and Diction in Selected Works of Stephen Crane: The Language of New York City and Its Rural Environs" (*DAI* 31:5426A).

vi. Naturalism and the Late Nineteenth Century

As an introduction for the student to the meanings of the term in its international literary context, *Naturalism* by Lilian R. Furst and Pete R. Skrine in the Critical Idiom series (London, Methuen) is admirable. It is a brief and accurate synthesis of critical opinion on a hotly debated term in literary history drawing on British, American, and European materials. "American Naturalism, An Appraisal" by Rodrique E. Labrie (*MarkhamR* 2:88–90) traces the meaning of the idea in American literature without contributing anything new on the topic and, through over-generalization, he commits a few errors. Although purely concerned with the philosophic "naturalism" of such a thinker as John Dewey rather than its literary expression, in "The Puritan Backgrounds of American Naturalism" (*Thought* 45[1970]: 502–20) Robert J. Roth concludes that "In addition to the vast influence of science, American naturalism owes its origins in large part to a reaction against elements in traditional American religion." Malcolm Cowley's classic essay "A Natural History of American Naturalism" of 1947 is reprinted in a revised form in his collected writings, *A Many-Windowed House.*

The most valuable item about Frank Norris to appear this year is William Dillingham's essay on Norris scholarship in *Fifteen American Authors* (pp. 307–32), an intelligent assessment, the final conclusion of which appears to be that much necessary work remains to be done before Norris's achievement is clearly understood. Bryant N. Wyatt, in "Naturalism As Expediency in the Novels of Frank Norris" (*MarkhamR* 2:83–87), once again reexamines Norris's naturalistic elements to conclude that he merely used naturalism as an expedient device, a conclusion not really satisfactory. Stuart L. Burns argues that "The Rapist [of the first Angèle] in Frank Norris's *The Octopus*" (*AL* 42:567–69), although not explicitly identified, is Father Sarria. James B. Stronks, in "Frank Norris's *McTeague*: A Possible Source in H. C. Bunner" (*NCF* 25:474–78), suggests that the Grannis-Baker subplot may have been borrowed from Bunner's popular story of the 1890s, "The Love-Letters of Smith." "Frank Norris and 'The Newspaper Experience'" by Joseph Katz (*ALR* 4:73–77) makes the point that Norris missed the literary training of writing for newspapers shared by Crane and Dreiser, but as an unpublished letter indicates, he believed that a writer learns by doing, not by being taught. John K. Swensson provides an edited text and a thorough analysis of an unpublished sketch in "'The Great Corner in Hannibal and St. Jo.': A Previously Unpublished Short Story by Frank Norris" (*ALR* 4:205–06). Hilliard I. Beller, "Values and Antinomies in the Novels of Frank Norris" (*DAI* 31:6589A), examines his philosophical inconsistencies as reflected in the fiction.

Twayne's U.S. Authors Series included three titles this year focusing on late nineteenth-century writers who are just beginning to receive serious critical attention: *S. Weir Mitchell* by Joseph P. Lovering, *Henry Blake Fuller* by John Pilkington, Jr., and *Robert Herrick* by Louis J. Budd. The less significant of the three was S. Weir Mitchell, eminent neurologist and popular novelist of the 1890s, whom H. L. Mencken called one of the "beloved of the women's clubs and literary monthlies." Both Fuller and Herrick were central figures on the American literary scene in the last decade of the nineteenth century and opening decades of the twentieth. All three volumes are competently done and, as the first full-scale assessments of the three as artists, especially welcome. A general survey of Herrick's reputation and career is "Robert Herrick, American Novelist" by Lawrence Jay Dessner (*MarkhamR* 3:10–14). Another general but usefully succinct analysis of a writer of the time is Louis Hasley's "George Ade, Realist, Fabulist" (*Four Quarters* 19[1970]:25–32).

In an illuminating discussion, "The Dilemma in Chesnutt's *The Marrow of Tradition*" (*Phylon* 32:31–38), John M. Reilly finds that Charles Waddell Chesnutt established irony as the predominant mode of perception in black fiction, and in his best work, *The Marrow of Tradition*, the conflict between perception and aspiration provides its underlying dynamics. In another perceptive essay, "The Art of *The Conjure Woman*" (*AL* 43:384–98), Richard E. Baldwin determines that "Chesnutt aimed to modify white minds to feel the equality of the black man, and with the conjure tales he developed a perfect vehicle for his artistic needs." He backs up his thesis with sound explications of the fiction in this vein. Both critiques considerably advance our appreciation of Chesnutt's accomplishment.

Two final items directly related to the Utopian mood of the late nineteenth century are a dissertation, Alexander J. Stupple, Jr., "Utopian Humanism in American Fiction, 1888–1900" (*DAI* 32:3273A), which deals mainly with Edward Bellamy, Ignatius Donnelly, and Mark Twain; and an article, "Three Kansas Utopian Novels of 1890" by Ben Fuson (*Extrapolation* 12[1970]:7–24), which summarizes three simultaneously published Utopian fantasies: *Willmoth the Wanderer* by Charles Curtis Dail, *A.D. 2000* by Alvarado Fuller, and *The Auroraphone* by Cyrus Cole. In his apologetic preface for his story about a man who lived for millions of years and explored Saturn, Venus, and the Earth, C. C. Dail said, "Although it is the Author's first effort, it will be found to Amuse, Instruct, and Please the Reader from the first to the last Page in the Book." It is regrettable that so little of the scholarship this year fulfills even one of Dail's modest goals, but neither has Utopia arrived, after all.

Virginia Commonwealth University

11. Poe and Nineteenth-Century Poetry

Patrick F. Quinn

For the past few years in the headnote to this chapter I have indicated the topics that appeared to be of special interest to students of Poe, and I have also made annual mention of the relative dearth of scholarly and critical material bearing on some of Poe's important contemporaries and successors. The situation is different this year. No book-length studies of Poe were published in 1971. Articles and essays on him were, as usual, numerous; but with few exceptions they were not of distinguished quality, and in them I could discern no significant new tendency or continuing emphasis. In the context of this chapter it seems that 1971 was an important year not for Poe but for Bryant, who may well have found his definitive biographer in Charles H. Brown; for Lowell, the subject of a minutely informative study by Edward Wagenknecht; also for Whittier, whose achievement as a poet was discussed in an essay of unusual critical authority by Robert Penn Warren; and for one lesser light, Christopher Pearse Cranch, whose poems, after a long period of almost total neglect, were republished in a one-volume scholarly edition.

i. Poe

a. **Bibliography and biography.**   No major new contributions under either heading were expected in 1971 and none turned up. In his "Edgar Allan Poe: Current Bibliography" (*PoeS* 4:38–44) Richard P. Benton provided another of his thorough annual lists, with almost every item succinctly summarized and occasionally evaluated. Dissertations and important reviews are caught up in this wide net which usefully supplements the Poe columns in the *MLA Bibliog-*

raphy. In its turn Benton's work is supplemented by "Fugitive Poe References: A Bibliography" (*PoeS* 4:44–46) in which Judy Osowski continues her posting of interesting brief references to Poe, some of which she discovers in very unlikely places (e.g., an article about Jayne Mansfield in *Film Culture Reader* [1970]).

Among Poe's acquaintances in the late 1830s was Thomas Wyatt, a compiler of books about natural history. That the Poe-Wyatt relationship did not end in 1839 or 1840, as has been assumed, is shown by a newly discovered Poe letter, dated 1 April 1841. In "Beyond the Tamarind Tree: A New Poe Letter" (*AL* 42:468–77) Joseph J. Moldenhauer calls attention to this document, which, despite its meagre intrinsic interest, he is able to annotate in extraordinary detail. Another Poe acquaintance, whose *Reminiscences of a Very Old Man* (1899) casts some light on the last years of Poe's life, was the engraver and publisher John Sartain. In "John Sartain and E. A. Poe" (*PoeS* 4:21–23) Richard Tuerk gives an account of this friendship so as to set in context a brief memoir about Poe which Sartain wrote for the *Boston Evening Transcript* in 1893. Tuerk comments on the significance, real though minor, of this hitherto unnoticed item. Of similar interest is an article by M. D. McElroy, "Poe's Last Partner: E. H. N. Patterson of Oquawka, Illinois" (*PLL* 7:252–71). As far back as Woodberry, biographers of Poe have alluded to Patterson, the young newspaper editor in Illinois who offered to subsidize and publish the literary magazine that Poe for so long had hoped to establish. This article, based on material in the Oquawka *Spectator*, brings Patterson into clearer focus. He was an enthusiastic admirer of Poe's writings, including *Eureka*, and "a discerning, respectful friend who helped circulate [Poe's] name and works on the frontier."

b. **Sources, allusions, influences.** Not unexpectedly, the name of Burton J. Pollin is the first to come up under this heading. Of work published by him in 1971 two examples are noteworthy: "Politics and History in Poe's 'Mellonta Tauta': Two Allusions Explained" (*SSF* 8:627–31), and "Poe's Use of Material from Bernardin De Saint-Pierre's *Etudes*" (*RomN* 21:1–8). In the first article Pollin describes the unsuccessful effort made by the Washington Monument Association of New York in the 1840s to develop public interest in financing a memorial to George Washington. The project lasted only long enough to lay the cornerstone, in a spectacular ceremony. Poe's allusion to this fiasco and what it implied about democratic fickleness is fairly obvious in "Mellonta Tauta." A more cryptic allusion, to "the great American poet, Benton," is construed as pertaining to the Missouri senator Thomas Hart Benton. The wheels-within-wheels situation here is clarified by Pollin: Benton was an advocate of the financial policies of Jackson, policies which resulted in economic depression and the demise of journals that Poe was hoping—in February 1837—to find employment on. In the other article Pollin describes some matters of interest in Saint-Pierre's once popular work, published in English translation in Worcester and Philadelphia, *Etudes de la nature*, "a strange mixture," Pollin calls it, "of close personal observation of natural phenomena and of weird fantasy." Among the matters that interested Saint-Pierre were the phenomena of ocean currents and polar ice caps, and the possibility of sending messages in glass bottles on the ocean currents. This brings us, of course, to "MS. Found in a Bottle," two details of which Pollin ventures to explain, the weird captain encountered by the narrator when aboard the second ship, and the unintelligible language employed by its ghostly crew. In a nutshell: "Is there any doubt that the language was Spanish and that [the captain] was Christopher Columbus . . . ?"

Guesswork continues as to how Poe came to write his most famous poem. In "Another Source for 'The Raven'" (*AN&Q* 9:85–87) Allen F. Stein points to a blackbird with the right credentials, to be found in Cornelius Mathews's *The Career of Puffer Hopkins*. Nominations also continue to be made as to possible sources of *Arthur Gordon Pym*; a new addition to the list is J. N. Reynold's *Voyage of the Potomac*. Daniel J. Tyson shows that in the fourth chapter of this account of a round-the-world voyage made by an American commercial vessel Poe found some material, a few hundred words worth, which he made use of in chapter 14 of *Pym*. In his article, "J. N. Reynolds' *Voyage of the Potomac*: Another Source for *The Narrative of Arthur Gordon Pym*" (*PoeS* 4:35–37), Tyson also makes some other suggestions, less well sustained.

A French seventeenth-century priest and man of letters, Dominique Bouhours, achieved some fame through his *La Manière de bien penser*, an anthology with commentary designed to bring out the superiority of the classics to modern literature in Italian and Spanish. In "Pinakidia" Poe borrowed from this work, hinting in his introductory remarks that he was doing so. Edgar C. Knowlton, Jr., looks closely at some instances of Poe's use of the Bouhours anthology in his "Poe's Debt to Father Bouhours" (*PoeS* 4:27–29). Whether some of this French critic's ideas may have assisted in the formation of Poe's literary theory is not investigated, but Knowlton does show that Barzun last year implied too low an estimate of Poe's knowledge of French (see *ALS 1970*, pp. 218–19), and he reaffirms the opinion that French literature and literary criticism "played a significant role in the development of Poe as critic and writer."

What amounts to an extensive and thoughtful gloss on an allusion that very few of Poe's readers would recognize is Sanford E. Marovitz's "Poe's Reception of C. W. Webber's Gothic Western, 'Jack Long; or, The Shot in the Eye'" (*PoeS* 4:11–13). In his November 1847 review of Hawthorne Poe referred to Webber's book as "one of the happiest and best-sustained tales I have seen." It was praised in this way, Marovitz believes, not simply because of its well-constructed plot but also because of the presence in the story of certain "dark elements" that Poe probably found congenial.

c. **General studies.** For someone who has maintained more than a casual interest in Poe there is no urgent need to consult the chapter which deals with him in *Eight American Authors* (pp. 3–36), for in writing this chapter Jay B. Hubbell obviously had in mind a nonspecialist audience for whom a broad introduction, at once selective and objective, would be useful. The chapter is organized in the usual way: bibliography, editions, biography, and so on, with major emphasis given to the commentary Poe's work has received, especially in recent years. Of the critical essays on Poe written in this country prior to 1900 Hubbell finds only six or so that are intrinsically worth reading, whereas currently the situation is rather one of an *embarras de richesse*. As Hubbell puts it: "We are now—in academic circles at least—in the midst of a Poe revival." His report on the activities of that revival reflects, among other things, the increased attention being given Poe's humorous and satiric tales, the importance ascribed to the colloquies and to *Eureka,* and the relative lack of interest in Poe's poetry. Of course in making this survey Hubbell leaves a few stones unturned, but he does so, one assumes, as a result of discrimination rather than oversight. What seems to me a matter for query is not the range of the survey nor the substance of what is said, but, occasionally, the *how*. In an effort to sustain the note of objectivity Hubbell implies in effect that he has almost no opinions of his own. For instance, how does he evaluate recent books on Poe by, to name three, Buranelli, Davidson, Jacobs? All we are told about them is what some other people have said, how Braddy commented on Buranelli, what Jacobs said of Davidson, how Stovall reviewed Jacobs. Such information is not necessarily superfluous but it does not replace first-person statement of original response. However, we do find direct and, indeed, authoritative expression of opinion when Hubbell in the final section of the chapter extends a guiding hand. "The young scholar," he writes, "who feels that only trivial or unattractive subjects remain to be investigated needs to be reassured. There are important topics that have not been adequately studied, and there are obsolescent studies which need to be done over in the light of new materials and changed critical points of view."

One important topic of continuing interest to Poe scholars whether young or old is the contrast between the often bizarre material of Poe's fiction and the high degree of control with which this material is treated. Complicating the matter is the strong likelihood that the material in question was not freely invented by Poe but was, rather, obligatory for him, and that to give expression to it amounted virtually to a psychic necessity. And, third, there is the paradox that such *self-centered* writing has been able to evoke so nearly universal a response. This cluster of questions is taken up by Paul Schwaber in a ruminative and loose-jointed essay, "On Reading Poe" (*L&P* 21: 81–99). One of Schwaber's conclusions is that "Poe's best fiction emanates from his darkest recesses and reaches ours, but it does so only by becoming acceptable, through the creative activity of his ego and the critical activity of ours—which is to say by finding fascinating and proper form as art." The one firm basis for this judgment is a careful account—half paraphrase, half analysis—of "The Fall of the House of Usher." One could wish for more evidence than this and also for some precise indications as to what Schwaber means by Poe's "best fiction." In addition to "Usher," only "The Murders in the Rue Morgue" is dealt with at any length, and even it is less analyzed than summarized. Meanwhile, though, Schwaber is not reluctant to generalize, saying, for example: "Poe's stories are flowers of sterility and death, which because of their narrative art enable us to experience the joys of sadism, masochism, and necrophilia without having even to be sick." It can be inferred from this that Schwaber associates himself with the Krutch-Bonaparte school of inquiry. Like those earlier exponents of psychoanalytic interpretation he stresses the hypothesis that the dying mother obsession all but governed Poe's creative as well as emotional life. But like most Poe commentators, whatever their orientation, Schwaber finds it hard to resist overstatement. Thus he says that Poe's writings (now notice the verb) "abound in lakes and oceans that swallow up men, boats, and mansions—or at least threaten to. Do not they too suggest the lost and always sought-for mother with whom he unconsciously yearned to unite?" Speculations more original than this, with something of an Eriksonian cast, occur elsewhere in Schwaber's essay when he suggests that there was an Allan component in Poe's psychological life, and that in that life the "failed father" role was a factor of some importance.

Another topic of continuing interest is Poe's cosmopolitan fame and the reasons for it. In Hubbell's chapter on Poe this topic is capably surveyed, necessarily in brief compass. One aspect of the topic is glanced at by G. A. Cevasco in "*A Rebours* and Poe's Reputation in France" (*RomN* 13:255–61). His thesis is that Huysmans's novel, published in 1884, succeeded in what Baudelaire, for all his efforts, had not quite managed to bring off: the establishing of Poe's name as a great name in France. The thesis may be right, but one is disconcerted by the skimpy documentation. An extensive review of the history of Poe's fortunes in France may be found in Jean Alexander's *Affidavits of Genius*: *Edgar Allan Poe and the French Critics, 1847–1924* (Port Washington, N.Y., Kennikat). Essentially, the book is an anthology of commentaries on Poe, beginning with the Forgues article of 1846 and ending with Valéry's variations on a theme from *Eureka*. All told, fifteen French writers are represented, most of them—despite the book's subtitle—novelists and poets primarily. It is the editor's hypothesis that "the professional critical mind necessarily begins to perceive patterns later (sometimes a hundred years later) than the creative mind." Whatever the validity of the principle behind it, the selection is an excellent one, both as a documentary history of French attitudes toward Poe over an eighty-year period and because of the intrinsic interest that a good many of these critiques have. In her spacious introduction to the book Miss Alexander fills out the various contexts—"The Outlaw," "The American," "The Poet"—in which these discussions of Poe were written. The sequence of these contexts im-

plies a dialectical progression as Baudelaire's challenging affirmation
of Poe's newness was in time countered, by the cultural old guard,
with a repudiation of Poe on grounds of his archetypically *American*
quality. But this brought about a kind of synthesis:

> It is a fine irony that in reacting against America and natural-
> ism (both being fundamentally materialistic) the most un-
> materialistic and nonrational school of French poetry should
> choose an American as standard-bearer and chief witness
> against America, and yet that it should use America's own
> tools of sensation, science, and the untrammeled spirit of con-
> quest. This was the paradoxical and fruitful situation of Sym-
> bolism. [p. 49]

In the final section of her introduction Miss Alexander discusses
Poe's poetry and his theory of poetry in relation to the Symbolist
aesthetic. Although a large assertion is sometimes left tantalizingly
undeveloped—such as that only the most subtle of the Symbolists,
Mallarmé, was able fully to understand the "Symbolism" of Poe's
better poems—this section seemed to me more original and illuminating than the others. The emphasis here as elsewhere is on Poe as a
catalyst during several stages of French literary history. But here,
for the first time, some of Poe's work, specifically "The Valley of
Unrest" and two or three other poems, is discussed on its own merits
though within the framework of French Symbolism. The readings
that result are valuable per se, and they also help to clarify Miss
Alexander's puzzling prefatory remark that Poe's international reputation rests on his poems rather than on his work in fiction.

A different but similarly eccentric position is taken by Haldeen
Braddy: "When posterity enters final judgment, Poe may well be
acclaimed, not so much as storyteller and poet, but as an inventive
critic." This is the theme of his essay "Edgar Allan Poe's Last Bid for
Fame" (*Studies in Medieval, Renaissance, American Literature*, pp.
134–42). Braddy contends that it was not enough for Poe that he
became widely known for his stories and poems. Towards the end of
his life he was fired by a new ambition, to become famous as a literary critic, to become nothing less than "the literary arbiter of his
age." Was such an ambition realistically warranted? Braddy seems
to think it was. But I am bothered, for one thing, by his treatment of
the chronology of the case; and I find it hard to believe that a critic's

credentials are in good order if, as Braddy says of Poe, "many of his critical judgments . . . revealed a positive flair for error in evaluating the lasting qualities of contemporary authors."

To show the extent of Poe's impact upon twentieth-century literary criticism in English is the purpose of William L. Howarth's anthology *Twentieth Century Interpretations of Poe's Tales* (Englewood Cliffs, N.J., Prentice-Hall). A larger collection would certainly provide a better reflection of that impact, but Howarth's selection can easily be supplemented by looking up the items mentioned in his bibliography. His introduction to the book, in keeping with current convention, is primarily an essay in interpretation rather than a functional introduction to the material he as editor has assembled. In this essay Howarth has some provocative, not to say odd, suggestions about how "Usher" and "William Wilson" might be read. He offers a precise definition of the basic theme of Poe's fiction: it is "man's search for identity or self-knowledge." As for the art of fiction as Poe understood it, here the essential thing is structure, with every detail of the work taking its place in the completion of a preestablished design: "Each event forms a link in the unbroken chain of plot; beginning posits end; middle connects both; end fulfills beginning." Individually, the tales reflect this methodicity; and Poe's fiction as a whole, Howarth asserts, has a similar neatness. He finds it divisible into three stages (early, middle, late) having three different fictional objectives (criticism, speculation, analysis), as Poe moved triadically from "grotesques" through "arabesques" to the tales of ratiocination.

An essay in Italian on the subject of Poe's interest for twentieth-century readers traverses familiar ground in rather routine fashion. Marilla Battilana's "Edgar Allan Poe, nostro contemporaneo" (*ACF* 8,ii[1969]:1–10) accentuates the role of the unconscious, and its expression in oneiric symbols, in Poe's work. This, it is claimed, is probably the basis of his appeal for modern readers. Not a new suggestion, certainly; and I think that the other considerations touched on in this article have been more adequately dealt with in discussions of Poe by Tate, Davidson, and Hirsch.

d. **Individual stories.** In keeping with what I take to be the major current trend in Poe studies, the premise of which is that comedy, satire, and irony are far more important elements in Poe's work than has hitherto been realized, are two articles, one endorsing this pre-

mise as warmly as the other disputes it. On the one hand: David
Ketterer's "Poe's Use of the Hoax and the Unity of 'Hans Pfaall'"
(*Criticism* 13:377–85); on the other: Benjamin F. Fisher's "Poe's
'Metzengerstein': Not a Hoax" (*AL* 42:487–94). Ketterer in his article gives a good deal of space to speculating about Poe's interest in
the literary hoax as a mode of satire, a form expressive of American
folk humor, and, most importantly, a way of conveying his ironic
opinion about the human need for self-deception. Poe's preoccupation with hoax presides to greater or less degree, it is argued, over
the entire spectrum of Poe's fiction, whether the subheading be "grotesque," "arabesque," or "ratiocinative." As for "Hans Pfaall," Ketterer concedes that it reads rather like a mish-mash: "What appears
to begin as a humorous satire on the limitations of idiopathic perception . . . slides into the factual ballast characteristic of a hoax, yet the
hoax gradually assumes the force of a genuine scientific treatise."
Ketterer attempts to show that the story's apparent contradictions
in intention and tone are resolvable into a fundamental unity when
set in the context of Poe's understanding of hoax. (Nowhere, though,
does Ketterer deal with a more basic issue: what a bore "Hans Phaall"
is.) "Metzengerstein" is not top-drawer Poe, either. But at least it is
much shorter, is outlandish in a less juvenile way, and might well be
a story that would gather attention even if someone less famous than
Poe had been its author. In his discussion of it Fisher is concerned
with showing cause why the story should be read not for comic effect,
intended or otherwise, nor as a burlesque of popular horror fiction,
but as a serious exercise in the Gothic genre. In developing this view
Fisher comes down hard on the point that when Poe revised "Metzengerstein" for later publication in what we now have as its final text
he deleted bits of gratuitous sensationalism, eliminated clichés of
the horror genre, and toned down the evocations of stock responses.
His conclusion is that "as a direct descendant of *The Castle of
Otranto*, Poe's tale seems quite close in tone, situation, character, and
props to its sober ancestor." Fisher's case is a good one; but also well
argued is the opposite position, taken by G. R. Thompson (see *ALS
1970*, p. 208).

   Although not all readers of Poe concur on the patent superiority
of "The Oval Portrait" over its first version, "Life in Death," most
would agree with Richard W. Dowell, who starts from this assumption in "The Ironic History of Poe's 'Life in Death': A Literary Skele-

ton in the Closet" (*AL* 42:478–86). The story appeared in the April 1842 issue of *Graham's*, just before Poe ended his editorship there. Dowell's question is why Poe, who had wanted to do particularly well as editor of *Graham's* so as to acquire backing for an independent magazine of his own, could have been so perverse as to publish a story which fell far short of his own standards. The answer Dowell proposes involves several factors, the one of major interest being Poe's professional relationship to Hawthorne. A review of *Twice-Told Tales* was to have appeared in the April 1842 issue; Poe, however—distraught over Virginia's illness—was unable to write the review, and instead of it he published "Life in Death," which was ready. But then to review Hawthorne in the next issue, on the heels of "Life in Death," was to draw possibly embarassing attention to the similarity between that story and Hawthorne's "The Portrait of Edward Randolph." In each story, Dowell points out, "the central object is a portrait originally enshrouded in darkness; when each painting is ultimately illuminated, a tragic face appears, so lifelike that the observers are momentarily stunned. Also, in each case, there is a tale of tyranny connected with the portrait, explaining the look of sadness on the subject's face." An awkward situation, but the review did appear, propounding criteria hardly exemplified in "Life in Death."

Until recently, one could assume agreement among readers of Poe that of his more famous stories the one least in need of interpretation is "The Gold Bug." It has been generally agreed also that Poe's interest in cryptography accounts for his intellectual motive in writing the story, the pecuniary motive being the prize of $100 offered by a Philadelphia newspaper, which prize Poe won. But since the appearance of Jean Ricardou's extraordinary analysis of "The Gold Bug" (see *ALS 1968*, p. 171) one feels less sure that the story is as transparent in every respect as it has been assumed to be. For instance, did Poe decide in advance that a story about a treasure-hunt would be the only appropriate entry in a competition for a monetary prize offered by the *Philadelphia Dollar Newspaper*? Ricardou's knack of bringing up such unexpected questions as this is matched in an article by Barton Levi St. Armand: "Poe's 'Sober Mystification': The Uses of Alchemy in 'The Gold Bug'" (*PoeS* 4:1–7). After pointing to the evidence in "Von Kempelen and His Discovery" that Poe knew a thing or two about the alchemical tradition, St. Armand turns to examine a number of apparently innocuous details in "The Gold Bug": Poe's choice of a tulip tree, the importance given to the seventh limb thereof, the names assigned to Legrand's servant (Jupiter) and to his dog (Wolf). St. Armand's contention is that Poe used alchemical lore as an undercurrent, or ground bass, in the story. Thus the tulip, rather than some other tree, is cited because it is an especially good instance of the transmutation process, with its leaves changing from yellowish-green in the spring to clear yellow in the autumn (when the action of the story takes place). In a word, the tulip tree is an especially *golden* tree. The seventh limb on it is singled out because the number seven is the highest digit in alchemical arithmetic, equivalent to the seventh rung in the alchemical ladder, which ascends from tin to gold. Tin is the base metal associated with the planet Jupiter; and in alchemical symbolism the dog, or wolf, is the acid which in the transmuting process eats away the last metallic impurities and reveals the sought-for gold. So at the climax, Legrand's dog, Wolf, having evaded Jupiter's restraint on him, leaps into the hole that has been dug, removes some irrelevant residues and so prepares for the final revelation. After examining some additional evidence—the color symbolism, for example—which he finds consonant with his thesis, St. Armand takes a more daring step. "The Gold Bug," he says, is "about" transmutation in a still wider sense:

> Just as the lead bullet is changed to the heavier gold bug, which then yields the ponderous, glittering treasure, so does Poe transmute and domesticate traditional symbols of the Western alchemical tradition. Goethe's Faust appears as an American entomologist and cryptographer, the Philosopher's Stone becomes Captain Kidd's treasure, and the pervading spirit of ominous revelation, Mercurius, assumes the shadowy form of Captain Kidd himself. [p. 6]

Poe, then, if Ricardou and St. Armand are on the right track, devised this story about a cryptogram and buried treasure in such a way that the reader must do some deciphering himself if he is to come upon the trove of possible meanings that lie buried in the text. No wonder Nabokov is an admirer of Poe!

There is no consensus about the meaning of the shrouded human figure which suddenly looms up in the final paragraph of Pym's narrative. In a new reading of the story, "Imagination and Perversity in

The Narrative of Arthur Gordon Pym" (*TSLL* 21:267–80), Joseph
J. Moldenhauer identifies this figure as death: "The chasm into which
Pym and Peters ... rush 'embraces' them; the phantasm which towers
above is maternal. Dying to life, they are born into death." This
sounds perverse, as Moldenhauer no doubt intended it to, for in
what he sees as the logic of the narrative perversity is of the essence.
One of *Pym's* themes is the convertibility or even identity of destruction and deliverance. Another, given central attention in this essay,
is "the coincidence or even equation of perversity and creative imagination." According to Moldenhauer, this theme, or principle, is operative in almost all of Poe's fiction, which is as much about art as are
his critical essays. In this reading, therefore, Gordon Pym represents
the artistic mind, the artistic imagination. Thus representative, he is
the central fact in the story, indeed *is* the story, its topography and
its other characters being projections of him. Accordingly, Pym is
not at all a passive figure, as some other commentators have alleged.
Rather he is the creator, who "steadily 'acts' by himself or through
alter-egos in the drama of self-destruction." There are a number of
persuasive suggestions in Moldenhauer's argument, but he does
push it a bit far, as when he calls the dog, Tiger, "another grotesque
... another Pym double." Credulity is strained also by the interpretation made of Dirk Peters. Moldenhauer sees him as "resembling an
artist in his excitability, capriciousness, and rumored insanity"; but
he is to be more strongly associated with the imp of the perverse.
One recalls, however, that instead of presiding over a manifestation
of the perversity impulse—when Pym on a Tsalalian cliff succumbed
to a longing to fall—Peters acted promptly to circumvent it.

In his edition of "The Fall of the House of Usher" for the Merrill
Literary Casebook series (Columbus, Ohio, Merrill), Eric W. Carlson has assembled the views of fourteen commentators, from D. H.
Lawrence to James M. Cox, set up the usual apparatus of a casebook,
and provided a short introductory essay of his own. At one point in
this essay he sounds a familiar chord: "Analyst of the soul of man,
Poe is the intuitive artist listening to the voice of his own deeper preconscious. Through introspection and soul-searching, in his 'arabesques' he dramatized the Gothic terror that 'is not of Germany but of
the soul.'" But what of the case at hand, "Usher," when placed in
the context of fourteen different opinions about it? Confronting this
problem, Carlson suggests foraging beyond the immediate text in

order to gather evidence of the author's outlook and mode of thought, evidence which can then be used as a kind of lens through which to read the story in question. Carlson illustrates this procedure, starting from Poe's division of "the world of mind" into Intellect, Taste, and Moral Sense, and going on, very rapidly, to mention such other matters as what Poe meant by "psychal fancies," by identity with "the Heart Divine," and what the ending of "Ligeia" is all about. I found it too fast a shuffle; and I doubt that this kind of essay is the best way to introduce a casebook to the student audience for whom it is presumably intended.

The standard interpreter of "William Wilson" sees it as a fairly obvious moral tale of a man's struggle with, evasions of, and final disastrous victory over, his own conscience. Told in the first person, the tale formulates no overt didactic point, but a moralistic inference of some kind seems very much in order. In "The Other William Wilson" (*ATQ* 10:17–26), Thomas F. Walsh does not rule out this interpretation but he seeks to diminish its authority and to offer some new proposals. In doing this he emphasizes the mythical associations of the *Doppelgänger* phenomenon, its associations with death and the diabolical, and, without dehydrating the story appreciably, he puts it in the context of some recent psychological theorizing about "autoscopic hallucination" (i.e., awareness of the double's presence causing a feeling of depersonalization, loss of identity). As the opening move in his argument Walsh makes the point that if it was his conscience that Wilson killed, why is his moral sense so alive, why does he give such strident expression to his feelings of guilt? It is clear that his moral sense has survived his double's death. And of what does he feel guilty? Not of his double's murder, for that event served merely as prologue to Wilson's "later years of unspeakable misery and unpardonable crime." The irony here is that the career of crime caused the misery it was supposed to eliminate. Walsh notices a parallel irony in the accusations Wilson makes against his double. He characterizes himself as a fiend in his attempt to ruin a fellow student at Oxford; fiendishness he projects onto the double, whom he sees as an "evil destiny" and a "pestilence," a force determined to ruin *him*. Similarly, in his earlier school years he resented the double's refusal to submit to his "will" and "arbitrary dictation"; later on it is Wilson who is reluctant to submit to what he calls his double's "inscrutable tyranny" and "arbitrary will." With all the emphasis given to *will* in the text as the title of the story, it seems appropriate to read it as Walsh does, as more a psychological than a moral allegory.

In "Poe's Ethereal Ligeia" (*BRMMLA* 24[1970]:170–76) Jack L. Davis and June H. Davis, before offering a theory of their own, comment on the large amount of interpretation this story has received. Basically, there are two ways of reading "Ligeia": either as a literal tale of a supernatural occurrence or as an allegory of some kind having to do probably with a psychological experience. The pivotal matter is whether or not one finds the narrator credible. The Davises do not. They see his story as evidence of a deranged mind that happens only occasionally to be in alignment with reality. To make out what actually took place the reader must follow up on the clues inadvertently dropped by the narrator and try to transpose his improbable narration into an intelligible key. What the Davis reading proposes is that Ligeia was indeed "ethereal," that she existed only as an opium-induced hallucination. But this hallucination was so indispensable to the narrator that he murdered his real wife (Rowena) "under the mad delusion that he [was] thereby providing a body for the imaginary Ligeia to inhabit."

The mysterious phrase "death watches in the wall" which occurs at a key moment in "The Tell-Tale Heart" was given a full explication a few years ago (see *ALS 1969*, p. 192). The phrase is dealt with again in a short note by E. Arthur Robinson, "Thoreau and the Deathwatch in Poe's 'The Tell-Tale Heart'" (*PoeS* 4:14–16). Robinson notices that the words "the death watch in the wall" appear in Thoreau's "Natural History of Massachusetts," which was published in the July 1842 issue of *The Dial*; and he shows that there are some good reasons to suspect that Poe came upon the phrase in this appearance of it. But within the similarity what counts is the difference: Thoreau and Poe both "use an obscure insect to symbolize inexorable changes of nature, in one instance to serve a transcendental joy in union with universal currents, and in the other a Gothic terror of destruction."

ii. Bryant, Whittier, Lowell, Longfellow, and Others

In his bibliographical essay on Bryant in *Fifteen American Authors* (pp. 37–62), James E. Rocks says that "the most important scholarly and critical writing on Bryant has appeared in the last forty years; the best of it has focused on Bryant as a product of his heritage and his age and has made a valuable contribution to our knowledge of American cultural history in the nineteenth century." Written before the publication of Charles H. Brown's *William Cullen Bryant* (New York, Scribner's), this observation proves to be quite apropos of that book, for its orientation is much more towards the life and times of Bryant than towards his mind and art. A large and unusually handsome volume, in the production of which it would seem that no expense was spared, and behind the writing of which there is evident an equal resolve to make a contribution of lasting interest, Brown's *Bryant* belongs with such solid biographical studies as those of Ola Winslow on Edwards and Ralph Rusk on Emerson. Like them, it focuses on facts. It reserves relatively little space for interpretation, speculation, and, in general, matters of opinion. Bryant was in his day a famous poet, a household word. Was he also a good poet? Which are his best poems? Brown does not say. Or what of the man's human quality? On this point much of the evidence is unfriendly. Lowell, Longfellow, and Bayard Taylor were put off by his glacial reserve. His son-in-law and first biographer characterized him as deficient in sympathy, as indeed "a little malignant." But Poe found Bryant generous and noble, and Bryant's notorious coldness of manner was explained away by another of his acquaintances as the consequence of strong feelings sedulously repressed. Who of these best understood Bryant's personality? Disappointingly, Brown offers no guidance in this area. But in the measure to which facts, massively and intelligently assembled, *do* speak for themselves, this meticulously researched account of Bryant's busy life is magisterial.

But not exhaustive. One amusing episode in Bryant's career, not mentioned in this new biography, is described by Ottavio M. Casale in "Bryant's Proposed Address to the Emperor of Brazil" (*ESQ* 63: 10–12). In 1876 the Emperor of Brazil, a man of unexpectedly ardent democratic and humanitarian sympathies, having arrived in New York harbor, declined to participate in the elaborate ceremony of reception that had been prepared for him. At 81 the Grover Whalen of his day, Bryant was left with an undeliverable welcoming address on his hands because the emperor, busy in visiting schools and hospitals, kept to a tight schedule of his own. A historical episode of far greater moment was the war with Mexico. Bernard Weinstein reviews Bryant's attitudes in "Bryant, Annexation, and the Mexican War" (*ESQ* 63:19–24), and he makes a more incisive judgment than Brown does as to how Bryant behaved. Once military victory was in sight, his tone became high-minded; but in 1846–1847 Bryant's editorials in the *Post* were, in Weinstein's opinion, the rationalizations of a racist and an imperialist.

In the introduction to his edition of Whittier in the Laurel Poetry series (New York, Dell, 1960), Donald Hall described Whittier as "that rare creature, a peasant poet," nominated nostalgia as *"the* great American subject," and mentioned Winfield Townley Scott as the author of the one good modern essay on Whittier's poems. In what is surely the other good modern essay on this subject, Robert Penn Warren's long introduction to his *John Greenleaf Whittier: An Appraisal and a Selection* (Minneapolis, Univ. of Minn. Press), the "peasant poet" suggestion is very firmly put aside. There are folk elements in Whittier's work, Warren agrees, but he finds Whittier no more a peasant poet than Faulkner is a peasant novelist. Like Faulkner—and, for that matter, like Cooper, Hawthorne, and Melville— Whittier, though he lacked the sense of historical and philosophic irony of those writers, had a deep intuition of what it meant to be an American. Moved by a feeling more profound than nostalgia, Whittier saw the problem of past and future as not only a personal one but one confronting America; and Whittier came to see also "that man's fate is that he must learn to accept and use his past completely, knowingly, rather than to permit himself to be used, ignorantly, by it." One of Warren's major points is that these insights were developed by Whittier *after* he had turned his attention from poetry to politics. When he did this, at age 26, by repudiating the merely poetical, he became able to ground his work on experience and thus become a genuine poet. The first substantial evidence is "Ichabod," in 1850. Warren comments fully on this poem and on a number of others, including *Snow-Bound.* His selection is made up of the thirty-six poems he considers Whittier's best. Karl Keller contributes a useful review of scholarship in the Whittier chapter of *Eight American Authors* (pp. 357–86).

Some opinions expressed by Robert A. Rees in the Lowell chapter of *Fifteen American Authors* (pp. 285–305) are that Duberman's biographical study is outstanding, that there is good critical commentary in Howard's book, that Lowell's diversity and versatility make him an elusive subject for both biographer and critic, and that it is time for a new effort "to evaluate and interpret all of Lowell's character and personality." To do so along psychoanalytic lines, however, would be, Rees warns, "foolish and dangerous."

After reading Edward Wagenknecht's *James Russell Lowell: Portrait of a Many-Sided Man* (New York, Oxford) I decided that this warning is unduly shrill. Lowell's character and personality are precisely what Wagenknecht is interested in interpreting and evaluating, and in doing so he stays quite clear of psychoanalytic theory and the application thereof. But what theory is used instead? Wagenknecht calls his study a "psychograph," but in what ways he understands the discipline of psychology is not made clear. He calls attention to, among other things, Lowell's Peter Pan temperament, his fear of a proclivity to insanity, the ambiguous character of the intense obsession with Jews which afflicted him in later life—on this topic Wagenknecht straightens out Beatty's misleading account—and he cites Lowell as "probably the only one of the classical New England writers who was ever in serious danger of suicide." Given these symptoms, it seems not impossible that an inquiry along psychoanalytic lines into the man and his problems might prove to be illuminating, which the Wagenknecht portrait is not. Essentially, it is only informative.

But it is so on an almost encyclopedic scale. Typical is the way in which Lowell's attitude towards nature is systematically canvassed: from landscapes and the seasons on through oceans and rivers to animal life, specifically Lowell's dog and the squirrels at Elmwood. Lowell "loved the Elmwood squirrels," Wagenknecht writes, "though I think he loved the birds more; birds and trees, I should say, were his two great passions in nature." An equally thorough inventory is taken of Lowell's religious views; but, again, the viewpoint is mainly statistical: "I have noticed [in Lowell's poems] only one reference to the Virgin Birth." The prose may not be memorable for its urbanity but it does present a great deal of data in a very orderly way, with each chapter neatly fitted into the one after it. Biographical details are taken care of in the opening chapter; in the following ones different aspects of Lowell's endowment, temperament, literary career, and convictions are examined. Neither a biography nor a critical study, the book was written on the assumption that Lowell was an artist, or enough of an artist, to warrant our continued interest in him. Rarely, therefore, is an evaluative comment made about anything Lowell wrote. What we have, then, is an assemblage of data set together to form a well-planned mosaic.

A relatively minor contribution, neatly done, is David Paroissien's "James Russell Lowell: The Fireside Traveler" (*SA* 15[1969]:61–74). Paroissien fills out a chapter in Lowell's life, the year (1851–1852) of his first visit to Europe. The basic text in the case is Lowell's "Leaves from My Journal in Italy and Elsewhere," in his *Fireside Travels*. Paroissien brings out how Lowell, in contrast with his Italophile friend W. W. Story, anticipated some of the iconoclastic responses of *Innocents Abroad*. But this is only part of the story. Henry James, as Paroissien himself points out, effectively summarized the situation when he said of Lowell: "If he was American enough in Europe, in America he was abundantly European."

Reviewing the development and the present state of Longfellow studies in *Fifteen American Authors* (pp. 263–83), Richard D. Rust decides, largely on quantitative grounds, that interest in Longfellow has taken an upward turn in the past ten years. The evidence is the output during this period of forty-seven articles, five books, four scholarly editions, and two doctoral dissertations. At least two more items can now be added to this list. John Griffith's "Longfellow and Herder and the Sense of History" (*TSLL* 13:249–65) alludes as if in passing to Constance Rourke's remark that no American writing tests Herder's theory that a fine art can be built upon folk art, but the essay as a whole is a persuasive reply to Rourke. Using "Hiawatha" and "Miles Standish" as his principal exhibits, Griffith argues that it is Herder's view of history (lucidly sketched by him) that is closest to Longfellow's. Cecelia Tichi in "Longfellow's Motives for the Structure of 'Hiawatha'" (*AL* 42:548–53) proposes that the value of cultural continuity is what informs that poem. In outline, its plot implies a progressive movement: mastery over the environment is followed by civilization and eventually by the apotheosis thereof, the advent of Christianity (when the white missionaries arrive). This is not *quite* so culturally chauvinistic as might appear, for although the white race is destined to supplant the Indians, "still the latter are as [Longfellow] presents them worthy in their own native culture of an historic European on-grafting in America."

Barry Menikoff brings up to date the summary of scholarship on Oliver Wendell Holmes in *Eight American Authors* (pp. 207–28).

For sixty-eight years of his long life (1797–1883) George Moses Horton was a slave in North Carolina. Verbally precocious to an unusual degree, he became a "natural" poet and a serious one. Three collections of his work, all of them dedicated to the theme of anti-slavery, appeared in his lifetime. He hoped by such publication to earn enough to purchase his freedom. A full account of his life and his work as a poet is given by W. Edward Farrison in "George Moses Horton: Poet for Freedom" (*CLAJ* 14:227–41; see also Richard Walser on Horton, *ALS 1966*, pp. 145–46).

By far a better known name, but perhaps almost as forgotten as a poet, is Christopher Pearse Cranch. The three volumes of verse he wrote are now available in *Collected Poems, 1835–1892*, edited with an introduction and index by Joseph M. DeFalco (SF&R). Although it is quite in order for an editor to feel partisan about the material he is working with, too emphatic a selling job tends to arouse skepticism. With the first sentence of his introduction DeFalco made me skeptical: "By any estimate, Christopher Pearse Cranch must be ranked as one of the five major Transcendentalist poets." And a concluding remark is in the same key: "This is not a variorum edition because it was impossible to include the variant readings." But who needs a variorum edition of so minor an author? DeFalco's introduction should be supplemented by the more impartial and analytic discussion of Cranch in J. C. Levenson's essay on him (see *AL* 21:415–26).

Wellesley College

12. Fiction: 1900 to the 1930s

Warren French

As a time of harvest 1971 was noteworthy for the unusual number of books and collections of essays about individual authors. As we approach the hundredth anniversaries of the births of many of the writers considered in this chapter, we can expect more studies of varied scope and worth. Let us hope that other centennials will elicit such illuminating tributes as Robert Penn Warren's *Homage to Theodore Dreiser on the Centennial of His Birth*.

i. General Studies

There are still few new general studies of the fiction of this period, though the increasing study of separate authors and the development of new critical techniques demonstrates the need for comprehensive reassessments. Three books, however, that make vast historical and geographical sweeps contain significant analyses of writers of this period.

Since Wayne Charles Miller's *An Armed America: Its Face in Fiction* (New York, New York Univ. Press [1970]) considers the whole history of the American novel, it can be dealt with adequately only in the chapter on "Themes, Topics, and Criticism." The fourth chapter, however, places often neglected novels like Dalton's Trumbo's *Johnny Got His Gun* (1939) and Laurence Stallings's *Plumes* (1924) alongside the better known books of Faulkner, Hemingway, and Dos Passos as the work of those who, "for the first time since Melville," deal critically "with an entire social structure through a consideration of a military situation" (p. 99). Another chapter on Marquand and Cozzens will be discussed below in section ii.

Charles A. Hoyt's *Minor American Novelists* ranges from Charles Brockden Brown to Edward Lewis Wallant, but includes chapters on James Branch Cabell, Nathanael West, and John Dickson Carr. *The Politics of Twentieth Century Novelists*, edited by George A. Panichas (New York, Hawthorn), falls largely within the scope of this chapter, but considers British and continental authors as well as Dreiser, Sherwood Anderson, Dos Passos and Steinbeck.

One new book to fall entirely within the period discussed by this essay is *The American Novel and the Nineteen Twenties*, edited by Malcolm Bradbury and David Palmer (London, Edward Arnold), with four general essays and studies of Sherwood Anderson, Dos Passos, Lewis, West, Faulkner, Fitzgerald and Hemingway. Bradbury's prefatory "Style of Life, Style of Art, and the American Novelist" (pp. 11–35) ties together the essays that follow with the generalization that while these writers "sought, above all, style, the literary and emotional economy appropriate to a new age," the crisis they faced is less one of "perception and language" than of "consciousness, the strain of living in a modernizing world" (pp. 14, 16). Lawrence W. Levine's "Progress and Nostalgia: The Self Image of the Nineteen Twenties" (pp. 37–56) stresses especially the way in which the popular arts of the decade reflected "the central paradox of American history"—"a belief in progress coupled with a dread of change" (p. 38). Henry Dan Piper's "Social Criticism in the American Novel in the Nineteen Twenties" (pp. 59–83) discusses Dreiser's and Anderson's influence upon Faulkner, Fitzgerald, and Hemingway, because all shared "the belief that it was the writer's responsibility to expose and hopefully to correct the shortcomings and injustices of contemporary American society" (p. 61). Eric Mottram's "The Hostile Environment and the Survival Artist: A Note on the Twenties" (pp. 233–62) discusses the way in which after World War I, perceptive Americans—especially the writers among them—functioned "as pathologists of the decadence created and maintained by politicians, economists, theoretical historians, churchmen and the activists of the military-business nexus" (p. 262).

Writings about individual authors will be considered, as before, under six general headings, though it has become necessary to subdivide one group in order to reflect the attention now being focused upon the "Harlem Renaissance" of the 1920s.

ii. Inheritors of the Genteel Tradition

All three grand ladies of the early years of this century are subjects of new books. Two of these focus on the early works of Ellen Glasgow.

J. R. Raper's *Without Shelter: The Early Career of Ellen Glasgow* (Baton Rouge, La. State Univ. Press) concentrates upon her "use of the complex realism associated with Darwin as a central tool to strip away the veneers of southern ideology," because of her finding "in the theories of the great evolutionist a confirmation and illumination of her own intuitions regarding human nature" (p. 13). Raper concludes that "beyond commonplace success and failure, four general possibilities for human conduct especially interested Ellen Glasgow." Finding that of these evasion was unsound and irony unsuccessful, she envisioned that man could realistically comprehend his place in the universe only with either "a sense of universal conflict or an intuition of unity" (p. 251)—attitudes still as important today as at the time of the great debate over Darwin.

Raper's analysis clashes with Marion K. Richards's statement in *Ellen Glasgow's Development as a Novelist* (SAmL 24) that the novelist's interest in Darwinian science was "transitory" and that her "scientific, philosophical, and political explorations did nothing to strengthen her work," which is best read as a comedy of manners (p. 193). Despite a painstaking tracing of the relationship of the themes of Ellen Glasgow's major works to her emotional development, Richards's account seems perfunctory and shallow beside Raper's.

Blair Rouse's "Ellen Glasgow, The Novelist in America" (*Cabellian* 4:25–35) deals not so much with Miss Glasgow as with the role of the novelist in America, although Rouse stresses her representative and somewhat contradictory concern, on the one hand, not with "the code of Virginia, but with the world we call civilized" and, on the other, with her lack of readers and literary friends in her native Richmond.

Of the two new books about Wharton, Louis Auchincloss's *Edith Wharton, A Woman of Her Time* (New York, Viking) is not so much a critical study as a lavish gallery of pictures of persons and places connected with her life; but it closes with a perceptive defense of her work as an integral part of the American Dream, because she realized that "the social game was played without rules, and this made her one of the few novelists before Proust who could describe it with profundity" (p. 191). Such speculations about Mrs. Wharton and her world seem never to have occurred to Geoffrey Walton, whose *Edith Wharton: A Critical Interpretation* (Rutherford, N.J.,

Fairleigh Dickinson Univ. Press, 1970) reads like the transcription
of a series of lectures during the 1930s by an Ivy League professor
whose popularity rested upon his providing students with plot summaries and long quotations that served as substitutes for reading the
works themselves. Walton's animus is clear from a concluding statement that "Edith Wharton made a distinctively upper-class contribution to literature, more distinctively so than James's because she
was more concerned with social detail." As a result, he adds, her
work at the present time "presents something of a challenge to
appreciation" (p. 204).

Part of the nature of this challenge is specifically suggested by
Jo A. McManis's "Edith Wharton's Hymns to Respectability" (*SoR*
7:986–93), which quite convincingly questions the motivations behind the self-sacrificial aspects of Mrs. Wharton's characters and
argues that her writing is—as she once described George Eliot's—"a
continuous hymn to respectability," because—possibly subconsciously
—"she never ceased to revere the law she transgressed."

Indirect support for McManis's conclusions is provided by two
similar articles in the *Markham Review*, suggesting that in structuring
her major novels Wharton may have worked out tensions in the
struggle between herself and society that she could not consciously
face. Michael W. Vella's "Technique and Theme in *The House of
Mirth*" (2,iii[1970]:[17–20]) describes the episodic structure of the
novel as being based upon the presentation of a series of "illuminating
incidents" that show the limitations of Lily Bart's character to be
also those of the constricting society in which she seeks to flourish.
John J. Murphy's "The Satiric Structure of *The Age of Innocence*"
(2,iii[1970]:[1–4]) argues that the form of the novel—which turns
satiric after Archer rejects Ellen—reflects the structure of the trap
that he built for himself by slothfully accomodating himself to his
traditional society. A similar tribute to the interrelationship of theme
and structure in a short story is Margaret B. McDowell's "Edith
Wharton's 'After Holbein': 'A Paradigm of the Human Condition,' "
(*JNT* 1:49–58), which sees this work—like Holbein's set of narrative
drawings—as an allegorical dance of death, the tragedy of which is
the pointless lives that the principal characters have led.

Two books about Willa Cather have also appeared, but neither
has any place in a scholarly library, since both are superficial and
derivative accounts for young readers (Barbara Bonham's *Willa*

Cather, New York, Chilton [1970]; and Ruth Crone's *Willa Cather, The Woman and Her Works*, New York, Scribner's [1970]). Entirely missing from such books is any recognition of the importance of the analysis made in essays like David Stouck's "Perspective as Structure and Theme in *My Ántonia*" (*TSLL* 12:285–94), which points out that "skillful ordering of temporal and spatial elements is one of the important compositional devices" used "to evoke the emotional response shared by narrator and reader," a response which ultimately illuminates what is transient and what endures as memorable in the incommunicable past.

Blanche Gelfant stresses equally the negative aspects of remembrance of the past in "The Forgotten Reaping Hook: Sex in *My Ántonia*" (*AL* 43:60–82), which argues that we must begin to look to the novel "not only for its beauty of art and for its affirmation of history, but also, and instructively, for its negations and evasions," because the novel reveals a fear of sex as a threat to loss of self—the autonomy that Cather undoubtedly correctly believed was essential to her success as an artist.

That this concern with autonomy may, however, have become an obsession is stressed in James Woodress's "Willa Cather Seen Clear" (*PLL* 7:96–109). Reviewing what we have learned through the University of Nebraska's recent publications of Cather's early papers (see *ALS 1970*, p. 225), Woodress points out the roadblocks that the novelist set up to keep biographers and critics at bay and argues convincingly that she went to "excessive and self-defeating" lengths to maintain her privacy.

Recent attention to neglected male exponents of the genteel tradition suggests why they have failed to be of sustained critical interest, despite flashes of popularity. John Fox, Jr.,'s credentials as a genteel writer are enunciated by Warren I. Titus's *John Fox, Jr.* (*TUSAS* 174): "In his longer works especially, his propensity is for Victorian gentility" (p. 123). This propensity is illustrated by a "Personal Sketch" written in 1908, which Harriet R. Holman reproduces in "John Fox, Jr.: Appraisal and Self-Appraisal" (*SLJ* 3,ii,18–38), a modest document about the author's boyhood that helps—along with Titus's study—to correct inaccuracies in previous accounts. Titus's deftly written book makes no extravagant claims for his subject, observing only that Fox was born too late to share the popularity of the genteel "local colorists" of the nineteenth century.

Central to any study of the writer who transported the genteel tradition to the Wild West is Neal Lambert's "Owen Wister's Virginian: The Genesis of a Cultural Hero" (*WAL* 6:99–107), which points out that by creating a character who is both frontiersman and gentleman, Wister united "successful affirmations of essentially contradictory systems of values" in a cultural symbol that involved both our notions about a beneficent wilderness and our commitment to civilization. Lambert's complementary "Owen Wister's Lin McLean: The Failure of the Vernacular Hero" (*WAL* 5:219–32) suggests that Wister achieved commercial success by falsifying his own impressions of the West through his downgrading of the true Westerner who proved "incompatible with too many of the elements of life that Wister himself valued."

James Ballowe's "Marquand and Santayana: Apley and Alden" (*MarkhamR* 2:92–94) exemplifies through a study of two authors a split of the kind that Wister could not face in himself, explaining that audiences could not face the implications of Oliver's death in George Santayana's *The Last Puritan* as "symbolic of the vitiation of the life and mind and spirit of America"; whereas Marquand's "genial caricature of George Apley restored to American readers the illusion that like other value systems puritanism's presence or absence does not have any appreciable consequences on their lives."

In one of the most important analyses of the lingering adherents to the genteel tradition Wayne Charles Miller in *An Armed America* seemingly inadvertently suggests a reason why these exponents failed to maintain a hold on the American imagination. Miller compares both Marquand's and James Gould Cozzens's work to sociologist Morris Janowitz's *The Professional Soldier: A Social and Political Portrait* (1960). Of Marquand's *Melville Goodwin, U.S.A.*, Miller writes, "With a cool objectivity approximating the social scientist's, Marquand, nine years before the publication of Janowitz's findings, reaches most of the same conclusions in an evocative and sympathetic rendering of Goodwin" (p. 180). Of Cozzens's *Guard of Honor*, Miller writes, "It is significant that Janowitz, the sociologist, dismisses most military novels as somewhat peevish protests but has nothing but praise for Cozzens' work" (p. 189). These comments need to be viewed in the light of Miller's earlier concession that Marquand's novel "generated little controversy or interest" (p. 179). When novelists and sociologists agree, why not simply read the sociologists

—as readers have increasingly tended to do? The "cool, reserved, and practical" adherents to the genteel tradition simply serve no distinctive function as writers of fiction.

H. P. Lovecraft, the final decadent issue of New England gentility, receives an elaborate tribute from French admirers in *Lovecraft* (Paris, Editions de l'Herne, 1969) an oversized, 379–page volume containing previously unpublished stories and poems, as well as eighteen French appreciations and thirteen translated American tributes. The material is too extensive and repetitive to analyze here, but the tone that dominates the book is embodied in editor François Truchaud's "The Dream Quest of H. P. Lovecraft" (pp. 15–25), which concludes with the explanation that the dream of Lovecraft never ends, because the world is made of dreams and is in a state of perpetual creation—in the image of Lovcraft and his lyric quests.

iii. The Redskins

Robert Penn Warren's *Homage to Theodore Dreiser on the Centennial of His Birth* (New York, Random House) is one of those uncommon works that reminds us how vital literary criticism can be. Warren obviously finds Dreiser's work vulgar and distasteful, yet—like Ellen Moers—he is fascinated by the energy and imaginative power of the man. Warren refutes especially those who find Dreiser's work artless and formless, asking of *An American Tragedy,*

> But ultimately how do we know the "power" or the "compassion"—know them differently, that is, from the power or compassion we may read into a news story—except by Dreiser's control? Except, in other words, by the rhythmic organization of his materials, the vibrance which is the life of fictional illusion, the tension among elements, and the mutual interpenetration in meaning of part and whole which gives us the sense of preternatural fulfillment? Except, in short, by art? [pp. 117–18]

Especially perceptive is Warren's analysis of the structure of *Sister Carrie*, concluding: "To sum up, the apparently casual structure of mere chronicle is set against a very firm and complex structure of thematic contrast and parallelism, and in the tension between these two principles of structure—the narrative and the thematic—

the vital rhythm of the novel is defined" (p. 37). Curiously, considering that Warren is one of the fathers of the rigorously objective New Criticism, his homage to Dreiser is an intensely personal testimony of the influence upon him of some of Dreiser's works—especially the neglected Cowperwood trilogy.

Warren's essay also appears in the *Southern Review* (7:345–410) along with an important formal analysis of Dreiser's work, Warwick Wadlington's "Pathos and Dreiser" (7:411–29), which argues that Dreiser is an accomplished writer in "the pathetic tradition." Wadlington considers the distinction between pathos and tragedy similar to Northrop Frye's distinction between high and low mimetic tragedy, but even closer to Robert Heilman's distinction between tragedy and melodrama. "In tragedy," Wadlington contends, "our attention is focused upon a man who suffers disjunction within himself; in pathos, more upon a man who suffers disjunction with his world." He illustrates the distinction through an analysis of Jennie Gerhardt, who "undergoes little of any real growth in the novel," because the "new life" she faces at the end is not a "symbolic rebirth, but only a new attempt to find a harmonious relationship with the world."

Two other essays seek to determine the source of Dreiser's unique power through formal analysis. Daryl C. Dance's "Sentimentalism in Dreiser's Heroines, Carrie and Jennie" (*CLAJ* 14[1970]:127–42) argues that Dreiser intentionally parodies "the conventional plot, theme, and characters of the sentimental novel . . . in such a way as to blaspheme the purpose and meaning of those old melodramas," by showing that true virtue could never be rewarded in a society that punishes not the sinful, but the weak. William J. Handy's *Modern Fiction: A Formalist Approach* (Carbondale, So. Ill. Univ. Press) discusses Dreiser along with Joyce, Faulkner, Hemingway, Malamud, and Bellow, applying to each the theory that "since the essential power of the fictional work resides in its texture, in the forms through which the artist constructs and relates his scenes and episodes, criticism becomes a matter of consciousness, of bringing to awareness the nondiscursive meaning embodied in the presentational writing" (p. 28). Applying this principle to *Sister Carrie*, Handy finds that the often puzzling literary power of the novel "lies in the singular way Dreiser's sensibility" gives voice in every scene to his "unwavering conviction that humanity can truly be achieved" (p. 66).

In the light of these analyses, R. N. Mookerjee's assertion in "The Literary Naturalist as Humanist: The Last Phase of Theodore Dreiser" (*MQ* 12:369–81) that the final works exhibit a strong humanism despite Dreiser's claims of remaining an uncompromising realist, though sound, is familiar and thinly developed. More useful is Mookerjee's well-informed explanation in "Dreiser's Use of Hindu Thought in *The Stoic*" (*AL* 43:273–78) that the treatment of Eastern mysticism, especially yoga, is superficial and "betrays a lack of any real understanding of the subtleties."

Two critics focus on Dreiser's use of popular art forms—especially Augustin Daly's melodrama *Under the Gaslight*—in *Sister Carrie*. In "Gaslight and Magic Lamp in *Sister Carrie*" (*PMLA* 86:236–40), Hugh Witemyer buttresses his conclusion that "Dreiser's youthful experience of the theater . . . helped him greatly in presenting his sad but sympathetic vision of radical American immaturity" with the observation that "arousal of sexual desire in *Sister Carrie* nearly always takes place in theaters," probably because the characters "habitually see themselves and others as actors in a private drama of fantasy and daydream." Sheila Hope Jurnak's "Popular Art Forms in *Sister Carrie*" (*TSLL* 12:313–20) extends basically the same thesis by pointing out that Dreiser's references to popular works that embody moral platitudes show his intention to suggest that "while popular culture incorporates the common man's fiction into literary form, true art strips away illusion and displays the actual."

The theatrical quality of the novel is also suggested by Jerome M. Loving's conclusion in "The Rocking Chair Structure of *Sister Carrie*" (*DN* 2,i:7–10) that by using such a simple device as a rocking chair "for his stage property, Dreiser has focused the attention of his readers relentlessly on the power of material things to betray the essential spirit as the wellspring of happiness." This issue of the *Newsletter* also contains the text of a ballad about Chester Gillette's killing of Grace Brown, which inspired *An American Tragedy* (pp. 5–6), and an interview with Richard Lehan (pp. 11–17).

The first issue of *Proof* contains not only Donald Pizer's heavily annotated "The Publications of Theodore Dreiser: A Checklist" (1:247–92), but also Joseph Katz's "Dummy: *The 'Genius'* by Theodore Dreiser" (1:330–57), an illustrated account of the ways in which the preliminary pages and two chapters of text contained in a salesman's dummy designed to promote the novel in advance of publication differ from the first edition.

Two pieces of detective work by Philip L. Gerber will intrigue those concerned with the prototypes of fictional characters: "Dreiser's Financier: A Genesis" (*JML* 1:354–74) documents the inspiration that the career of Charles Tyson Yerkes provided for the character of Frank Cowperwood, and "The Alabaster Protégé: Dreiser and Berenice Fleming" (*AL* 43:217–30) explores the similarities between Yerkes's protégé, Emile Grigsby, and Cowperwood's Berenice.

Tributes to Dreiser during his centennial year appeared all over the world. These evidences of his international influence will become accessible to American scholars only if a collection of translations is made. Meanwhile two final tributes by American critics make 1971 a year of remarkably solid achievement. Robert Elias's emended edition of *Theodore Dreiser: Apostle of Nature* (Ithaca, N.Y., Cornell Univ. Press [1970]) corrects misstatements in the original edition (1949) and adds an updated version of Elias's survey of Dreiser scholarship for *Fifteen Modern American Authors* (1969).

In his contribution to *The Politics* (pp. 231–50), Sheldon Grebstein maintains that, often as Dreiser's politics have been examined, three phases have not received proper attention: first, "Dreiser's portrayal of political events in his novels as conspiracies in which the private interests and motives of the select few prevail over the professed common ideals and public welfare" (p. 232); second, Dreiser's obsessive fear of sexual conduct arousing adverse public opinion; third, an ambivalence between a liberal faith in reform and a reactionary, fatalistic view of character in his novels, leading to "an underlying identification with the strong, however deep and genuine his pity for the weak" (p. 244).

Jack London is becoming the subject of comparative studies. Arnold Chapman's "Between Fire and Ice: A Theme in Jack London and Horacio Quiroga" (*Symposium* 24[1970]:17–26) argues that in both stories, "The Anglo-Saxon invader of the wilderness embodies the pragmatic, extroverted, outward-directed will" necessary for the continuance of a culture that seeks to dominate the environment and that both authors feared that this unnatural striving would cause the intruder "to be expelled like a foreign body from healthy tissue." T. E. M. Boll's "*The Divine Fire* (1904) and *Martin Eden* (1909)"

(*ELT* 14:115–17) argues that London may have gotten the idea of his novel from May Sinclair's earlier work, whose hero could have given Eden "an example by having founded his intensified creativity upon a philosophical system that is a dynamic monism."

Despite the evidence to the contrary, critical writing can still be fun. Jonathan H. Spinner's "Jack London's *Martin Eden*: The Development of the Existential Hero" (*MichA* 3,i[1970]:43–48) begins "*Martin Eden* is one of the first novels that documents . . . the final collapse of the Horatio Alger legend" and presents one of the first scenes in the new American drama of "the existential dilemma of the modern anti-hero." Spinner goes on to prove that no other novel of the period could have shocked readers with such a hopeless picture as Eden's first finding that hard work does not lead to success and then discovering that he is alienated from both the middle class and the socialists. Further discouragement is found, James K. Bowen argues, in "Jack London's 'To Build a Fire': Epistemology and the White Wilderness" (*WAL* 5:287–89) in London's implication that "animals survive through instinct; men of limited mental capacity fail."

A long neglected member of the "tribe" that came to Greenwich Village in the 1920s from the Midwest receives sympathetic treatment in John E. Hart's *Floyd Dell* (TUSAS 184), which acknowledges that Dell's work has been almost forgotten. Rather than reviving interest in it, however, Hart's account suggests why it has met this fate. In a diary that he kept after moving to Washington, D.C. during the Depression to work "regular hours" shuffling papers for the Federal Arts Project, Dell wrote, "I am still as proud of my governmental reports, as of anything I have ever written" (p. 165). Who would be inspired to turn to the novels?

Two articles provide footnotes to the still unwritten history of the most outspoken and prolific of the "redskins," Upton Sinclair. Peter A. Sorderbergh's "Upton Sinclair and Hollywood" (*MQ* 11[1970]: 173–91) describes the running battle between Sinclair and the Hollywood moguls, who moved to California about the same time, culminating in the novelist's attack in *Upton Sinclair Presents William Fox* and the film studios' campaign against his election as governor on the Democratic ticket in 1934. Antanas Musteikis's "The Lithuanian Heroes of *The Jungle*" (*Lituanus* 17,ii:27–38) points out Sinclair's lack of knowledge of the Lithuanian culture of his main characters, as evidenced especially by the unlikelihood of Jurgis Rudkus's rapid switch from conservative farmer to ardent socialist.

Lawrence J. Dessner's "Robert Herrick, American Novelist" (*MarkhamR* 3:10–14) justifies the usual neglect of the novelist by observing that his "basic assumptions are historically egocentric and philosophically naive," "an elaborate apologia for his own life and conduct." In the face of Dessner's analysis, George P. Spangler's "Robert Herrick's *Waste*: Summary of a Career and an Age" (*CRAS* 2:26–36) sounds quite naïve when it claims that the novel's record of a long quest for salvation reaching a dead end is "definitive not only of Herrick's final despair, but of the utter inadequacy" of traditional American idealistic individualism for coping with the realities of the urban, industrial country that faced Herrick's generation.

Reinhold Echter's "O. Henry's *Sound and Fury*" (*NS* 20:370–79) reprints in English this short conversation between a writer and his secretary, then makes in German the large claim that it is especially suited for classroom use because of the way in which O. Henry uses the two characters' misunderstanding of each other's remarks to dramatize his parodistic-satirical concerns. One turns with relief from such pompous overstatement to the lyrical understatement of D'Arcy McNickle's *Indian Man: A Life of Oliver LaFarge* (Bloomington, Ind. Univ. Press), an account of this gentle scholar's efforts to achieve a rapprochement between the genteel tradition and the true "redskins." It contains some very interesting information on the composition and publication of LaFarge's best remembered novel, the Pulitzer-Prize winning *Laughing Boy* (1929).

iv. The Iconoclasts—The Provinces

The recently developing interest in demonstrating that Sherwood Anderson's *Winesburg, Ohio* is more than just a collection of short stories (see *ALS 1968*, pp. 186–87) reaches a peak in Forrest L. Ingram's *Representative Short Story Cycles of the Twentieth Century* (The Hague, Mouton), a revision of a 1967 dissertation. Ingram argues for the use of the term *short story cycle* to distinguish groups of stories "so linked to each other by their author that the reader's successive experience on various levels of the pattern of the whole significantly modifies his experience of each of its component parts" (p.

19). He discusses Faulkner's *The Unvanquished,* Kafka's *Ein Hungerkünstler,* and *Winesburg,* along with shorter accounts of Steinbeck's *The Pastures of Heaven* and other cycles. The unity of Anderson's work, Ingram maintains, lies not just in the "constant narrative voice," repetition of verbal and thematic patterns, or "the pseudorealistic locale," but in the associational linkings between the stories as they are arranged to indicate George Willard's preparation "for his mythic journey out of the land of fragmented personalities and ruined dreams into manhood and maturity" (p. 147).

Ingram is not the only one concerned about defining the form of a work like *Winesburg.* The two most imaginative dissertations recently reported deal with the same problem and propose other labels for a new genre. *Winesburg* provides the common denominator between Ingram's book and Raymond J. Silverman's "The Short Story Composite: Forms, Functions, and Applications" (*DAI* 31[1970]: 6633A), which also studies Steinbeck's *The Pastures of Heaven* and Hemingway's *In Our Time;* and Dallas M. Lemmon's "The Rovelle, or the Novel of Interrelated Stories: M. Lermontov, G. Keller, S. Anderson" (*DAI* 31[1970]:3510A). On the basis of priority, simplicity, and euphony, Ingram's *short story cycle* appears to be the most acceptable term.

Yet another analysis of the genre does not propose a label. In "The Process of Observation: *Winesburg, Ohio* and *The Golden Apples*" (*UR* 37:304,293–98—the first pages of this article and another are reversed), Robert S. Pawlowski maintains that both collections "present an event or series of events in much the same way as the [Cubist] painter presents a geometric line, . . . so loosely connected that the viewer is at a loss to learn at once their specific relationship to each other and to the design as a whole." Barry Bort's "*Winesburg, Ohio*: The Escape from Isolation" (*MQ* 11[1970]:443–56) considers the book only as a study of the impossibility of communication, suggesting that it is not "a chronicle of self-discovery," but the revelation of the rare achievement of a human community.

So much attention is being focused on *Winesburg* that overviews of Anderson's work are rare. Brian Way in *The American Novel and the Nineteen Twenties* (pp. 107–26) speculates, however, on the reasons why the bulk of Anderson's work is "characterized by extremes of foolishness, sentimentality, and technical incompetence." Way finds that beyond the shaky grasp of fictional technique and narrow range, Anderson's work suffers from "a lack of adequate subject matter," because "he tends to lose himself in ecstatic tenuities, moments in life for which he claims some great spiritual, emotional, or poetic intensity, but at which nothing clearly demonstrable happens" (p. 121).

Ray Lewis White's contribution to *The Politics* (pp. 251–62) stresses Anderson's belief in "apolitical art," which led him to evade commitment on political issues until the Depression of the 1930s. Even then he refused to write propaganda or join the Communist party. "His own life was singularly free of partisan politics," White sums up, "and yet he followed the general course of the United States into social reform in the 1930's. Needed reforms made, he resumed his role as artist" (p. 262).

Admirers of James Branch Cabell may resent his being included in *Minor American Novelists* (pp. 41–66), but yet be pleased by Fred B. Millet's spirited and penetrating argument that Cabell "was anti-realistic, because he believed that what it is customary to call realism is not true to life, since it ignores man's capacity for dreaming of worlds and lives more rewarding and satisfying than those dull drab daily life offers" (p. 45). Millet attributes the decline in Cabell's popularity to the seeming irrelevance of his ironies during the years of serious social concerns in the 1930s and 1940s.

It is disappointing to learn that after spring 1972, a principal evidence of the resurgence of interest in Cabell, *The Cabellian: A Journal of the Second American Renaissance* will be discontinued, for this elegant semiannual has provided an attractive model for organs of such groups as the Cabell Society. Yet one must wonder that devoted editor Julius Rothman has been able to find the time and energy to set such a high standard for four years.

While much of the 1971 issues is devoted to biographical and bibliographical materials (the autumn issue is especially rich in photographs of Cabell and his homes), Dorothy B. Schlegel and others have provided noteworthy considerations of the novelist's reputation. Miss Schlegel's "Cabell and His Critics" (3,ii:50–63) reviews Cabell's exasperation with critics, especially Virginians, and concludes that "Cabell and his public both had good reasons for feeling hostile to each other. Cabell accused humanity of stupidity and dullness; humanity retaliated by accusing the author of ineptitude and egotism." Virginians were further offended by Cabell's violating their code of

ethics by "putting their little peccadillos into print." Miss Schlegel's
"Cabell's Comic Masks" (4:1–8) discusses the way in which recent
emphasis upon the comic elements in Cabell's vision have served "to
hide the deep sense of tragedy which lay at the heart of his work," a
situation attributable to the novelist's having decided that "man
should make the best of a bad situation and find what solace he can
from creature comforts." Lin C. Siegle's "Dating in *Figures of Earth*"
(4,i:17–21) provides detailed references to the use Cabell made of
the dates of significant pagan and Christian festivals in "signposting"
the life of Manuel the Redeemer.

Edgar E. MacDonald's "Cabell's Game of Hide and Seek" (4,i:9–
16) leads directly to a consideration of Louis Untermeyer's *James
Branch Cabell: The Man and His Masks* (Richmond, Whittet and
Shepperson [1970]), both of which emphasize the many faces that
Cabell turned to the public. MacDonald ends his account of Cabell's
not wholly successful efforts "to whip his diverse essays, poems, tales,
and novels into a 'Biography of Universal Man'" with a description of
a hypothetical thesis that Louis Untermeyer once proposed, titled
something like "The Psychogenesis of a Poet; or, Cabell the Masque-
rader," which would "detail the steps Cabell has taken, as a result of
early associative disappointments, to repress or at least to disguise
the poet in himself—and it will be disclosed how he has failed." Untermeyer's short book, a private printing of an address delivered before the first meeting of the Associates of the James Branch Cabell
Library of Virginia Commonwealth University, is really an abbrevi-
ated version of that thesis—a series of recollections of Cabell that
includes the acute observation that though Cabell and Sinclair Lewis
seem opposite poles of American writing, Untermeyer "can think of
no contemporaries who had so much in common and who differed so
widely in what they said and did about it." Ironically, Lewis objected to Cabell's "irreverent burlesque" of the very things Lewis
himself hated.

Untermeyer's comment that "Lewis, supposedly anti-sentimental,
was full of naive sentimentality," is supported by George H. Douglas's observation in "*Main Street* after Fifty Years" (*PrS* 44:338–48)
that upon its semicentennial Lewis's famous "satire" seems a "gentle
book, full of optimism and naïvete." In another revaluation "Sinclair
Lewis and the Drama of Dissociation" (*The American Novel*, pp.
84–105), Howell Daniels observes that, although in the twenties

"Lewis's sociological fictions made their primary appeal through the satiric observation of phases of contemporary life," often the novels were elevated "above the level of mere destructive comment on contemporary folly" by creating "a fictitious Middle America with its own geography and history" (p. 104).

The leading article in the third annual *Sinclair Lewis Newsletter* is Jack L. Davis's "Mark Schorer and Sinclair Lewis" (pp. 3–9), which reviews the whole relationship between the men and points out that because of Schorer's New Critical bias, he failed to penetrate the consciousness of his subject in either the biography or scattered critical pieces.

v. The Iconoclasts: New York and the Harlem Renaissance

Interest is growing not only in the black writers of the 1920s, but also in the influence of John Dos Passos's novels of the period. In *An Armed America*, Wayne Charles Miller suggests that it was not Cummings or Hemingway, but Dos Passos in *Three Soldiers*, who established the form that "most of the novels occasioned by World War II and the Korean War have taken" (p. 109). W. Gordon Milne in *The Politics* (pp. 263–77) also traces a consistent pattern in Dos Passos's apparently shifting political positions back to his revolt against the enslavement of the individual in *Three Soldiers*. While the "various stereotypes" attached to Dos Passos have fitted for a time, Milne argues, underlying these phases has been "an unflagging credo, a faith in the individual sturdiness of plain people" (p. 265).

Brian Lee's "History and John Dos Passos" (*The American Novel*, pp. 196–213) begins with the assertion that "Dos Passos's best fiction has a pessimism different in kind and more profound than that found in the works of any of his American contemporaries" and attributes it to Dos Passos's feeling that the social tragedy of our times is that all his characters are becoming automata because "twentieth-century man has created physical and spiritual environments for himself which will not allow him to go on living as a human being" (p. 213).

Leon L. Titche, Jr., agrees with this interpretation in "Döblin and Dos Passos: Aspects of the City Novel" (*MFS* 17:125–35), observing that the characters in *Manhattan Transfer* suffer a collective defeat at the hands of the city. Titche stresses that while in Alfred Döblin's *Berlin Alexanderplatz* (1929) "the character is outside the social periphery, battering to get in," in Dos Passos's novel, "the characters are within, fighting to get out." John M. Reilly is less convincing when he attempts in "Dos Passos *Et Al.*: An Experiment in Radical Fiction" (*MQ* 12:413–24) to attribute the experimental structure of *Manhattan Transfer* to a short-lived effort to create a Marxist conceptual pattern for viewing fragmented contemporary experience that failed because no social or political revolution followed in the United States. In *Dos Passos, the Critics, and the Writer's Intention* (Carbondale, So. Ill. Univ. Press), editor Allen Belkind brings together seventeen articles about Dos Passos and adds a lengthy preface reviewing the trends in criticism of the novelist.

This growing stream of writing about Dos Passos is only a trickle compared to the torrent unleashed by the rediscovery of the Harlem Renaissance, especially of Jean Toomer's *Cane*. Nathan Irvin Huggins's *Harlem Renaissance* (New York, Oxford Univ. Press) treats fiction only in passing, but provides for the first time a full-scale history of this much discussed episode against which the novels may be placed in a cultural context from which they are often wrenched. Especially useful are Huggins's discussion of the novels of Carl Van Vechten, the white writer most closely associated with the renaissance, and Wallace Thurman, whose *Infants of the Spring* (1932) is treated as an "obituary" of the renaissance.

Huggins points out that Van Vechten's *Nigger Heaven* (1926) was a historic event, because it was the first "generally read novel" to abandon traditional stereotypes of the Negro, although Van Vechten never reconciled his contradictory assumptions that the reader had to reject these stereotypes while accepting another of the Negro as "a natural primitive." Gerald Haslam's "Wallace Thurman: A Western Renaissance Man" (*WAL* 6:53–59) concurs in Huggins's judgment of *Infants of the Spring* as "brooding over the failure of the New Negro Movement to accomplish more," but deals at greater length with Thurman's earlier *The Blacker the Berry*, in which the novelist—himself born in Salt Lake City—compares the treatment of a young black girl in Los Angeles and New York with that she received in her native Idaho. Dorothy West's "Elephant's Dance: A Memoir of Wallace Thurman" (*BlackW* 20,i[1970]:77–85) complements these studies with an account of the life of this promising young writer who died of tuberculosis at thirty-two.

Like most writers on the Harlem Renaissance, Huggins devotes a good deal of space to Jean Toomer's *Cane*, still the major rediscovery of the recent wave of interest in the period. Huggins considers Toomer the only Harlem writer who was "self-consciously *avant garde*" (p. 180), and he reads Toomer's answer in the novel to the quest for Negro identity as finding one's roots in a Southern homeland and looking into "the fulness of the past without shame or fear," an effort more powerful and provocative than attempts to find black models in the white Protestant ethic or African primitivism.

Darwin T. Turner's *In a Minor Chord: Three Afro-American Writers and Their Search for Identity* (Carbondale, So. Ill. Univ. Press) deals at much greater length with Toomer. (The other two writers are Countee Cullen and Zora Neale Hurston.) Setting the novel into a context of an extended discussion of Toomer's life—something few other critics have done, Turner takes what has previously been the accepted view that *Cane* is not even an experimental novel, but "a collection of character sketches, short pieces, poems, and a play" (p. 14). Toomer, Turner feels, never learned "to translate his philosophy into an idiom comprehensible to the uninitiated" (p. 13), partly as a result of the increasingly detrimental influence of philosopher George Gurdjieff on Toomer's rarely considered later works.

Other critics persist, however, in expounding theories that treat *Cane* as a unified novel. Two analyses in *Studies in the Novel* present contrastingly pessimistic and optimistic views of the work. John M. Reilly's "The Search for Black Redemption: Jean Toomer's *Cane*" (2[1970]:312–24) argues that in the first section Toomer establishes the conditions for black redemption, but in the second part shows the increased inhibition of spontaneous life, and in the third part has Kabnis emerge as a horrible example, the victim of the sin of racial oppression, who has become like the sin itself "a foe of life." William C. Fischer's "The Aggregate Man in Jean Toomer's *Cane*" (3:190–215), on the other hand, concludes that while many of the male characters are egotistically isolated and emotionally paralyzed by "the reality of racial bloodletting," they are counterbalanced by others whose strength and sensitivity permit them "to survive as an ongoing inspiration."

Others line up with Fischer, determined to read *Cane* positively. Rafael A. Cancel's "Male and Female Interrelationships in Toomer's *Cane*" (*NALF* 15:25–31) finds Toomer envisioning the Negro woman—in contrast to the man—as "possessing all the primitive instincts and lust for life that refuse to be contained in a sterile and mechanistic world." Sister Mary Kathryn Grant's "Images of Celebration in *Cane*" (*NALF* 5:32–34,36) finds such images frequent in the first two parts of the novel, though those in the North are "usually generated" by memories of the South. Finally, in part 3, Kabnis must return South "to discover his identity and to discover celebration." In the bluntest challenge to earlier criticism, Bernard Bell maintains in "A Key to the Poems in *Cane*" (*CLAJ* 14:251–58) that all these poems are functional, communicating the spiritual core of the novel, which anticipates the theories of Gurdjieff and suggests the "metaphysical forces necessary to bring the crass material of American society and the sensuality of man's nature into harmony."

Some short articles deal with specific parts of the work. Patricia Chase's "The Women in *Cane*" (*CLAJ* 14:249–73) argues that there is no aspect of woman that Toomer does not weave into his archetypal vision. Hargis Westerfield's "Jean Toomer's 'Fern': A Mythical Dimension" (*CLAJ* 14:274–76) manipulates Judeo-Christian imagery to suggest that Fernie May Rosen may be an implicit avatar of the Jewish Mother of God. Edward E. Waldron's "The Search for Identity in Jean Toomer's 'Esther'" (*CLAJ* 14:277–80) argues that the light-skinned Negro girl who rejects both the white world of America and "the lost world of Africa" is "left in Limbo, with not even a hell in sight."

Toomer is not alone in the limelight, though in view of his place there Frank Durham's collection of reprinted *Studies in "Cane"* (Columbus, Ohio, Charles E. Merrill) appears premature. *Langston Hughes, Black Genius: A Critical Evaluation*, edited by Therman B. O'Daniel (New York, William Morrow) adds to a number of reprinted pieces, six hitherto unpublished essays, two of which deal with Hughes's fiction. Eugenia W. Collier's "A Pain in His Soul: Simple as Epic Hero" (pp. 120–31) describes as Hughes's "greatest contribution to American culture" the Simple sketches, which she considers "a black epic" comparable to *Beowulf*. Harry L. Jones's "Rhetorical Embellishment in Hughes's Simple Stories" (pp. 132–44) catalogues details that demonstrate that the stories "make full use of the best prescriptions and proscriptions of the best writers on rhetoric through the ages."

Critics continue to divide sharply over the merits of James Weldon Johnson's "Autobiography of an Ex-Coloured Man" (see *ALS 1970*, p. 239), presenting this time contrasting views of Johnson's use of irony. Robert E. Fleming contends in "Irony as a Key to Johnson's *The Autobiography of an Ex-Coloured Man*" (*AL* 43:83–96) that the novel is set apart from others dealing with the tragic mulatto because Johnson replaces the stereotyped black with a complex character and conveys a vision of black life "through irony rather than by means of the heavy-handed propagandistic techniques of his predecessors." Marvin P. Garrett argues, however, in "Early Recollections and Structural Irony in *The Autobiography of an Ex-Colored Man*" (*Crit* 13,ii:5–14) that Alfred Adler's theories about the effects of early memories on the neurotic's concept of the world "provide an excellent perspective" from which to consider Johnson's psychological portrait of a "morally obtuse and self-centered character," motivated by "an excessive concern with self-protection."

vi. The Expatriates

Future critics of fiction are going to have to come to terms with William Gass's *Fiction and the Figures of Life* (New York, Knopf, 1970). The author of the novel *Omensetter's Luck* offers theories about the nature of fiction and its relationship to life, centered on the concepts that "the aim of the artist ought to be to bring into the world objects which do not already exist there, and objects which are especially worthy of love" and that we should try to understand works of art "in order to know *them* better, not in order to know something else" (p. 284). This insistence upon a critical concern with contemplation rather than communication applies particularly well to the writings of Gertrude Stein. Gass argues that "none of the literary innovators who were her contemporaries attempted anything like the revolution she proposed." Whereas *Finnegans Wake*, for example, is "a work of learning," which "can be penetrated by stages," in Miss Stein's work "the deep clear bottom is visible at once," so that "she reads easily when an impatient mind does not hasten the eye" (pp. 87, 96).

Norman Weinstein's *Gertrude Stein and the Literature of the Modern Consciousness* (New York, Ungar [1970])—despite a promising title—uses approaches that Gass would reject to examine Miss Stein's writing in the light of twentieth-century theories of language and "to present possible systems" through which the works might be elucidated. Finding his efforts frustrated by the impossibility of summarizing her experiments in the Aristotelian language patterns that they break through, he suggests that her importance lies in the possibilities that her works opened to artists who followed her, yet he reaches no specific conclusions. Jane Mayhall's speculations on *Things as They Are* (Miss Stein's first novel, written in 1903 but not published until 1950) in *Rediscoveries* (pp. 197–208) are, on the other hand, quite dogmatic in calling this lesbian love story Miss Stein's "most daring book," after which she replaced reason and emotion by "brilliant word games, and tantalizing dissociative patterns" (p. 207).

Gass would probably also reject Strother B. Purdy's "Gertrude Stein at Marienbad" (*PMLA* 85[1970]:1096–1105), which evokes Miss Stein's memory only to argue that her works are generally unread because she "was imposing on the printed word something that it could not bear—but which the visual image could," so that her theories are only "realizable by a film," like Resnais's *L'année dernière à Marienbad*, from a script by Robbe-Grillet.

While Edward B. Mitchell has found it worthwhile to collect fourteen articles by critics like George Orwell and Philip Rahv in *Henry Miller: Three Decades of Criticism* (New York, New York Univ. Press) and Harold T. McCarthy argues in "Henry Miller's Democratic Vistas" (*AQ* 23:221–35) that Miller unconsciously echoes a famous exchange between Henry James and William Dean Howells by arguing that "the only experience which has significance is that which becomes art," Peter L. Hays feels obliged to argue that Miller is not an artist at all, but a dangerous anarchist, because of "his celebration of life, energy, passion, ecstasy, and his condemnation of anything that restricts free enjoyment." Hays may be writing tongue in cheek; but, if so, he is unrewardingly heavy-handed in "The Danger of Henry Miller" (*ArQ* 27:251–58).

Two other writers who take Miller seriously relate him to past and present proponents of mystical visions. Paul R. Jackson's "Henry Miller, Emerson, and the Divided Self" (*AL* 42:231–41) suggests that Osmanli, the young soapbox orator in *Sexus,* may be a version of Emerson's Osman, who appears to have suggested to Miller "the possibility for dramatizing the simultaneous levels he felt in his divided self." Wilhelm Höck's "Leben nach der Geburt: Samuel Beckett und Henry Miller: Einzelgänger der literarischen Moderne" (*Hochland* 63:365–77) concludes that the two writers certainly come together—though Miller speaks out what is disguised in Beckett—in constantly questioning whether in the possibility of death there is a possibility of rebirth.

An often neglected expatriate receives affectionate attention in Wallace Stegner's essay on Glenway Wescott's *Good-bye, Wisconsin* (*Rediscoveries*, pp. 47–56, reprinted from *SoR* 6[1970]:674–81), which blames the neglect of this "quintessential expression" of the protest against the Midwest in the 1920s upon its being "one of the last major expressions of what we too glibly call the revolt from the village." Stegner finds, however, that the stories in this book "survive the time and impulse that produced them," because of the tension in them between "village philistinism and artistic aspiration, crude hurtful stories and a controlled and subtle telling."

A principal source of information about the expatriate set continues to be *Under the Sign of Pisces: Anaïs Nin and Her Circle*, edited by Richard Centing and Benjamin Franklin V. John Tytell's "Anais Nin and 'The Fall of the House of Usher'" (2,i:5–11) argues that Roderick Usher and Jeanne, "the weary protagonist" of *Under a Glass Bell*, both suggest "the logical development of the symboliste hero: an hysteria of hypersensitivity causing excesses which result in the annihilation of sensibility." Philip K. Jason's "Teaching *A Spy in the House of Love*" (2,iii:7–15) discusses two baroque elements of the work—the way in which "the musical nature of Sabina's life may suggest that the various episodes in the novella should be viewed as variations on a theme" and the way in which the many images of circularity actually characterize the narrative technique. Other issues are devoted to biographical and bibliographical materials, including Miss Nin's view on women's liberation (2,i:1–4). Editor Centing also provides an introduction to Evelyn J. Hinz's *The Mirror and the Garden: Realism and Reality in the Writings of Anais Nin* (Columbus, Ohio State Univ. Libraries), which brilliantly demonstrates that the novelist finds the naturalist's mirror "a symbol of neurosis on the psychological level"—"two dimensional, static, and stylized"—and prefers "the garden as symbolic of all that is natural and positive in life and art"—"the symbol of psychic health" (p. 14).

vii. The Cosmogonists—Porter, Steinbeck, West, Wilder, Wolfe

A major disappointment is M. M. Liberman's *Katherine Anne Porter's Fiction* (Detroit, Wayne State Univ. Press). Liberman attracted attention several years ago with two defenses of *Ship of Fools*, which the novelist herself commended (see *ALS 1966*, p. 162; *ALS 1968*, p. 193). To this material, now combined in a single essay, Liberman has added only six highly contentious readings of shorter works. Liberman's brilliant command of Miss Porter's work is shown by such an explanation as:

> The failure of love, that is, the incapacity to imagine fully another's humanity, to act upon such imagination with a degree of generosity, and to abjure that vicious counterfeit of love, sentimentality, is by now so pervasive a theme in modern writing as to be something like a common topic. As treated in *Ship of Fools*, it surprised friends and repelled strangers, but it need not have, since it had its logical antecedent in Miss Porter's earlier work. [p. 47]

He has, however, failed to provide the overall view of Miss Porter's work that his title and the pretentious format promise.

Ten writers join to present a surprisingly unified study in *Steinbeck, The Man and His Work*, edited by Richard Astro and Tetsumaro Hayashi (Corvallis, Oregon State Univ. Press), the proceedings of a 1970 Steinbeck conference. Half of the ten papers are general studies. James P. Degnan's "In Definite Battle: Steinbeck and California's Land Monopolists" (pp. 65–74) deals with the background of the California novels; the others develop critical theses.

Peter Lisca's "Escape and Commitment: Two Poles of the Steinbeck Hero" (pp. 75–88) reaches the conclusion that Steinbeck's last novels present "neither the individualized or communal escapes of his early work and the immediate post-war novels, nor the inspired, Christ-like sacrificial commitment of his proletarian fiction," but rather the importance of the observation that he made on marine ecology in *Sea of Cortez*, "there would seem to be only one commandment for living things: survive!" (p. 88).

Charles Shively's "John Steinbeck: From the Tide Pool to the

Loyal Community" (pp. 25–34) argues that while it cannot be proved that philosopher Josiah Royce influenced Steinbeck, both men developed their world-views along the same line, aiming at "a unification in which man's sense of purpose and dignity can be restored." Charles R. Metzger's "Steinbeck's Mexican-Americans" (pp. 141–55) counters the frequent charge that Steinbeck's treatment of *paisanos* is "romantic and sentimental" with the argument that while it is romantic, it is hardly sentimental because "it actually fits the facts of life as life was conducted by the kinds of real persons who provided Steinbeck with models for his fictional characters" (p. 146). John Ditsky's "Faulkner Land and Steinbeck Country" (pp. 11–23) makes a separation of the two men's work in terms of quality partly on the basis of Steinbeck's "inability to see the insufficiency of treating Nature's relationship with men merely through the repetition of certain devices" rather than developing like Faulkner "a set of valid prior assumptions about man and the land which his fiction might then illustrate" (p. 23).

The newest estimate of Steinbeck's achievement is James Gray's *John Steinbeck* (UMPAW 94). The retired literary editor of the *Chicago Daily News* begins his pamphlet with the assertion that "it says something significant about the importance of Steinbeck's work that the testimony must be examined on several different levels of interest," something that can be said of few American writers "up to the very recent phantasmagorical/psychedelic experimentation with forms of fiction" (p.12). Gray's praise for Steinbeck's use of his "story-telling skill" as means of trying "to identify the place of man in the world" concludes with the judgment that the novelist "might be called a moral ecologist, obsessively concerned with man's spiritual struggle to adjust himself to his environment" (pp. 41, 44). In the light of these remarks it is not surprising that the late Lawrence William Jones finds in "Steinbeck and Zola: Theory and Practice of the Experimental Novel" (*StQ* 4:95–101) that neither author was able "to live up to the extreme demands of objectivity and impersonality that Zola imposed upon the novelist." In "Music from a Dark Cave: Organic Form in Steinbeck's Fiction" (*JNT* 1:59–67), however, John Ditsky finds that Steinbeck might be called "naturalistic" in the sense that for him "the ultimately most successful formal development was one which was *organic*," relying upon "the coincidence of narrative plan and 'natural' growth patterns," especially his favorite devices of "music and the dark cave in Nature" used in many works from *Cup of Gold* to *The Winter of Our Discontent.*

In *The Politics* (pp. 296–306), Warren French portrays Steinbeck as "representative of an American type of great influence during the first two decades following World War II, the Stevenson Democrat" (p. 297) and concludes that Steinbeck's admission "that it was more difficult in the 1960s than in the 1930s to determine who was an underdog" shows that the novelist's thinking "had not become sophisticated enough to deal with the subtle problems of an age of affluence," a failure of private vision that reflected "a general failure of American politics" (pp. 304–05). Interesting light is thrown on Steinbeck's politics by John Kenneth Galbraith's reprinting in *Economics, Peace and Laughter* (Boston, Houghton Mifflin) a letter from Steinbeck announcing that he is "against all governments" and pleading that Galbraith not accept an appointment as ambassador to India, citing as a precedent his own refusal to work for Darryl F. Zanuck of Twentieth Century-Fox (p. 325).

The debate continues over "The Leader of the People," with Bruce K. Martin (who apparently wrote before earlier pieces were published—see *ALS 1970*, p. 245) expressing dismay at the lack of attention to the work and arguing in " 'The Leader of the People' Reexamined" (*SSF* 8:423–32) that the grandfather's stories represent to Jody a welcome escape from a dull existence, but that the boy finally comes to regard the stories not so much as a solution to his problems as a means of comforting the grandfather whose plight parallels his own.

Not much else has been written recently about Steinbeck's other work of the 1930s. William Goldhurst's "*Of Mice and Men*: John Steinbeck's Parable of the Curse of Cain" (*WAL* 6:123–35) theorizes that "viewed in the light of its mythic and allegorical implications, *Of Mice and Men* is a story about the nature of man's fate in a fallen world, with particular emphasis upon the question: is man destined to live alone, a solitary wanderer . . . ?" George Henry Spies III's "John Steinbeck's *In Dubious Battle* and Robert Penn Warren's *Night Rider*" (*StQ* 4:48–55) points out that the novels are alike in having protagonists who are "dehumanized through their complete devotion to the 'cause' " and in not really having "endings," since the mass movements the dead heroes represented "will undoubtedly continue forever in one form or another."

Leonard Lutwack in *Heroic Fiction: The Epic Tradition and American Novels of the Twentieth Century* (Carbondale, So. Ill. Univ. Press) discusses *The Grapes of Wrath* as one of a small group of works that illustrate how in modern America, "the epic tradition and the novel have been of mutual benefit, the deficiencies of one being corrected by the virtues of the other" (p. 12). Observing that Steinbeck's novel has a two-part theme, "the education of a people and the education of its emerging leaders" (p. 48), Lutwack finds that of all Steinbeck's characters only Tom Joad "affirms the possibility of a hero arising out of the anonymity of twentieth-century economic strife and still bearing the signs of an ancient dedication" (p. 63).

Steinbeck's often neglected postwar "Monterey" novels are scrutinized in two contributions to *Steinbeck, The Man and His Work*. Robert M. Benton's "The Ecological Nature of *Cannery Row*" (pp. 131–39) speculates that "perhaps the solution to the structural difficulty of the novel can be found in the commensal relationships portrayed when those relationships are seen in connection with the central metaphor of the tide pools and Steinbeck's acknowledged interest in ecology" (p. 134). Even Steinbeck's flimsiest novel finds a defender in Robert DeMott, who argues in "Steinbeck and the Creative Process: First Manifesto to End the Bringdown against *Sweet Thursday*" (pp. 157–78) that the novel is about the writing of a novel and that "its theme and deep structural principle are creativity and the condition of the artist" (pp. 162–63). Considering the same works, Richard Astro in "Steinbeck's Bittersweet Thursday" (*StQ* 4:36–48) concentrates on the changes in the characters and neighborhood between *Cannery Row* and *Sweet Thursday* and observes that "rendered nearly hopeless by the decayed world of the new Cannery Row, Dock is no longer Steinbeck's fictional *persona*, but merely his ironic victim," whose fate seems less tragic than pathetic.

Principal beneficiary of increasing interest in Steinbeck's later fiction is *East of Eden*. Lester J. Marks's "*East of Eden*: 'Thou Mayest'" (*StQ* 4:3–18) repeats the argument in his earlier book that the novel is the apex of Steinbeck's development, because in it for the first time he goes beyond "affirming that man is great because he can *survive*" to present a vision of man triumphant over evil. Pascal Covici, Jr.,'s "From Commitment to Choice: Double Vision and the Problem of Vitality for John Steinbeck" (*The Fifties*, pp. 63–71) maintains further that Steinbeck's work has not been properly judged because Steinbeck's fiction in the 1950s revolves around the issue of "individual choice" rather than the universal commitment he was concerned with in the 1930s: "the matter of the family" replaces "the matter of the land" in Steinbeck's American myth.

Attention is also turning to Steinbeck's work in genres other than the novel. Richard Astro—who has been making an extensive study of Steinbeck's relationship with Ed Ricketts—warns in "Steinbeck and Ricketts: Escape or Commitment in *The Sea of Cortez?*" (*WAL* 6:109–21) that analyses of Steinbeck's fiction based on statements made in "The Log" from *The Sea of Cortez* "are likely to court disaster" because this log contains "Ricketts' fundamental notions" about science, life, and man in general, some of which Steinbeck shared, but some of which he rejected.

Steinbeck's film scripts are also receiving attention. Robert E. Morsberger's "Steinbeck's Zapata: Rebel vs. Revolutionary" (*Steinbeck, The Man and His Work*, pp. 43–63) finds that *Viva Zapata!* is not a digression into Hollywood hackwork, but a powerful story that brings into final focus questions about the relationship of issues to individuals and to leaders of people that Steinbeck had been struggling with for years. Metzger also considers "The Film Version of Steinbeck's *The Pearl*" (*StQ* 4:88–92) in an account of the proceedings of the Steinbeck Conference held at San Jose State College, February 26–28, 1971. Metzger finds that the film weakens Steinbeck's parable by watering down three major themes—the importance of manhood, survival, and self-defense—and failing to stress adequately "the really big parable theme of hope." Herbert Kline's "On John Steinbeck" (*StQ* 4:80–88) reports the film directors recollections at the same conference of his collaboration with Steinbeck on *The Forgotten Village*. Much information about film versions of all Steinbeck's works is found in Michael Burrows's *John Steinbeck and His Films* (St. Austell, Cornwall, Primestyle, Ltd.), which is not a formal essay, but a valuable collection of notes and quotations from correspondence.

Two other very useful references tools have appeared. Tetsumaro Hayashi's *John Steinbeck: A Guide to the Doctoral Dissertations* (Muncie, Ind., Ball State Univ.), the first in a projected annual series of Steinbeck monographs, summarizes the sixteen studies completed between 1946 and 1969. Sakae Morioka has abstracted and translated from the Japanese (*StQ* 4:116–19) the six articles appearing in the special Steinbeck memorial number of *EigoS* (April 1969). The most intriguing of these, Ryusei Iseri's "*East of Eden*—Steinbeck's View of Man," finds that the "Thou Mayest" thinking in the novel resembles that of the Hokke and Kegon sects of Buddhism.

Like Robert Elias, James F. Light has updated his standard critical study, *Nathanael West: An Interpretative Study* (2nd ed., Evanston, Ill., Northwestern Univ. Press) by expanding the text and adding a survey of scholarship, especially the books that have appeared since his pioneering study in 1961.

Two essays take a quizzical look at the relationship of West's work to various mass media. Joan Zlotnick's "The Medium is the Message, Or Is It?: A Study of Nathanael West's Comic Strip Novel" (*JPC* 5:236–40) points out that *Miss Lonelyhearts* was originally planned as a comic strip and resembles one in several respects. "If Miss Lonelyhearts' spiritual and sexual failure," Zlotnick concludes, "is an emblem of the inability of the American male to assert himself in our culture and if West diagnoses this failure as symptomatic of a sick society, it is ironic that he should make this diagnosis in the style of the comic strip, which reflects and reinforces this sickness it calls normality." T. R. Steiner's "West's Lemuel and the American Dream" (*SoR* 7:994–1006) finds that the villain of *A Cool Million* is not such a monstrous demagogue as Whipple, but "the popular imagination which makes it easier for them to thrive," because it needs "Horatio Alger, racial stereotypes, pulp pornography." West's tone is deliberately crude because "if our dreams derive from the popular imagination, they inevitably embody and reflect the quality of that imagination."

Helen Petrullo compares the novel with two contemporary works, Sinclair Lewis's *It Can't Happen Here* and James Thurber's *The Last Flower*, in "Clichés and Three Political Satires of the Thirties" (*SNL* 8:109–17) and finds all three not simply "topical debunkings," but works of permanent literary merit. Bruce Olsen apparently disagrees because in "Nathanael West: The Use of Cynicism" (*Minor American Novelists*, pp. 81–94), he observes that West "was too close to a philosophy of value to achieve objectivity" (p. 94), as is especially apparent in *The Day of the Locust*, which fails "as do many novels, in the confusion between moral earnestness and effective structure" (p. 91). Jonathan Raban's "A Surfeit of Commodities: The Novels of

Nathanael West" (*The American Novel*, pp. 214–31) expresses a similar view more harshly, calling West's work "pathetically incomplete," never getting beyond the point of hysterically imitating the klaxon of the ambulance carrying the bodies away from Apocalypse.

Carter M. Cramer would call such opinions "misreadings" of West's work as "novels" rather than what Northrop Frye calls "anatomies." In "The World of Nathanael West: A Critical Interpretation" (*ESRS* 19,iv:5–71), Cramer concludes that *The Day of the Locust* is "a masterpiece of the demonic mode" that makes West not just an artist, but a moralist condemning violence as the American way of life. Similarly, Nathan A. Scott, Jr., in *Nathanael West* (CWCP) admits that West's vision is narrow and violent, but compares him to Kafka and Borges, arguing that it is "just by virtue of his very immoderateness and extremism that he was able to throw some light on the chaos of our time" (p. 42). In what Scott,—extending Lionel Abel's term *metatheatre*,—calls *metafictions*, he sees West asserting that "our life is, willy-nilly, a work of improvisation, of invention, of art" (p. 19).

Louis O. Perez's "Wilder and Cervantes: In the Spirit of the Tapestry" (*Symposium* 25:249–59) describes "important thematic and artistic similarities" between *Don Quixote* and *The Eighth Day*, "particularly in regard to the function of the tapestry," which conveys their message—"the irrevocable fact that we are all involved in mankind and all our acts are not only recorded in the great tapestry of history but influence directly or indirectly the lives of others."

In *Fiction and the Figures of Life*, William Gass asks, apropos of the social value of fiction, "How would you like to be replaced by your medical dossier? Your analyst's notes?" William U. Snyder's *Thomas Wolfe: Ulysses and Narcissus* (Athens, Ohio Univ. Press) comes perilously close to replacing Wolfe with exactly the things Gass mentions. An authority on nondirective counselling, Snyder produces a psychological analysis of Wolfe from his writings and reports that Wolfe's relationships with other men were colored by his search for a father substitute that was ultimately frustrated because Wolfe "could not remain dependent and keep his self-respect" (p. 97). As far as Wolfe's relationships with women were concerned, Snyder observes that "since Tom was scornful of both masturbation and homosexuality and could not tolerate the idea of sex with a good woman," he became a Don Juan type wanderer (p. 182). Snyder concludes with the diagnosis that Wolfe can be classified as a psychoneurotic with "severe labile and cyclical" emotional features and "evidences of paranoidal behavior of subpsychotic intensity" (p. 219). From a different point of view, Cambridge undergraduate Michael O'Brien in "Thomas Wolfe and the Problem of Southern Identity" (*SAQ* 70:102–11) compares Wolfe's leaving the South to an English working-class boy's "slowly, and usually neurotically, leaving aside his social origins."

Wolfe was the subject of the first South Atlantic Graduate English Conference at the University of Georgia, April 10–12, 1969. The proceedings of this gathering appear in *Thomas Wolfe and the Glass of Time*, edited by Paschal Reeves (Athens, Univ. of Ga. Press), in which three important critics present extensions of their earlier work. Richard S. Kennedy's "Thomas Wolfe's Fiction: The Question of Genre" (p. 1–44) broods over the problem of applying Northrop Frye's critical terminology to lyric works of fiction that need to be classified on the basis of structure rather than characterization and proposes for Wolfe's work the term *fictional thesaurus*—"a long literary work made up of short units in prose or verse in which the parts are joined together by association of ideas rather than by probable or necessary development" (p. 28). It would be interesting to see the term applied to Jean Toomer's *Cane*, as Kennedy suggests it should be.

Richard S. Walser's "The Angel and the Ghost" (pp. 45–77) concludes that, viewed in terms of these major symbols, *Look Homeward, Angel* "is an investigation into the essentials of creativity"— the ghost representing "the inspiration of art" and the angel "the permanence of art," both of which "must affirm themselves if man is to be capable of the creative act" and both of which are manifested in Ben, "symbol of the sacrificial intermediary" (p. 67). C. Hugh Holman's "Thomas Wolfe: Rhetorical Hope and Dramatic Despair" (pp. 78–112) discusses the two distinct modes of writing in *Look Homeward, Angel* and points out that, while the novelist in the dramatic passages "portrays a dispiriting and despairing world," the poet-seer in the rhetorical passages "lifts his voice to chant the ideal and the promise of America" (p. 95). The book also includes reminiscences by Wolfe's brother Fred and transcripts of several forum discussions.

viii. Richard Wright and the Tough and Tender Thirties

Because of the growing number of new periodicals devoted to black writing, comments on Richard Wright outnumber those on all others writing about the troubled world of the 1930s. Recent essays have concentrated on individual works or groups of works, however, rather than adding new overviews of his career to the many produced during the last few years. Enormously helpful in bringing order to the burgeoning study of Wright is John M. Reilly's "Richard Wright: An Essay in Bibliography" (*RALS* 1:131–80), which follows the format of the surveys in *Fifteen Modern American Authors* (1969).

Attention is turning particularly to the early writings about Mississippi, which Martha Stephens in "Richard Wright's Fiction: A Reassessment" (*GaR* 25:450–70) praises as "classic studies" of the black in his native South or a Northern ghetto. She calls attention especially to Wright's "unswerving attention to immediate experiences of one individual" in *Lawd Today, Uncle Tom's Children,* and the first two sections of *Native Son.* Keneth Kinnamon's "*Lawd Today:* Richard Wright's Apprentice Novel" (*SBL* 2,ii:16–18) also praises Wright's vividly real picture of black life on Chicago's South Side in the 1930s, but concludes that the material fails to fuse. John M. Reilly's "Richard Wright's Experiment in Naturalism" (*SBL* 2,iii:14–17) charges more specifically that "in writing *Lawd Today,* Wright found the demands of naturalism upon his narrative manner revealed the inadequacy of naturalistic assumptions."

In one of the most perceptive and important analyses yet to appear of a Wright story, Blyden Jackson argues in "Richard Wright in a Moment of Truth" (*SLJ* 3,ii:3–17) that "Big Boy Leaves Home" belies Wright's consciously avowed intention to depict the quality of will the Negro must possess to live and die in a country which denies him his humanity and that instead, "whether Wright so intended or not, the lynching of Bobo is symbolically a rite of castration . . . the ultimate indignity that can be inflicted upon an individual." In this lynching, "all lynchings are explained, and all race prejudice. Both are truly acts of castration." John Timmerman's "Symbolism as a Syndetic Device in Richard Wright's 'Long Black Song'" (*CLAJ* 14:291–97) also objects cogently to Edwin Berry Burgum's interpretation of Sarah as a victim of loneliness, deserted by an Uncle Tom-mish Silas, and presents Silas as a proud black man who has elected to perish with his dream farm, leaving Sarah to face hopelessly the nightmare she has created.

Defending the final section of *Native Son* against its many critics, Edward Kearns argues in "The 'Fate' Section of *Native Son*" (*ConL* 12:146–55) that despite the abstractness, this section "is a logical and necessary extension of Wright's thematic strategy, because once Bigger has acted and begun to establish his identity, he must conceptualize the meaning of his act if it is to have any value."

David Bakish's "Underground in an Ambiguous Dreamworld" (*SBL* 2,iii:18–23) champions "The Man Who Lived Underground" as Wright's best work, using it as evidence that the author himself always lived underground, "struggling with an ambiguous identity" and—like his protagonist—found it difficult to distinguish between dream and reality. Much light is shed on this story by Michel Fabre's "Richard Wright: The Man Who Lived Underground" (*SNNTS* 3:165–79), which reports that it does not derive from Dostoevski, but is based upon an account in *True Detective* (August 1941) of Herbert C. Wright, a Los Angeles white, who did live underground and robbed businesses in 1931 and 1932. Fabre reads the story as an "existential parable" presenting the humanist message that while an individual can impose masks upon himself, "man acquires his identity from other men."

Turning to Wright's poorly regarded later fiction, Lewis A. Lawson contends in "Cross Damon: Kirkegaardian Man of Dread" (*CLAJ* 14:298–316) that in *The Outsider*, Wright offers "essentially a Christian, rather than an atheistic, existential view," since at the end Cross accepts the guilt that frees him to seek atonement.

Turning to a neglected contemporary of Wright's, Darwin T. Turner in *In a Minor Chord* examines the career of Zora Neale Hurston (pp. 89–120), a perpetual wanderer who Turner feels "deliberately assumed a role designed to gain assistance from white people." Although in her best work, *Moses, Man of the Mountain* (1939), she found "a format in which she could best utilize her talents for writing satire, irony, and dialect" (p. 109), Turner concludes that, "superficial and shallow in her artistic and social judgments, she became neither an impeccable raconteur nor a scholar" (p. 120).

Work on other "tough guy" writers can be briefly reported. James J. Thompson, Jr.,'s "Erskine Caldwell and Southern Religion" (*SHR*

5:33–44) points out that three themes—"sexuality, degenerated ethical standards, and fatalism"—characterize Caldwell's writing about
both respectable middle-class Protestants and poor white fundamen-
talists. Richard B. Sale's "An Interview in Florida with Erskine Caldwell" (*SNNTS* 3:316–31) contains some comments of Caldwell's on
the increasing size of Southern revival sessions that make heavy use
of music.

Harold Billings's *A Bibliography of Edward Dahlberg* (Austin,
Univ. of Texas Press) brings to light the fact that there is still no
book-length study of Dahlberg and only a scattering of critical articles about him, despite many effusive tributes. Dahlberg himself
provides an introduction for Billings's work and carries his personal
history forward through his quarrels with the Communist party in
the 1930s in *The Confessions of Edward Dahlberg* (New York, George
Braziller).

For *Rediscoveries* (pp. 67–74), Irwin Shaw recalls Daniel Fuchs's
Homage to Blenholt (1936) as an ancestor of *Portnoy's Complaint*,
dramatizing the gentle reproach to an America that disturbs the individual's peace and affronts his dignity that is "the underlying theme
of a whole school of Jewish-American writing from Odets to Roth."
Warren Eyster, also in *Rediscoveries* (pp. 134–46), asks whether
Humphrey Cobb's antiwar novel, *Paths of Glory* (1935), deserved its
obscure fate, since "*no* writer has ever exposed the power structure
that exists within modern armies more relentlessly than Cobb."

Lee J. Richmond's "A Time to Mourn and a Time to Dance;
Horace McCoy's *They Shoot Horses, Don't They?*" (*TCL* 17:91–100)
calls this recently revived novel "indisputably the best example of
absurdist existentialism in American fiction," except for some of
Nathanael West's work, and explores its reputation among French
existentialists. Charles Child Walcutt's *John O'Hara* (UMPAW 80,
1969) finds the subject "a good and extraordinarily important writer
of short stories and an inferior novelist," who ranks with Trollope,
Balzac, Galsworthy, and James T. Farrell. The novels are weak, Walcutt maintains, because "the serious American writer . . . generally
rejects the standard American values of business and status, without
which the relations among individuals, already more intricately various and slippery than they might be if our manners were more uniform, become difficult to manage in the sustained action of a full
novel" (p. 7).

The first book-length study of Farrell is Edgar M. Branch's *James T. Farrell* (TUSAS 185). Some day I hope someone may have the fortitude to explore the remarkable way in which the landmark Twayne series has so often managed to find critics who reflect the characteristics of the authors they deal with, as in the example of this book, which concludes unapologetically with the assertion that at the age of 68, "Farrell has not realized the full potential in his vision" (p. 171), though Branch admits that the cycles centering on Studs Lonigan and Danny O'Neill—completed thirty years ago—are "Farrell's major contribution to American literature" (p. 167). The problem is that both Farrell and Branch throw away their best lines. Speaking of the Studs Lonigan trilogy, for example, Branch brilliantly observes that "what most of the characters . . . lack in magnanimity, they amply possess in personal aggrandizement" (p. 59) and "from the initial illusions of the young 'hard guy' mugging in the mirror to the dying hallucinations of the defeated weakling, Studs's life is a progress in unreality" (p. 71); but Branch himself fails to point out—whether from lack of perception or toughness—that these observations are true of Americans generally, so that the enormously productive Farrell has never managed to establish himself as either a popular or elite author because he strikes too sensitive a nerve in portraying the average American, without being able himself to transcend that average.

A long section on Caroline Gordon in the *Southern Review* is the principal source of tributes in 1971 to the regional writers of the 1930s. Radcliffe Squires's "The Underground Stream: A Note on Caroline Gordon's Fiction" (7:467–79) traces the use of underground water in her novels as a symbol of the salvation that is not available from a decadent society as metaphorically appropriate for that which is hidden but potential in man. Ashley Brown's "*None Shall Look Back*: The Novel as History" (7:480–94) discusses the way in which this novel uses *War and Peace* as a model for dealing with both one Kentucky family's experiences during the Civil War and the war in the western theatre as an action beyond any individual's comprehension. Thomas H. Landers's "The Function of Ritual in Caroline Gordon's *Green Centuries*" (7:495–508) traces the way in which the differences between two societies—"the amorphous, individualistic society of the pioneers, and the formalized, communal society of the Cherokees"—are contrasted through the destructive debasement of the white man's imported rituals and the community-binding effect of the persisting Indian rituals. The section also includes "Always Summer" (7:430–46), Miss Gordon's reminiscences of growing up in Virginia, and Catharine B. Baum and Floyd C. Watkins's "Caroline Gordon and 'The Captive': An Interview" (7:447–62), the author's recollections of writing the story of an Indian captivity. Miss Gordon is also saluted in Brainard Cheney's essay on *The Malefactors* (*Rediscoveries*, pp. 232–44) as "tomorrow's prophet" at "the eleventh hour of our interregnum," when man, "in his prolonged revolt against the human predicament, begins to find his way once more back toward maturity."

Also in *Rediscoveries* (pp. 17–28), Robert Penn Warren relates the dramatic origins of Andrew Lytle's *The Long Night* and observes that this story of individual vengeance against a background of the Civil War "is more like a ballad than a novel—a quintessential poetry of action, pathos, humor, and doom," not a record, but Southern society's paradoxical dream of itself.

Turning to that leviathan of regionalism, Floyd C. Watkins writes about "*Gone with the Wind* as Vulgar Literature" (*SLJ* 2,ii[1970]: 80–103), arguing that "good historical novels are in some way meditative" and that Miss Mitchell's is bad because "it creates a myth which seems to ease the hunger of all extravagantly Southern and little romantic souls, but it propagandizes history, fails to grasp the depth and complexity of human evil and the significances of those who prevail."

Moving northward, we find extended attention devoted to another writer often overlooked by critics in Clifford D. Edwards's *Conrad Richter's Ohio Trilogy: Its Ideas, Themes, and Relationship to Literary Tradition* (SAmL 18[1970]), which traces the philosophical theories of "psycho-energies" that led Richter "to consider the human organism (mind and body) to be somewhat like a bio-electrical dynamo" (p. 31). If this dynamo increases its production of creative energy, man is led away from animalism toward the spiritual level. In the trilogy, Edwards finds that *The Trees* and *The Fields* show how man's steady conflict with natural adversity on the frontier causes the pioneers to develop a unique ethical courage; whereas *The Town* shows the destruction of these values by "the sordid forces of economic materialism and collectivism" (p. 190).

The far West lost perhaps its major literary atrist when Walter

Van Tilburg Clark died in 1971, shortly after the publication of Max
Westbrook's critical study (see *ALS 1970*, pp. 229–30) at last demonstrated the extent of Clark's achievement. Westbrook pays tribute to
Clark in *Western American Literature* (6:190), a journal that earlier
in the year carried two new analyses of Clark's work. Concentrating
on Clark's first novel in "Nature and the Nature of Man in *The Ox-
Bow Incident*" (*WAL* 5:253–64), Robert W. Cochran concludes that,
though Clark recognized "unflinchingly man's capacity for cruelty
and cowardice," he led the reader "beyond a too curious contemplation" of them to a contemplation of the emotional equilibrium of Art
Croft. Paul Stein's "Cowboys and Unicorns: The Novels of Walter
Van Tilburg Clark" (*WAL* 5:265–75) traces through the three works
a progress from "regionalism" to "sur-regionalism," from a study in
The Ox-Bow Incident of "the failure of individuals under the pressure of particularized societal forces," through a turning inward
"with yet a lingering glance at environmental influence" in *The City
of Trembling Leaves*, to a portrayal of man standing alone, "facing
the challenge of life on the bare stage of nature" in *The Track of
the Cat*.

Surely "sur-regional" in its implications is Hollis Summers's tribute to William Maxwell's *They Came Like Swallows* (*Rediscoveries*,
pp. 87–94) as a novel that "dramatizes the difference between sentiment and sentimentality." "I have come away from *They Came Like
Swallows* believing it," Summers concludes, articulating the faith
that one hopes underlies all critical encounters with literature.

Indiana University–Purdue University at Indianapolis

13. Fiction: The 1930s to the Present

James H. Justus

The year's work evidences no startling revaluations of major figures (with the notable exception of Warren French's retrospect of Salinger), although there is considerable vitality in the work on younger writers like Vonnegut, Hawkes, and a clutch of new generation black novelists. In varying permutations, there is still great interest in black humor—its historical antecedents as well as its bases in existentialism. Dissertations on O'Connor (four), Malamud (three), Styron (three), and Vonnegut (three) continue to be popular—with continued interest in Barth, Hawkes, Nabokov, Updike, Warren, and Welty (two each); but there is an obvious increase in dissertations on groups of writers in varying combinations and in thematic and generic studies (black writing, the military novel, writers of the absurd, social criticism, and others).

i. General Studies

The most significant critical contribution to contemporary American fiction this year is Tony Tanner's *City of Words: American Fiction, 1950–1970* (New York, Harper and Row), a book of essays on individual writers whose common obsession is the "problematical and ambiguous relationship of the self to patterns of all kinds—social, psychological, linguistic," and Tanner's emphasis is on their struggles to leave idiosyncratic marks on a language which they find inflexible. From the first, says Tanner, American writers have suspected that the verbal constructs which men call "descriptions of reality" are "tenuous, arbitrary, and even illusory," a concern seemingly not shared by their English counterparts. The "need for forms and suspicion of forms seem to be problematically linked emotions," especially crucial for recent writers. Tanner's choices to illustrate his thesis are persuasive, though they obviously support it better than some writers whom he ignores—Styron, O'Connor, Baldwin, among others.[1]

Jerry H. Bryant's *The Open Decision: The Contemporary American Novel and Its Intellectual Background* (New York, Free Press) should have been an important book, since Bryant ambitiously tackles the enormous complexities of modern science, social science, and philosophy as keys to the image of reality which informs so much recent literature; but the prose is dispirited and repetitious, and the substance is disappointingly familiar. Bryant announces that he is not content with tracing the impact of existentialism on American fiction since World War II, but fails to broaden that promising dissatisfaction into anything really new. The "open decision" of the title turns out to be little more than existential commitment to the achievement of the "highest possible intensity of individuality"—the full consciousness of oneself as different from the world of which one is a part. This principle assumes "that reality lies in the individual, that the individual is subjective and ambiguous, that the preferred state is to be as much an individual as possible, that such individuality requires 'true consciousness,' that from true consciousness emerges a concern for others and a sense of human solidarity." Most recent critics have written out of just such an understanding of our contemporary literature. Bryant fills in his generalized contours not with sustained specificities but with categories (the war novel, the "hip" novel, the business novel) in which he restates what others have stated before.

Leonard Lutwack achieves the unlikely distinction of writing a book that is simultaneously too ambitious and too restricted. *Heroic Fiction: The Epic Tradition and American Novels of the Twentieth Century* (Carbondale, So. Ill. Univ. Press) devotes its most substantial segment to Saul Bellow (see below), with separate and unsatisfactory treatments of *Invisible Man, The Naked and the Dead,* and *The Sot-Weed Factor.* Journeys and rebirth rituals abound, however, in other books as well: "cyclical renewal of life is the grand theme of American epic novels" (and, we might add, of many novels not

1. Periodical versions of some of the chapters in *City of Words* have been noted previously: on Burroughs (*ALS 1966*, p. 182), Malamud (*ALS 1969*, p. 242), Mailer (*ALS 1970*, p. 266), and Vonnegut (*ALS 1970*, pp. 277–78). Other relevant segments will be discussed below.

heroic). There is something slapdash and arbitrary about *Heroic Fiction.* Its thesis loses definition because of the tendency to absorb moods, genres, and styles; and the illustrative titles are not inevitable choices: why not a chapter on "The Odysseys of Eugene Gant" or some treatment of Dos Passos and Faulkner, perhaps even the Lanny Budd novels of Upton Sinclair?

Allen Guttmann's study, *The Jewish Writer in America: Assimilation and the Crisis of Identity* (New York, Oxford Univ. Press), is as sociological and cultural as it is literary. Its weakness is its method, which Guttmann calls "a combination of paraphrase and analysis," but which turns out to be plot summary and a disproportionate reliance upon other reviewers and critics. Its strengths—historical sweep and an authoritative command earned from wide and diverse reading —are best seen in the accounts of movements and minor figures for which background and plot summaries are functional: brief lives (Ludwig Lewisohn), postwar emphasis on "Peoplehood" (Herman Wouk, Chaim Potok), writer-radicals and proletarians (Daniel De-Leon, Michael Gold), and black humorists (Stanley Elkin, Bruce Jay Friedman). The sections on more important writers—Mailer, Roth, Malamud—are perfunctorily critical, but the longest single chapter is a sensible, though familiar, sketch of Bellow's career (see below).

The *schlemiel* as a literary figure comes into his own with two complementary studies, both of which attempt definitions based on distinctions among related types of the fool, trace its cultural and literary ancestry (in both oral and written forms), and account for the transformation of a European type into its American version. Sanford Pinsker's *The Schlemiel as Metaphor: Studies in the Yiddish and American Jewish Novel* (Carbondale, So. Ill. Univ. Press), is the richer of the two, being both more literary in orientation and more detailed in critical evaluation. After a separate treatment of Mendele and Sholom Aleichem, Pinsker concentrates on representative works by I. B. Singer, Malamud, and Bellow.[2] Ruth R. Wisse's *The Schlemiel as Modern Hero* (Chicago, Univ. of Chicago Press) is studded with so many jokes and tales that it resembles a *Yidisher Folklor,* but it is especially valuable in its thesis: that only in the 1950s, when America began to "experience itself as a 'loser'" was the figure elevated into

2. Two segments in earlier published versions have previously been noted: on Singer (*ALS 1969,* p. 237) and Malamud (*ALS 1969,* p. 242).

national prominence from his parochial setting and that his progress was checked in the late 1960s because of ideological polarization and the resistance in the dominant culture to ironic accommodationism. Wisse's most important chapter is devoted to Bellow (see below), but there are interesting observations on Singer (who makes the *schlemiel* "a character of semifantastic fiction"), Mendele (who makes the type "not a hero manqué, but a challenge to the whole accepted notion of heroism"), and such "unredeemed" *schlemiels* as Malamud's Fidelman and Roth's Portnoy. (Norman Podhoretz's *Making It* is described as the "unmaking of a schlemiel.")

Southern white novelists since the *Brown* vs. *Board of Education* decision have seriously overcompensated for the racial situation before 1954, says Floyd C. Watkins in *The Death of Art: Black and White in the Recent Southern Novel* (Athens, Univ. of Ga. Press, 1970). After sampling forty-two novels, he finds that race "distinguishes the good guys and the bad almost as accurately as the white and black hats did in old Western movies." Good comes from the Negro himself, "acting in full freedom of the will," while bad in him is "sociologically determined and is attributable to the evils caused by a white society." Because the philosophical inconsistency of such a bias makes the black man "responsible for his goodness, not responsible for his evil," aesthetic credibility is compromised. Watkins's study, taking its evidence from fiction ranging widely in quality, is ironically an extension of the work on Negro stereotypes by Sterling Brown and Nancy Tischler.

Although it is an anthology of previously published pieces, *The Sounder Few* deserves special mention. Of the nine pertinent essays here, three are first-rate: Walter Sullivan's astute assessment of Flannery O'Connor (pp. 101–19), Benedict Kiely's dazzling summary of John Barth (pp. 195–210), and George Garrett's brilliant reading of Wright Morris (pp. 263–80). But none is dull, and there are many unexpected dividends. Walter Sullivan's "Southern Writers in the Modern World: Death by Melancholy" (*SoR* 6[1970]:907–19) is a spirited attack, from a position unabashedly moral, on the emptiness and mediocrity of Southern literature produced by the generation which matured after 1945.

Kingsley Widmer's "The Beat in the Rise of the Populist Culture" (*The Fifties*, pp. 155–73) is an important study in the genesis and continuity of the counter-culture, despite a tone which hovers indecisively between outright sympathy and objective analysis. The diction is akin to the slogans, chants, and holistic aphorisms made famous by his subject; but Widmer's essay contains admirable insights into the movement's characteristic forms (confessions) and its outstanding honorific figure (the holy fool), as well as assorted bonuses: a fine one-paragraph summation of Mailer and the most intelligent account yet of Kerouac. We may not "need" this cultural revolution in precisely the way Widmer imagines, but he is right in his analysis of it.

ii. Norman Mailer

For some time now critics have increasingly sought for the literary and cultural sources of Mailer's ideas, language, and techniques. Richard Foster made a convincing case for seeing Mailer in the Fitzgerald tradition (see *ALS 1968*, p. 211); and now most of the substantial pieces in a special collection of essays devoted to Mailer, the autumn number of *Modern Fiction Studies* (Vol. 17), are studies of sources and influences.

Donald L. Kaufmann's "The Long Happy Life of Norman Mailer" (pp. 347–59) is an evaluative comparison of Mailer and Hemingway, a promising task which unfortunately comes to nothing. Although he cites similarities in language, authorial tone, the uses of sex, violence, and death as well as the possibilities for heroism, Kaufmann finally decides that such connections are "more imaginary than real." (Kaufmann also contributes a negligible note on *Of a Fire on the Moon*, "Mailer's Lunar Bits and Pieces," pp. 451–54, composed in a relentlessly modish style.) In a more impressive essay, "Norman Mailer and John Dos Passos: The Question of Influence" (pp. 361–74), John M. Muste disputes previous claims (1) that the innovative devices of *U.S.A.* are the sources of Mailer's flashbacks in *The Naked and the Dead*, (2) that Mailer's novel is "panoramic-naturalist," and (3) that it, like *U.S.A.*, is a novel of social protest. Although the argument is convincing, Muste's most important observation is that unlike novels of World War I, which assume that war is a "monstrous and accidental mistake," those inspired by World War II tend to see war as a natural outgrowth of modern civilization generally.

Richard D. Finholt, in " 'Otherwise How Explain?' Norman Mailer's New Cosmology" (pp. 375–86), takes a scientific tack by arguing that in *An American Dream* and *Why Are We in Vietnam?* Mailer transcends the tenets of the post-Darwinian naturalism of his earlier career to embrace a supernaturalism based on the notion of God as "the manifestation of the primordial field." And two critics discuss the cultural influences behind *Vietnam*. Roger Ramsey ("Current and Recurrent: The Vietnam Novel," pp. 415–31) sees schizophrenia as its dominant theme, and the sources are both richly and disturbingly varied: the war, Reichian psychology, race, technology, the new anthropology, McLuhanism. Richard Pearce ("Norman Mailer's *Why Are We in Vietnam?*: A Radical Critique of Frontier Values," pp. 409–14) sees considerably more than contemporary culture behind "this surprisingly complex novel"—the tall tale, Huck Finn, pastoralism, Ike McCaslin—but Mailer heightens and intensifies these attitudes beyond the compass of his literary predecessors.

Other essays in this *MFS* number, in addition to Laura Adams's "A Selected Checklist" (pp. 455–63), include separate studies of the early fiction. David F. Burg believes that Valsen, a "Sisyphusian hero, a rebel-victim," is "The Hero of *The Naked and the Dead*" (pp. 387–401), but, perhaps more importantly, he insists upon reading this first novel in its own context rather than in light of Mailer's later development. John Stark, in *"Barbary Shore*: The Basis of Mailer's Best Work"* (pp. 403–08), contends that Mailer's Manicheanism, though subsumed in more interesting psychological conflicts in later books, appears as a capitalism-Marxism dichotomy in his second novel, and what later will be surrealistic techniques show up as allegory and polemic.[3]

Mailer is old-hat for the "new man of the left," says Robert Merideth in "The 45-Second Piss: A Left Critique of Norman Mailer and *The Armies of the Night*"(pp. 433–49). Though better written than its cousins, the smudged and earnest mimeographed newsletters of new left organizations, it is symptomatic of the unsubstantial allegiance that besets leftist students as well as middle-American sports fans. Merideth's Mailer is something of a straw man: Just how many serious readers of any political persuasion take *Armies of the Night* as a "model" for a "left moving into" the new decade? Whoever be-

---

3. In "The Passing of Arthur in Norman Mailer's *Barbary Shore*" (*RS* 39: 54–58), L. Moffitt Cecil suggests that the Arthurian Compact and the Russian revolution are complementary referents in this novel, making it a lament for man's failure to achieve peace and order.

lieves that that work is *not* "ego-oriented" or compulsively concerned with "image"? And, except for ideologues, who is pained that its author's radicalism is "limited" and part-time? To an "unreconstructed American imagination," says Merideth, Mailer remains a compelling figure; but for those who have surmounted the "melodramatic existentialism" that was once so liberating, his language and his "feeling and perception" are now hopelessly stale.

For those of the left who still feel tempted to follow Mailer into the reconstructed 1970s, Merideth's polemic should be balanced by John D. Champoli's "Norman Mailer and *The Armies of the Night*" (*MSE* 3,i:17–21), an admiring account of the "enormous psychic and artistic reconstitution" which Mailer forged in this "novel." Champoli believes its unique achievement lies in its author's refusal to adopt "the comforting banalities of moral seriousness or the comic cynicisms of black humor." And in his third contribution on Mailer this year, "Catch-23: The Mystery of Fact (Norman Mailer's Final Novel?)" (*TCL* 17:247–56), Donald L. Kaufmann characterizes *Why Are We in Vietnam?* as "a cross between a leftist polemic and a political novel," with some of the "tonal acrobatics" of the earlier nonfiction. With D. J., Mailer's quest for a hero takes an atavistic turn; dominated by the naked voice of raw consciousness, this "final novel"— a blast of "pop dynamics"—ends a twenty-year experimentation with language.

Morton L. Ross sees three defining concerns in his comparison of "Thoreau and Mailer: The Mission of the Rooster" (*WHR* 25:47– 56): a demand for life "awakened into the immediate present," a preoccupation with self as the "necessary symbol" for that awakened life, and an interest in writing "a prose protean enough to record the awakened self." Both writers show delight in their own voices, which Ross describes as "extravagant, rambunctious, and exuberant." Similarly, William Hoffa links Mailer to a subjectivist tradition—Edwards, Franklin, Whitman and others whose autobiographical works turn "inward upon the naked self in order to see the outside world" reflected in it. "In Norman Mailer: *Advertisements for Myself*, or A Portrait of the Artist as a Disgruntled Counter-Puncher" (*The Fifties*, pp. 73–82), Hoffa sees this transitional book as Mailer's first successful attempt in developing his most congenial narrative center—the subjective ego—and even the double table of contents (chronological and generic) functions as a projection of Mailer's newly found candor.

In what amounts to an overview of Mailer's career, Robert F. Lucid has edited two volumes. *The Long Patrol: 25 Years of Writing from the Work of Norman Mailer* (New York, World) is a fat sampler of excerpts from the beginning to *Of a Fire on the Moon*, including perhaps more poems than most Mailer admirers really need. *Norman Mailer: The Man and His Work* (Boston, Little, Brown) contains more than a dozen previously published essays of varying quality and pertinence, a *Playboy* interview, a chronology, and a valuable checklist of primary materials. Lucid contributes a fine essay of his own in an introduction that makes Mailer a "public writer" in the tradition of Irving, Mark Twain, and Stephen Crane.

iii. Saul Bellow, Bernard Malamud, J. D. Salinger

Citing "underworld" episodes, journey motifs, and the encyclopedic treasuries of wisdom, Leonard Lutwack, in "Bellow's Odysseys" (*Heroic Fiction*, pp. 88–121), finds the Odyssean figure throughout Bellow's works. If elevating renegades and castaways into epic heroes was a bold maneuver for Melville, it is merely elusive in Bellow: though the Bellovian hero performs nothing heroic, he achieves a conception of himself "that is not unheroic." Wilhelm (*Seize the Day*) is a "tentative" epic hero, Henderson is a "full-blown serio-comic Odysseus," Herzog a "compromise," and Artur Sammler is Bellow's "farewell to the theme of the contemporary Odysseus." Except for *Henderson*, with which the motif works well enough, Lutwack must deal in so many transpositions and strained equations that the entire effort seems wasted.

In this light, it is tonic to have Allen Guttmann's reminder that Bellow's novels repeatedly insist upon the validity and the worth "of the ordinary as well as the heroic" (*The Jewish Writer in America*, pp. 178–221). Augie March, a "cocky penitent" for whom "marginality is possibility," comes to the end of his adventures as the "Columbus of the commonplace"; and the richly realized *Herzog* documents the modest rewards of "marginality understood and overcome."

An equally fruitful line of exploration is Sanford Pinsker's discussion of Bellow's "psychological" *schlemiels* (*The Schlemiel as Metaphor*, pp. 125–57), characters of "attitude" who think they are inadequate "regardless of their actual condition." Unlike Eliot's Prufrock, Bellow's *schlemiels* can bring to their dilemmas "a special heritage of endurance" and a conviction that the dilemmas have independent values of their own without ironic juxtaposition "with a richer past."

In "The Disappointments of Maturity: Bellow's *The Adventures of Augie March* (*The Fifties*, pp. 83–92), David R. Jones declares that Bellow's first popular novel has not worn well. More important than its obvious weaknesses—its bloated, simile-heavy prose and its broken-backed structure—is its lack of a central ingredient: "at that place in its creation where the imagination should have fired the material into life, a vagueness crept in." The holiday nature of its composition, like Augie's own larkiness, provides no focus for its protagonist's character and no sense of life for his favorite city, Chicago. But for Tony Tanner (*City of Words*, pp. 64–84), that sense of stasis is functional; what makes Augie run is the succession of involvements in "versions, visions, fabrications" of reality and not reality itself. The paradox at the center of the novel is that too much autonomy involves loss of the world and too little leads to the loss of self. Tanner sees Augie finally in a borderland between society and the void, "in some way fixed, yet at large in the desperate expansiveness of his own rhetoric."

Renewal through imagination—a notion familiar in Blake, Wordsworth, and Coleridge—is the subject of "The Romantic Self and *Henderson the Rain King*" (*BuR* 19,ii:125–46). Daniel Majdiak argues for Bellow's belief that resources in the romantic image of self as unified and independent, though extravagant, still are available to man in creating a desirable self, and Bellow's most comprehensive rationale for his opposition to the fashionable nihilism of the modernists is found in *Henderson*. Henderson is also a literary "limper," according to Peter L. Hays's *The Limping Hero: Grotesques in Literature* (New York, New York Univ. Press), a study of the "archetype" of the character whose maiming is symbolically crucial in the works in which they appear. Other texts important to Hays's study are Malamud's *The Assistant* and *The Fixer* and Styron's *The Long March*.

Despite the fact that the Africa of *Henderson* is "an original creation," Eusebio L. Rodrigues, in "Bellow's Africa" (*AL* 43:242–56), demonstrates that Bellow derived the factual matter for his novel from the nineteenth-century travel documentaries of Sir Richard Burton, Frederick Forbes, and others, and from the anthropological texts of his mentor, Melville Herskovits. Two critics discuss the symbolic role of the African tribes in Henderson's search for psychic wholeness. As his title indicates, "Life Against Death in *Henderson the Rain King*" (*MFS* 17:193–205), Donald W. Markos uses Norman O. Brown to explicate the conflicting human instincts of loving acceptance (Arnewi) and aggressive resentment (Wariri) in the protagonist. And as her title might not indicate, Judith Moss's "The Body as Symbol in Saul Bellow's *Henderson the Rain King*" (*L&P* 20[1970]: 51–61) is written in "the light of Freudian conversion symptomatology." Henderson projects onto the African landscape and its two tribes conflicting aspects of himself, the "passive-dependent-oral" (Arnewi) and the "active-violent-anal" (Wariri); and his body metaphorically generates "the dual theme of regeneration and recovery."

Ruth R. Wisse (*The Schlemiel as Modern Hero*, pp. 92–107) sees *Dangling Man* as Bellow's challenge to Hemingwayesque values and therefore a turning point in our cultural history; but her most valuable observations concern Herzog. Though he is Bellow's most typical *schlemiel*, he is given a sensuous, evocative background missing in earlier types, and his role explains the "complacent" resolution of the novel: in all empirical tests, the *schlemiel* may fail, "but he never fails in his final self-acceptance."

Gabriel Josipovici's "Bellow & Herzog" (*Encounter* 37,v:49–55) is a sane philosophical analysis of the two "beliefs" which Herzog tries to overcome—crisis ethics and "potato love." Realizing the infinite complexity of even the fools around him, Herzog refuses to judge and is thus inhibited from any action; in "formulating the formulator," Bellow is able to write the book that Herzog never will.

Concentrating on *The Natural* and *The Assistant* in "From Bernard Malamud, with Discipline and with Love" (*The Fifties*, pp. 133–43), William Freedman sees the function of discipline as a tribal virtue for refining man's instinctual behavior. "What Roy Hobbes childishly destroys, Frank Alpine maturely accepts"—the necessity for submitting oneself to the father's will. In "The Double Theme in Malamud's *Assistant*: Dostoevsky with Irony" (*Mosaic* 4,iii:89–102), Norman Leer focuses on "the nature and possibilities of expiation in a post-Dostoevskian world." Malamud borrows not only a pattern of guilt and expiation from *Crime and Punishment*; he also uses narrative devices emerging from a dualistic psychology to suggest the dualism of characters in both internal and external manifestations.

In "Bernard Malamud: The Novel of Redemption" (*SHR* 5:309–18), Fred L. Standley professes to see a new mood of affirmation in recent literature, especially in Malamud, for whose composite protagonist "redemption is posited as a real and live option." *The Fixer* weaves together all the emphases of the previous novels—"the fall, reconciliation with community, reconciliation with familial tradition, and reconciliation of the fragmented self-concept."

"Structure and Content in Malamud's *Pictures of Fidelman*" (*ConnR* 5,i:26–36) is mostly a synoptic piece by Robert E. Ducharme, who believes the subtitle, *An Exhibition*, is the key to this "picaresque chronicle" of an American artist manqué caught in frozen moments like "pictorial tableaux." But Barbara F. Lefcowitz, in "The *Hybris* of Neurosis: Malamud's *Pictures of Fidelman*" (*L&P* 20[1970]:115–20), sees this recent book as a "unique fusion of pathology and comedy"; and Malamud's parody of neurosis is the unifying device linking the failure of both Fidelman's private and public worlds.

"Salinger imposed upon a tacky age the style that it liked," says Warren French in "The Age of Salinger" (*The Fifties*, pp. 1–39), a long retrospect which admirably sets this novelist's contributions in their cultural context. Holden Caulfield offered an image of unromantic resignation in a fresh idiom, and Seymour Glass that of the possibilities of dying nobly. Both figures are "triumphant and defeated" characters who spoke to a youthful generation guided, often unconsciously, by the premise that one "could not retain his integrity and stay alive." Salinger's popularity has declined, concludes French, because the earlier books spoke better to a passive generation than to the later activist one.

Anthony Quagliano's "*Hapworth 16, 1924*: A Problem in Hagiography" (*UDR* 8,ii:35–43) argues that Salinger meant Seymour to be an "enlightened man" whose act of suicide probably signifies the attainment of the highest spirituality. Salinger, in urging us "to opt for the halo," is writing a biography of a contemporary American saint. Seymour's suicide is similarly "explained" by Gordon E. Slethaug, in "Seymour: A Clarification" (*Renascence* 23:115–28), as a dedicated commitment to "a divinely ordained pattern of life." To prove Seymour's exemplary life, Slethaug spends a good bit of time talking about his intuition, compassion, childlike love, and delight in all life—qualities which have never been much in doubt. Bernice Goldstein and Sanford Goldstein, in "Some Zen References in Salinger" (*LE&W* 15:83–95), see key episodes of "Seymour: An Introduction" and "Raise High the Roof Beam, Carpenters" deriving from Salinger's reading in R. H. Blyth and Eugen Herrigel.

iv. John Barth and Thomas Pynchon

Richard Boyd Hauck, in "These Fruitful Fruitless Odysseys: John Barth" (*A Cheerful Nihilism*, pp. 201–36), discusses all the dimensions of Barth as storyteller, the tendency of his stories to become cyclical, his use of all the narrative tricks (ancient and modern), and his happy struggle with the philosophical dilemmas of creating worlds that are not surrogates of reality but alternate versions. Although his is a fine introduction to Barth generally, Hauck is particularly incisive in his treatment of *The Sot-Weed Factor* and Burlingame, the "definitive absurd creator" who teaches Ebenezer that "multiplicity is beautiful" and us all that the unsolemn view of the world, like the pox, is a disease: "once contracted, it can never be cured."

Gerhard Joseph's *John Barth* (UMPAW 91[1970]) proposes that at the heart of all of Barth's work are the configurations of the *Bildungsroman*, but his "real narrative passion is reserved for voracious clashes of mind." Although he sees parodic flourishes of such classical modernists as Frazer, Freud, Wittgenstein, Jung, and Sartre in most of the fiction, Joseph suggests that Barth "suffers with his characters from a tendency to simplify an emotionally intricate, fully human confrontation into an intellectual scheme." This pamphlet is particularly helpful in its segment on the short fiction.

The belief in a verifiable moral vision is the target of Barth's aesthetic, says Campbell Tatham in "John Barth and the Aesthetics of Artifice" (*ConL* 12:60–73). Unlike some of his contemporaries who assume the primacy of a moral imperative, Barth emphasizes art as artifact, and his novels are all "commentaries" on fictive theory. In "John Barth and Festive Comedy: The Failure of Imagination in *The Sot-Weed Factor*" (*XUS* 10,i:3–15), John C. Bean finds a serious discrepancy between the matter and the manner of Barth's third novel; though the structure and style suggest festive comedy, they are imposed on an "essentially non-festive world." Because the dominant mood of "rigidity, fear of experience, resistance to change" precludes any movement toward love and reunion, Barth leaves us cranky and sour.

Two critics concentrate on Barth's rhetoric. Tony Tanner (*City of Words*, pp. 230–59) says that though Barth is an "impressario of fictions," his formal problem is the ambiguity of "provisional form," the arbitrariness of human life duplicated in arbitrariness in fiction-making. Forming words into patterns is for Horner (*End of the Road*) not a search for stabilizing what he knows of the world but a form of play which he prefers to other forms. The disclaimers, introductions, and cover letters in *Giles Goat-Boy* are Barth's announcement that he can "equivocate about, trivialize and undermine" his own prodigious inventions. Barth comes close to excluding the possibility "that *any* particular section of his rhetoric can be taken seriously."

Peter Mercer, however, sees significant distinctions in "The Rhetoric of *Giles Goat-Boy*" (*Novel* 4:147–58). Splendidly precise in isolating and illustrating the various registers and styles in the novel, Mercer also makes sense of the structure. The movement of *Giles* depends upon a series of linguistic engagements with the self-conscious archaism of the hero, including numerous parodies of the rhetorics of American society, "from the grunting of near-animality to the sterile articulacy of academicism."

Stephen L. Tanner, in "John Barth's Hamlet" (*SWR* 56:347–54), explores the ending of *The Floating Opera*, often called sentimental and unconvincing, in light of the two related themes in the novel—"the conflict between the mind and the heart" and "the to-be-or-not-to-be question." Some readers may remain skeptical that Barth's resolution is justified. Masao Shimura assumes that Barth is more European than American in fictional attitudes, techniques, and themes; but in "John Barth, *The End of the Road*, and the Tradition of American Fiction" (*SELit* Eng. no.:73–87), he proposes certain links with *The Scarlet Letter* and Faulkner's *The Wild Palms*—having mostly to do with adulterous triangles and contrapuntal structures associated with what Shimura calls "baroquism."

Tony Tanner's essay on Pynchon (*City of Words*, pp. 153–80) is primarily an investigation of "entropy" and its association with the larger patterns of Manicheanism: "demonized reality, with evil as an inexplicable and anonymous force beaming in on people for no discoverable reason." Stencil in *V.* is a "vacancy filled in with the colours of his obsessions, not a self, but in truth a stencil," and Profane, the rootless wanderer, is as unaware of clues and patterns as Stencil is obsessed with them. Pynchon's world, says Tanner, is crowded with fetishistic constructions that pass for reality, and *The Crying of Lot 49*, which he sees as an addendum to *V.*, reveals Pynchon's ambivalences about his own fiction making.

In "Pynchon's Tapestries on the Western Wall" (*MFS* 17:207–20), Roger B. Henkle sees both novels as contemporary versions of the romantic epic, with its loose structure, fictionalized reinterpretations of earlier cultures, and a love of literary invention for its own sake. Henkle assesses Pynchon's works in terms of their literary antecedents (Joyce, Nabokov, West), cultural influences (Robert Graves, Leslie Fiedler), and biographical facts (Pynchon's work with the Boeing company). For those interested in Pynchon, Henkle's essay is an excellent place to begin.

Anne Mangel, in "Maxwell's Demon, Entropy, Information: *The Crying of Lot 49*" (*TriQ* 20:194–208), sees the basis of Pynchon's writing not in traditional mythologies or religious patterns but in scientific and technological concepts. Pynchon distrusts and radically separates himself from such moderns as Eliot and Joyce, who because they saw art as "perhaps the last way to impose order on a chaotic world" produced static and closed systems of their own.

v. Joseph Heller and Kurt Vonnegut, Jr.

Thomas Allen Nelson breaks little new ground in "Theme and Structure in *Catch-22*" (*Renascence* 23:173–82); most readers would agree that the inability to locate moral responsibility in a world recognizing only self-aggrandizement is Heller's most crucial theme, and some have seen cycles of events which in their incremental recurrence grow more serious as an important formal device.

What sets *Catch-22* above other absurdist books inspired by Sartre and early Camus are the experimental techniques which dramatize rather than merely describe their view of the human condition, says Jean E. Kennard in "Joseph Heller: At War with Absurdity" (*Mosaic* 4,iii:75–87). Sweden, though representative of a sane world, may be a false note in the resolution. Thomas Blues is firmer in his belief that Heller sentimentalizes Yossarian's decision to flee to Sweden by emphasizing the "adventurous" precedent of Orr, the systems man whose escape is a technological rather than a moral achievement. There is, says Blues, a discrepancy between the organic center of the novel and its mechanically complete resolution ("The Moral Structure of *Catch-22*," *SNNTS* 3:64–79).

Ernest W. Ranly's "What Are People For? Man, Fate and Kurt Vonnegut" (*Commonweal* 94:207–11) is a casual philosophical inquiry into the deeper questions of Vonnegut's science fiction: what is the nature of man, and is there a grand design which accommodates him? Ranly finds evidence that Vonnegut would like to have man free "to be undependable, inefficient, unpredictable and nondurable," but that he is too caught up in the intellectual presuppositions of science to allow him that luxury; the mechanization of man is both the subject and the method of Vonnegut's parables.

Stanley Schatt argues that Vonnegut is not a science fiction writer but a social critic, and in "The Whale and the Cross: Vonnegut's Jonah and Christ Figures" (*SWR* 56:29–42) he traces the development of those ambivalent, complex personae who struggle between the forces of benevolence and malevolence, who are puzzled by the difficulty of loving mankind once they know its weakness. In another essay, "The World of Kurt Vonnegut, Jr." (*Crit* 12,iii:54–69), Schatt examines the epistemology throughout most of the works, arguing that Vonnegut's attempt to deal with reality is "pragmatic and pluralistic," not nihilistic.

Two others sound less sanguine. In "The Unconfirmed Thesis: Kurt Vonnegut, Black Humor, and Contemporary Art" (*Crit* 12,iii:5–28), Max F. Schulz links the novelist to the black humorists' consciously formulated "metaphysics of dissonance." The pattern is reflected in the other arts as a world view that celebrates "strategies of self-repudiation," the grappling with the nature of a world in which reality consists of "arbitrary mental constructs" and selfhood is realized in chance relationships. Using *Mother Night* and *Cat's Cradle* as his chief examples, Jerome Klinkowitz finds Vonnegut more inventive and prolific than his fellow black humorists. In "Kurt Vonnegut, Jr. and the Crime of His Times" (*Crit* 12,iii:38–53) he describes Bokononism as a "religion after alienation" because it removes evil from the self and deposits it in a finite, real existence, not one reflective of "Ideal Man." In interpreting Bokononism as a way to relieve man's unbearable egocentric responsibility for the world's problems, Klinkowitz shows no inclination to regard it as anything but serious.

Two lesser but noteworthy pieces are Mary Sue Schriber's "You've Come a Long Way, Babbitt! From Zenith to Ilium" (*TCL* 17:101–06), which argues that the frustrated "American quest for paradise" is the issue in both *Babbitt* and *Player Piano*; and Leonard J. Leff's "Utopia Reconstructed: Alienation in Vonnegut's *God Bless You, Mr. Rosewater*" (*Crit* 12,iii:29–37), the thesis of which is that Vonnegut's disparate attacks on the nonproductive upper classes, the misuse of art, and the raw power of big government are all illustrative of the alienating and dehumanizing power of money. Stanley Schatt and Jerome Klinkowitz have also prepared a useful "Kurt Vonnegut Checklist" (*Crit* 12,iii:70–76) covering the primary works and the "important reviews and essays" concerning them.

vi. Vladimir Nabokov

In *Vladimir Nabokov* (UMPAW 96), Julian Moynahan says that, like Proust, Nabokov is a "preterist" artist, one who tough-mindedly controls the past for a goal far greater than that of the "nostalgist"—not self-discovery or regional identity, but the "discovery and definition of human consciousness, conceived as the master key to the riddle of reality. . . ." *Speak, Memory* is thus an important work, with its explicit argument for the necessity for heightening awareness, for discovering patterns, themes, and repetitions that suggest transcendence into the freedom of the timeless; but Nabokov's "master idea" in the fiction too is man's ability to break out of his imprisonment in consciousness and time through the gift of image making. Moynahan demonstrates the admirable quality, rare among Nabokov buffs, of taking his subject seriously without falling into either solemnity or coterie wittiness.

Nabokov's world "breathes with a teasing and unseen deception," says William Woodin Rowe, and his *Nabokov's Deceptive World* (New York, New York Univ. Press) is an investigation of the subtle, complex, multidimensional "mechanisms" of Nabokov's special "telling." Two chapters are devoted to stylistic effects whose origins are to be found in the Russian language and Nabokov's predecessors (Gogol, Apukhtin, Pushkin). Rowe explores Nabokov's phonetic deftness; his use of strategic details; his use of devices for creating "a reciprocal relationship between the real and the unreal"; and the use of sexual puns, sports, and games to suggest sexual meanings.

Rowe's book is more assembled than written, but its wealth of solid information makes it a valuable companion piece to Carl Proffer's earlier book on *Lolita* (see *ALS 1968*, p. 209).

Charles Nicol's "Pnin's History (*Novel* 4:197–208) is a good explication of the Nabokovian technique of "associational cross-references," which in *Pnin* revolve around the Cinderella story. Two clusters (*squirrel* and *glass*) testify to Pnin's triumph: that Pnin and Victor "qualify as father and son under every test but flesh itself." Nicol appends to this fine essay a somewhat arbitrary coda on Nabokov as Pnin's antagonist and competitor.

Martha Banta, in "Benjamin, Edgar, Humbert, and Jay" (*YR* 60:532–49), explores gracefully the imaginative implications and expansions of the Franklinian fable and the Poesque dream in *Lolita* and *The Great Gatsby*. The common yearning she finds is for a reality which merges the prosaic with the sublime, the pragmatic with the idealistic; but defeat is assured, primarily because of the "external dream milieu" which modern America provides and nourishes.

. *Ada* is a confession, a quest for redemption even in the face of the knowledge that there is no hope of existence "in life or after death," says Sissela Bok; the unsurprising but earnest thesis in "Redemption Through Art in Nabokov's *Ada*" (*Crit* 12,iii:110–20) is that the world of this novel is not a "nulliverse," a world comprised of randomness, but an artfully contrived unity of depth, intensity, and meaning. John F. Fleischauer, in "Simultaneity in Nabokov's Prose Style" (*Style* 5:57–69), contends that narrative action in the fiction is linked by points in space rather than points in time; attention to structure, syntax, and description shows that in terms of ordering, Nabokov is closer to Hegel than to Bergson.

Albert Parry's "Introducing Nabokov to America" (*TQ* 14,i:16–26) is a reminiscence by the former writer for Mencken's *American Mercury* who first wrote of Nabokov in 1933; and "Memory's Defense: The Real Life of Vladimir Nabokov's Berlin" (*YR* 60:241–50) is Robert C. Williams's investigation of the Berlin years of Nabokov's exile (1922–1937) as the generative force for the later works. Despite some hopeful nagging from Alfred Appel, Jr., in his "Conversations with Nabokov" (*Novel* 4:209–22), the Russian reveals his lack of sympathy with the French New Novel ("a little heap of dust and fluff in a fouled pigeon-hole"); but he willingly talks of his fondness for American silent film comedians and his varied opinions on detective stories, cinematic sexual scenes, and late Picasso. Chess problems, he also declares, have the same virtues as other worthwhile art: "originality, invention, harmony, conciseness, complexity, and splendid insincerity."

vii. Flannery O'Connor and J. F. Powers

"Flannery O'Connor: Realist of Distances" (*RANAM* 4:69–78) is Marion Montgomery's tribute to the author who understood that the basis for enduring art was not merely craftsmanship but a vision of "man's place in the world," an awareness so rare as to be thought of as grotesque. Humor is possible for O'Connor, Montgomery believes, because, like Dante and Chaucer, she views "the prospect of Hell from a position beyond terror and pity." Another piece by Montgomery, "In Defense of Flannery O'Connor's Dragon" (*GaR* 25:302–16), is primarily an analysis of the New Left and its connections with O'Connor's moral arraignment of hypocrisy.

In "Flannery O'Connor's Vision: The Violence of Revelation" (*The Fifties*, pp. 111–20), Kenneth Frieling argues that the epiphantic moment favored by O'Connor necessitates the short story form, in which the mystery of grace is presented as illustration, not extended explanation most often required of the novel.

Louise Blackwell contends that O'Connor's most successful stories are humorous in the traditional sense, by which she means a humor which has a surprise effect on the reader, which effectively uses dialect for emphasis, and which has stylistic economy. In "Humor and Irony in the Works of Flannery O'Connor" (*RANAM* 4:61–68), she finds that the least successful ones are those in which the author's hostility breaks through the humorous frame. This is an important subject which this piece barely begins to analyze. Paul Levine's "Flannery O'Connor: The Soul of the Grotesque" (*Minor American Novelists*, pp. 95–117) is a convenient summary of O'Connor's work, linking it to Sherwood Anderson and Nathanael West.

J. H. Dorenkamp finds that "The Unity of *Morte D'Urban*" (*UDR* 8,ii:29–34) is best seen as that of a baroque painting in which compositional elements continually lead the eye of the beholder beyond the frame rather than allowing it to rest on a given point within the picture. The centrifugal unity is revealed by the intersection of "vari-

ous circles"—the Order, the diocese, Billy Cosgrove, the Twaites—
and the tantalizing possibilities along "roads not taken."

In "Wanderers in the Wasteland: The Characters of J. F. Powers"
(*BaratR* 6,i:38–48), Rosemary M. Laughlin compares the priests and
nuns in Powers's world to Galahad; their failure to find the Grail
makes Powers a tragic writer rather than a "satiric moralist or man-
nerist." David M. La Guardia's "A Critical Dilemma: J. F. Powers
and the Durability of Catholic Fiction" (*Challenges*, pp. 265–76)
is a familiar topic by now: whether parochial material inhibits "universal human response." As we might have guessed, Powers's catholicism involves problems "not wholly aesthetic, not wholly religious." The dredging prose confounds rather than clarifies such
problems.

viii. Robert Penn Warren and William Styron

Henry D. Herring discusses "Politics in the Novels of Robert Penn
Warren" (*RANAM* 4:48–60) and finds politics in all the fiction except *The Cave* and the short stories. The political sphere "encourages
violence, deception, arrogance, and misuse of power," says Herring,
and thus the meaning of politics in Warren's novels "is the inability of
men to cooperate even for their mutual benefit in creating a unified
society." Written in a heavy-handed, governmental prose, this essay
contains little that is new.

The connection between "Adam's Lobectomy Operation and the
Meaning of *All the King's Men*" (*PMLA* 86:84–89) is in its strategic
placement in Jack Burden's search for "the true nature of man and
evil," says James C. Simmons. The preceding West Coast sleep is a
"symbolic lobectomy," and Burden's theory increases his distance
and remoteness through a process of dehumanization. In "Robert
Penn Warren as Allegorist: The Example of *Wilderness*" (*Rendezvous* 6,i:13–21), Allen Shepherd sees the seventh novel as Warren's
first in which "character and action grow out of meaning"; with its
curious mingling of Bunyanesque allegory and conventional novelistic
technique, *Wilderness* has both "mimetic thinness and instructive
clarity."

Richard Pearce's *William Styron* (UMPAW 98) is a nicely unified
pamphlet which places *The Long March* in a thematically central

place in Styron's career. Characterizing all the work is the feeling of war as the condition of life, a postwar perspective that makes Styron as close to Heller as to Mailer. If Christian humanism is a given, so is the apocalyptic view that "denies the possibility of knowledge, order, or salvation." Pearce makes an important distinction between the traditional apocalyptic view (linear and temporal) and the new one which is ahistorical and nonrational.

Appropriately placed in a section called "Polemics," Joan Mellen's "William Styron: The Absence of Social Definition" (*Novel* 4:159–70) is a thoughtful article which deplores the novelist's "dissembling attitude toward social and historical" dimensions of his subjects and his tendency to declaim rather than dramatize social contexts. She sees in all of his works empty nostalgia, disembodied *Angst*, intellectual clichés borrowed from other writers. In the end, Mellen's attack is extended to Mailer, Bellow, Updike, and others ("a school of sorts, whatever their particular quarrels with each other") who languish in metaphysical despair and the "gratuitous assertiveness of existential will," and concludes with the charge that a "serious American literature of the postwar period has yet to appear."

"William Styron: Heritage and Conscience (*HSE* 5:121–36) is largely on *Lie Down in Darkness* in which Charlotte Kretzoi traces the deterioration in three generations of Loftises and the concomitant intensity of guilt. Feeling responsible for the sorry present, the "questing" heroes display guilt which really "belongs to the tragic inheritance that forces them to commit sins." It is unlikely that Styron, whether as a Christian, traditional Southerner, or existentialist, would be willing to take such an easy way out. In "Rebellion of Wrath and Laughter: Styron's *Set This House on Fire*" (*SoR* 7:1007–20), Marc L. Ratner contends that by means of cartoon-like characters and caricatures, gothic excesses, bombast, and burlesque, Styron's third novel is not tragedy but satire. The book is a confessional psychodrama as well as a satire on the romantic-puritan character of American life. Although it suffers from an occluded sense of definition and wobbly generic distinctions, Ratner's essay contains valuable observations.

Nancy M. Tischler has assembled a symposium on *The Confessions of Nat Turner* (*BaratR* 6,i:3–37)—five essays gathered from the 1969 MLA seminar on Religion and Literature and "A Letter from William Styron" commenting on them. Jean S. Mullen's "Styron's Nat Turner: A Search for Humanity" (pp. 6–11), primarily a summary of the controversy over the novel, makes the point that the "hard message" of the book is the necessity for forgiveness. The most learned piece is Dalma H. Brunauer's "Black and White: The Archetypal Myth and Its Development" (pp. 12–20), which attempts to disentangle the confusion surrounding the concepts of "black, dark and evil on the one hand and white, light and good on the other." Through an examination of Babylonian, Sumerian, and Hebrew myths, Brunaur concludes that the contrast is not a matter of pigmentation but of the presence or absence of sunlight and that the symbolic dichotomy dates only from the Middle Ages.

In "Nat Turner's Mysticism" (pp. 21–24), Blair Whitney stresses Turner's incapacity for adopting a revolutionist's role because of his reluctance to act except in accordance with his sporadic mystic experiences, and even his religion is too personal to inspire disciples after his death. Patricia R. Cannon's "Nat Turner: God, Man, or Beast?" (pp. 25–28) demonstrates that Styron's biblical "pastiche" yields only two of the possible aspects of Christ—the ritual scapegoat and the suffering saviour. But even though he is only a "messiah *manqué*," the fact that a novelist wrote the book in biblical terms implies the "salvific function of the Nat Turner legend." Sanford Pinsker also finds that Styron gradually shifts his hero from the role of Old Testament prophet to an avatar of Christ, but he makes the unmystical observation in "Christ as Revolutionary / Revolutionary as Christ: The Hero in Bernard Malamud's *The Fixer* and William Styron's *The Confessions of Nat Turner*" (pp. 29–37) that Turner's sexual vacillations "are a sort of shorthand way of representing the tensions between Nat's commitment to the spiritual and his growing attraction to the fleshly."

Allen Shepherd, in "'Hopeless Paradox' and *The Confessions of Nat Turner* (*RANAM* 4:87–91), focuses on the protagonist's recurring dream and connects it to the dilemma of his being simultaneously a freedman and a slave; it represents the paradox of a man who looks with contempt upon those he would lead to freedom, who rebels against dehumanization by mass killing, who kills the only woman he has ever loved, and who is ordered to be executed by the only man who ever understands him. Bruce Curtis's "Fiction, Myth and History in William Styron's *Nat Turner*" (*UCQ* 16,ii:27–32) is a shallow little piece which attempts to prove that John Hersey's *The Algiers Motel Incident*, a "nonfictional study of black boys in Detroit," is more effective than Styron's fictional study of a black man in Virginia because it is more "credible." If anyone missed the recriminatory *Nat Turner* debates (1967–1969), John White's summary article is useful; "The Novelist as Historian: William Styron and American Negro Slavery" (*JAmS* 4:233–45) turns up nothing new, but White attempts to detach himself from the imbroglio and tests the novel against scholarship on slavery, for which he gives Styron high marks.

ix. Eudora Welty and Carson McCullers

American students will find little of usefulness in Marie-Antoinette Manz-Kunz's *Eudora Welty: Aspects of Reality in Her Short Fiction* (Zurich, Franke Verlag) that they cannot find in older, less ponderous studies. Not noticeably coherent, this book is a series of readings of various stories, and the critic's ambitious subject—the examination of "reality" measured through Welty's "mimetic procedure"—is as elusive here as it turns out to be in other similar enterprises. The sections on *The Golden Apples* are helpful and sensible; and there are some interesting observations—such as those on the consonance of the personal rhythm of life with the rhythm of nature in "A Worn Path"— but even here, the articulation is murky and pretentious.

Anne M. Masserand explores the contradictory attractions of the home and the journey in "Eudora Welty's Travellers: The Journey Theme in Her Short Stories" (*SLJ* 3,ii:39–48). Variations of "the Marvellous Stranger" recur often in the short fiction, as a bringer of news who impels others to leave home in order to keep in touch with "vital forces" that can be gained only by journeying. Grant Moss, Jr.,'s "'A Worn Path' Retrod" (*CLAJ* 15:144–52) is a general appreciation of Welty's "small affirmative statement about the human spirit," especially as symbolized by Old Phoenix. M. E. Bradford sees the central issue in Welty's recent novel as "cultural survival." In "Looking Down from a High Place: The Serenity of Miss Welty's *Losing Battles*" (*RANAM* 4:92–97), Bradford sees the mood as elegiac, which, as a mode of aesthetic perception, invariably rests upon "an affirmation of good losing. . . ." Teachers of "Petrified Man" may be interested in checking W. Keith Kraus's suggestion (*Expl* 29:item 63) that Mrs. Fletcher's name comes from a turn-of-the-century food faddist.

Joseph R. Millichap's "The Realistic Structure of *The Heart Is a*

Lonely Hunter" (*TCL* 17:11–17) is a succinct, intelligent essay that shows an impressive knowledge of McCullers's first book, often dismissed as a modern gothic allegory. The mill city, argues Millichap, is described as a microcosmic social world, and the "legendary" style is carefully contrived to show the failure of communication and the resultant violence in modern society. Janice T. Moore speculates that the fowl imagery in *The Ballad of the Sad Cafe* underscores Lymon's propensity toward evil (*Expl* 29[1970]:item 27).

McCullers's conception of human reality approaches that of Greek tragedy from a Christian perspective, says Yvette Rivière in "L'Aliénation dans les romans de Carson McCullers" (*RANAM* 4:79–86), which contains an especially perceptive sketch of the social and economic sources of the vagabond type as well as the literary (Natty Bumppo, Huck Finn, and the heroes of Jack Kerouac). Of considerable importance is *The Mortgaged Heart: Carson McCullers*, edited by Margarita G. Smith (Boston, Houghton Mifflin), a collection of previously published but uncollected work, mostly stories (including a few student selections from the NYU years), with an interesting group of essays and even some poetry. The introduction by McCullers's sister is commendably informative.

x. Truman Capote and Walker Percy

In *The Worlds of Truman Capote* (New York, Stein and Day, [1970]), William L. Nance sees Capote's fiction shifting markedly after *Other Voices, Other Rooms*: from the stress on confinement and "intensified and distorted consciousness" to liberation with unconventional wanderers seeking some ideal of happiness. If his is a fiction of nostalgia, says Nance, "A Christmas Memory" is one of his most satisfying works; but he nevertheless devotes a large proportion of his book to the principles behind and the execution of *In Cold Blood*. Although the documentary novelist may be doomed to wander between the poles of journalistic factuality and imaginative power, Capote attempted "to force the poles together" simply by not keeping his research distinct from his deepest personal life. Nance is perceptive when he discusses the problem of dramatized narrators and impersonal narration and in showing how a blending of chance and art in this nonfiction novel extends character types, themes, and emotional tones from Capote's earlier fiction. Nance's book, however, is most alive when it is most gossipy—with stories of Capote's misadventures in stage work, of his journalistic work prior to *In Cold Blood*, of how he behaves at home, on talk shows, and as host of five hundred close friends at the Plaza Hotel. Nance's book may not win any awards from the deep readers of the world, but then neither will his subject.

Donald Pizer also explores the nonfiction novel in "Documentary Narrative as Art: William Manchester and Truman Capote" (*JML* 2:105–18), an exercise in definition as well as an evaluative comparison. The form, says Pizer, lays great stress on seemingly verifiable detail and chronology; since he juxtaposes two of the most verifiable aspects of experience—"objects and the movement of the clock"—the author of documentary narrative attests to his credibility as storyteller by constantly appealing to his story's principal components. Manchester's *Death of a President* fails as art because its author is so totally absorbed in event as event, while Capote's *In Cold Blood* succeeds in explaining event as meaning.

Simone Vauthier's "Le Temps et la mort dans *The Moviegoer*" (*RANAM* 4:98–115) is yet another treatment of *rotation* and *repetition*, two of Bolling's existential tactics, but the discussion proceeds with authority and style. Vauthier, who observes that Bolling's quest is always conducted in the implicit presence of death, sees the conclusion as less optimistic and as more fabricated than the narrative line makes it appear to be.

In comparing the protagonists of "Percy's *The Moviegoer* and Warren's *All the King's Men*" (*NMW* 4:2–14), Allen Shepherd finds, among other things, that Bolling and Burden both use comparable means to similar ends, each arriving finally at a "somewhat suspect redemptory epilogue." Communion, says Shepherd, is the key to the sought-after resolution in both novels.

Two critics discuss the importance of William Alexander Percy in the novelist's cultural and philosophical development. Jim Van Cleave, in "Versions of Percy" (*SoR*[1970]:990–1010), sees Bolling's inability "to talk the same language as his Aunt Emily" a dramatized version of the distance between the idealism of the older Percy and the tortured existential realism of his nephew. The biographical relationships and the tensions between the two Percys are, however, forgotten halfway through a much too prolix essay. Clearer, and more accurate in its facts, is Lewis A. Lawson's "Walker Percy's

Southern Stoic" (*SLJ* 3,i:5–31), which shows the enabling dialectic to be between the Stoic attitude as it was suited to an earlier South and a rejection of it as irrelevant to a generation which must cherish the self, not merely the view, of another. Such a dialectic lies behind the father-son relationships in both *The Moviegoer* and *The Last Gentleman.*

In "An Interview with Walker Percy" (*GaR* 25:317–32), the novelist admits to John Carr that "ideological divisions" existed between his views and those of the elder Percy. In his fine tribute to "my uncle, who was also my adoptive father," Percy touches on other subjects —the relative intensity and chronology of the influence on him of Kierkegaard, Sartre, and Marx. Carr's is a more ambitious and fuller interview than Charles T. Bunting's "An Afternoon with Walker Percy" (*NMW* 4:43–61), which nevertheless gives an important glimpse into what Percy calls the "agony of the craft, of getting it right."

xi. James Agee and John Updike

In an impressive analysis of Agee's "severe aesthetic," "The Plot Against Fiction: *Let Us Now Praise Famous Men*" (*SLJ* 4,i:48–67), Eugene Chesnick characterizes Agee's as a romantic vision which distrusts the imagination, a faculty deified by ordinary romantics, and stakes everything on consciousness, the immediate apprehension of created being. What begins as a project to capture the real world in a new way—consciousness untainted by imagination—evolves into a study of authorial anxieties; this genreless work, concludes Chesnick, answers Agee's need to define an interior self even as he worries the objective exterior reality of Alabama tenants into shape.

Two critics have called for a new corrected edition of Agee's posthumous novel. Gene W. Ruoff argues that "*A Death in the Family*: Agee's 'Unfinished' Novel" (*The Fifties*, pp. 121–32) is not nearly so unfinished as its editors assumed when they issued it in 1957. The two lengthy sequences "of limited internal coherence" belong to Agee's collected prose, not to this novel, and the decision to incorporate them, says Ruoff, is misplaced devotion to the author. Victor A. Kramer, in "The Manuscript and the Text of James Agee's *A Death in the Family*" (*PBSA* 65:257–66), finds errors as well as editorial alterations in the present text and gives as sample evidence a list of misreadings from the first chapter.

For the second edition of *Letters of James Agee to Father Flye* (Boston, Houghton Mifflin), the kind of casually assembled volume that sends bibliographers up the wall, Flye includes "some" of his letters to Agee from 1938 to 1950, and Robert Phelps contributes an appreciative reminiscence of both men.

Two books with special emphases give readings of Updike that remain partial. Rachael C. Burchard's *John Updike: Yea Sayings* (Carbondale, So. Ill. Univ. Press) is a simplistic account of the importance of affirmative Christianity in the novelist's works. In *The Poorhouse Fair* both Conner and Hook are seen as inadequate because of that "missing ingredient"; *Rabbit, Run* is about a moral derelict whose Christian intuition (as well as instruction) allows the novel to end somehow with a "sudden unreasonable but optimistic lift"; and *The Centaur* resolves itself similarly with the transcendent Sagittarius epilogue. In an overlong and curiously misdirected chapter, we are treated to an irrelevant defense of *Couples* against charges that Updike wrote it for shock value and to an incredible argument that the novel is a "modern art form of many dimensions" which exploits "multidimensional media."

Larry E. Taylor's thesis in *Pastoral and Anti-Pastoral Patterns in John Updike's Fiction* (Carbondale, So. Ill. Univ. Press) is not merely that pastoral is an important element in Updike's work but that pastoral patterns exist as a "strong, historically traceable current in the American literary tradition." Taylor gives a splendid treatment of the early stories and *The Poorhouse Fair*, in which the pastoral mode dominates and of the antipastoral *Rabbit, Run*, with its fableistic and satiric aspects; his account of the structure and language of *The Centaur* is almost good enough to convince us that it is Updike's finest work. Finally, however, neither Burchard's affirmative tests nor Taylor's pastoral patterns do much to show us Updike's artistic uniqueness.

Tony Tanner (*City of Words*, pp. 273–94) dislikes Updike's indiscriminate use of "myth" to describe the St. Stephen story (*The Poorhouse Fair*), Peter Rabbit (*Rabbit, Run*), and Chiron (*The Centaur*) and finds little credence in the religious referents for the material clutter which ensnares his characters. Though he admires Updike's acceptance of suburbia as his given world without the radical repatterning of actual society, he still finds a feeling of "cosmic vertigo" beneath the lacquered realism of the surfaces.

David Myers, in "The Questing Fear: Christian Allegory in John Updike's *The Centaur*" (*TCL* 17:73–82), believes the structure in this novel to be based on the allegory of the victory of goodness over death. Although Greek myth is pervasive in whimsical allusion, satire, and surrealist nightmare, only the relevance of Christian allegory accommodates its varied manifestations. In "Updike's *Couples*: Eros Demythologized" (*TCL* 17:235–46), Robert Detweiler discusses what he believes to be a relativistic perspective in Updike's novel based on the "atomic motions and electromagnetic force fields of the Einsteinian universe," a perspective which can be seen in plotting, point of view, and fictive texture and which insists upon pluralistic customs, ideas, models. The final vision suggests Tillich's "Gestalt of space" as well as the "autonomous secularism" that informs most of the novel.

xii. Ralph Ellison and Other Black Writers

Tony Tanner (*City of Words*, pp. 50–63) believes musical improvisation to be Ellison's model for his difficult balancing act in *Invisible Man* between Procrustean molds and Protean fluidity; the protagonist's tack is to learn the patterning power of his own mind, not the patterns of the external world, which means a rejection of both the surface identities of Norton and Brother Jack and the subterranean fluidity of Rinehart. Marcia R. Lieberman, however, sees Ellison's protagonist as continuing a European literary tradition, the "Simple Simon who scarcely perceives reality and thus can barely fend for himself in a world of foxes and wolves." In "Moral Innocents: Ellison's *Invisible Man* and *Candide*" (*CLAJ* 15:64–79), she draws parallels between Voltaire's *ingénu* and the narrative structure, point of view, and moral intention of *Candide* and that of Ellison's "sceptical and conservative book."

In "The Journey Towards Castration: Interracial Sexual Stereotypes in Ellison's *Invisible Man*" (*JAmS* 4:227–31), Frederick L. Radford examines four episodes which show Ellison's use of white sexual myths and black counter-myths. The battle royal (Ellison's brilliant substitute for the obligatory lynch scene) and the confrontation between Norton and Trueblood (demonstrating "white sexual hypocrisy and black sexual honesty") are subtle and distanced art. Ellison is less successful, says Radford, in his use of black counter-myths of the white woman.

Two important checklists appeared. Bernard Benoit and Michel Fabre's "A Bibliography of Ralph Ellison's Published Writings" (*SBL* 2,iii:25–28) supersedes R. S. Lillard's 1968 bibliography in the *American Book Collector*; it locates a few new items between 1937 and 1967 as well as some items after 1968 and up to June 1971. Jacqueline Covo's "Ralph Waldo Ellison: Bibliographic Essays and Finding List of American Criticism, 1952–1964" (*CLAJ* 15:171–96) is a valuable adjunct to Benoit and Fabre. J. D. Bell discusses Ellison's allusion to the old Dixieland song, "Ballin' the Jack," in the epilogue of *Invisible Man* (*Expl* 29[1970], item 19); and Ronald G. Rollins speculates on the significance of the name of Lucius Brockway (*Expl* 30, item 22).[4]

Apropos the complaint that black writing is almost entirely a literature of protest, Raman K. Singh flatly declares in "The Black Novel and Its Tradition" (*ColQ* 20:23–29) that "*all* literature is protest writ large." After playing fast and loose with his key term (Shakespeare and Eliot emerge as significant protest writers), Singh distinguishes the black novel from "the American novel" by the nature of the quest for identity: white protagonists tend to lose their identities while black ones find theirs. Even the illustrative use of Jean Toomer and William Demby fails to make a coherent case for this approach.

Stephen B. Bennett and William W. Nichols do better with "Violence in Afro-American Fiction: An Hypothesis" (*MFS* 17:221–28), in which they explore the equation between "violent assertion and self-realization." Unlike the romanticized violence of white-dominated pop culture, the "creative violence" in the fiction of Ellison, Baldwin, Wright, and Bontemps often allows a character to discover his humanity. They suggest that apocalyptic rage associated with recent black militancy has long been a part of the imagination of the best black writers.

In "The Black Aesthetic in White America" (*PR* 38:376–95), Morris Dickstein charges that no white critics have responsibly engaged black writing of the past decade, partly as a response to the

4. Teachers of Ellison's novel will find Ronald Gottesman's compilation, *Studies in "Invisible Man"* (Columbus, Ohio, Charles E. Merrill), a useful, compact anthology of seven previously published essays and the *Paris Review* interview with Ellison.

Keep Out signs posted by militant blacks. James Alan McPherson and Cecil Brown, among others, are seen as a vigorous new generation of black writers "who may help find a new solution to the problem of literature and ideology." In "From Protest to Paradox: The Black Writer at Mid Century" (*The Fifties*, pp. 217–40), C. W. E. Bigsby argues that Baldwin and Ellison are important for the 1950s because they saw in the racial situation not materials for the naturalistic and proletarian novels, both outworn forms, but "a powerful image of alienation, absurdity and anomie which spoke to a wider audience than that commanded by either the self-confident exoticism of the Negro Renaissance or the simplistic commitment of the Depression era." This acute summary essay also deals briefly with William Gardner Smith, Willard Motley, John O. Killens, and William Demby.

Nancy M. Tischler extends her work on black stereotypes with "The Metamorphosis of the Brute Negro" (*RANAM* 4:3–11). From his beginnings in Thomas Dixon and his less brutal manifestations in Julia Peterkin and T. S. Stribling, the type has become in the hands of Wright, Ellison, and Baldwin the classic American hero—"proud, virile, outspoken, emotional" but also "full of hidden longings, uprooted from his origins." Nancy Y. Hoffman makes admirable insights into William Demby's best-known novel through a discussion of its avant-garde experiments. "Technique in Demby's *The Catacombs*" (*SBL* 2,ii:10–13) associates this black writer with Borges and Nabokov (in the blurring of categories of reality and fantasy), Teilhard (in the confessional aspects), and McLuhan (in the use of techniques simulating simultaneity of time through newspaper headlines).

Frances S. Foster writes a general introduction to "Charles Wright: Black Black Humorist" (*CLAJ* 15:44–53), suggesting that the author of *The Wig* belongs to the school of Bruce Jay Friedman and Thomas Berger. In "Black Jesus: A Study of Kelley's *A Different Drummer*" (*SBL* 2,ii:13–15), Robert L. Nadeau argues that William M. Kelley's attack on the stereotypical views of blacks seen through the social and economic structures of American society derives from the Transcendentalists' affirmation of self-reliance.

Robert E. McDowell has guest-edited a special number of *Studies in the Novel* devoted to black novelists, and perhaps its most valuable item is "A Checklist of Books and Essays About American Negro Novelists" (*SNNTS* 3:219–36). It includes general discussions as well as works on individual authors, and its compilers are McDowell and

George Fortenberry. Albert Gerard's "The Sons of Ham," translated by Judith H. McDowell (*SNNTS* 3:148–64), is mainly devoted to Baldwin, who in *Another Country* achieves the fundamental aim of the Afro-American novel—showing how the Negro emerges "as a modality of the condition of man." While it fails to advance our understanding of Baldwin very substantially, it is a measured and graceful contribution.

Eldridge Cleaver and LeRoi Jones are the particular targets of John V. Hagopian's "Mau-Mauing the Literary Establishment" (*SNNTS* 3:135–47): what may have been appropriate in the war against racial injustice (sloganeering, intimidation) has, says Hagopian, only trivialized and corrupted most black literature of recent vintage. Nick Aaron Ford, on the other hand, in "A Note on Ishmael Reed: Revolutionary Novelist" (*SNNTS* 3:216–18), finds noteworthy and sufficient that the author of *The Free-Lance Pallbearers* is not the best but merely the "most revolutionary" of recent black novelists. Finally, Charles D. Peavy, in "The Black Revolutionary Novel, 1899–1969" (*SNNTS* 3:180–89), contends that black fiction of the late 1960s, supposedly influenced by increased social militancy, actually is a continuation of a seminal work of 1899, Sutton Griggs's *Imperium in Imperio*—about a black students' revolt at a Tennessee Negro college.

xiii. Others

a. **John Hawkes.**   Don Greiner is surely right in believing that black humor, though it rejects stable social norms and cultivates violence in a perspective of detachment, still is able "to suggest hope," but his "Strange Laughter: The Comedy of John Hawkes" (*SWR* 56:318–28) is finally better at showing how traditional theories of comedy fail to explain black humor than in developing a persuasive alternative explanation. In addition to Hawkes, Greiner uses O'Connor, Heller, West, and others as illustrative cases.

According to Tony Tanner (*City of Words*, pp. 202–29), time becomes subordinate to topography in the fiction of Hawkes, who regards with suspicion landscapes that once were considered stable and conducive to values. In demonstrating how Hawkes's mannered foregrounds are carefully sculpted as formalized shapes of man's deepest urgencies, Tanner is particularly good in his discussion of the symbolic functions of the two islands in *Second Skin*. The technical articulaton of those urgencies in two "anxiety dreams" is the subject of "John Hawkes and the Dream-Work of *The Lime Twig* and *Second Skin*" (*L&P* 21:149–60), in which John C. Stubbs argues that the source of Hawkes's power lies in the delicate balance achieved between "conscious ordering and liberated visualizations of the unconscious."

b. **J. P. Donleavy.** In "The Evolution of Donleavy's Hero" (*Crit* 12,iii:95–109), Dean Cohen traces the functional use of the folktale of the gingerbread man, the simple story that becomes a terrifying fable of man's course through life, a progress from danger to danger until he is finally devoured. In this imaginative essay, Cohen traces the continuities of character and the escalation of horror from *The Ginger Man* to *The Saddest Summer of Samuel S.*

Another approach to Donleavy's hero is "The Novelist as Clown: The Fiction of J. P. Donleavy" (*Meanjin* 29 [1970]:108–14) by Maurice Vintner, who sees this novelist's rogues in a great comic tradition, blending "comedy and mockery and fine irony and farce with loss and grief and real loneliness to provide a comment on life." But for all his variations on the rogue hero, says Thomas LeClair, all of Donleavy's novels are obsessively concerned with death ("A Case of Death: The Fiction of J. P. Donleavy," *ConL* 12:329–44); the very extremity of death in *The Ginger Man* accounts for its power, and Donleavy's retreat from it in succeeding novels accounts for both the sentimentality and slackness of technique.

c. **Philip Roth and James Purdy.** Tony Tanner reads *Herzog* and *Portnoy's Complaint* as "crucial novels" in an increasingly popular genre—the confession of self-analysis (*City of Words*, pp. 295–321). Both Bellow and Roth strive to touch the reader's impulse to participate in retrospective discontent with the self. Roth's novel, says Tanner, is not a profound analysis of the "lower depths of the psyche," since most of the energy behind it is in "recomposing the 'decomposing' self"; without "latent content" because its hero is determined to dredge everything to the surface, the reality of the novel lies only in the "nervous inventiveness" of its rhetoric. Eileen Z. Cohen's "Alex in Wonderland, or *Portnoy's Complaint*" (*TCL* 17:161–68) is a somewhat improbable comparison of Lewis Carroll's Alice and Roth's protagonist: both "must wander through their nightmare visions to discover who they are."

In his fine essay on James Purdy (*City of Words*, pp. 85–108), Tanner finds that his fiction is haunted by gradual and mysterious collapse, an "inward vanishing and fading away," in which both characters and their actions are attenuated. All the novels concern the deprivations common to those who must accommodate to an "overwhelmingly literate and verbalizing world."

In a similar vein, Donald Pease, in "James Purdy: Shaman in Nowhere Land" (*The Fifties*, pp. 145–54), sees the keynote of Purdy's work to be the "impossibility of rebirth in America." He is especially good in tracing the evidences of social infantilism in *Malcolm*—totemic identifications, gratuitous ceremonies, fairy-tale longings, and the like.

Indiana University

14. Poetry: 1900 to the 1930s

Richard Crowder

Pound and Crane received most of the important critical attention this year. The usually popular Frost was given a rest. After the spurt of his centennial Robinson was again the object of few studies. As for the total output, in addition to biographies and critical investigations of varying quality, scholars produced such helps as a concordance, bibliographies, and a reissued index. The *Explicator* (Vol. 29) published six items on Frost, three each on Cummings and Robinson, and one each on Crane and Ransom. That no one tried an analysis of a passage in Pound is interesting: the problems are numerous and complex; a single page of explication would hardly be a pinprick.

On the other hand, Pound was most popular with graduate students (seven dissertations). Frost and Crane were next (five), followed by Jeffers (four), then MacLeish, Robinson, and Cummings (two), and Millay, Ransom, and Cullen (one). These total thirty, as contrasted with only eighteen last year.

i. General

Allen Tate edited *Six American Poets from Emily Dickinson to the Present* (Minneapolis, Univ. of Minn. Press), which reprints the UMPAW pamphlets on Dickinson, Robinson, Marianne Moore, Aiken, Cummings, and Crane, with some useful editorial additions. The bibliographies are grouped together at the back. A good index has been added, which will make the essays much easier to use than they were in pamphlet form. Tate has written a six-page introduction, in which he classifies Robinson as "pre-modernist"; Aiken, Cummings, and Crane as "modernist"; and Moore as "unique" like Dickinson. He devotes considerable space to Aiken, whom he places "above Pound . . . and at the top with Eliot." He predicts that time will prove three other poets among the best of this generation: Ransom, Van Doren, and Wheelock.

In "Bacchus and Merlin: The Dialectic of Romantic Poetry in America" (*SoR* 7:140–75), Harold Bloom sees the romantic tradition as set by Emerson's "Merlin" and "Bacchus" and continued by Robinson and Crane with others. He defines that tradition as the "interplay between the assertion of imagination's autonomy, and a shrewd skepticism of any phenomenon reaching too far into the unconditioned."

Igor Zhuravlev's "The Relationships Between Socialist Poetry in the U.S.A. at the Beginning of the Twentieth Century and the Graphic Arts of the Socialist Press" (*ZAA* 18[1970]:168–82) is an interesting oddity, politically oriented. After pointing to such obvious connections as Markham's "The Man with the Hoe" with the Millet painting and Sandburg's "The Walking Man of Rodin" with the statue of John the Baptist, the author shows the influence of "allegorical drawings . . . in the socialist press" on the verse of an acquaintance of Jack London, F. Bamford. Arturo Giovannitti's "When the Great Day Came" (1918) is traced to Delacroix's "Revolution." The comic-strip character Henry Dubb is shown to have been introduced into songs and verses of the time (D. Guiles, F. Adkins, R. Leemans, A. Stirnson). Zhuravlev has been led into the paths of banality for the sake of propaganda.

ii. Ezra Pound

In *Discretions* (Boston, Little, Brown) Pound's illegitimate daughter (by Olga Rudge), Mary de Rachewiltz, tells the story of her growing up in Italy: the northern mountains and Rapallo, her marriage to an Italian, half Russian, their restoration of a remote castle. Intimate family anecdotes bring light to bear on obscure lines in the *Cantos*. There is a three-page list of "citations" (showing that the author quotes more lines from the second half of the *Cantos* than from the first) but no index. The style is too "literary" to be palatable; sometimes indeed it borders on the simpering, with references to Mamme, Tatte, Mamile, Tattile, Babbo, and Moidile; and attempts at local color through the employment of Italian and other foreign languages are irritating. The final effect is at the edge of the gush of an adoring (and prejudiced) teen-aged daughter. One ought to read this book and study its pictures, but Moidile's stylistic eccentricities are hard to take.

Last year in this chapter we noted excerpts from Hugh Kenner's *The Pound Era* (Berkeley, Univ. of Calif. Press) as they appeared in various periodicals. Now the big study has been published in toto. It centers on Pound himself—the restless explorer and inventor, the poet whose insistence on concision led the way out of the mazes of fin-de-siècle verbosity, the polemicist on economics whose life in Rapallo shielded him to such an extent that he never comprehended the shift in actuality from gold to credit in the modern world of finance and industry. This book also pictures Joyce, Picasso, Eliot, Wyndham Lewis, and other notable figures of the first half of the century and what they had in common—a sense of design even in the midst of a period of seemingly chaotic change. The central paradox is the side-by-side existence of metamorphosis and constancy. With brilliant hindsight Kenner sees through the revolutionary movements —for example, Pound's imagism and vorticism and Picasso's "distortions"—to the always present truths they expressed and represented. He makes telling use of the views of contemporaneous art historians, scientists, anthropologists, and philologists to give credence to his thesis and includes helpful photographs of relevant paintings, drawings, and sculptures. Always he returns to Pound, who gives new, twentieth-century meaning to the phrase "tradition and permanence." Concerning Pound's years at St. Elizabeth's, Kenner concentrates on the art that came from incarceration. Despite occasional Poundian peculiarities of style, this book will be indispensable to a profounder reading of the *Cantos*.

The same press has published a second good book on Pound, *The ZBC of Ezra Pound* by Christine Brooke-Rose. Like *The Pound Era* this book bears the stylistic influence of its subject, possibly unnecessarily, but it nevertheless serves the excellent purpose of taking serious beginners by the hand and leading them along the intricate trails that discourage the untutored. Miss Brooke-Rose starts with a quotation from the admittedly difficult canto 98. "Yes, yes, it can be explicated," she promises. Then she quotes Pound's opinions on teaching and learning, leaning largely on *Guide to Kulchur*. Throughout her book she draws from the best critics (Kenner, de Nagy, Davie, et al.) sometimes differing with them, sometimes depending on them for

support and clarification. Chronologically she pursues very thoroughly Pound's growth and development from *A Lume Spento* to the first
of the *Cantos*. She discusses his experiences in translating, the function
of Chinese ideograms and other visual effects, his reliance on early
French love poetry and other sources. Whereas Kenner analyzes the
poetry that emerged from St. Elizabeth's, Miss Brooke-Rose devotes a
good deal of space to the conditions of the imprisonment itself, to
Pound's suffering after World War II (never self-pitying), to the
Bollingen controversy, and to other matters of biography—constantly
following her master's admonishment of making it new. The author
claims frankly that "Pound has never regarded *The Cantos* as telling
the absolute dogmatic truth about anything." On page 265 she invites
the reader to return to page 2 and reread the quotation from canto
98. By this time, it is her intention, he will be caught up in the fascina-
tions of the work of Pound and will be ready to strike out on his own
through the labyrinths. The titles of the twelve chapters are quotations from Pound that gradually illuminate his point of view and
close with "There is no substitute for a lifetime."

In "The View Beyond the Dinghey," Frederick K. Sanders (*SR*
79:433–60) reviews nine recent books about Pound (1966–1969).
Sanders maintains that in college anthologies Pound has been too
scantily represented. He finds some parallels between Pound and
our own Vietnam protestors and between Pound's "enormous self-
confidence" and Milton's. It is the poetry of both men, however, and
not the polemics, which will be their permanent contribution to civilization. Sanders relates Pound to Paul Klee in their "search for the
permanent elements in man's earliest understanding." He admits,
however, that the clarification of Pound's vision of a world civilization
is far from finished but insists that Pound was always loyal to the
United States, that he had a large interest in exploring for his native
country what is involved in taking a major part in the world's cultural
maturation.

In "A Peacock Dinner: The Homage of Pound and Yeats to Wilfrid Scawen Blunt" (*JML* 1:303–10) William T. Going describes the
tribute to Blunt organized by Pound and sponsored by Yeats in January 1914. Going thinks Pound was not attracted to Blunt's poems so
much as to his candid attacks on England's foreign policy—especially
in India, Egypt, and Ireland. In a clarifying footnote Eric Homberger in "Pound, Ford and 'Prose': The Making of a Modern Poet"

(*JAmS* 5:281–92), disagrees with Herbert N. Schneidau's opinion that Pound's "image" was an intensified version of Ford Madox Ford's "impression." He says that Ford's influence was in another direction —in the insistence that the vocabulary of poetry should be identical with that of prose. Homberger traces the effect of Ford on Pound from an essay of Ford's which Pound forwarded to Harriet Monroe, "Impressionism—Some Speculations," the thesis being the necessity of "rendering one's own time in the terms of one's own time." By 1916 Pound had come to the view that he must have the attitude of a scientist in order to protect himself from the prudish morality of the England of the period. By so doing, he had alienated himself from the school of conventional poets in order to become "modern." In the ongoing debate as to who was responsible for Pound's release from St. Elizabeth's, Ronald H. Bayes, in "Who Sprung Ezra? Continued Speculation" (*Univ. of Portland Rev.* 20[1968]:47–48), says that Senator Richard L. Neuberger of Oregon requested "the Legislative Service" to investigate the matter. Neuberger's letters to Bayes are now in the Houghton Library.

Several new Pound letters were published recently. Stanislaw Helsztynski presents "Ezra Pound's Letters to a Polish Scholar" (*KN* 17[1970]:299–323). The article includes four letters to Mme. Stephane de Yankowska (in London) and forty-five letters to her brother, Stanislaw "Stan" Wiktor Jankowski (in California, later in Maryland, then in Australia). Writing from St. Elizabeth's, Pound arranged for Jankowski to stay with friends in Urbana, Maryland, so that he could supervise the Pole's translation of *Benjamin Minor* by Richard (i.e., Ricardus, Prior S. Victoris Parisiensis.) He tried, without success, to secure Jankowski a professorship in East Pakistan. The letters are marked by Pound's usual verve, liberality, impetuosity, learning, and eccentricity. Donald E. Herdick publishes "A New Letter by Ezra Pound about T. S. Eliot" (*MR* 12:287–92). The recipient was Clarence Stratton, an English teacher in a Cleveland high school, to whom Pound discloses that he has been successful in getting publicity in the *New York Times* for his "Bel Esprit," a movement to interest 30 people in giving Eliot financial support for several years so that he would no longer have to work at Lloyd's Bank. The "Bel Esprit" idea had been derived from similar programs for French writers in Paris, but it testifies to Pound's unflagging generosity towards his fellow writers and artists.

John L. Brown, in "Ezra Pound, Comparatist" (*YCGL* 20:37–47), points out that from the time of the publication of *The Spirit of Romance* (1910) Pound was a convinced comparatist. Though he frequently recommended translations, he wondered how a modern man could even think if he knew only one language. He scorned such college courses as American literature: "You might as well give courses in 'American chemistry.'" Brown discusses Pound's concern with the other arts, especially painting and music. Because of his devotion to the practical side of making poems, he was interested in comparative prosody, even to the point of speculation about the verse structures of the Hittites and the Babylonians. Pound had great faith in art as the expression of the permanence and unity of human qualities (not just American or English or French).

Lillian Feder supports the thesis that the images of death in Pound's poetry often rise from repression and rage brought on by a spiritual and emotional frigidity in the unconscious minds of the mythical personae. Her essay is called "The Voice from Hades in the Poetry of Ezra Pound" (*MQR* 10:167–86). The function of Hell as means of purification as developed by Pound is the subject of Wolfhard Hlawatsch's "Ezra Pounds Weg zum Licht: Eine Interpretation von *Canto XV*" (*NS* 18[1969]:551–57). Drawing from the *Divine Comedy*, Pound demonstrates the depravity and ignorance of the current world. He wants to reestablish man's consciousness of the evils of profiteering. With his eyes on the mirror (compare Athena-Perseus-Medusa), man can find the way to the Light. In addition Hlawatsch suggests that in this canto there are parallels with the tenets of Islam. Hell can be a useful experience in cleansing man of worldly corruption. Ron Baar criticizes Pound's vigor in attacking illicit money-making. In "Ezra Pound: Poet as Historian" (*AL* 42:531–43) Baar declares that in cantos 37, 88, and 89, where Pound is describing the Bank War of the early nineteenth century, the poet "overstates his case beyond defense." Daniel Cory has some "Second Thoughts on Ezra Pound" (*Encounter* 37,iv:86–92) as he replies to critics of an earlier essay of his in which, he insists, he was quoting Pound's exact words from their conversation in Venice. He is sure that the poet has "certain misgivings" about parts of the *Cantos*. As for Cory's own "intellectual equipment," his critics apparently object to his approach: he simply has read—very carefully—what Pound has written, without studying any commentaries or critiques resulting from the research of others. Cory is almost sarcastic about "the academic racket." He enjoys "the moments of splendour" in the *Cantos*, but frankly finds them rare. (Perhaps an occasional naif in our midst is good for us all.)

Scholars will be glad to know that the University of California Press (Berkeley) has reissued the *Annotated Index to the Cantos of Ezra Pound: Cantos I–LXXXIV* (1957), compiled by John H. Edwards and William W. Vasse, assisted by John J. Espey and Frederick Peachy. Furthermore, Jeannette Lander's critical *Ezra Pound*, first published in Berlin (Colloquium [1968]), is now available in America (New York, Ungar).

iii. Hart Crane

In reviewing two biographical works about Crane, Paul L. Mariani ("Words for Hart Crane," *HSL* 3:150–53) thinks Susan Jenkins Brown's book is lightweight and John E. Unterecker's sometimes too heavyweight. (Both books were reviewed in *ALS 1969*.) One of Unterecker's contributions, however, is to emphasize the meditative side of the poet, for Crane was not always a roaring, self-indulgent celebrant of the flesh. Mariani suggests a need for "a study of Crane's baroque sensibility," an analysis of the poet's vision, "even some old-fashioned *explication de texte*." Crane, he reminds us, is as yet far from canonized.

Several essays deal with influences and parallels. Marc Simon, in "Hart Crane and Samuel B. Greenberg: An Emblematic Interlude" (*ConL* 12:166–72) points out that Crane first read Greenberg's poetry in 1923, after which he wrote "Emblems of Conduct," borrowing a few phrases from six of the older writer's poems and paralleling his techniques of repetition. To a special issue of the Birmingham-Southern College *Bulletin* (63,ii)—*Essays in Honor of Richebourg Gaillard McWilliams*, edited by Howard Creed, Robert W. Houston contributes "Hart Crane and Arthur Rimbaud: A Comparison" (pp. 13–19). The author shows how the two poets use similar imagery with similar frequency and intensity: "an odd collection . . . waters, wings, Negroes . . . , idealized female figures . . . , Indians, cities, bridges, polar regions, intense colors, flowers." Houston examines the function in both writers of the journey as symbol in the search for personal identity and poetic source, concentrating chiefly on "Voyages" and "Le Bateau ivre." Another apparent influence on Crane was the painter Joseph Stella. George Knox, in "Crane and Stella: Conjunction of Painterly and Poetic Worlds" (*TSLL* 12:689–707), sees a similarity of visionary aspect in Stella's painting of Brooklyn Bridge and *The Bridge*.

In "Hart Crane's Use of 'Symphonic Form'" (*A-A* 2[1970]:15–29), Elizabeth Huberman demonstrates how Crane prefigures his themes in *The Bridge*, then states them, then calls them back through "repetition, parallel and variation." His "telescoped language" gives the impression that multiple meanings are being expressed simultaneously, as in a symphony. The author examines "Faustus and Helen" as an early example of this form of composition. Having gone beyond the compression of the short lyric, Crane had now found space for complexity of detail but clarity of the whole. As he approached the problems of *The Bridge*, he saw "symphonic form" as the solution to the need for contrasting and condensing "into a single frame many large-scale elements far distant from each other in nature, time, and place." With the pervading theme of Columbus, Crane binds the parts of the poem together "into a single whole" by means of "recurrences, variations, and transformations." The symphonic "sounding together" of the various themes gives the work "sweep and movement" so that ambiguity, sentimentality, and obscurity are minimized "in the full choir of meaning." In "The Theory of Relativity and *The Bridge*" (*HSL* 3:108–15) James C. Cowan seeks out possible allusions to Einstein's theory. In Cowan's opinion the bridge suggests for Crane "universal law beyond itself, . . . the constant velocity of light, as it takes its curvilinear path through world space." When the poet describes his bridge as "One arc synoptic of all tides below," he is clearly delineating the function of the Einstein theory, Cowan believes.

M. D. Uroff contributes two Crane studies. "Hart Crane's 'Recitative'" (*CP* 3[1970]:22–27) is "a relative early statement" of a dominant theme: "the restorative powers of the poet's vision in a dark and divided world." The poem is structured like a formal oration leading into a final summation. Even if the structure is uncomplex, the idea is paradoxically "complex and exceedingly direct" at the same time.

The poet assumes a stance of representative man seen from three different angles: as "isolated artist," as "man among men," and as "poet" addressing himself. The author, in looking at the poem stanza by stanza, finds a means of the poet's securing unity through "inspired vision." Her other essay is entitled "The Imagery of Violence in Hart Crane's Poetry" (*AL* 43:200–16). Violence, she says, is central to the poet's work. His art destroys, is violent, in order to achieve purity and ecstasy. Among his metaphors are a consuming and purifying fire, a destructive wind, and "the act of breakage," which generates the "energy and meaning of life." The author illustrates her point with several poems, including, of course, "The Broken Tower," which is the subject of another article, by George Knox—" 'Sight, Sound and Flesh': Synoptic View from Crane's Tower" (*MarkhamR* 3:1–10). In an effort to get at what the poem is a summary of, Knox reviews the interpretations of earlier readers and quotes from Peggy Baird's explanation. After citing imagery from earlier poems as well as letters to various friends and mentioning the influence of Jessie Weston's *From Ritual to Romance,* he concludes that "the bell-ringing was a summational symbolic act" and states emphatically that "the tower and the lake in the last stanza are penis and vagina." The ringing of the bells "was a crucial and climacteric intersection of the symbolic and the existential, the desire and the vision, the hope and the ultimate despair." This is an ingenious and candid reading that ought to provoke debate.

Richard P. Sugg, in "The Imagination's White Buildings and 'Quaker Hill' " (*ErasmusR* 1:145–55), sees in the "Quaker Hill" section of *The Bridge* a continuation from Crane's first book of poems of the search for some kind of "architectural embodiment within the world of the real." He sees in the poem the necessity of moving beyond stoic acceptance of death (Quakerism) toward affirmation of love and flesh. The poet is not rejecting the intellect, but seeks unity by means of "movement from intellect *through* flesh to the act of imagination," the construction of a satisfying "poetic architecture equivalent with the imagination's living truth." Richard Hutson, in "Hart Crane's 'Black Tambourine' " (*LWU* 3[1970]:31–36), finds society looking at the poet as inevitably a participant in the "timelessness of uselessness." Having confronted himself thus frankly, the poet, through both subject and form, converts "his humiliation and frustration into art."

iv. Robert Frost and E. A. Robinson

An anonymous reviewer in *TLS* ("A Writer of Poems: The Life and Work of Robert Frost," 16 April:433–34) is disturbed by Lawrance Thompson's hanging out the dirty laundry in *Robert Frost: The Years of Triumph* (see *ALS 1970*, 288–89). He maintains that the reader does not know Frost's good poems any the better for being told of the "nastiness" in the poet's life. The reviewer also considers *The Poetry of Robert Frost*, edited by Edward Connery Lathem, and is of the opinion that the poetry (particularly after *New Hampshire*, 1923) has a tendency toward "decline." In all of Frost's eleven books only about thirty poems are worthy to be included in "the canon of virtue." The rest are marred by sentimentality. In this Britisher's view, Frost is just a minor poet to whom, however reluctantly, one often returns. As if in response to this negative critic, A. M. Sampley, in "The Myth and the Quest: The Stature of Robert Frost" (*SAQ* 70:287–98), finds in Frost a poet who recognizes and confronts his natural loneliness and wins a victory over his apprehensions, with the result of a sound integrity.

"Robert Frost's Quarrel with Science and Technology" (*GaR* 25:182–205) is investigated by John T. Hiers. Technology and science have benefited mankind but do not explain the problems involved in hate and love. Frost would appear to support the Christian doctrine of faith through all trials rather than the ultimate pessimism of materialism. Man's need is to impose on his universe an order beyond the reach of technology and science. That there is difficulty in giving Frost a fair reading is the opinion of Lewis M. Dabney in "Mortality and Nature: A Cycle of Frost's Lyrics" (*Private Dealings*, pp. 11–31). Dabney says that modern man is uneasy with the pastoral tradition, from which Frost takes his "universal imagery and music of man's fate." The poet's chief theme is the need to accept death as the limit of humanity, no matter how difficult it is to swallow the doctrine. His own direction is toward classical equanimity. Dabney illustrates his point through the seasonal poems, from the invitations of "The Pasture" and "Come In" and the spring poems such as "Two Tramps in Mud-Time" and "Nothing Gold Can Stay" through such summer poems as "Hyla Brook" and "The Oven Bird" and the autumnal pieces (e.g., "After Apple Picking" and "A Leaf Treader") to such winter poems as "Desert Places" and "Stopping by Woods on a Snowy Evening," which "properly completes his cycle." According to Dabney, this last poem shows that, in spite of the inevitable oncoming of death, man can still refresh his spirit in nature, even though such renewal underscores "his isolation in the universe."

Two poems are individually treated, "The Oven Bird" and "Mending Wall." George Monteiro ("Robert Frost's Solitary Singer," *NEQ* 44:134–40) says that "The Oven Bird" is central to the early poetry. Though the world has "diminished," the poet who resists compliance and even transposes to another key if necessary will prove durable, even though he no longer sings in the lyric mode of the tradition. In "Frost's Wall: The View from the Other Side" (*NEQ* 44:653–56), Charles N. Watson, Jr., provides a new, though tentative, reading of "Mending Wall," which poem Frost placed in *North of Boston* as a dramatic monologue (not, as usually classified, a "meditative lyric"). If read thus, argues Watson, one will see that the monologue subtly exposes the speaker as the blind one, not the neighbor, who has understood ("thought of it so well") his father's saying and has decided to live by it. Watson wisely uses "perhaps" in this interpretation.

Frost, of course, was a conscious craftsman. C. Vimala Rao, in "The 'Other Mood': A Note on the Prose of Robert Frost" (*LCrit* 8,iv[1969]:63–69), comments that this poet's wisdom about how a poem comes into being springs from intuition rather than from such learning as Eliot and Arnold drew on. His prose has the "informality and homeliness" of his verse, suggesting more than it explicitly states. Josephine Grieder discusses Frost's comments on and emendations of Pound's "Portrait d'une Femme" ("Robert Frost on Ezra Pound," *NEQ* 44:301–05). He underscored redundancies and made "humorous but critically observant" notes on idiom, phrasing, and word selection. Pound probably never saw these marginalia, which illustrate, however, says the author, Frost's own acuity.

Vrest Orton's *Vermont Afternoons with Robert Frost* (Rutland, Vt., Charles E. Tuttle) provides a slight introductory essay of nineteen brief pages, which give no detailed account of Orton's visits with Frost. The friendship began in 1930. Except for "a couple of times after that" the visits ended in 1955. The book quotes from nine letters to Orton (1930–1931), showing the poet's basic conservatism, his concern with ailing members of his family, and his commitment to friendship with Orton. There are four photographs and several pages of Orton's own verse. ("The ideas were told me by Robert Frost. The form is mine.")

A welcome new reference book is Edward Connery Lathem's *A Concordance to the Poetry of Robert Frost* (New York, Holt Information Services).

As for E. A. Robinson, Ellsworth Barnard ("The Man Who Died Twice," *HSL* 3:154–56), favorable in general towards Louis O. Coxe's *Edwin Arlington Robinson: The Life of Poetry* (see *ALS 1969*, pp. 261–62), is nevertheless puzzled by Coxe's confidence in identifying the subject of "For a Dead Lady" as the poet's mother and his accepting the aging ladies in "Veteran Sirens" as prostitutes. Barnard admits that Robinson is not currently stylish, but feels satisfaction in the way critics continue to write about him because he is a sound poet.

Three individual poems are the subjects of separate articles. Bertrand F. Richards studies the perplexities of "Luke Havergal" in " 'No, There Is Not a Dawn . . .' " (*CLQ* 9:367–74). Because of the generally recognized fascination for Robinson with proper names, Richards sees in "Luke" a reference to Luke 4:23: "Physician, heal thyself" and a connotation of indecision as in *lukewarm*. "Havergal" suggests, on the one hand, the possession of a girl and, on the other, a reference to bitterness (gall). Not pretending to solve the riddle of the poem, Richards considers three possible ways of taking it: (1) "lost love and suicide"; (2) the constant dying of all mankind; and (3) the poet's own despair at the loss (real or imagined) of creative ability. Joseph H. Harkey argues that Eben Flood's second moon is a harvest moon of the past, a synecdochic illusion of times and friends past and gone ("Mr. Flood's Two Moons," *MTJ* 15:20–21). The old man is not tipsy, for after his third drink he dispells the illusion and is "again alone." Harkey sees Flood as not pitiful so much as pathetic, close to tragic, for he has lost friends, happiness, and honor. These two essays are boldly speculative and open to differences of opinion.

N. E. Dunn does not depart so boldly from the customary readings of *Lancelot* (" 'Wreck and Yesterday': The Meaning of Failure in *Lancelot*," *CLQ* 9:349–56), but presents, however, a fresh view of the book. The people of Camelot do not live up to the responsibilities of love, a weakness which carries over to the moral code and commitment of society as a whole, where chivalry has lost strength in succumbing to adultery. Though Lancelot himself recognizes the need for transcendent vision, he gives in to self-indulgence. An individual must discipline his "human" weaknesses if he expects to reach "happiness and fulfillment." Dunn sees parallels between the situation in *Lancelot* and the circumstances of our own time. (We recall that the poet himself said that there was a nebulous relationship between his book and the world of World War I.)

Beginning with *Captain Craig* (1902), says Arthur M. Sampley ("The Power or the Glory: The Dilemma of Edwin Arlington Robinson," *CLQ* 9:357–66), Robinson stressed what was to be his central thesis: that a man must create his own values, regardless of society's opinions. *Merlin* (1917) has man in a complex position where he cannot renounce his responsibilities to society. Like Dunn, Sampley sees *Lancelot* (1920) as indicating the moral necessity of self-renunciation for the sake of society, though *Tristram* (1927) returns to the self-determination of *Captain Craig*. In the long poems after *Tristram* Robinson is less confident in the power of the self to resist stresses in making decisions. (The characters in the many earlier shorter poems are divided about equally between those who can and those who cannot overcome adversity in finding fulfillment.) In spite of his increasing caution about man's ability to establish independent values, "Robinson respected the lonely man groping out his own way." This is an intelligent study of one of the poet's pervading convictions.

Four other items are bibliographical in nature. William White, in "Robinson in Leary's *Articles* . . . *1950–1967*" (*CLQ* 9:374–75), corrects twelve misprints in Leary's list of Robinson essays, but concludes that, even so, there is in every instance a useful clue to counteract the error. Richard Cary ("Additions to the Robinson Collection," *CLQ* 9:377–82) continues his inventory of the Colby College Library wealth of Robinsoniana, including, among other items, nineteen letters from Robinson, three letters to Robinson, and twenty-two letters about Robinson. John W. Pye's *Edwin Arlington Robinson: A Bio-Bibliography* (Hartford, Conn., Watkinson Library, Trinity College [1970]) is a catalogue of the 1969 exhibit of materials in the H. Bacon Collamore Collection at Trinity College. As the continuation of Charles Beecher Hogan's indispensable 1936 *Bibliography*, William White's *Edwin Arlington Robinson: A Supplementary Bibliography* (Kent, Ohio, Kent State Univ. Press) is invaluable. For the most part White follows Hogan's organization and style, which differs somewhat from the MLA and Chicago style manuals. He has filled in

Hogan's inevitable omissions, has included Lillian Lippincott's additional entries in her 1937 *Bibliography*, and has incorporated Hogan's
own additions in the *PBSA*. Probably more important than bringing
these materials together in one volume is White's listing of the titles
of books, articles, and reviews published since Hogan's last work. In
a word, this book and Hogan's 1936 work provide a virtually complete coverage of everything of bibliographical interest to Robinson
scholars to the beginning of 1971. It is highly recommended.

v. Cummings, MacLeish, Ransom, and Davidson

The Cummings material is composed of brief explications. Winfried
Schleiner's "Drei Gedichte von E. E. Cummings" (*LWU* 2[1969]:
27–37), aimed at teachers below college level, is slight. The author
sees "maggie and milly and molly and may" as a quest poem; "my
sweet old etcetera" ends in scatalogical surprise. The author maintains that the obscenity in "i sing of Olaf" is not used exclusively in
conjunction with irony and satire though these are present in the
poem. "Cummings' Last Poem: An Explication" (*LWU* 3[1970]:106–
08) by Jane Donahue examines the last work in *73 Poems* as a statement of the poet's ultimate trust in a lover's insight and capacity
for perceiving the oneness of the universe and for going beyond the
conventional views of the materialist and the idealist. Love, "the
axis of the universe," makes possible "a wholly new order of experience and values." The last word, *believe*, underscores the credal
quality of the poem. Jan Aarts ("A Note on the Interpretation of
'he danced his did,'" (*JL* 7:71–73) applies linguistic techniques to
this half line and emerges with the meaning "he rejoiced in his past
actions." He thinks his fellow linguists sometimes forget (naively?)
that a good poet's departure from orthodox grammar often enhances
his central meaning.

Grover Smith's *Archibald MacLeish* (UMPAW 99) says that
MacLeish has maintained a high level of craftsmanship, but not at
the expense of communication, though his early poems sometimes
make more music than sense. As he turned from musicality, MacLeish
developed "conscious symbolism; witty, almost metaphysical strategies of argument; compressed and intense implications," following
partly in the path of Eliot. In the 1920s he realized that he had to
control his rhetorical predilections through form, and to form he

gave more and more care. Smith's pamphlet follows the usual UMPAW pattern of a chronological description of MacLeish's books, discussing, for example, the "social implications" of his work in the thirties. The author calls attention to the poet's war work, with the resulting long lapse between *America Was Promises* (1939) and *Actfive and Other Poems* (1948). In the few pages devoted to the plays, *J. B.* is labelled "eloquent, superbly theatrical" and *Herakles*, "brittle." Though on the whole MacLeish's standards have been "classical and aristocratic," exclusiveness has been suppressed in favor of humanity and its condition. Like the other pamphlets in the series, this one is chiefly introductory in nature.

Two articles examine the plays. In "The Games God Plays with Man: A Discussion of *J.B.*" (*The Fifties*, pp. 249–59), Sy Kahn studies plot and character from the point of view of a play director. He finds Nickles "the most powerful and attractive spokesman in the play for the agony of man." The tension lies, however, in *J. B.*'s freedom to choose between suicide and living. God's games are beyond human comprehension; so, if J. B. lives, he must expect suffering which can be tempered by an indecipherable belief in constant renewal. Kahn contrasts MacLeish with the Jewish novelist, Elie Wiesel, who, because of his miraculous survival from the Nazi death camps, creates characters "more finely tuned to their agony and anger than the characters in *J. B.*" MacLeish did not, of course, have to play the Jews' game with God at high risk and high stakes and could not bring their agonized experience to his writing. "MacLeish's *Herakles*: Myth for the Modern World," by C. J. Gianakaris (*CentR* 15:445–63), says that this may not be a successful play, but it does warn rather profoundly against allowing technology to triumph over moral commitment as man confronts his frustrations in his search for meaning in existence.

James E. Magner's *John Crowe Ransom: Critical Principles and Preocupations* (The Hague: Mouton) discusses Ransom as an "ontological particularist." Magner explores the influences on Ransom's point of view and dwells at some length on Yvor Winters's conservative reaction to that stance. In a chapter on "The Material Object, the Cause and Nature of the Poem," Magner contrasts Ransom's "metaphorical knowledge" with Richards's "psychic harmony," and Ransom's "poetic dualism" with Brooks's "poetic unity." The author then defines Ransom's ideas about the making of a poem and considers his classifications of poems according to "types" and "ends," his groupings of his contemporaries (Pound, Stevens, Frost, et al.), and his rating of twentieth-century critics. (Magner points out, for example, that, though Ransom agrees with Blackmur in "his attitude toward life, poetry, and art," he finds fault with Blackmur's failure to construct a clear definition of "his critical position." Magner's conclusion is that Ransom lacks rich "philosophic vision" and "the finely honed critical scalpel of a Blackmur," but like Eliot he has insights born of "a deep and far-ranging sensibility." This book is an exhaustive analysis and should be a major work for both Ransom scholars and historians of American criticism.

In "Writers in Crisis" (*Roots* 1[1970]:160–66) Gladys J. Curry rehashes the familiar connections between Ransom's "Philomela" and the unhappy paucity of traditional values in modern American society. Ashley Brown ("Landscape into Art: Henry James and John Crowe Ransom," *SR* 79:206–12) sees a debt in the poem "Old Mansion" to the chapter on Charleston, South Carolina, in James's *The American Scene*. Whereas, however, James stresses space and description, Ransom is interested in the differences between the past and the present South. Reviewing Ransom's *Selected Poems* (1969), Robert Buffington finds an inclination in Ransom to include some earlier poems excluded from previous collections ("The Poetry of the Master's Old Age," *GaR* 25:5–16). Buffington is glad that Ransom has not done much tinkering with his best poems, in spite of an ever-present temptation to revise. In the several extensive changes Buffington detects a preference for shifting words and phrases and a turn toward choppy rhythm and unwarranted terseness. Some passages even approach doggerel. Instead of resolving the ambiguities in "Here Lies a Lady," the poet ignores them. Ransom's belief that there should be limits to the use of irony has weakened his reworked verse.

Thomas Daniel Young and M. Thomas Inge worked together in the preparation of *Donald Davidson* (TUSAS 190). The first chapter reads like an extended obituary, giving the facts of Davidson's life through World War I. Though the second chapter continues the life story, it is more interesting because of its descriptive analysis of the early poems, works of an apprentice, but showing more and more control and presenting an initial statement of his absorption in the deterioration of the postwar world and hinting at his later quest "for a rightful heritage." Chapter 3 discusses his longest poem, *The Tall*

Men, in which he tries to bring his present self into unity with not only his own past but the history of Tennessee and the South. He is now determined to speak out for the necessity of struggling to retain the spiritual values of his heritage as a shield against the destructive power of materialism (symbolized by the industrialism of the North). In chapter 4 the authors show how, in *Lee in the Mountains and Other Poems,* Davidson repeats his utter disdain for men who turn from a "sacred tradition" to the clawing battles in the act of amassing fortunes. The answer appears to be "religious resignation." In Robert E. Lee Davidson finds the ideal symbol, "the noblest of the tall men." *The Long Street* contains many of his best-crafted poems. Marked by an "affirmation of faith" and a "plea for truth and justice," they are more restrained and tolerant than his earlier poems. Then, the last chapter discusses Davidson's prose—reviews, lucid and civilized, and essays, devoted chiefly to supporting Agrarianism as a way of life. Most of the book is about the poetry, for the authors are convinced that Davidson will at last be recognized as a successful poet "because of the totality of [his] vision, the seriousness of his intent, and the integrity of his craftsmanship." This is the first book-length study of a solid Southern poet.

vi. Black Poets

"The Vagabond Motif in the Writings of Claude McKay" is the title of an article by Sister Mary Conroy (*NALF* 5:15–23), who describes McKay's version of love as "the orgastic moment." Sex is his metaphor for the escape implied in vagabondage, but it also expresses the black man's hope of attaining, at least spiritually, "his racial homeland," of which woman is the soil. Converted to Christianity towards the end of his life, McKay found in the church a hope for securing harmony between black and white. The sonnets of this period express his yearning in this direction as well as a faith in "ultimate solace."

Margaret Perry's *Bio-Bibliography of Countee P. Cullen, 1903–1946* (Westport, Conn., Greenwood Publishing Corp.), after a sympathetic introduction by Don M. Wolfe, traces the details of Cullen's life, emphasizing his loyalty to his family and friends, his quiet tenderness of spirit, and his gentle dignity, all of which are apparent in his most characteristic lyrics. In a chapter on "The Poetry of Cullen: An Explanation" the author comments that, as poet, Cullen was unique, partly because among blacks he had a penchant unusually strong for the traditional forms, partly because he did not make a special effort to be a black poet. His weakness lay in his reliance upon ready-made phrases, but when he rose above them his freshness and expression of emotion were easily identified. The author finds some resemblance to Millay in the early poems and thinks of Keats as an influence. What she does not say, but might, is that with careful selection Cullen could be well represented by a few good poems. A chapter in the book is devoted to "Contemporary Reviews of Cullen's Work" and there is a bibliography. Walter C. Daniel writes of "Countee Cullen as Literary Critic" (CLAJ 14:281–90). From November 1926 to March 1928 Cullen was literary critic for *Opportunity*, in a column called "The Dark Tower." He encouraged the use of Negro materials and the evaluation of Negro life by white Americans. Whether they liked it or not, he admonished blacks to make a good impression on whites and not try to interest whites in every phase of the black experience. His influence was sizable on black writing both in what he said and in what he allowed to be published in *Opportunity*.

James Presley says nothing new in "Langston Hughes: A Personal Farewell" (SWR 54:79–84). He reviews the life and work of Hughes, who died in 1967. Hughes had trouble as a literary man "because he was black" and because he "had a small and fickle public, if one at all." His work was never "uniformly fine," but much is worth rediscovery: humor, protest, class struggle, and folk poetry. Frances E. Kearns stresses Hughes's irritation at the slow pace of racial reform, especially in his last poems ("The Un-angry Langston Hughes," YR 50[1970]:154–60), but his characteristic attitude is expressed by his character "Simple": "White folks is the cause of a lot of inconvenience in my life."

Julian C. Carey, in "Jesse B. Semple Revisited and Revised" (Phylon 32:158–63), sees that Hughes's best-known character realizes that the black man is not the problem in racism, for he knows himself to be a human being, a laboring man who happens to be "colored." In "Two American Poets: Their Influence on the Contemporary Art-Song" (XUS 10:33–43), Sister Marie Yestadt says no doubt Hughes's use of jazz and blues rhythms in his poetry attracted composers like John Alden Carpenter. The "Black Pierrot" theme interested other composers: Howard Swanson, William Grant Still, and Jean Berger.

(The other poet the author considers is Whitman.) Hans Finger's "Zwei Beispiele moderner amerikanischer Negerlyrik: Langston Hughes, 'Mother to Son' und Russell Atkins, 'Poem'" (*LWU* 2[1969]: 38–46) concludes that three characteristics of the Negro lyric, judging at least from these two poems, are references to black history, the use of Negro speech idiom, and reliance on spirituals and blues both for symbol and for rhythm.

vii. Jeffers, Sandburg, and Others

Arthur B. Coffin's *Robinson Jeffers, Poet of Inhumanism* (Madison, Univ. of Wis. Press) is not a study of Jeffers's religion or psychology, though he urges other scholars to pursue these areas. He himself attempts to recount the poet's ideological growth towards "inhumanism" and so to focus on "the dynamics of intellect" in the poems and to contribute to "the final assessment" of the poet's point of view during an era of alienation and search. Though Jeffers firmly believed in the superior truth of poetry as it centers on man's experience, for him the traditional forms were a hindrance; hence his more "organic structure." Contrary to the opinions of some early readers, Coffin finds Jeffers in basic disagreement with Schopenhauer in the matters of "the will, Nature, and death"; more sympathetic rather with Nietzsche, whose influence the author traces through three central chapters with careful citations and discussions of the poetry. He concludes that Jeffers "moved beyond most of Nietzsche's formal doctrine" (of the revaluation of values) to the materialism of Lucretius. On his way to this judgment, Coffin examines the influence of Vico, Spengler, Petrie, Havelock Ellis, and the writers of Greek tragedy. Nietzsche had been useful in clearing out the hackneyed traditions and misconceptions. Then from Lucretius the poet derived a congenial position—that the order of nature supplies a "transhuman magnificence" in which man would do well to put his faith. This book is a sound and significant addition to the slowly growing body of Jeffers studies.

According to Kenneth S. Rothwell ("In Search of a Western Epic: Neihardt, Sandburg, and Jaffe as Regionalists and 'Astoriadists,'" *KanQ* 2[1970]:53–63) the word *Astoriad* (derived from Irving's *Astoria*) refers to a work that turns history, saga, and tale into epic, dealing with "themes of settlement and conquest." John G. Neihardt is both "epicist" and "regionalist." Whereas he recreates "physical

environment," Dan Jaffe reconstructs regional history and Carl Sandburg evokes " the people of the region." The author considers Neihardt's *A Cycle of the West* in terms of epic, though he concedes that
Neihardt was "not entirely successful as either folk poet or literary
epicist." Sandburg's *The People, Yes* fits the pattern of an Astoriad,
although it has more popular that literary appeal. Dan Jaffe, a young
college teacher, in *Dan Freeman* (1967), describes the career of
a pioneer. Rothwell classes this last work with Charles Olson's *Maximus* and Williams's *Paterson*. In the works of his selected poets (and
others) Rothwell sees emerging "an epic theme of the past, but meta-
morphosed to fit modern reality." In " 'Behold the Proverbs of a People': A Florilegium of Proverbs in Carl Sandburg's Poem, 'Good Morning, America' " (*SFQ* 35:160–68) Wolfgang Mieder makes the evident
observation that Sandburg's multiplicity of proverbs can be explained
by the nature of his craft and the purpose of his writing. Mieder
examines section 11 of "Good Morning, America" and finds Sandburg
describing the American people through the characteristic aphorisms
common to all of them—often basic, simple, nonmetaphorical. Many
grow out of money-consciousness. He avoids monotony by changing,
for example, an imperative to an interrogative. When he does quote
metaphorical proverbs, he changes the language: e.g., "the grass is
longer in the backyard." Mieder attaches a list of proverbs, citing the
standard authorities for sources.

Giving himself the topic of "Vachel Lindsay and His Heroes" (*Ill.
State Univ. Journal* 32,v[1970]:22–57) David L. Bradbury considers
(alphabetically from Alexander to Woodrow Wilson) sixty-four "heroes and brave dreamers"—painstakingly identifying the kind and degree of interest Lindsay found in each. The result is pedantic and
unprofound.

Elmer Diktonius, the Finno-Swedish poet, was extraordinarily attracted to the work of Edgar Lee Masters about 1923. This is the
discovery of George C. Schoolfield in "Elmer Diktonius and Edgar
Lee Masters" (*Americana Norvegica* 3:307–27). In two enthusiastic
essays Diktonius showed a genuine adoration for *Spoon River Anthology* (using a sports reporter's diction in his analysis). He used
Masters's poems as support for his own free style and his tendency to
descend to the depths of pessimism. He also translated a group of the
epitaphs, choosing principally those of "the prominent or educated
male populace of Spoon River" and the "respectable" women. In a

book of poems with, among others, "portraits" of Dostoevsky, Nietzsche, and Strindberg, Diktonius included a poem on Masters, which, according to Schoolfield, distorts the character of the American by settling on a serene, peaceful tone, ignoring the violence and ugliness to be found in many of the Spoon River epitaphs.

Though Conrad Aiken shows how old age can be rich, contemporary critics are ignoring him because he is too closely aligned with the conventions of the last century. This is the opinion of Benjamin DeMott as stated in "Life Carved to a Pointed End" (*SatR* 54,30 Jan.:23–25). In "Edna St. Vincent Millay: 'Nobody's Own'" (*CLQ* 9:297–310), reviewing Millay's life in Greenwich Village and her subsequent marriage to the compliant Eugen Boissevain, J. Gassman makes the obvious comparison between Millay and today's liberated woman.

Thomas Ford, in *"The American Rhythm*: Mary Austin's Poetic Principle" (*WAL* 5[1970]:3–14), examines Mrs. Austin's book of 1923 and finds her opinion to be that the rhythms of American verse are original, not derivative from Europe. Sandburg, Lindsay, and the Sherwood Anderson of *Mid-American Chants* (1918) were influenced by the American Indian. Ford thinks that in her own book, her translations of Indian songs, though faithful to the idea, lack the probable lyric quality of the originals. He admits that Mrs. Austin's absorption in Indian art and social problems "may have prejudiced her view," but he is rather sympathetic toward her insistence on a common bond between Indian poetry and the American verse of her day—rhythms developed from a "non-logical and non-literary source," from "the energy and pulses inherent in the land itself." This theory is hardly in the mainstream of American critical thinking.

Kenneth Fields discusses "Past Masters: Walter Conrad Arensburg and Donald Evans" (*SoR* 6[1970]:317–39). As minor poets of the first twenty years of the century with acknowledged limitations, they nevertheless refined the language inherited from the fin de siècle. According to Fields, their ultimate style was adopted by Stevens, among others. Arensburg wrote delicately and softly, Evans, satirically (his later poems being bad imitations of Robinson's ironical portraits). Fields notes Arensburg's debt to the aesthetics of England and France, but claims that his work, as background, was important to the development of Pound, Eliot, Williams, and Stevens. In spite of his striving after a "straightforward" style, Evans's best work was through the indirections of irony. Both poets possessed "great talent" and were "on occasion brilliant." Finally, Louis Hasley, in "The Golden Trashery of Ogden Nashery" (*ArQ* 27:241–50), admits that Nash's contribution to our literature may not have been stupendous, but his forms and his techniques have made an "ineradicable" impression on the style of humorous verse.

Purdue University

15. Poetry: The 1930s to the Present

A. Kingsley Weatherhead

i. General

Essays about recent poetry in general that must be recorded here include Roy Harvey Pearce, "The Burden of Romanticism: Toward the New Poetry: (*IowaR* 2,ii:109–28) which sheds light from a new angle on this topic. From the later eighteenth century on, the theory of poetry has been romanticist, passing through stages centering respectively on myth, symbol, and language. The obligation accepted by modern poets of the generation of Eliot, Stevens, and Williams was to "preserve, refine, and extend our language" and to teach their successors to use it toward the end of "that great romantic vision: the transformation of the humanism of the one into the humanism of the many." Examples of poems from W. D. Snodgrass, Gregory Corso, James Wright, Gary Snyder and others show these poets going beyond Williams in presenting the contours of experience so carefully as to make it ours, sharing with the reader rather than talking to him. "Contemporary American Poetry: The Radical Tradition," by A. Poulin, Jr. (*CP* 3,ii[1970]:5–21) is a general survey which makes useful discriminations and an interesting if unconvincing argument against the claim of Donald Hall (in his 1962 anthology) that contemporary poets have destroyed their own past. In "The Age of Interpretation and the Moment of Immediacy: Contemporary Art vs. History" (*ELH* 37[1970]:287–313), Herbert N. Schneidau makes engaging comments on some of the curious features of our immediate culture and relates new developments in art to the efforts of various kinds of modern poetry to come at reality itself, annihilating the traditional distance between art and life and joining the attack upon other norms of the past. In "The Poetics of the Physical World" (*IowaR* 2,iii:113–26), on the other hand, Galway Kinnell asks why it seems that in the modern poem the less formal beauty there is, the more it becomes possible to discover the glory of the ordinary. In addition to fixed form the modern poem has discarded the inner conventions, whose function was to break down the mystery of human feelings according to formulae and bring us to terms with them.

A number of review essays and chronicles survey recent work and trends in poetry. Laurence Lieberman, in "Recent Poetry: Exiles and Disinterments" (*YR* 61:82–100) comments on the latest volumes of Stanley Kunitz, Richard Howard, Theodore Weiss, Howard Moss, and A. R. Ammons and relates them to the poets' earlier work. Another series of poets, Robert Penn Warren, Richard Tillinghast, Alicia Ostriker, George MacBeth, John Hollander, and Rolfe Humphries, are discussed by Harry Morris in "The Passions of Poets," (*SR* 79:301–09). In the *MR* annual review of poetry, "The Home Book of Modern Verse 1970" (*MR* 12:689–708), Josephine Miles glances at a wide variety of poems, some of which show new departures in language. Poets seem "relatively uninterested and uninteresting in many means," but they are concerned with ends. In "Here Today: A Poetry Chronicle" (*HudR* 24:320–36) Hayden Carruth complains of the triteness of the "common American style" as descended originally from Pound and Williams and coming down through Olson, Duncan, Creeley, and Levertov. He reviews new work by Howard, Ammons, James Wright, and others. Richmond Lattimore, in "Poetry Chronicle" (*HudR* 24:499–510) notices the collections of Robert Fitzgerald and Howard Moss, new work by Adrienne Rich and Galway Kinnell, and one or two volumes of translations.

The December 1970–January 1971 issue of *Les Lettres Nouvelles* is entitled *41 poètes américains d'aujourd'hui* and it reproduces poems and occasional prose passages of practicing American poets. The poems are printed in English and French on facing pages; and the volume as a whole, surveying from afar, provides a useful map of our territory, dividing it into sections, "Some Elders" (Lowell, Berryman, Olson, and others), "Black Mountain" (Duncan, Levertov, Creeley, Blackburn, and others), "After the Beat Generation" (Ginsberg, Snyder, LeRoi Jones, McClure, Wieners), "The New York School" (Ashbery, Schuyler, Koch), "The New Subjectivity" (Simpson, Bly, Wright, Stafford, Kinnell, Merwin, and others), and "New Tendencies" (Aram Saroyan, Lyman Andrews, David Shapiro, and others). Each section is headed by an introductory essay by the editor of the issue, Serge Fauchereau. There are biographical notes, occasional brief critical pieces reprinted from American sources, and a few photographs. *Private Dealings: Eight Modern American Writers* by David J. Burrows, Lewis M. Dabney, Milne Holton, and Grosvenor E. Powell (Stockholm, Almqvist and Wiksell, 1970) is a collection of essays—two by each author—directed to a sophisticated but not wholly academic Swedish audience. The essays on Stevens, Williams, and Robert Lowell are general rather than specialized, but their usefulness will not by any means be limited to those who are being introduced to these poets and have not yet encountered the scholarship. In "Wallace Stevens and the Pressures of Reality" (pp. 32–49) Grosvenor Powell illustrates the "ambiguous intercourse" between world and mind in Stevens. In "To Hit Love Aslant: Poetry and William Carlos Williams" (pp. 50–69), Milne Holton emphasizes the concept of engagement between individual imagination and object. He finds an example of field composition in "The Locust Tree in Flower." The same critic, in "Unlikeness: The Poetry of Robert Lowell" (pp. 115–45), makes a fine survey of the work up to and including *Near the Ocean*, which, perceptive throughout, is particularly valuable in its economical demonstration of the unity of *Life Studies*.

Black American Poetry Since 1944: A Preliminary Checklist by Frank Deodene and William P. French (Chatham, N.J., The Chatham Bookseller) lists first editions of books of poetry and pamphlets of over five pages by black authors in the United States that were published between 1944 and spring 1971, thus covering the period following that covered in Dorothy B. Porter's *North American Negro Poets: A Bibliographical Checklist of Their Writings, 1760–1944* (1945). The names of anthologies substantially devoted to black poetry are also included. "The Motif of Dynamic Change in Black Revolutionary Poetry," by A. Russel Brooks (*CLAJ* 15:7–17) concerns the varieties of the change motif and the notes of expectancy in the black poetry of today. The aim of R. Roderick Palmer, in "The Poetry of Three Revolutionists: Don L. Lee, Sonia Sanchez, and Nikki Giovanni" (*CLAJ* 15:25–36), is to refute by examples from these three poets the contention referred to by Addison Gayle in the preface to *Black Expression* (see *ALS 1970*, p. 378), that black literature is "simplistic, immature, and unimportant." "New Black Poetry: A Double-Edged Sword" by Bernard W. Bell (*CLAJ* 15:37–43) claims that the hatred of the new black poets is "a valid though increasingly ineffective poetic stance"; the poetry is "rooted in a love of black people and an affirmation of life." This is a useful brief survey of the evolution of the poetry, which notes among other factors the cultural forces that have acted upon it since the twenties.

Two articles on rock may be noted: in "Modern Songs as Lyric Poetry: Euphony, Rhythm, Metre and Rhyme" (*Style* 4[1970]:245–51) Mary Mountain Ferri studies examples of rock poetry from Paul Simon, Bob Dylan, and Leonard Cohen in terms of traditional poetic technique. The relation of rock to the public imagination is explored by Frank D. McConnell in "Rock and the Politics of Frivolity" (*MR* 12:119–34).

Todd Gitlin, in "The Return of Political Poetry" (*Commonweal* 94:375–80) pays some attention to Robert Bly and Denise Levertov and then suggests directions in which political poetry ought to move.

ii. William Carlos Williams

Williams has been the object of some significant scholarship and criticism during the year. There is first *William Carlos Williams: The American Background* (London: Cambridge Univ. Press) by Mike Weaver, which is the first book to appear devoted exclusively to the influences of his background. Weaver considers "personal, literary, aesthetic, intellectual, and social" factors—including family, earlier literature, contemporary aesthetic notions, theories of sex, Vorticism, Dewey, Kandinsky, Whitehead, Antheil, imagists, objectivists, precisionists, communism, social credit, puritanism, relativity. The book does not embark upon criticism, though obviously it will be indispensable to all future critics of this poet. Researched over some years, it is a far ranging and thorough study. One index of the diligence of the work that has gone into it is that Weaver has consulted over four hundred fugitive little magazines in England, France, and the United States; another, that he has gathered unpublished Williams material from ten university and city libraries in the Eastern and Midwestern parts of this country. Many little known and unknown facts are assembled here. One part of the background Weaver presents is a precedent to *Paterson* that Williams does not acknowledge: *Passaic, a Group of Poems Touching that River* (1842), a volume of a hundred and fifty pages by a nineteenth-century doctor, Thomas Ward, from which some substantial selections are reprinted in an appendix. He also produces an early oil painting of the river by Williams and, among other plates with various relationships to Williams's writing, a photograph of *Fata Morgana* by Paul Tchelichew, which is an anthropomorphic landscape like that described at the beginning of *Paterson*, and the *National Geographic* photograph of the six wives of the Mangebetou chief that Williams remembered later in the same work. A second appendix locates the sources of some eighty to ninety passages in *Paterson*, from some of which it is very likely that further interpretations of this endlessly discussable work may germinate.

A *Companion to William Carlos Williams's "Paterson"* by Benjamin Sankey (Berkeley, Univ. of Calif. Press) opens with some twenty pages which discuss "The Poet's Job," "The City of Paterson," "Method and Principal Symbols" and other subjects, the consideration of which, though not new to the criticism of Williams, is here made in straightforward prose. It furnishes an excellent introduction to this or any other study of *Paterson*. The concluding pages of the book, again in the clear terms of intelligent criticism, essay an understanding of why Williams proceeded as he did: and they make an evaluation of his success. Between these two parts, Professor Sankey offers a passage-by-passage commentary on the poem with summaries of its larger and smaller sections. Some of the summaries are particularly useful—on the role and place of Klaus Ehrens, for example, or on the intentions behind *Paterson V*. The commentary has insights, some of them enhanced by Professor Sankey's study of Williams's drafts and other notes at Buffalo and Yale, which reveal the contribution of the parts of the poem to the whole. The lack of an index is regrettable.

No study of Williams's poetry can proceed far without some careful consideration of his prose. His theories of poetry he applied to his prose; and he declines most of the time to recognise a distinction between the two modes. More than any other writer of like importance he combined them. It is appropriate, therefore, that with *The Prose of William Carlos Williams* (Middletown, Conn., Wesleyan Univ. Press [1970]) Linda W. Wagner should significantly complement her pioneer work in the poetry. She discusses *Kora in Hell*; *Spring and All*, which is a mixture of poems and prose pieces; *The Great American Novel*; the essays; *In the American Grain*; the conventional novel, *A Voyage to Pagany*; the shorter fiction; the plays, the autobiography; the later full-length novels. She comments also upon the poetry at various stages of Williams's career: the unity of his work,

she says, "makes possible one emphasis of this study, that on the interrelationships between his prose and his poetry." *Paterson* is, of course,
considered, and "Asphodel, That Greeny Flower," with other later
poems "primarily because his writing in prose as well as in poetry
comes to its natural and easy culmination in them." Earlier appearances of some parts of the book have been noticed in this annual. As
a whole, it provides a full and perceptive accounting of the individual
works it includes and of the whole developing sweep of Williams's
career. It is clearly written.

The William Carlos Williams special number of *JML* (1,iv)
contains a Williams chronology, a bibliography, and a number of important articles. Joseph Evans Slate, in "Kora in Opacity: Williams'
Improvisations" (pp. 463–76), gives a sensitive account of the nature
of *Kora in Hell*, discussing also its genesis and its reception by Ezra
Pound, René Taupin, and the Baroness Von Freytag-Loringhoven.
In "Williams' 'Two Pendants: for the Ears' " (pp. 477–92), Neil Myers
makes a close study of this poem. James K. Guimond, in "William
Carlos Williams and the Past: Some Clarifications" (pp. 493–502),
explains the general hostility to the past and shows at the same time
how Williams admired certain historic figures who sometimes re-
volted against the conventions of their times and sometimes reflected
the vitality of the contemporary life. In "*Paterson*: Landscape and
Dream" (pp. 523–48) Sister Bernetta Quinn notes the function of the
dream in the poem and scans its landscape, repeatedly turning up interesting details hitherto unremarked. "Suffused-Encircling Shapes
of Mind: Inhabited Space in Williams," by Cary Nelson (pp. 549–
64) discusses space, which is "inhabited by consciousness," and the
poet's "sense of the poem as an inhabited object." Some new perceptions are recorded by James C. Cowan in "The Image of Water in
Paterson" (pp. 503–11). In "The Measured Dance: Williams' 'Pictures from Brueghel' " (pp. 565–77), Joel Conarroe studies the late
sequence of poems related to the Brueghel paintings, considering both
the pattern of the whole—its ascents and descents—and the details in
individual poems as they arise from details in the canvasses. One of
the more engaging articles is "*Paterson*: A Plan for Action" (pp.
512–22), in which Louis L. Martz adjusts the accepted ideas about
the development of *Paterson*, observing that with the first three books
we have a work that "holds together with a dominant symbolism and
a soaring climax." Williams wished, however, for something less

formally composed, and book 4 is not a conclusion but a set of new beginnings. Paul Ramsey's article, "William Carlos Williams as Metrist: Theory and Practice" (pp. 578–92) is a clear, commonsensical treatment of Williams's metrics, which have not regularly been approached with such penetrating intelligence. In the extensive discussions of two poems, "Metric Figure" and "The Yachts," and in his broader comments on Williams as a whole, Ramsey goes beyond metrics into other observations, all made with sensibility and described with verve. " 'A Celebration of the Light': Selected Checklist of Writings about William Carlos Williams" (pp. 593–642) by Jack Hardie concludes this issue of *JML*. This remarkable bibliography begins with a list of over five hundred general studies and reviews, each item annotated. Then follow lists of discussions on individual works: not only for larger works such as *Paterson* and *In the American Grain* but for two hundred shorter poems commentaries are listed, and many of these items are again annotated.

An interesting and useful article on literary form may be considered here, since *Paterson* is one of its chief exhibits. In "Process and Product: A Study of Modern Literary Form" by Donald M. Kartiganer (*MR* 12:297–328,789–816) many of the significant features of process literature are assembled and discussed. In this mode the artist strives to identify art with life and to create the illusion of a work in the very act of being written; in product literature, on the other hand, there is an artistic framework, a sense of rigorous authorial control and completeness. Among other implications noted in process poetry is that the subject of the poem becomes the poet's own efforts to create poetry and that creative assistance is expected of the reader. *Paterson* shows some of the characteristics of process poetry insofar as the poet collects fragments which he is not authorized to order, "the key to poetry and life being the ability to cherish the independent existence of reality: the only appropriate form is the refusal of form" (p. 311). In the light of this concept of process and product Kartiganer considers a number of other phenomena: the parallel methods of Freud and Jung respectively, the position of the imagists in this spectrum, and the fusion of the two modes in Eliot, Conrad, and Faulkner. It is an enterprising and admirably illuminating presentation. Catharine Savage, in "Michel Butor and *Paterson*" (*FMLS* 7:126–33), shows how Williams's poem appealed to Butor in the construction of his *Mobile*, essentially for its method of dealing with the heterogeneity of the American culture by images in a field of relationships; she notices also a number of similar elements in the two works. The same critic, under the name Catharine S. Brosman, discusses Butor's debt to Williams again in "A Source and Parallel of Michel Butor's *Mobile: In the American Grain*" (*MLR* 66:315–21). G. Morris Donaldson, in "William Carlos Williams: *Paterson*, Books I and II" (*WCR* 5,i[1970]:3–10), notes the changes made between original manuscripts and final form and discusses the reasons for them. "William Carlos Williams: A Review of Research and Criticism," by Linda W. Wagner (*RALS* 1:17–29) consists of sections on bibliography, editions, manuscripts and letters, biography, and criticism and surveys this terrain with urbane commentary.

iii. Robert Lowell

Robert Lowell by Richard J. Fein (TUSAS 176[1970]), is a thorough, sensible, and eminently readable account of this poet. Fein deals with the individual volumes by studying closely those works central to the poet's meaning and development. Backing off from this kind of criticism, however, he repeatedly looks over Lowell's work as a whole, drawing out its main themes, its obsessions, its character; and then, beyond Lowell, he occasionally makes statements or offers suggestions on the relation of the poetry to the culture that constitutes its context. Fein treats both the familiar Lowell poems and many which have had little attention; and his generalizations are perceptive and shrewd. In commenting upon *Life Studies*, for example, he epitomizes Lowell's career at this point as measuring the development of modern poetry "from the hard surface, the intellectually brilliant writing (replete with self-conscious literary references)" to one that is "low-keyed, approaching the informalities and laxities of prose"; from "a religiously charged and traditionally formed poetry to an unrelenting secular search for the self in terms of a language that works like a safety razor that adjusts and readjusts the edges of its blade" (p. 69). This is a good critical and scholarly work.

The Public Poetry of Robert Lowell by Patrick Cosgrave (London, Gollancz [1970]) is a very different kind of study. With dissatisfaction at much of the criticism on Lowell, Cosgrave seeks to establish the poet in a tradition. There are two lines in the English tradition: the line of wit, from Shakespeare, through Ben Jonson, and the metaphysical poets; and the line of gravity, from Shakespeare, through Pope, Samuel Johnson, and Yeats, to Lowell. Johnson is the pivotal figure because at a significant moment in the history of English literature he originated a procedure that Lowell was to follow: the involvement of personality in the act of judgment in the public poem. Cosgrave returns repeatedly to this feature as he proceeds through the canon. At the same time he relates poems to a theory of poetics. His studies of individual poems, each extended and made with minute attention, are original and valuable. "Waking Early Sunday Morning," in Cosgrave's view Lowell's greatest "and one of the greatest as well as the most important for the future of contemporary poems," shows Lowell going "clearly over, technically as well as spiritually, to the inheritance of Yeats. In doing so he has finally abandoned the corrupting influence on him of the school of Eliot [Eliot and Pound belonging to the line of wit], a school which has come near to ruining modern poetry in English but which, with 'Waking Early Sunday Morning,' may well be on the point of final exclusion from influence in the development of English literature" (pp. 10–11). The manner adopted by Cosgrave in analyzing poems, his concern with "rational structure," his condemnation of the "vice" of imitative form, and his strictures on "misused talent" (and, in passing, his observation that hedonism ruined Stevens) would have left us in little doubt as to the identity of his mentor in criticism, even if he had not at the outset declared Yvor Winters to be the greatest critic of the century. He is indebted to Winters for his account of the moral and absolutist theory of poetry, for his denunciation of Eliot, and perhaps for his style which is strong and generally unrelieved by uncertainty. But he is free to differ, and he does so most noticeably in his admiration of Yeats. The book is a new voice in Lowell studies.

There are a handful of significant articles to report. Building upon his work in *PCP* of the previous year (see *ALS 1970*, p. 320), Thomas Vogler, in a long article, "Robert Lowell: Payment Gat He Nane" (*IowaR* 2,iii:64–95), discusses some passages from the *Aeneid* at length in order to illuminate the idea that Lowell's poetry is an attempt to redeem suffering through art. A good deal of new light is thrown on the individual poems of *Lord Weary's Castle*, which represents a modern exile, reenacting Dante's journey through hell, looking for the Word, the "payment," the conception that justifies suffering, in the detritus of a fallen world. To "The Greatness and Horror of Empire: Robert Lowell's *Near the Ocean*" (1967), reprinted in *The Sounder Few* (pp. 213–31), Daniel Hoffman adds an afterword (pp. 232–42). In it he notes the changes Lowell has made in his own revision of "Endecott and the Red Cross"; he takes issue with John Simon and his condemnation of Lowell's adaptations (see *ALS 1968*, p. 250); and he adds a note on *Notebooks 1967–68*, which expresses a life now "purified of the trivial and revealed as a thrust toward an understanding of the center of his own time." New light is shed by Paul Kavanagh, in "The Nation Past and Present: A Study of Robert Lowell's 'For the Union Dead'" (*JAmS* 5:93–101), who studies the historical relevance of Colonel Shaw, noting particularly the similarities and differences between Lowell's poem and that of J. Russell Lowell, "Memoriae Positum," which also celebrates the death of Shaw. Kavanagh concludes that Robert Lowell's poem is ambiguous in its treatment of the Shaw material, that he is "far less certain as to the relevance of liberalism either to the historical development of American society, or to the disintegrating contemporary scene" and that he is "forced to accept the unreality of claims made for the racial equality, either supposedly realized or hoped for." In "Baudelaire and the Poetry of Robert Lowell" (*TCL* 17:257–74), Steven Axelrod contends that *Imitations* centers on Baudelaire, who defined the modern mood of spiritual exhaustion and psychological extremity; before then Lowell's reliance on him had been minor; after, in *For the Union Dead* and *Near the Ocean*, it is of major importance. "Robert Lowell and Wallace Stevens on Sunday Morning" (*UR* 37:268–72) by Elizabeth Lunz is an interesting reading of Lowell's "Waking Early Sunday Morning" as "a specific answer to the errors of Stevens's 'Sunday Morning.'" Reviewing *Notebook 1967–68* in "The Consistency of Robert Lowell" (*SoR* 7:338–44) George Lensing emphasizes the unity in Lowell's work to date, citing particularly the moral outrage, the personal torment, and the sense of man's innate depravity. "Reading Robert Lowell," by David Bromwich (*Commentary* 52,ii:78–83) is a review article which surveys Lowell's work in general terms up to *Notebook*, which it studies in some detail.

iv. Wallace Stevens

The most important publication on Stevens was a gathering of essays in an issue of the *Southern Review* (7,iii) collectively titled "Wallace

Stevens and the Romantic Heritage." There is remarkably little overlapping in the individually contributed material. We keep coming
back to some of the same poems, of course; but even here, there is
variety in the commentary. There are first the vivid miscellaneous
details in Holly Stevens's "Bits of Remembered Time" (pp. 651–57),
which are engaging because one automatically relates them to poems
—the modest wine cellar, for instance, the imported plants. On reading that his social life at home was restricted, one wonders, as Miss
Stevens does, whether this situation gave rise to the poetry. She
quotes from "Arrival at the Waldorf": "Where the wild poem is a
substitute / For the woman one loves or ought to love, / One wild
rhapsody a fake for another." An important new approach to the
early poetry is provided in "*Harmonium* and William James" (pp.
658–82) by Margaret Peterson, who finds sources or impulses for
poems in the contemporary opposition to German idealism, in Stevens's nostalgia for Catholicism, and in antirationalism. Appealing to
parallel passages in James, Mrs. Peterson develops new transcriptions
of Stevens's "symbolic shorthand" and is able to offer significant interpretations of hitherto unpenetrated poems or alternatives to earlier
"hedonistic" readings. Her readings of "The Emperor of Ice-Cream,"
"Disillusionment of Ten O'Clock," and "Metaphors of a Magnifico"
are particularly instructive. In "The Wallace Stevens Vulgates" (pp.
699–726), James McMichael discusses five poems from *Harmonium*
in which the dialectic of reality and imagination is operative. He has
subjected them to unusually close scrutiny and has new observations
to make, even about "Sunday Morning," where it is not easy to add
to all that has already been said. In later poems, Stevens merely
describes the dialectic—"he would rather tell us about the theoretical
properties of the imagination than realize its powers by verbally
wrestling with those elements that his ontology tells him are real"
(p. 723). Doris L. Eder, "Wallace Stevens: The War Between Mind
and Eye," (pp. 749–64) is a short article on the prose of Stevens, the
role of philosophy in his work, and some critical pitfalls. Some of the
ground covered is not new; but discussing such matters in Stevens as
his belief about metaphor, his relating of concrete to abstraction, his
phenomenalism, and the monism attributed to him, Professor Eder is
valuable for the clarity and economy with which she writes, from a
position some way this side of the idolatry only too familiar in
Stevens criticism. The idea of the mind's separation from reality is

the starting point of Kenneth Fields's informed essay, "Postures of the Nerves: Reflection of the Nineteenth Century in the Poems of Wallace Stevens" (pp. 778–824). When Stevens wished to look directly at reality it was often represented by a woman, who resembled Pre-Raphaelite "stunners" in their vague rapt attitudes, their loose gowns, their habitual postures before mirrors, and their disembodiment. The pursuit of this theme leads Fields into parts of the Stevens terrain untrodden—into poems hitherto uncriticized, and into the legacies of Hegel, Pater, Descartes, and others.

Two essays on geographical implications in Stevens are of interest. Jan Pinkerton, "Wallace Stevens in the Tropics: A Conservative Protest" (YR 60:215–27), finds that the use of tropical scenes and images in this poet is an appeal to the primitive warm lethargic enjoyment of life as a conservative protest against change and progress in the industrious puritan North. In evoking the exotic for such a purpose, Stevens is associated with Hawthorne, Melville, and Henry Adams; and like them he felt secure only in his own less threatening culture. "Wallace Stevens: America the Primordial" (MLQ 32:73–88) by Dwight Eddins discusses the significance of the American continent as subject and symbol in Stevens. The landscape dictates that man must assert his imaginative power to find human significance where there is only natural chaos. Eddins refines upon the distinction between North and South made in earlier criticism and contributes new important readings to certain relevant poems, including "Sunday Morning" and "Farewell to Florida." "Wallace Stevens' 'Sunday Morning'" (Edda 70[1970]:105–16) is a lecture in Norwegian by Jan W. Dietrichson which gives a careful analytic description of the poem, its content and form, concluding that it is a product of the nineteenth century, belonging to Stevens's early phase and marking its close. In "The Arrangement of Harmonium" (ELH 37[1970]:456–73) William W. Bevis demonstrates the effects of fragmentation, incongruity, and mystification that Stevens deliberately achieved in his volumes by juxtaposing poems that were from quite different periods and were different in mood and in the meanings that the symbols are made to bear. "Wallace Stevens' Letters of Rock and Water," by George S. Lensing, in Essays (pp. 320–30), shows how letters constituted the "workshop" from which poems emerged, correspondents bringing to life in the poet's imagination foreign places he had not visited. Edward Guereschi, in "Wallace Stevens and the

Poetics of Secular Grace" (*ErasmusR* 1:131–45), describes secular grace as the "redemptive and affirmative qualities" in poetry and proceeds to statements about three poems, "The Comedian as the Letter C," "The Man with the Blue Guitar," and "Notes Toward a Supreme Fiction." New glosses for the terms *reality* and *imagination* are deduced from Stevens's prose, in "Political Realities and Poetic Release: Prose Statements by Wallace Stevens" (NEQ 44:575–601), by Jan Pinkerton, who suggests that Stevens's intellect, as the *Letters* now reveal, had not so philosophical a bent as critics have supposed and that "reality" should be construed rather straightforwardly as socialism, taxes, violence, and other novel unpleasantnesses of the world, to which poetry, or imagination (though this word undergoes a strange semantic modulation) could serve as antidote. Some characteristics and implications of the duality in Stevens are briefly suggested in "The Meta-Metaphysical Vision of Wallace Stevens," by Marianna Bankert (*Renascence* 24:47–53). Joseph N. Riddel, "Stevens on Imagination—The Point of Departure" in *The Quest for Imagination: Essays in Twentieth-Century Aesthetic Criticism*, edited by O. B. Hardison, Jr. (Cleveland, Press of Case Western Reserve Univ., pp. 55–85), probes the complexities of the imagination in this poet. *The Merrill Checklist of Wallace Stevens*, compiled by Theodore L. Huguelet (Columbus, Ohio, Charles E. Merrill [1970]) is selective. It lists works by Stevens, including letters, the important biographical and critical books and articles about him.

v. Theodore Roethke

The sense of some hitherto obscure passages is revealed (or its absence explained) in "Theodore Roethke's *Praise to the End!* Poems," by John Vernon (*IowaR* 2:60–79), who finds that both the sequence and the individual poems are informed by the alternation of regression and progression, the body and the world first becoming amorphous, language reduced to mere sound, and time to timelessness, then the achieved wholeness flowing back into each part. In "Texture and Form in Theodore Roethke's Greenhouse Poems" (*MLQ* 32:409–24), John D. Boyd analyses some representative poems, noting particularly the reconciliation of opposites, the organic unity, and the functions of sound patterns. John Hobbs, in "The Poet as His Own Interpreter: Roethke on 'In a Dark Time'" (*CE* 33:55–66), makes a thorough and useful study of the poem, taking into consideration the poet's own remarks on it. "A Phenomenological Glance at a Few Lines of Roethke," by Matthew Corrigan (*MPS* 2:165–74) studies some stanzas from Roethke's "The Lost Son" for what they show of the development of self-consciousness.

The Northwest Review devoted its summer issue (11,iii) to a series of articles on this poet. In "Theodore Roethke and Tradition: 'The Pure Serene of Memory in One Man'" (pp. 1–18) Jenijoy La Belle locates some of the influences on Roethke, citing comparable passages from earlier poets. Coburn Freer's "Theodore Roethke's Love Poetry" (pp. 42–66) describes the genesis and development of the love poems in the canon, illuminating the themes of love and burden in them by appealing to the parable of the Prodigal Son, a repeated motif in Roethke, and in particular to Rilke's exegesis of it. In "Kenneth Burke and Theodore Roethke's 'Lost Son' Poems" (pp. 67–96), Brendan Galvin, arguing the wide influence of Burke's critical writings, uses them to interpret and illuminate passages of the poems. "Bibliographic Notes on the Creative Process and Sources of Roethke's 'The Lost Son' Sequence" (pp. 97–111) by James R. McLeod has first a commentary on the critical reception of Roethke's volumes as they appeared, which pays particular attention to the propriety of psychological criticism and to the question of the influences of Freud and Jung. The bibliography gives the places and dates of the first appearances of the poem of "The Lost Son" and "Praise to the End," biographical and critical comments, comments and readings by Roethke, and manuscript locations. One of the most penetrating studies in the issue is a brief article by Arnold Stein, "Roethke's Memory: Actions, Visions, and Revisions" (pp. 19–31) which, considering the "pure serene of memory," examines in particular two passages, each a scene from the greenhouse, in "Meditations of an Old Woman" and "The Rose," along with the early sketches of each in the *Notebooks*. Roethke bade his students "'beware the poetry of moments'"; and the captured moment in perfected expression in the former of the two passages, Stein suggests, "points toward a mute inner failure"; it is intact, complete in itself, not a wave or a waver, but a form going nowhere."

"The use of an author's correspondence, manuscripts, and notebooks is of considerable importance to scholars and critics," says James Richard McLeod, introducing *Theodore Roethke: A Manuscript Checklist* (Kent, Ohio: Kent State Univ. Press). In addition to manuscripts of poems, Roethke left some two hundred spiral note-books, and thousands of letters to and from hundreds of correspon-dents. This volume describes the filing of the notebooks, and it lo-cates the manuscript of every poem and of each letter Roethke wrote in one or other of nineteen repositories in the United States and Canada. It is a painstaking achievement; one foresees much benefit coming from it—the kind, for example, that has accrued to William Carlos Williams criticism from the study of his rough drafts.

The Wild Prayer of Longing: Poetry and the Sacred by Nathan A. Scott Jr. (New Haven, Conn., Yale Univ. Press) may be consid-ered here; for its main statement is illustrated to the extent of one-third of the length of the book by a study of Roethke. Scott is con-sistently rewarding for his ability to identify ideas and impulses in the very contemporary world and then relate them to the literary and artistic phenomena to which they have given rise. Here he traces the decline of figural literature and the alienation of the world without. Then he notes the rebirth of "savage thought" and the effort of the avant-garde forms of all the arts to reconceive the world as offering the "possibility of life under the law of participation" (p. 31). Things in the ordinary world may convey some illumination of the "mystery of existence" if we engage in "meditative thinking," Heidegger's term for an imaginative process that dislocates normal pragmatic thought and brings us into the neighborhood of Being. Roethke probably never read Heidegger, but in his poetic vision he reflects what Heidegger exemplifies in philosophy. His joy and his impulse to sing are respons-es to what he hears from "a world whose presence is itself conveyed as a kind of music" (p. 81); and he offers a great example of the sacramental conception of the world, important to this generation on account of its widespread anxiety to discover in things an indwelling sanctity which will authorize participation.

vi. Tate, Eberhart, and Jarrell

Allen Tate: A Literary Biography (New York, Pegasus) by Radcliffe Squires combines biography and literary criticism in a good balance. There are the staple ingredients of the poetic career—residence in Paris, domestic arrangements, poverty and debts, creative writing ap-pointments in universities. Squires deals with the important literary associations and gives concise accounts of the Fugitive and Agrarian

movements and the row over the award of the Bollingen Prize to
Ezra Pound. He is particularly good at assembling, here and there
throughout the book, the factors that make up what he calls "the
uneasy compound" of Tate's thought. Tate's respect for the classics,
for tradition, and for sacred myths, on the one hand, and his abhor-
rence of positivism, his distaste for romanticism and for humanism, on
the other, establish him as a central figure of his age—an age now
formally closed, Squires suggests, by one of Tate's own poems. And
one's sense of the whole period is augmented by this book. Squires
deals with Tate's prose and poetry, relating various pieces to facts in
the biography and to the ideas Tate was nourishing at the time of
composition. He is regularly alert and knowledgeable in commenting
upon individual poems; but sometimes among the critical observations, deriving perhaps from his own practice as a poet, he is able to
offer insights of unusual value, such, for example, as the ideas on
poetry's own separate life or those on popularity in poetry. This is an
unpretentious book written with economy, an agile style, and unob-
trusive wit. It is exactly what a literary biography should be.

In the beginning of *Richard Eberhart: The Progress of an American Poet* (New York, Oxford Univ. Press) Joel H. Roache looks at certain poems which represent stages in the development of this poet and
observes, with the proper caveats, that his eye turns progressively
outward toward "the existential human condition" away from ab-
stractions of the spirit. The direction of his work is related to that of
his career: Eberhart began in poetry before it received any widespread subsidy from universities and has remained with it to reap
these fruits. Roache considers him representative of American poetry
and its shifting place in society. He is interested in its quotidian
housekeeping problems and has collected many details of Eberhart's
publication record—which journals rejected poems, which accepted,
and later, which commissioned them; the negotiations with publishing houses here and in England; et cetera. He has usefully reviewed
the criticism of Eberhart and supplied a bibliography of his work and
work about him.

Daniel Hoffman's article on Richard Eberhart (see *ALS 1964*,
p. 211) is reprinted in *The Sounder Few*, with an afterword (pp. 74–
80), in which Hoffman notes in Eberhart's latest volume, *Shifts of
Being*, the "consistent and unbelievable unevenness" of his work: it

communicates a sense of wonder and in some parts moves naturally; in others, rhymes and rhythms are strained and diction forced.

The Poetry of Randall Jarrell by Suzanne Ferguson (Baton Rouge, La. State Univ. Press) is the first book on Jarrell by a single author. She treats the six volumes of poetry chronologically, tracing the development of themes and subjects, selecting for close study from each volume the most significant and characteristic poems. The commentary reveals the impact on the poetry of Jarrell's reading, which was vast, his models, his critical precepts, and his personal life. Changes between worksheets and finished poems and between the various editions of the latter are noted. Although it often appears quite simple, a good deal of Jarrell's poetry is mysterious and resists interpretation more strongly than that of his contemporaries or his models. Thus one senses the material inadequacy of paraphrase, of which there is a good deal here. Professor Ferguson says that perhaps Jarrell's obscurity "was a part of his idea of fashionableness, because it does not seem to result from the attempt to say something new and difficult . . . but from an idea that it is all right, maybe even a good thing, for poems to be difficult" (p. 35). If the mystery is not due to fashionable meretriciousness, on the other hand, nor, as may be, to his own uncertainty, it may in some cases seem a disservice to crowd it out and cast clear light upon what the poet instinctively or deliberately left in penumbra. Emphasis, however, must rest upon the value of Professor Ferguson's sensitive analyses throughout the book.

"A Check List of Criticism on Randall Jarrell, 1941–1970: With an Introduction and a List of His Major Works" (*BNYPL* 75:176–94) by Dure Jo Gillikin includes lists of Jarrell's books—poetry, essays, fiction, children's books, translations—and books he edited, in addition to articles and book reviews about him.

vii. Olson, Ginsberg, Levertov, Creeley, Rexroth

"A Gathering for Charles Olson (*MR* 12:33–68) reports remembered anecdotes by a friend and a teacher. It includes "Olson/His Poetry" (pp. 45–57) in which, defending this poet against the strictures of conventional critics, M. L. Rosenthal delivers some arresting observations, with an ability, now familiar, to distinguish the qualities by which new departures in verse may be described. The following is an example: "His [Olson's] greatest immediate predecessors had been forced to let their sense of form make way for another sense—that of the process creating an *illusion* of form. Their insistence was nevertheless on the ultimate, if possibly desolate, expectation of humanized form that would dominate mere process. They felt, and both resisted and yielded to, the great, new pull toward the void: reality abandoned by the human imagination" (pp. 49–50). In "Charles Olson: A Preface" (pp. 57–68), William Aiken finds the main theme of the poems, the idea of defining man by reference to space, embodied in "The Kingfishers," "In Cold Hell, in Thicket," and in *The Maximus Poems*. There are redeeming poetic features in the "pedantry and personal history" of these last. *Athanor* 2 contains some anecdotes and images in "I remember Olson" by Albert Cook (pp. 47–48) and a description of the influence on Olson of Professor Frederick Merk, in "Merk and Olson" by Ralph Maud (pp. 49–51). In a third piece in this issue, "Olson and His Ages" (pp. 52–57) Linda Wagner makes some interesting observations, weighing among other matters the question of Olson's debt to predecessors, concluding that his "mentors were never Pound and Williams; they were rather Melville, Shakespeare, Dante." Despite its brevity this article contributes important comments on the work of this poet. Ann Charters, in "I Maximus: Charles Olson as Mythologist" (*MPS* 2:49–60), discusses the concept of myth and the debts to Jung that shape the ideas in *The Maximus Poems*. In "Melville: To Him, Olson" (*MPS* 2:61–95), Martin Y. Pops considers Olson's *Call Me Ishmael* not only as scholarship and criticism but as "an extrapolation of *Moby-Dick* as a species of Projective Verse," which performs a rite and demands reader participation. His study leads Pops into observations about Olson's general poetic principles and practice.

As the jacket claims, *A Bibliography of Works by Allen Ginsberg: October, 1943–July 1, 1967*, compiled by George Dowden (San Francisco, City Lights), is a Gargantuan labor of love, partly because of the mere abundance of Ginsberg's work and partly because of the particular difficulties that arise in cataloguing it: in his preface Dowden mentions "the hazards of international little press publishing, the disappearance of revolutionary editors in some countries, lost newspaper interviews, poems and prose left with editors and forgotten, mimeographed ephemera, etc. . . . Some Czech and Cuban items are missing, as nobody would reply from those countries after Ginsberg had been expelled ('They're scared')" (p. xiii). There are peculiari-ties about the bibliography: Dowden includes not only the conven-tional lists of poems and prose, first appearances, records and tapes, et cetera, but in addition a list of the drawings and paintings which have the poet as subject, with a description of each and its location (unless stolen), and also a section entitled " 'Some Mantras' as tran-scribed and explained by Allen Ginsberg." There is an index, and there are photographs of the covers of books by Ginsberg and of Ginsberg's person. An unusual and engaging compilation. In Alison Colbert's "A Talk with Allen Ginsberg" (*PR* 38:289–309) the poet gives his account of the origin of his Blake album. He recalls the influence of Williams upon his own breakthrough into a poetry identi-cal with speech and discusses what he had learned from Kerouac. The most interesting part of the interview describes the entry of the Buddhist ideas into literature in the early fifties and how they con-verged with propositions of Blake and Williams.

George Bowering's "Denise Levertov" (*AntigR* 7:76–87) a brief, thoughtful survey, quotes from her work at various stages and com-pares her repeatedly with Anne Bradstreet and Emily Dickinson, her most important predecessors.

"Robert Creeley: A Checklist 1946–1970" by Lee Ann Johnson (*TCL* 17:181–98) lists both the poet's works and also criticism and reviews of it.

In "The Poetry of Kenneth Rexroth" (*AR* 31:405–22), Gordon K. Grigsby deplores the lack of attention this poetry has drawn and surveys it, noting particularly its absorption of Chinese poetry and its acceptance of time and mortality.

viii. Wilbur, Donald Hall, James Dickey, Marianne Moore, Nemerov, Winters, Berryman, Plath, Elizabeth Bishop

In "When the Gloves Are Off," a review article of Richard Wilbur's *Walking to Sleep* (*Review* 26:35–44), Clive James is perceptive in locating and demonstrating technical excellences in the earlier poems; but he considers the poet's work, which unlike that of others does not lend itself to cope suddenly with the new troubled situation, to be somewhat hermetic and off balance. "The Beautiful Changes in Richard Wilbur's Poetry" (*ConL* 12:74–87), on the other hand, is an original approach in which John P. Farrell explores the respective sig-

nificance in the poems of two kinds of change, disintegrative and metaphoric, and defends Wilbur against the charge that he is aloof from
modern reality. Charles F. Duffy's " 'Intricate Neural Grace': The
Esthetic of Richard Wilbur" (*CP* 4,i:41–50) is a useful short study of
Wilbur's aesthetic made by exploring poems that speculate on art and
life.

"Donald Hall's Poetry" by Ralph J. Mills, Jr. (*IowaR* 2:82–123)
is an extensive survey, from the early poems that show the wit and
irony characteristic of the New Criticism generation to the most recent ones which attend upon and express the voice of inward experience. Like that of so many others in the last fifteen years, the direction of this poetry has been toward openness. It is not easily inspected
and discussed: it deliberately cultivates reverie and irrational sequences of images and thus yields little to the kinds of logical analysis
familiar in college instruction for thirty years. Mills calls to his aid
terms from dream psychology and from Jung generally: and while he
has the sensibility and the subtlety of style to describe much of what
is going on in a number of Hall's poems (including a long commentary on "The Alligator Bride"), he also has the discretion that re-
strains him from destroying them in total explications. By the precepts and examples in this essay we can learn to read Hall's poems.
At the same time, Mills keeps before us other strains of poetry that
belong to the same genre, both predecessors and contemporaries, as-
sociating Hall particularly with Robert Bly, James Wright, Louis
Simpson, and W. S. Merwin among other poets in English and, for
some things, with William Stafford and Galway Kinnell. There are
more examples of Hall's poems and further discussion in another,
briefer survey by Mills titled "Poems of the Deep Mind" (*TPJ* 4,ii:16–
25). The same issue of this journal, which is entirely devoted to
Donald Hall, contains "Some Notes on *The Alligator Bride, Poems
New and Selected*" (pp. 49–55) in which William Matthews dwells
on other features in Hall: the search in the new world for origins, the
relationship between parents and children, the death our children
will visit upon us. A number of passages from "An Interview with
Donald Hall" by Scott Chisholm (pp. 26–48) will, no doubt, be
quoted frequently in discussions about the new poetic departure for
which Hall is the main spokesman. He speaks of poems in which
"there is always something going on of which I was not aware." He
says, "poems begin in a passive way, a phrase comes to me, or some

words come to me. . . . This happens in certain moods"; ". . . it would seem that the surrealist poem is suited to the times. . . ." "In the last ten years or so, American poetry has joined international modernism. It has not harvested the fruits of Pound and Williams, it has harvested the fruits of the great early painters of this century and of the poets from Spain and France and Germany" (p. 33).

James Dickey, The Critic as Poet: An Annotated Bibliography with an Introductory Essay by Eileen Glancy (Troy, N.Y., Whitston Publishing Co.) lists poetry and prose of this author, along with criticism about him, briefly annotated. In the introductory essay, Eileen Glancy confers on Dickey the laureateship of being poet-critic of the decade (following Randall Jarrell) and applies his critical criteria to his poetic practices.

Justin Replogle, "Marianne Moore and the Art of Intonation" (*ConL* 12:1–17) is a sensitive article about the tunes in the poet's voice, expressed with subdued and becoming wit. Miss Moore's intonation contours are much stronger than those of most poets; an unusually large amount of her meaning comes through her tunes, to which she alerts her reader by various devices.

Not previously noted in *ALS*, Julia Randall's 1969 essay, "Genius of the Shore: The Poetry of Howard Nemerov," is reprinted in *The Sounder Few* (pp. 345–56). In it she surveys in general the "candid vision" of this poet, and claims that *The Blue Swallows* "is far and away the most significant and least recognized volume of poems of the sixties," an estimate which, even if ambiguous, serves to remind us of the merit of Nemerov's work and also that merit is never properly measured by the mere volume of criticism published.

Howard Kaye, "The Post-Symbolist Poetry of Yvor Winters" (*SoR* 7:176–97) outlines briefly the kinds of verse Winters wrote throughout his career and gives examples; by 1934 he had developed his abstract style in which he wrote intermittently for the rest of his life. The abstract style being insufficient, however, he also wrote in what he called the post-symbolist style, which gives " 'the sharp sensory detail contained in a poem or passage of such a nature that the detail is charged with meaning without our being told of the meaning explicitly, or is described in language indicating such meaning indirectly but clearly.' " Most of this article is devoted to studying examples of Winter's post-symbolist poetry: complex matters are dealt with in a style of gratifying clarity.

"Berryman's *The Dream Songs*" (*SR* 79:464–69), a review-article by Larry P. Vonalt, sorts out the shifting identity of Henry and his relation to the poet and then briefly surveys themes in the poem. It concerns Henry's losses; his fear of extinction and hence his need for fame; his spiritual death and rebirth. It is "one of the most significant religious poems of the twentieth century." In "Slithy Tome" (*Agenda* 9,i:52–61) Peter Dale reviews Berryman's *Dream Songs* and proceeds frugally and with English reasonableness from word order and other verbal oddities to the question of the subject: a poem about a poet writing a poem which is the poem written by the poet" (p. 59). W. B. Patrick, "Berryman's 77 Dream Songs: 'Spare Now a Cagey John / A Whilom' " (*SHR* 5:113–19) proceeds in a vein opened by William Wasserstrom (see *ALS 1968*, p. 257), studying among other matters the relationship between Stephen Crane and Henry in *The Dream Songs*, and suggesting that Henry had problems similar to Crane's.

In "Sylvia Plath's Crossing the Water: Some Reflections" (*CritQ* 13:165–72) Ted Hughes prints and makes individual comments upon nine poems from about forty which Sylvia Plath wrote between *The Colossus* and *Ariel* which would, he says, have made a fine book. But habitually dissatisfied with her own past achievements, she was looking ahead to a new style and failed to collect these poems, which have a beauty of their own. Hughes describes them aptly enough as "little safe planets floating near the solar conflagration of *Ariel*." In "The Rise of the Angel: Life Through Death in the Poetry of Sylvia Plath" (*MSE* 3:34–39) William Meissner finds the poet of *Ariel* seeking spiritual purity through suffering and death.

Book reviews in *The Review* are most often good, brief critical surveys. Though the wit is a little labored, "Everything's Rainbow" (25:51–57), a review of the *Complete Poems* of Elizabeth Bishop by Clive James, is characteristic. James points to the precision in the poems but concludes, "If 'precision' is the cardinal word in our aesthetic vocabulary, we will be praising her for the very thing that she has striven (correctly, in my view, although not often successfully) to transcend."

ix. Others

In "Laura Riding's Poems" (*CQ* 5:302–08), a review, Michael Kirkham makes a brief but careful study of the peculiar style of this poetry, illustrating it by reprinting and analyzing the poem "Afternoon."

The work of Wendell Berry, who returned from New York to farmland in Kentucky, has begun to attract attention, due in part, no doubt, to its topical commentary on the human violation of nature. In a balanced introductory essay, "The Hunter's Trail: Poems by Wendell Berry" (*IowaR* 1,i[1970]:90–99), Kenneth Field observes that close harmony with nature is a condition of grace in the work of this poet. His early volumes were ornate and literary, his voice still fails him when he writes on public issues, and he has fewer subjects and fewer kinds of rhythm than he ought. But for five or six solid poems he is distinguished from his contemporaries. Two essays in *MPS* also introduce this poet: John Ditzy, "Wendell Berry: Homage to the Apple Tree" (2,i:7–15) and Robert Hass, "Wendell Berry: Finding the Land" (2,i:16–38), the latter dealing particularly with Berry's relation to nature, to the land, and its loss.

"The Poetry of Carl Rakosi" by L. S. Dembo (*IowaR* 2,i:72–80) is a brief summary of the main characteristics of this poet, supplied with examples that show how the Wallace Stevens flourishes of the early work are still present in the later, where Rakosi turns more attentively to subject matter.

"A Bibliography of Richard Wright's Works" by Michel Fabre and Edward Margolies (*NewL* 38,ii:155–69) includes the places and dates of the publication of Wright's individual poems.

Ann Colley in "Don L. Lee's 'But He Was Cool Or: He Even Stopped for Green Lights': An Example of the New Black Aesthetic" (*CP* 4,ii:20–27), emphasizing that it is a black audience Lee has in mind for the poem, shows how he tries to free himself from white poetic conventions in this satire by using free verse, unconventional rhythms deliberately notated, and colloquial language.

In "The Progress of Lewis Turco" (*MPS* 2:115–24) William Heyen documents development from stiff and methodical verse to an openness in which the reader senses his own existence.

University of Oregon

16. Drama

Walter J. Meserve

i. Histories, Anthologies, Indexes, Dissertations

No effective scholarly work dealing with the full scope of American drama or theatre appeared in 1971. Scholars interested in any historical perspective limited themselves to the modern period, and their works will be discussed in that section of this essay. The one volume that attempted the broader view is Marion Geisinger's *Plays, Players, & Playwrights: An Illustrated History of the Theatre* (New York, Hart Publishing Co.), a beautiful book surveying Western theatre beginning with the Greeks and including more than 400 sketches and photos. Of the 726 pages more than 300 treat early American theatre, twentieth-century American theatre, and the American musical theatre. This imbalance might prove attractive to the American specialist, but it must be understood that the work is a commercial rather than scholarly venture. There is no bibliography, no source identification for photos, a lack of dates when they seem necessary (for the Federal Theatre, for example), and no reference to modern black theatre or black dramatists. At its worst, however, it is misleading. Burgoyne's *The Blockade of Boston* is a weak illustration of American drama during the Revolution; Dunlap's *History* is "invaluable" only if its limitations are understood; saying that a lack of copyright prevented Mrs. Stowe from reaping a fortune from *Uncle Tom's Cabin* does not describe the situation accurately.

Two other books that present general views of particular aspects of American drama should be noted briefly. Nellie McCaslin's *Theatre for Children in the United States* (Norman, Univ. of Okla. Press) provides a history of children's theatre in America since 1903. Under numerous headings which suggest her episodic and encyclopedic approach, she lists and gives scattered but copious information on producing agencies and financial backing for children's theatre. College and university productions seem proportionately slighted, while the organization of the book indicates that a better history of children's theatre and drama in America should be written. Louis L. Williams's *The American Passion Play, A Study and a History* (Bloomington, Ill., American Passion Play, Inc., 1970) is more of a public relations volume for a particular passion play than a study of the subject, but it does provide much interesting information on *The American Passion Play* by Delmar D. Darrah, performed yearly since 1924 in Bloomington, Illinois—production problems, characters, scenes, and spectacles. Its special pleading and its repetitious and sentimental writing style, however, demonstrate its basic unscholarly approach, although the volume begins with a suggestion of the history of passion plays and concludes with a good overview of the passion play in America.

Best American Plays, Sixth Series 1963–1967 (New York, Crown Publishers) appeared, edited by the late John Gassner and Clive Barnes, who provided a most interesting introduction as well as one-page introductions for each of the seventeen plays. American drama has come a long way since this series started. This volume is the first to include a musical, an off-Broadway play, and plays with those Anglo-Saxon four-letter words. It is also a comment on New York theatre that Barnes advises playwrights with adventurous or unusual plays to take them to London rather than New York.

In the category of indexes there are two new ones to be noted. Carl J. Marder III has provided "An Index to *Personal Recollections of the Drama*, by Henry Dickinson Stone" (*TD* 3,i–ii:65–80) which basically indexes proper nouns. "A Subject Index to *Drama Survey*, 1961–1968" (*TD* 3,i–ii:81–100) by Peter H. Clough is divided into articles organized under twelve subtypes plus book reviewers, and record reviews. The index is good to have, but this one is a reminder that present-day economics has forced such journals as *Drama Survey* and *Drama Critique* to cease publication.

In 1971 there were more than thirty dissertations on subjects related to American drama and theatre. A good number of them dealt with particular dramatists: the reception of Edward Albee's plays in Germany, O'Neill's New England cycle, O'Neill's methods of characterizing the secret self, character and value in the plays of Archibald MacLeish, the plays of Bronson Howard, the poetic dramas of Robinson Jeffers, Philip Barry and his critics, man and society in the plays of Arthur Miller, style and language in Miller's plays, Laurence Stal-

lings and war, six plays of Tennessee Williams, and the work of LeRoi
Jones. As the need for an assessment of American dramatic criticism is
more urgently recognized, more dissertations appear. This year there
were studies of Wolcott Gibbs, Harold Clurman, and George Jean
Nathan. For the student of American theatre there were dissertations
on the Detroit Theatre from 1862 through 1875, Harrison Grey Fiske's
management of the Manhattan Theatre from 1901 until 1906, the
Living Theatre, William Duffy's management of the Albany Theatre
from 1830 through 1835, and the acting careers of John Hodgkinson,
Olive Logan, and Alice Brady. Other dissertations dealt with such
topics as game structure in plays, the New Dramatists Committee, the
American family, musical comedy, dramatizations of American novels,
and the characterization of the American Indian in American plays
from 1830 through 1860.

ii. From the Beginning to 1860

To encourage the student to become serious about early American
drama, Julian Mates has provided what he terms "The Dramatic
Anchor: Research Opportunities in the American Drama Before
1800" (*EAL* 5,iii:76–79). Admitting that the possibilities are fewer
for the scholar than for the antiquarian, he briefly suggests sources
and emphasizes the need for research on repertory theatre and theatre managers. He makes a good point and, hopefully, students will
accept the challenge. Certainly, there is a need for intelligent curiosity, for the drama of the period does have its attraction, as the following
three essays suggest. In "William Byrd II: Comic Dramatist?" (*EAL*,
6,i:18–30) Carl R. Dolmetsch presents something more than a remote
possibility that Byrd had something to do with the composition of
The Careless Husband. If so—and the evidence is not overwhelming
—Byrd would replace Governor Hunter as America's first dramatist.
Attempting to show that a play may reveal both an historical period
and the political views of its author, Charles S. Watson fuses historical and literary criticism in "A Denunciation on the Stage of Spanish
Rule: James Workman's *Liberty in Louisiana* (1804)" (*LaHist*
2[1970]:245–58). Workman's attitudes as a judge and a Federalist
sympathizer are clearly shown in the farcical characters and episodes
of the play. In the third essay, "A Note on Robert Montgomery Bird's
Oralloossa" (*ELN* 9,i:46–49) Daniel R. Bronson argues with some

force that the failure of the play is offset by the strength of the title character, "a conservative white man who, in the 1830's, was able to perceive the phenomenon we now call black rage."

The architecture of various American theatres, the managers who produced plays, and the actors who drew the audience to those plays—these were the topics that interested most scholars of early nineteenth-century American theatre and drama. James R. Corey relates "Miss Cheer: American Actress, 1764–1768" (*RS* 39:137–43) to the theatre of her time. With considerable insight and charm the late Alan S. Downer discusses "Early American Professional Acting" (*TS* 12,ii:79–96). Converting the Hallams from theatrical outcasts to merchant adventurers and viewing Dunlap as a myth maker rather than a true historian, Downer tries to make early materials relevant to modern students. In a distinctly different view of acting, John L. Marsh looks at "Captain E. C. Williams and the Panoramic School of Acting" (*ETJ* 23:289–97). Researching scattered reviews, he draws some conclusions about the popularity and the narrative techniques of Williams, who was the owner and delineator of the "South Seas Whaling Voyage," a panorama which toured Eastern America for about ten years after 1858. The article provides an interesting glimpse of a peculiar aspect of American theatre.

There are two new book-length studies of early American theatre. West T. Hill, Jr., records *The Theatre in Early Kentucky, 1790–1820* (Lexington, Univ. Press of Ky.), including a bibliography and a list of performances during that period. Listing only three performance dates prior to 1800, he provides a well documented record of the first theatre in Lexington before going on to the work of Noble Luke Usher and the first Western theatre circuit—Lexington, Frankfort, and Louisville. Although chapter 6 concerning the Drakes is largely a retelling of Ludlow's *Dramatic Life*, Hill's overall picture of theatre in Kentucky is a significant addition to American theatre history. *Outside Broadway: A History of the Professional Theatre in Newark, New Jersey, from the Beginning to 1867* (Metuchen, N.J., Scarecrow Press, 1970) by Lester L. Moore makes good use of the periodicals of this period but tends to be sketchy, a bit pretentious, and not interestingly written. It provides a list of plays and players but lacks an index. A brief text of 124 pages, the history emphasizes the period from the building of the Concert Hall in 1847 through the Military Hall theatre during the early 1850s, Kate Fisher's Newark

Theatre in the mid-1860s, and the popular era of Waller's Opera House.

Of particular value to theatre historians is Julia Curtis's "The Architecture and Appearance of the Charleston Theatre, 1793–1833" (*ETJ* 23:1–12), which corrects widely accepted past descriptions of this building in a very scholarly and well-written fashion. Richard Stoddard's "Notes on John Joseph Holland, with a Design for the Baltimore Theatre, 1802" (*TS* 12,i:58–66) present particular information on an American scene painter along with one of his designs. As most theatre researchers know, the history of scene design and painting in America is recorded in a most hesitant and superficial manner.

Two bibliographic notes for the teacher of American drama are Gary Engle's description of "The Atkinson Collection of Ethiopian Drama at the University of Chicago" (*RALS* 1:181–99) and John Rothman's *The Origin and Development of Dramatic Criticism in the "New York Times," 1851–1880* (New York, Arno Press [1970]). Although not exactly what the title suggests, the thin volume provides bibliographic material on the reviewers as well as probable identification and a study of sample reviews.

iii. From 1860 Through 1915

For the period from the mid-nineteenth century through 1915 few scholars chose particular plays or playwrights on which to concentrate their efforts. Of the several popular late nineteenth-century men of the theatre only Dion Boucicault got into print. In "Boucicault on Dramatic Character" (*SSCJ* 37,i:73–83) Cleveland Harrison explains Boucicault as a follower of Aristotle, who believed in the appropriateness, consistency, and reality of character. Believing that the test of a dramatist or an actor was found in the characters he left to posterity, Boucicault considered the "quality of suffering" as the crucial link between character and actor but concerned himself with the feelings, appearance, and features of a character rather than his moral distinctions. Although Henry James had great difficulties as a dramatist during his life, his work has since attracted a number of assessments. In an essay which tells more about G. B. Shaw than James, "Shaw the Reviewer and James' *Guy Domville*" (*MD* 14:331–34), Joe B. Hatcher briefly reiterates Shaw's explanation of the audience's extreme bad manners and his statement that he admired the attempt to write a meaningful play—a quality he missed in others. Interestingly enough, Shaw also praised the work of a friend of James, William Dean Howells, whose plays had only slightly more success in the commercial theatre than James's. To show that James expressed the essence of the drama in his work, however, Robert Emmet Long compiled the "Adaptations of Henry James' Fiction for Drama, Opera, and Films; With a Checklist of New York Theatre Critics' Reviews" (*ALR* 4:268–78). His list includes thirteen plays, two operas, and four films.

A lesser and younger literary contemporary of James was George Ade, who also tried his hand with drama, yet with considerably greater success. Harold H. Kolb, Jr., in "George Ade (1866–1944)" (*ALR* 4:157–69), surveys Ade under the usual organizational headings in this journal. "Owen Davis, America's Forgotten Playwright" (*Players* 46[1970]:30–35) was briefly considered by Barry Williams, who pointed out Davis's most enviable accomplishments. In a brief but significant article in terms of the history of dramatic theory in America, Mike Mendelsohn assesses "Percy Mackaye's Dramatic Theories" (*BRMMLA* 24:85–89). Jerry V. Pickering suggests the importance of Moody's dramas as indicators of the social mileau in "William Vaughn Moody: The Dramatist as Social Philosopher" (*MD* 14:93–103). In a well-written argument, the author contends that Moody is summed up in his plays, where he attempts to reconcile his ideals and ideas with a changing society.

The most original and in many ways the best written essays concerned with the 1860–1915 period deal with those theatrical activities which are considered outside the legitimate theatre. Vaudeville, for example! Albert F. McLean's "U.S. Vaudeville and the Urban Comics," written for the new English journal, *Theatre Quarterly* (1,iv:47–52) is scarcely more than a quick survey of relatively well known information, especially if one knows Prof. McLean's other work; yet a survey has its place. Obviously more significant in the annals of vaudeville is Parker Zellers's *Tony Pastor: Dean of the Vaudeville Stage* (Ypsilanti, Eastern Mich. Univ. Press). In a thin volume of 118 pages, plus a selected bibliography, Zellers takes Pastor from his early days as a circus ringmaster, and then as a comic singer in 1860, through his success in family theatre, his move to Broadway, and on to Union Square, his competition with Keith and Albee, and his final years, 1896–1908, as a generous, well-liked manager somewhat removed from the everyday theatrical fight. Another distinctive form of the theatre in late nineteenth-century America was the Buffalo Bill play, whose major character, for which Ned Buntline provided the first impulse, was created upon the stage by William F. Cody. In an excellent article William S. E. Coleman explores the story of "Buffalo Bill on Stage" (*Players* 47:80–91).

Still another exceptional article on another aspect of late nineteenth- and early twentieth-century theatre is "The Indian Medicine Show" (*ETJ* 23:431–45) by Brooks McNamara. It all seems to have started in 1881 by John Healy, the first drummer for Kickapoo Indian Sagwa. By World War II the Medicine Show was virtually a thing of the past, but during those sixty intervening years, it was big entertainment, with variety shows and spectacle followed by the stock tale of the man who saved an Indian's life and received the secret of the medicine in return.

As these somewhat more individualistic aspects of the American theatre were created, developed to a certain prosperity, and were forgotten, the legitimate theatre was plying its slow way in and out of various kinds of artistic, moralistic, and commercial entanglements. One such difficulty is very interestingly presented by J. Richard Wills in "Olive Logan vs. the Nude Woman" (*Players* 47:36–43). As a playwright and actress, Miss Logan respected the theatre and its artists. After *The Black Crook*, certain productions of *Mazeppa*, and Lydia Thompson's British Blondes, however, she voiced her opinion about the demoralizing influence she sometimes found upon the stage. Immediately attacked for her views on female nudity that revealed legs, Logan soon had public opinion on her side; but any victory, she realized, would not last—and she was right. An eruption in 1881 of ministerial condemnation of the theatre is treated in Sandra Hupp's "Chicago's Church-Theatre Controversy" (*Players* 46:60–64).

Toward the end of the nineteenth century the Theatrical Syndicate gained control of much of the American theatre. Few managers or actors had the courage or the fortitude to contend with the syndicate, and those who did frequently regretted their action. In "New Orleans: Greenwall vs. the Syndicate" (*Players* 46:180–87) Shirley Harrison describes the gallant action of Henry Greenwall, manager of the Grand Opera House, as he engaged his own stock company, reduced admissions, and even built his own theatre in a vain attempt to fight the syndicate. Shortly after the syndicate got started, the United Booking Office working within the B. F. Keith Vaudeville Exchange, began to control every detail of vaudeville production. Frederich E. Snyder, "Theatre in a Package" (*TS* 12,i:34–45), describes the system as well as the formula for vaudeville productions. An essay and a slender book treat William Gillette, an actor and dramatist of this period. Yvonne Shafer's "A Sherlock Holmes of the Past: William Gillette's Later Years" (*Players* 46:229–35) briefly summarizes his career and samples reviews from his 1936–1937 season. Doris E. Cook's *Sherlock Holmes and Much More; or Some Facts about William Gillette* (Hartford, Conn. Historical Society [1970]) provides "some facts" and insight into his private and public attitudes, particularly after 1910, but not much more.

Of especial value is Daniel J. Watermeier's *Between Actor and Critic: Selected Letters of Edwin Booth and William Winter* (Princeton, N.J., Princeton Univ. Press), which supplements these important letters (1869–1890) with a sensitive introduction and useful annotations.

iv. Between the Two World Wars

Although the two decades between the world wars produced the plays which created for America a favorable position in the world theatre, only three of the dramatists consistently stimulate published scholarly research—O'Neill, Wilder, and Odets. Other dramatists who helped give American drama its modern reputation—Paul Green, Robert Sherwood, Philip Barry, Maxwell Anderson, S. N. Behrman, Lillian Hellman, William Saroyan, and Elmer Rice—receive only an occasional essay. That the amount of published research on American drama is slight and limited to few dramatists must be explained, in part, at least, by the lack of a journal which deals exclusively or primarily with American drama. The few drama journals which do exist tend to include all of drama or emphasize the modern period. Consequently, there are many gaps in the history and the assessment of American drama. Some of those are being filled each year, but it is a slow progress. Each year, too, more and more criticism treats the contemporary scene—which does not always warrant the effort. Yet obviously that is the kind of material that journals will publish.

The three books reviewed this year that offer general views of

modern American drama and theatre present the three most prevalent attitudes toward the subject: a concern for American musicals, a
New York critic's memories, and a despairing academic view of
things. Stanley Green's latest volume, *Ring Bells! Sing Songs! Broadway Musicals of the 1930's* (New Rochelle, N.Y., Arlington House),
is divided into two almost equal parts: pictures and commentary with
reference to the times and the people involved, and casts and credits
for all the musicals of this period. The second volume is Brooks Atkinson's *Broadway* (New York, Macmillan [1970]) which provides
knowledgeable observations and some anecdotal commentary on
actors, managers, critics, and playwrights from 1900 through 1950,
with a postscript for the contemporary scene. There is no bibliography, and the historical continuity within its three main chapters is
not clear. It is not essentially a scholarly work, nor was it meant to be;
but it will take its place among the volumes of opinions by America's
major theatre critics.

The third volume, Ruby Cohn's *Dialogue in American Drama*
(Bloomington, Ind. Univ. Press) represents a dominant scholarly
approach to American drama. The title is a bit ambiguous as she
examines "American dramatic dialogue of the past." With this objective, she assumes that "American drama—a written text that can be
taken seriously for stage and page—begins with O'Neill." The first essay in the volume, "The Wet Sponge of Eugene O'Neill," is excellent;
Long Day's Journey, Hughie, and *Iceman* are considered his masterpieces for dialogue. The essay on "The Articulate Victims of Arthur
Miller" seems to lack a coherent thesis, and the discussion does not
clearly substantiate the values with which the writer finally assesses
Miller's dialogue. In the dialogue of Tennessee Williams's plays Cohn
finds a weakness for symbols but a strength for the American stage in
his vocabulary and rhythm. Edward Albee is the "most skillful composer of dialogue," having a perfect contemporary, colloquial, stylized dialogue. Cohn next considers American novelists who have
written plays, finding that none of them wrote dialogue which reveals
a penetrating insight into how men think or feel. The chapter on
"Poets at Play" provides substantive but selective information. Primarily concerned with inadequacies, however, it avoids almost completely a discussion of the ways in which poetic language may emphasize a point or assist a crisis or climax in the drama. The writer's
greatest enthusiasm is reserved for the canon of LeRoi Jones, whose

"violent language" perhaps should be enjoyed though not to the exclusion of others. The idea behind Cohn's analysis is valid, although the atmosphere created is occasionally a bit snobbish. Perhaps most people, but certainly not all, would accept both her beginning assumption and her conclusion that the best of the American plays fall short of the best European plays and that the shortcoming is in the dialogue.

a. **Eugene O'Neill.** One book-length study this year, Horst Frenz's *Eugene O'Neill* (New York, Frederich Ungar), is a brief, 30,000-word volume first written in German (Berlin, Colloquium Verlag) then translated by Helen Sebba with revisions and additions by Frenz. It is a careful and workmanlike analysis of O'Neill's plays. Rolf Scheibler's *The Late Plays of Eugene O'Neill* (Bern, Francke Verlag [1970]) analyzes *A Touch of the Poet, Moon for the Misbegotten, Long Day's Journey,* and *The Iceman Cometh.* Scheibler attempts to show that O'Neill has clearly expressed ideas about society and that his views are "less negative than generally assumed." He seems a little overwhelmed with his analytical method but his structural analysis of particular scenes, along with his concern for symbols and images, is effective. Stressing the part that women play, Scheibler argues that the four dramas are related through the idea of "possessive idealism" and suggests "a strange light of comfort" in these late O'Neill plays. Jackson Bryer's *Merrill Checklist of Eugene O'Neill* (Columbus, Ohio, Charles E. Merrill) will be helpful for the beginning student of Eugene O'Neill.

A number of articles deal with particular O'Neill plays. Roger Asselineau describes "*Desire Under the Elms,* A Phase of Eugene O'Neill's Philosophy" (*Festschrift Rudolf Stamm,* pp. 277–83) as a clash between Cabot's Puritanism and Abbie's worship of Dionysus. Each O'Neill play, Asselineau argues, is an attempt to find God or some justification for the human condition, and *Desire* is a quiet affirmation of the dignity of man in what may be a godless universe. It is an intelligent and well-written essay, quite the opposite of Kenneth M. Rosen's "O'Neill's *Brown* and Wilde's *Gray*" (*MD* 13:347–55), which is one of those senseless exercises in matching points which reveal nothing about either artist. Claude R. Flory, "Notes on the Antecedents of *Anna Christie*" (*PMLA* 86:77–83) examines the play manuscript and refutes previous contentions concerning the experimental nature of the play and its relationship to "The Ole Davil" by showing conclusively that there is nothing experimental about the play and that at least ninety-five percent of the "Davil" play is identical with the published text of *Anna Christie*.

The best essay on O'Neill this year is John H. Stroupe's "*Marco Millions* and O'Neill's 'two part two-play' Form" (*MD* 13:382–92). Basing his evaluation on O'Neill's notes and a 1928 Theatre Guild prompt copy of the play, Stroupe shows O'Neill's writing process and explains how an earlier conceived dual interest in Polo's travel and education with his corrupting influence upon Chinese society became a criticism of American values once the play was condensed into a three-act form. Frederic I. Carpenter's "Focus on Eugene O'Neill's *The Iceman Cometh*, The Iceman Hath Come" (*American Dreams*, pp. 158–64) evokes some thought as he uses the play as a springboard for his own frequently wandering ideas and questions. His contentions concerning Hickey's name are not convincing, and there is a general inconclusiveness about the essay. Jackson R. Bryer's "Hell Is Other People: *Long Day's Journey into Night*" (*The Fifties*, pp. 261–70) is only slightly more satisfying. To Bryer the play is a tragedy based upon love and has four tragic characters, all of whom are both responsible and not responsible. Unfortunately, his enthusiastic and sometimes exciting claims are eliminated by his lack of supporting argument and clear evidence. Certainly, his conclusion that *Long Day's Journey* is one of the greatest plays in any language in any age is far too easily reached. This was not a strong year for scholarship on O'Neill.

b. **Glaspell, Wilder, Anderson.** Dramatists between the two world wars received only slight and limited attention this year. Susan Glaspell got a strong boost from Arthur E. Waterman—"Susan Glaspell (1882?–1948)" (*ALR* 4,ii:183–91)—in the established format of this journal. Waterman's past scholarship on Glaspell substantiates the opinions he offers here. Thornton Wilder was surveyed in the German series of which the previously mentioned O'Neill book is an example—Hermann Stresau, *Thornton Wilder* (New York, Frederich Ungar). Generally, the plays are slighted in this thin volume although the *Alcestiad* receives a full explanation. After a stimulating introductory chapter the book shows weaknesses in continuity, balance, and a tendency to overburden the assessment with philosophical or pseudo-philosophical complications. Michael D'Ambrosio's "Is 'Our Town' Really Our Town?" (*EngR* 22,i:20–22) doesn't really deal with the play, whereas Dieter Herms's "Zum Humor im epischen Theater Thornton Wilders" (*NS* 20:36–47) helps the American understand the European's appreciation of Wilder. Although Maxwell Anderson received scant attention this year, Laurence Avery's "Addenda to the Maxwell Anderson Bibliography: Monro's Chapbook" (*PBSA* 65: 408–11) is a significant item.

c. Odets and Rice. Works of Odets and Faulkner are compared in " 'Pylon,' 'Awake and Sing!' and the Apocalyptic Imagination" (*Criticism* 13,ii:131–41). Defining the apocalyptic imagination as "one which conceives and responds to structures that are not organic, have no controlling center, but are all the exploding surfaces of a totally circumferential form," Richard Pearce pleads his special view that of those works which reflect the social atmosphere of the thirties *Pylon* and *Awake and Sing!* develop "the vision of the apocalypse most fully." Gerald Weales's *Clifford Odets, Playwright* (New York, Pegasus) is a particularly effective addition to the several book-length studies of Odets in its extensive background research and analysis of *Waiting for Lefty* and *Awake and Sing*. Written with both fervor and feeling for the man and his plays, the book follows a chronological pattern, emphasizing the plays of the 1930s and arguing for a fair appraisal of "one of our most talented playwrights."

Frank Durham in *Elmer Rice* (*TUSAS* 167[1970] views him as a man in a dilemma: an artist trying to function in the marketplace. Despite the strictures of the Twayne format, Durham touches upon about thirty of the fifty plays which Rice wrote. He perceptively analyses *The Adding Machine* as Rice's best work and evaluates Rice's contribution to American drama in an organized and responsible fashion.

d. Theatre of the Twenties and Thirties. Two articles from recent years comment on the Provincetown Players. Robert K. Sarlos is concerned with the physical stage in "Wharf and Dome: Materials for a History of the Provincetown Players" (*ThR* 10,iii[1970]:163–78), complete with pictures and diagrams. In another essay, "Producing Principles and Practices of the Provincetown Players" (*ThR* 10,ii

[1969]:89–102) Sarlos finds the players characteristically American in their methods of casting plays and in their tolerance for individual dissent.

Of the articles on the thirties the most interesting is Gregory D. Kunesh's "The Blue Eagle Theatre: A Precedent for the Federal Theatre Project" (*Players* 46:268–71). More of a note than an essay, it points out that between May 1933, and May 1935, the National Alliance of the Theatre was involved in activity which deserves further attention. Heinz Bernard's "A Theatre for Lefty: USA in the 1930's" (*ThQ* 1,iv:53–56) is a very general survey of selected aspects of the left-wing theatre movement during the 1930s, with a section on the Living Newspaper productions in the Federal Theatre. Least impressive is Gil Lazier's wandering and trivial chronicle of a piece called *No Excuse*, which he and others created out of the passion brought on by the incidents at Kent State and Cambodia only to discover that audiences found it neither tasteful nor good drama. The essay is called "Living Newspaper 1970: Obituary for a Gentle Agit-Prop Play" (*ETJ* 23:135–51). It could hardly have fulfilled the editor's requirement of "distinguished contemporary scholarship and criticism."

v. After World War II

Ideas for a new American drama are constantly suggested, but thus far no single event or experimentation has marked the beginning of a new era. Hesitantly and with difficulties that are not readily described, American drama has progressed from what now might be called the exciting conservatism of Arthur Miller and Tennessee Williams through the reconstruction of absurdist drama in America and on to a growing interest in poetic drama and political drama. Perhaps the exotic or artistic experimentation with nudity or the emotionally vivid black drama and revolutionary theatre provides the climax.

Throughout this progress America's favorite stage entertainment, the musical, has prospered. To show its tremendous success in contemporary world theatre, Richard Altman with Merwyn Kaufman recounts *The Making of a Musical: "Fiddler on the Roof"* (New York, Crown Publishers), from its first out-of-town performances through its New York opening and on to the world tours and its last stop in Hollywood in November 1971. It is a chatty book with enough substance to give it some value for the student of American musicals. But there are also other musicals. In "The Rise and Fall of *Hair*" (*Dram* 43,ii:14–16) Tom Tumbusch makes some observations about the revolutionary quality of this musical, which is now pretty dull entertainment for many college students, and asks what new controversies will be thrust upon drama students, principals, and school boards when *Hair* is released for nonprofessional productions. Perhaps another new era will then have started.

The place of man in contemporary drama and theatre, the function of that drama and theatre in contemporary society, and the relevance of drama/theatre to man—these become significant issues for the drama/theatre scholar. In *Perspectives on Contemporary Theatre* (Baton Rouge, La. State Univ. Press) O. G. Brockett discusses the relationship between values in theatre and values in society and suggests the variety of forms in which committed art may appear. A redefinition of theatre, he feels, must relate to the larger issues in society for which the need for redefinition is symptomatic. In *Revolution as Theatre* (New York, Liveright) Robert Brustein collects some of his recent essays and adds an introduction which is well worth reading as an attempt to make the radical movement self conscious. This same radical movement is the object of Mordecai Gorelik's ire in "Social vs. Irrational Theatre" (*Players* 46:208–10). Openly opposed to the antiverbal theatre theorists as well as those "alienated playwrights who can see no difference between hot air and responsible thinking," Gorelik represents a healthy, conservative view of things.

The relevance of modern drama to modern man is an issue which a number of critics and scholars have faced. The attempt to discuss this issue within a traditional terminology, however, seems to create additional difficulties. Robert W. Corrigan edited and introduced *Tragedy: A Critical Anthology* (Boston, Houghton Mifflin) for which Glenn M. Loney provided the headnotes for individual plays. The weakness of the volume is apparent immediately in the differences of opinion between these two men. Corrigan provides general observations about tragedy as the conflict of a division in man's nature in which an "apparently" insoluble situation occurs, or he sees man doomed to defeat while enjoying a spirit which triumphs over his fate. With his comments, however, he gives Loney little on which to build an argument describing any of the American plays as tragedy.

Trying to use classical terminology, Loney somehow cannot make
Death of a Salesman a tragedy; he finds more difficulty with *Billy
Budd* and finally settles for "moral tragedy of mankind"; after finding
the action of *J. B.* tragic, he seemingly avoids the idea of tragedy in
his subsequent discussion. One must sympathize with the problem
which these men face and to which Brockett referred in his book.

Tragedy as a dramatic structure presents many difficulties for the
scholar, and there are many ways to look at any of the plays included
in the Corrigan-Loney anthology. Sy Kahn explains his directional
view of *J. B.* in "The Games God Plays With Man: A Discussion of
J. B." (*The Fifties*, pp. 249–59), viewing the play as a mid-twentieth-
century version of Job with Nickles as the powerful spokesman for
the relevant agony of man. Concerned with another MacLeish play
that challenges modern mankind to commit itself to relevant human
priorities, C. J. Gianakaris found a question as the controlling issue
in "MacLeish's *Herakles*: Myth for the Modern World" (*CentR* 15:
445–63): "What if you should labor mightily to attain the world
but lose your own soul in the process—what then?" This is a question
for all men—dramatist, director, actor, scholar, concerned individual
—and it provides one compelling reason why many essays are written
about contemporary drama.

a. **Arthur Miller.**   A short play by Miller, *Fame,* was published in
the *Yale Literary Magazine* (140:32–40). Meyer Rubin is a popular
playwright who is always being stopped for his autograph. In a bar
Abe, with his wife, recognizes Meyer as an old high school classmate,
but Meyer doesn't have the faintest idea who Abe is. As they talk,
Abe brags about his success in industry, discovers that Meyer is a
writer, and hints that he could help him out if Meyer ever needs
money. He even suggests that Meyer write plays because that is
where the money is. Then the discovery is made: Meyer is *the* Meyer
Rubin, eminently successful playwright. Built upon an irony, the
play's character and comedy add to its effect.

Articles on Miller's work this year were not outstanding. Ronald
Hayman, "Arthur Miller—Between Satire & Society" (*Encounter* 37,
v:73–79), considers Miller's well structured plays with his social
commitment and concludes that he is the "most Sartrean of living
dramatists." In "A Note on Arthur Miller's *The Price*" (*JAmS* 5:307–
10), Ralph Willett analyzes this latest play and concludes that Miller's

characters have not progressed in terms of accumulated insight. They have, he argues, no recognition beyond the acceptance of the future as repetition of the present. Nothing is added to Miller scholarship with Chester E. Eisinger's "Focus on Arthur Miller's *Death of a Salesman*, The Wrong Decision" (*American Dreams*, pp. 165–74) which offers only observations on the business success and the rural agrarian dreams.

b. **Tennessee Williams.** The most useful item in Williams scholarship this year is Jordan Y. Miller's *Twentieth Century Interpretations of "A Streetcar Named Desire"* (Englewood Cliffs, N.J., Prentice-Hall). Miller's introduction provides an excellent overview of the play although all might not agree that Blanche is a classical Aristotelian tragic figure. Another essay by Miller appears in *The Fifties* (pp. 241–48). Entitled *"Camino Real,"* the essay is a minor revision of an essay written for *American Dramatic Literature* (1961). The scattered and personal observations that are new, however, a personal denial of Williams's world, for example, are both unscholarly and ineffective. Another point of view on Williams's work, not completely new but intelligent and well-argued, is presented by Frank Durham in "Tennessee Williams, Theatre Poet in Prose" (*SAB* 36,ii:3–16). In portraying a "peculiar range of sensibility," Durham explains, the most successful dramatists have employed, "a new poetic drama which eschews verse for an eclectic but organic union of both verbal and non-verbal elements of the theatre." To illustrate this "plastic theatre" concept, Durham uses *The Glass Menagerie.*

c. **Edward Albee.** Popularity with critics and scholars is proving to be a fleeting enjoyment for Edward Albee. Quite clearly, the pattern of critics' interest and editors' preference is shifting. Albee is out; black drama is in. Relatively few American scholars commented on Albee's work. Ruby Cohn with "Albee's Box and Ours" (*MD* 14:137–43) was one. Accepting Albee's declaration that all dramatists make statements about the condition of man and the nature of the art form they use, Cohn argues that *Box-Mao-Box* makes a strong statement about Albee's art form and his use of language. He has, she writes in her own esoteric phrasing, "musicalized the structure and texture of drama." In another essay a most pretentious and ornate writing style very adequately obliterates any idea that could be taken seriously in Dorothy Dunlap Tolpegin's "The Two-Petaled Flower: A Commentary on Edward Albee's Play, *Tiny Alice*" (*CimR* 14:17–30). "Children and Childishness in the Plays of Edward Albee" (*Players* 46:252–56) by M. J. Kilker makes no enlightened assessment of Albee's plays. Looking through all of Albee's plays, the author sees childhood and children as a meaningless "positive factor" when it suggests innocence, promise, or enthusiasm and a "negative factor" when it is used as escape. Unfortunately, there is nothing on which to hang these factors. Sensing a direction in popular criticism, Sy Syna compares LeRoi Jones's *The Slave* and *Who's Afraid of Virginia Woolf?* for their devastating portrayals of professors—"The Old Prof Takes the Stage" (*Players* 46:76–79). He also clearly finds satisfaction in the portrayals and looks askance at critics who did not like them.

d. **Black Drama.** Black journals should obviously discuss black literature, theatre, or art. Now, however, scholarship on black drama and theatre has become a most acceptable province of the general academic journals, and white scholars have descended upon the general area in a manner which might surprise one unfamiliar with the opportunistic pattern of contemporary drama and theatre criticism. *Theatre Documentation* (3,i–ii:3–28) has published "The Negro in Twentieth Century American Drama: A Bibliography" by Clyde G. Sumpter. In each of four periods encompassed by the years from 1900 through 1969 he lists play collections, plays, articles, and unpublished materials—providing an acceptable working bibliography while showing a certain ignorance in his choice of title. Orley I. Holtan's "Sidney Brustein and the Plight of the American Intellectual" (*Players* 46:222–25) would seem to describe the critic's attempt to use black drama to explain a predominantly white problem—the necessity for commitment on the part of the intellectual in a corrupt society. George R. Adams, in "Black Militant Drama" (*AI* 28:107–28), argues that the "social topography of *A Raisin in the Sun, Dutchman* and *Blues for Mr. Charlie* presents "a map of American psycho-social behavior." With his slogan-oriented vocabulary, Adams comments that these plays have a "therapeutic lesson" for "us" (white America) which must be heeded if America is to "survive as an ongoing and healthy culture." The entire essay, unfortunately, is so full of psychoanalytic jargon that it becomes a meaningless rhetorical exercise. C. W. E. Bigsby's "Black Drama in the Seventies" (*KanQ* 3, ii:10–19) again shows the white critic's interest in black revolutionary theatre as excitingly creative while noting that what the black writer has to offer has little chance of acceptance in a white-oriented Broadway theatre.

Evaluation of black drama and theatre is a difficult task—perhaps impossible if the black scholars and critics are to be believed when they state so categorically that a white person cannot understand black drama. It may be, as Michael W. Kaufman writes, "The Delicate World of Reprobation: A Note on the Black Contemporary Theatre" (*ETJ* 23:446–59). There is, Kaufman states, that black political drama written only for blacks which repudiates all Western art and accepts only a racist separation. This drama portends a racial revision in theatre and insists that audiences can bring about that change. The black critic may look at certain plays from a particular viewpoint. In "Big Time Buck White" (*BlackW* 20,xii:72–74), for example, Johari Amini explains the negative or nonproductive effect this play has for blacks; it is simply not relevant to their condition. To his mind the title should be: *Check Out Your Mind—Is This What We Ought to Be?* For the true picture of black drama and theatre one should read Ed Bullins's journal, *Black Theatre*. Issue number 5, entitled "Waitin' for the 70's," includes fine reports on black theatre around the world as well as a particular report on Bullins's New Lafayette Theatre and interviews with a number of prominent black writers. LeRoi Jones's comments on the necessity of black theatre in black communities is an especially clear statement of the black dramatists' intentions. Collections of black plays may increase opportunities for understanding. Clinton F. Oliver and Stephanie Sills have edited *Contemporary Black Drama* (New York, Scribner's), which includes eight plays plus a rather traditional survey introduction by Oliver entitled "The Negro and the American Theatre." Lindsay Patterson's *Black Theatre, A 20th Century Collection of the Work of its Best Playwrights* (New York, Dodd, Mead) includes twelve plays, most of them written since World War II.

e. Black Drama: LeRoi Jones. As Walter W. Burford explains in "LeRoi Jones: From Existentialism to Apostle of Black Nationalism" (*Players* 47,ii:60–64) Jones "is without doubt the most important Black dramatist on the American scene." Interviewers such as Mi-

chael Coleman in "What is Black Theatre?" (*BlackW* 20,vi:32–36)
continue to ask his opinions. For most scholars *Dutchman* remains
his most important play while *The Slave* represents that important
point in his career where art became revolution. Together "the two
plays compose a ritual drama symbolizing LeRoi Jones' conviction
that history develops through cycles of race-war." This is the opinion
of John Lindberg in " 'Dutchman' and 'The Slave': Companions in
Revolution" (*BARev* 2,i–ii:101–07) as he discusses the themes of
search and sanity in these plays, each representing a stage in the
black revolution. John Ferguson analyzes "*Dutchman* and *The Slave*"
(*MD* 13:398–405) according to Aristotle and declares *Dutchman* a
good play and *The Slave* poor particularly in terms of character portrayal. Such an article, of course, provides good evidence for those
black critics who insist that a white audience cannot understand
black drama. More evidence appears in Julian C. Rice's extravagant
attempt—"LeRoi Jones' *Dutchman*: A Reading" (*ConL* 12:42–59)—
to understand the play as a poetic expression of the history of black
music. Going "beyond musicology," Jones, according to Rice, makes
psychological and social observations about "the essential nature of
the Negro's existence in this country." It is difficult to prove Rice
wrong in this final quoted comment—although Jones would resent the
word *Negro*—but how tolerant must journal readers be?

vi. New Directions

Looking into the past and making judgments is comparatively easy.
Contemporary reviewers consistently do this, e.g., Henry Hewes,
"Theatre in '71" (*SatR* 54,xxiv:14–19). The choice of an off-Broadway play, John Guare's *The House of Blue Leaves*, as the best American play of the year, however, may suggest something new about
American theatre as well as American drama. And meaningful new
directions are difficult to divine. Two years ago experimental drama
and theatre showed considerable strength. In fact, critics are beginning to sort out traditions within these experiments. Mardi Valge-
mae, who has gotten more "scholarly mileage" out of his interest in
expressionism than one would have thought possible, argues without
much force that the experimental, underground theatre of the 1960s
owes a basic debt to expressionism—"Expressionism and the New
American Drama" (*TCL* 17:227–34). Reacting to what he con-

siders a weakness in experimental drama, John Lahr writes about "America: The Collapsing Underground" (*Gambit* 17:64–69) and finds the future of American theatre in "performance theatre and the theatrical imagination of playwrights like Sam Shepard and LeRoi Jones." Another critic, Foster Hirsch—"Performance Theatre: *Diony-sus in 69* and *The Serpent*" (*KanQ* 3,ii:41–49)—exclaims in some horror that this kind of theatre must not replace dramatic literature. His reasoning that a theatre of gesture and event cannot express the human experience as well as the playwright's theatre will certainly appeal to critics of dramatic literature.

Another concern for the future is explained by Joan Goulianos in "Politics and Plays" (*KanQ* 3,ii:50–56). Having a particular political bias and a belief that drama should be politically relevant, she fears that plays like Lennox Raphael's *Che!* will "continue to be persecuted," while producers turn to safer plays such as *The Great White Hope*. These directions seem to involve new fears, but certainly this situation is not new. As far as scholarship in American drama and theatre is concerned, the newness that must be continually sought after may be described in terms of insight, accuracy, clarity of expression, coherence of argument, and substantial perspective.

Indiana University

17. Folklore

John T. Flanagan

Folklore bibliography continues to diversify and accumulate; it also appears in a variety of places. A 1970 volume by Charles H. Nilon, *Bibliography of Bibliographies in American Literature* (New York, Bowker) devotes some three pages to folklore, but the coverage is spotty and only brief and perfunctory annotation is provided. *A Classified Bibliography of the Periodical Literature of the Trans-Mississippi West, A Supplement* (1957–67) by Oscar Osburn Winther and Richard A. Van Orman (Bloomington, Ind. Univ. Press [1970]) includes scattered folklore material. Arranged geographically or topically (Civil War, fur trade, Indians) the book utilizes a number of subheadings. Folklore items are listed for several states and regions, and a number of other entries loosely labelled culture might be more appropriately called folklore. The compilation is generally useful and thorough. The *Annual Bibliography of English Language and Literature* edited by John Horden and James B. Misenheimer, Jr. (London, Modern Humanities Research Association) lists approximately 135 items under such labels as mythology, legend, folklore, topography, and local history. English and American items are jumbled together and Volume 44, like its predecessors, is hardly current. Although most of the citations reflect a 1969 publication, many items appeared four or five years earlier. The folklore section of the *American Quarterly* (23:378–81), compiled by James Penrod, Warren I. Titus, and Cratis Williams, includes some forty-one items, presumably limited to material with interdisciplinary value. The list is highly selective but provides useful brief annotations.

Two specialized bibliographies are especially significant. Don Yoder's "The Pennsylvania Germans: A Preliminary Reading List" (*PF* 21,ii:2–17) is an excellent summation of material available on all aspects of Pennsylvania German life and culture. Yoder deals not only with history and language but with religion, the arts, folkways, and the Pennsylvania Dutchman in fiction. The list incidentally complements a similar survey which Yoder did for the Amish in 1969. Donald Nugent in "Witchcraft Studies, 1959–1971: A Bibliographical Survey" (*JPC* 5:710–25) goes back to antiquity to glean material dealing with witchcraft in the Western world. The bulk of his listing is European, especially German, French, and English, but considerable American material is also included. Nugent says bluntly that "California is perhaps the most conspicuous focus of Western witchcraft today." His terse but lively comments on almost every item are helpful and interesting.

The *1970 MLA International Bibliography* lists almost 1500 items under such titles as prose narratives, folk poetry, folk games and toys, folk customs, and material folklore. The coverage is impressive, but since the classification is by type rather than by place of origin it is difficult to segregate American material. The excellent author index, however, can facilitate use of the book if the reader is familiar with the names of fellow workers in his field.

For the student of American folklore the most useful single compilation is Merle E. Simmons's annual contribution to the *Southern Folklore Quarterly* (35:173–323). Simmons retains his usual categories but explains the rationale of his work, citing both inclusions and omissions; he notes that he has rejected ephemeral popular magazine material, newspaper items, and brief notes. The largest divisions are general folklore with 292 items and "song game dance" with 264 items. There is a disproportionate emphasis on Hispanic folklore; on the other hand, the annotations are perceptive and extremely helpful.

Another kind of bibliography perhaps should be added here: Ronald L. Baker's "Folklore Courses and Programs in American Colleges and Universities" (*JAF* 84:221–29). Baker found that at least 175 American institutions of higher learning now offer courses in folklore and that students can earn doctoral degrees in folklore in three universities: Indiana, Texas, and Pennsylvania. The most popular course is the introduction to folklore, but this is closely followed by courses in the ballad and folksong and in the folktale. Leah A. Strong examines "American Folklore for the Undergraduate" (*NCarF* 19: 194–200) and pleads for inclusion of such a course in American studies curriculums, with description of such a course at Wesleyan College (Macon, Georgia).

i. History and Theory

An unusual amount of discussion of the history and theory of folklore saw publication in 1971, ranging from surveys of previous scholarship to new interpretations of genres and types. Despite the besetting sin of redundancy and pretentiousness, some of the essays are distinguished for their genuine insight.

In *American Folklore and the Historian* (Chicago, Univ. of Chicago Press) Richard M. Dorson presents twelve essays, all but one previously published, dealing with the theory of folklore, research opportunities in folklore, and folklore in its relationship to history and American studies. The essays are rich in scholarly bibliography and are vigorously, almost aggressively, written. Indeed the reader might be more willing to accept Dorson's arguments if Dorson occasionally admitted that he did not always have all the right answers to the problems he discusses.

Jan Harold Brunvand's "New Directions for the Study of American Folklore" (*Folklore* 82:25–35) distinguishes basically for a foreign audience the differences between research in the field on the two sides of the Atlantic Ocean. He contends that while the historic and geographic method does not seem suitable to the study of American folklore, folklorists who have stressed the regional background, the racial or religious slants, occupations, social classes, and popular culture have done important work. Brunvand's *A Guide for Collectors of Folklore in Utah* (Salt Lake City, Univ. of Utah Press) is obviously intended for use in a small and carefully limited area but has much larger utility.

William R. Ferris, Jr., in "The Collection of Racial Lore: Approaches and Problems" (*NYFQ* 27:261–79) explains his obstacles in collecting folklore in the Mississippi Delta country and his inability to move freely from one racial group to another without invoking mutual suspicion. He found that it was almost mandatory to establish some kind of personal rapport before he could begin his field work.

In "Superstitious Pigeons, Hydrophobia, and Conventional Wisdom" (*WF* 30:1–17) Kenneth L. Ketner urges folklorists to understand basic psychology before engaging in specialized kinds of research and suggests that in certain instances *conventional wisdom* is a term preferable to *superstition*. Ketner uses the madstone as an example of a widely accepted cure in folk medicine. It is interesting to note that when the madstone was successful its excellence was celebrated, but negative results were quietly ignored.

Linda Dégh and Andrew Vazsonyi in "Legend and Belief" (*Genre* 4:281–304) analyze the meaning of legend and discuss various familiar definitions. They argue that the objective truth of a legend is not primarily important since generally both the narrator and the audience are far removed from the legend's source, but there must be total or partial belief in the legend, even if the belief is limited to a few persons and the event may have occurred long ago. Hungarian legend sessions known to the authors confirm their argument.

In June of 1969 the University of California at Los Angeles sponsored a symposium on the American folk legend and invited various American and Canadian specialists to present papers. Subsequently Wayland D. Hand edited the papers in *American Folk Legend, A Symposium* (Berkeley, Univ. of Calif. Press). Lack of space prevents adequate treatment of the individual articles but it should be noted that Richard M. Dorson provided historical perspective; Linda Dégh, Herbert Halpert, Wayland D. Hand, Robert A. Georges, and Barre Toelken dealt with matters of definition, structure, and style; Horace P. Beck, Jan Brunvand, Alan Dundes, and Albert B. Friedman treated sociopsychological values; Don Yoder specifically considered saints' legends in Pennsylvania; D. K. Wilgus and Lynwood Montell analyzed a Civil War theme which survived in legendry and song; and Stanley L. Robe and Américo Paredes surveyed Hispanic material. Richard M. Dorson described the conference in "The UCLA Conference on American Folk Legend" (*NYFQ* 27:97–112).

Another symposium is devoted to New Perspectives in Folklore (*JAF* 84:3–167). The contributors of the thirteen papers include well known anthropologists and folklorists, whose subjects range from attempts to define the discipline to riddle analysis, local legends, Nez Percé myths, and Mexican genres of verbal behavior. Much of the discussion is abstract or redundant and not all of it is genuinely significant. Several examples must suffice.

The initial paper, Dan Ben-Amon's "Toward a Definition of Folklore in Context" (pp. 3–15), examines all previous definitions of folklore, finds them wanting in some way or another, and ends up by categorically rejecting the one quality which all the older definitions shared—tradition. To Ben-Amon folklore can be a body of knowledge, a mode of thought, or a kind of art. He then asserts that "folklore is artistic communication in small groups." The proposed definition is original but neither logical nor relevant and can only add to the present confusion.

Alan Dundes in "Folk Ideas as Units of World View" (pp. 93–103) effectively and persuasively points out that such a term as *myth* has different meanings to different people and that probably the same difficulty applies to proverbs, superstitions, and other conventional genre distinctions. As a consequence Dundes believes that a more useful term to denote "traditional notions that a group of people have about the nature of man, of the world, and of man's life in the world" might be *folk ideas*. But he warns that he is not proposing a new genre since he has already objected to the genres now commonly accepted. As examples of folk ideas he suggests the notion of unlimited good, buried treasure legends, and salvation through suffering. Folk ideas, finally, are not limited to folklore but appear in popular culture.

A somewhat narrower theme is developed impressively by Dennis Tedlock in his essay "On the Translation of Style in Oral Narrative" (pp. 114–33). Tedlock is concerned about the adequacy of translations of American Indian stories, specifically Zuni narratives, and he criticizes Frank H. Cushing for inserting material foreign to the stories and for expanding the texts which he collected. Despite the fact that Cushing's *Zuni Folk Tales* of 1901 has long been accepted as a major work in the field, Tedlock contends that the style is almost Victorian in its quaintness. In Tedlock's view Cushing's book and other such translations suffer from a neglect of oral style: the tone of voice, the degree of loudness, and especially pauses.

An article in a different journal, Carlos C. Drake's "Literary Criticism and Folklore" (*JPC* 5:289–97), might be considered as a kind of coda to this discussion. Drake points out that members of English departments generally distrust folklorists and recites some of the common charges made against them: intellectual shallowness, failure to preserve critical standards since much folklore is crude and inchoate, and a willingness to collect and classify rather than to evaluate. In contrast, Drake feels that folklore can be immediate rather than something ossified and remote; furthermore, he argues rather convincingly that students sent out into the field to collect folklore can learn more about actual literary processes than they could by plowing through the mass of criticism accumulating around certain novels.

One important book which appeared during the year must be mentioned even though it is neither new nor written by a North American. *The Concept of Folklore* by the distinguished Brazilian folklorist Paulo de Carvalho-Neto, translated by Jacques M. P. Wilson (Coral Gables, Univ. of Miami Press) originally appeared in Portuguese in 1956. In it the author expresses briefly his theory of folklore, which he defines as the "scientific study of the cultural acts of any people." These acts, according to Carvalho-Neto, are anonymous and noninstitutionalized. Eventually they become ancient, functional, and prelogical (by which he means emotional). The book is a brilliant exposition of these premises.

ii. Ballads

Both the traditional Scottish and English ballads originally imported to the United States and native American ballads continue to attract the attention of scholars. Norman L. McNeil in "Origins of 'Sir Patrick Spens'" (*Hunters & Healers*, pp. 65–72) speculates on the historicity of one of the most popular of the Child ballads. He remarks that although no such figure as the putative hero of the ballad appears in Scotch history, there are a number of situations which resemble the main story: namely, the death of various Scotch nobles by drowning en route to or from Norway. Certain events in both thirteenth- and sixteenth-century history are similar, but McNeil argues that the ballad is probably a conflation of incidents changed by several singers. Thomas G. Burton in "The Anglo-American Ballad: 'By Indirections Find Directions Out'" (*NCarF* 19:185–90) discusses versions of Child ballads 73 and 81. "The Brown Girl" and "Lord Daniel," sung by Mrs. Rena Hicks of Beech Mountain, North Carolina, differ in many details from the more familiar songs but retain the basic story pattern. Burton asked the singer questions about the behavior of the ballad characters and usually got affirmations. Thus these traditional songs provide a means of finding out contemporary views toward social conduct. In "The Ancestry of 'The House-Carpenter': A Study of the Family History of the American Forms of

Child 243" (*JAF* 84:414–27) Alisoun Gardner-Medwin proposes a
new theory for the dissemination in the United States of one of the
best known Child ballads. To her "The House-Carpenter" has a strong
Scottish element and it may have been brought across the Atlantic by
Scotch tobacco traders in the eighteenth century. She also suggests
the possibility that historical and textual study might reveal that other
ballads had similar patterns of development and travel.

The most complete study of a ballad published during the year
is Eleanor Long's *"The Maid" and "The Hangman": Myth and Tradition in a Popular Ballad* (Berkeley, Univ. of Calif. Press). The work
is commendably thorough, since variants, analogues, language, and
melodic traditions are all carefully examined. The author concludes
that the constant theme in European versions of the story is "rescue
from jeopardy, successively refused by family members and offered
by the protagonist's beloved, by the payment of ransom in some
form." Miss Long's work is primarily compilation and reference;
much of the text is unreadable.

Three minor American ballads stimulated articles. John Q. Anderson in " 'The Gatesville Murder': The Origin & Evolution of a
Ballad" (*Hunters & Healers*, pp. 73–81) reviews the evidence behind
the making of a song commemorating a murder. Although the ballad
is hardly memorable, it does illustrate ballad making in the late nineteenth century. Wayne E. Homan's "The Sorrow Song of Susan Cox"
(*PF* 20,iv:14–16) describes a well known broadside which told the
story of a girl executed in 1809 for killing her illegitimate baby. Peter
R. Aceves in "The Hillsville Tragedy in Court Record, Mass Media
and Folk Balladry: A Problem in Historical Documentation" (*KFQ*
16:1–38) gives an overly detailed account of a ballad relating to a
family feud in Hillsville, Virginia, in 1911. The treatment of the story
by various media is illuminating but the essay is redundant and need-
lessly long.

A more familiar ballad is the subject of a genetic essay by D. K.
Wilgus, "The Individual Song: 'Billy the Kid' " (*WF* 30:226–34).
The version that Wilgus traces was the product of the Rev. Andrew
Jenkins about 1927 and has survived both in oral tradition and on
commercial phonograph records. Evidence from song folios and folksong collections as well as recordings by Vernon Dalhart, Tex Ritter,
and Jimmie Driftwood attests its popularity. Wilgus reports that the
original author-composer benefited little from his product.

iii. Folk Song

The field of folk and popular song is so vast today that it seems inadvisable to attempt even a brief survey of scholarship in the field unless it is specifically connected with folklore. I have ignored notes and brief articles in trade magazines and have excluded most of the material published in periodicals devoted to popular culture.

George W. Ewing in "The Well-Tempered Lyre: Songs of the Temperance Movement" (*SWR* 56:139–55) reviews the origin of temperance verse, describes it at its heyday, and tries to explain its virtual disappearance after the repeal of prohibition. Ewing suggests some of the folklore associated with hard liquor and quotes stanzas from various songs but supplies virtually no documentation. Jean F. Gravelle in "The Civil War Songster of a Monroe County Farmer" (*NYFQ* 27:163–230) analyzes a manuscript of Civil War songs made by a New York farmer. Some are the familiar work of composers like George F. Root and Henry Clay Work but others are variants of traditional ballads. A few seem to be native compositions. Mrs. Gravelle describes each ballad and employs such categories as the sentimental love song and the drinking song. In "Whalemen and Their Songs: A Study of Folklore and Culture" (*NYFQ* 27:130–52) Elliott Oring examines songs known to whalers in both the northern Greenland fishery and the South Pacific and discusses the subject matter of the ditties. He contends that the whalers not only revealed a good part of their lives in what they sang but that they also reflected certain wish fulfillments. The dominantly feminine motifs in the scrimshaw carving done in the whalers' spare time are quite revealing. Oddly enough the author makes no reference to Melville in his article.

Roger D. Abrahams complemented an earlier account of the singing of Almeda Riddle of Cleburne County, Arkansas, by editing *A Singer and Her Songs: Almeda Riddle's Book of Ballads* (Baton Rouge, La. State Univ. Press [1970]). But the volume is really more than the singer's ballad repertoire since Mrs. Riddle comments and reminiscences in what is truly a folk autobiography. Some fifty-two ballad texts and tunes are presented. Mrs. Riddle insists that although she occasionally takes liberties with song material she does not tamper with old ballads. Also she obviously prefers songs which are either narrative or didactic.

The vogue of collecting autograph album verse continues. Ovid

S. Vickers in "Of Folk Verse and Friendship Books" (*MFR* 5:34–38) presents examples dealing mostly with love and friendship. George W. Boswell's "Autograph Album Verses" (*TFSB* 37:97–104) prints rhymes collected over the years by his students. The usual categories are preserved (friendship, love, praise, humor, insult) but no comment or interpretation is provided. Two examples will suffice: "When you see a lizard climbing a tree, Pull its tail and think of me" and "The river is up and logs are floating. Let's get married and quit this courting."

Several articles deal interestingly with music. C. P. Heaton in "The 5-String Banjo in North Carolina" (*SFQ* 35:62–82) emphasizes the importance of the Tarheel state in the development of banjo playing and provides a succinct history of the banjo from the time when Negroes brought the first crude instruments from Africa. Men eminent in the cultural development of the banjo are Frank Proffitt, who first popularized "Tom Dooley," J. E. Mainer, and above all Earl Scruggs. The many banjoists who attend country music conventions in North Carolina today are almost all devotees of the Scruggs style. William R. Ferris, Jr., in "Racial Repertoires Among Blues Performers" (*Ethnomusicology* 14[1970]:439–49) argues that many blues songs seem inappropriate for white audiences and are either emasculated or avoided by Negro performers. Not only are blues frequently obscene but they are often couched in language which a white audience would not understand (such phrases for example as "black cat bone," "John the conqueror root," and perhaps even "jelly roll"). Two singers from rural Mississippi, Scott Dunbar and James Thomas, provided over seventy songs for the collector. Albert Goldman in "Jazz Meets Rock" (*AtM* 227, Feb.:98–106) provides some perceptive comments on the development of jazz and makes the point that the jazz devotee will recognize trends and themes in the music whenever it is played by a veteran performer. He pays tribute to such jazz virtuosos as Charlie Parker, Ornette Coleman, and the drummer Elvin Jones.

An unusual article by Joe Dan Boyd, "Negro Sacred Harp Songsters in Mississippi" (*MFR* 5:60–83), compares methods used by white and black singers of *Sacred Harp* material and refers to the Pleasant Ridge Colored Musical Convention which has been meeting annually since 1898. Boyd comments that Negro Sacred Harpers sing slowly, indulge in harmonic foot-tapping, and not only applaud but comment loudly following a song.

The July number of *Western Folklore* (30:171–246) is devoted to articles dealing with commercialized folk music and hillbilly songs, much of the evidence deriving from the John Edwards Memorial Foundation at UCLA. Singers and records are discussed by Archie Green, Norman Cohen, and Bill C. Malone, and there is a useful survey of copyright problems by Guthrie T. Meade, Jr. The general focus of the issue is on discography.

An ingenious synthesis of folk ideology and music gives special significance to R. Serge Denisoff's *Great Day Coming: Folk Music and the American Left* (Urbana, Univ. of Ill. Press). Denisoff continues his investigation of fields previously covered in a series of articles by discussing the role of the Almanac Singers, the relation of radical thought to folk music, and the roots of both rural and urban folk consciousness. Radical folk songs derived in part from spirituals and hymn tunes, and performers like Lee Hays, Pete Seeger, and Woody Guthrie were closely linked with Communistic thinking at one time, although they had little influence on the labor movement. Denisoff is chiefly concerned with the ideology of folk musicians; he is correspondingly less interested in such matters as artistic values and melodic structure. His book gives an excellent account of the protest songs of the last twenty-five years but suffers from over-documentation.

iv. Folk Tales and Legends

Interest in folk narrative continues to spur collectors into discussing individual tales or compiling representative collections from specific areas. Each method has demonstrable utility. Wayland D. Hand in his "Migratory Legend of 'The Cut-Out Pullman': Saga of American Railroading" (*NYFQ* 27:231–35) supplies several accounts of trains separated at division points with passengers in one car and their clothes and baggage in another. The loss of personal property was a minor inconvenience, but occasionally when a sexual liaison had been formed there were more serious consequences. An English train was once labelled "The Flying Fornicator." The story of a Kentucky tombstone desecrated by vandals prompted Mildred Hatcher to write

"Different Versions of 'The Fingerless Statue,' A Folktale" (*KFR*
17:5–9). The woman commemorated by the statue was either guilty
of self-mutilation or was murdered; in either case the stone figure
had no fingers on her left hand. In "The Tale of the Mysterious Barrel
and Other 'Haint' Tales Collected in Big Springs" (*TFSB* 37:59–72)
Lourene Salmon provides material about a rural Baptist church in a
small Tennessee town which was the center of strange lights, sudden
prodigious rackets, and even apparitions. Even a century after such
occurrence they lingered in the minds of the community. As one
native remarked, "I don't believe in boogers, but I ain't sayin' I
wouldn't run." James E. Spears in "Five Original Negro Folk Vi-
gnettes" (*TFSB* 37:40–45) records several trivial Negro tales illustrating voodooism and conjuring.

More in the nature of the tall tale are two accounts from the West.
Roger L. Welsch in "The Myth of the Great American Desert" (*NH*
52:255–65) observes that Nebraska was in many ways a desert when
the white man first arrived but that conditions have radically changed.
He cites familiar stories such as the harness that alternately shrinks
and stretches, the flour that clings to the wall when the sack blows
away, and the voracious grasshoppers capable of devouring a team
of horses. Warren Clare, in "The Side-Rock Bolter, Splinter Cat and
Paulski Bunyanovitch" (*IY* 15:2–8), surveys the career of James
Stevens, one of the creators of the Paul Bunyan stories, and concentrates on the Stevens yarn purporting to prove that the fabulous
logger was really of Russian origin as confirmed by Vladivostock
newspapers. No such sources, of course, have ever been found.

Miscellaneous groups of legends have been collected in various
places. The staff-written "Boogers, Witches, and Haints" (*Foxfire*
5:28–48) includes booger or ghost tales from North Georgia which
involve mysterious fire balls, strange voices, and bewitched guns.
Some of the mysteries, to be sure, turn out to be pranks. William
Hugh Jansen, in "A Content-Classification of a Random Sample of
Legends, Mostly Local" (*KFQ* 16:81–96), analyzes some 211 student-
collected tales and utilizes some twenty-four subject categories, not
all of them mutually exclusive. Some categories such as speech de-
fects, medical experiences, and clever animals are listed without
examples, and the legends actually printed are little more than anecdotes. The January issue of *North Carolina Folklore* prints some
eleven stories gleaned from WPA records for the Tarheel state (19:3–

32). They are very brief but the informant is always listed and motifs are identified. One tale in particular, "The Banshee," is notable for its surprisingly literary style and for its singular subject—a ghostly woman wailing over a dead man and terrifying his killer. Banshees are not common in North Carolina. An entire issue of *Northeast Folklore* (12:1–70) is devoted to George W. Bauer's "Cree Tales and Beliefs." Bauer taught school in Fort George, Quebec, and used his opportunities to tape-record Cree legends and tales. These are of course Canadian stories but their animal protagonists—raccoon, beaver, moose—are well known south of the border.

Political legends are the substance of Robert B. Downs's amusing lecture, "Southern Political Humor and Folklore" (*SLib* 21:9–21). Downs uses published stories as his material but draws them from sources as varied as Crockett's autobiography, J. Frank Dobie's reminiscences, and a satirical book by James M. Cain.

Two compilations of Hoosier narratives appeared in *Indiana Folklore.* "Narratives from Early Indiana" (3[1970]:229–41), edited with an excellent introduction by Linda Dégh, proves that folk material can often lie neglected in early histories of a region. Several tales from William M. Cockrum's *Pioneer History of Indiana* (1907), notably "Lazy Hound," are in the best tradition of humorous folk narrative. Anthony Milanovich's "Serbian Tales from Blanford" (4:1–60) presents twelve magical tales of Serbian life collected from immigrants in a small mining town north of Terre Haute. Little is known about the narrators and the original Serbian texts have mostly disappeared, but curiously enough several of the stories have literary sources, notably "Cinderella" and "The Boy Who Fooled the Devil."

A somewhat conglomerate collection of anecdotes, descriptions, legends, and tales was published by George Carey under the title, "*A Faraway Time and Place, Lore of the Eastern Shore* (Washington, D.C., Robert B. Luce). Carey spent considerable time with the oyster dredgers and fishermen of the eastern side of Chesapeake Bay and visited Smith, Deal, and Tangier islands. From old skippers, commercial fishermen, and watermen of various sorts he compiled a miscellaneous volume rich in superstitions and tall tales. He observes that the old-fashioned, leisurely stories have disappeared in favor of short, succinct stories with obvious punch lines. But the weather and maritime lore of the region survives and is preserved in traditional fashion.

v. Folk Speech

Articles dealing with folk speech reflect a wide spectrum of interest since animal calls, dialect, occupational lingo, and even graffiti have attracted researchers. One book even deals with a whole language peculiar to one locality.

David W. Thompson in "Gee, Haw and Geehaw" (*PF* 20,4:47–57) discusses the cries or commands commonly used to direct horses or to frighten away cats and birds. These cries normally have no literal meaning but depend for their effect on the stress or vocal tone employed. Thompson found little help in etymology and denies any echoic value in terms like *gee* and *haw* and *sookey*. In addition some of the traditional commands are even contradictory. George W. Boswell in "Class Competition in Kentucky Dialect Study" (*KFR* 17:48–52) reports on Kentucky dialectal words still current but rapidly becoming moribund. He found that *peart* and *betwixt* are still utilized but that *redd up* and *troubly* (cloudy) and *fight* (in the sense of abuse) a baby are virtually obsolete. Earl F. Schrock, Jr., in "An Examination of the Dialect in *This Day and Time*" (*TFSB* 37:31–39) focuses his attention on a novel published by Anne W. Armstrong in 1930 which made considerable use of folk idiom and dialect. *This Day and Time* reflects accurately the double negatives, irregular verbs, false plurals, and solecisms commonly heard in East Tennessee; indeed Mrs. Armstrong sometimes sacrificed artistic effectiveness in her book for linguistic precision. But she was extraordinarily consistent in her efforts to record regional speech.

Joyce Gibson Roach's essay, "Diesel Smoke & Dangerous Curves: Folklore of the Trucking Industry" (*Hunters & Healers*, pp. 45–53), gives an interesting account of occupational speech. The author draws upon previous accounts of similar material and adds her own examples. She comments that some of the most vivid terms in truck drivers' speech are simple borrowings from such other occupational groups as cowboys, railroad men, sailors, and farmers. Negroes have also made involuntary contributions. Among the more typical examples are the following: *swamper* (nondriving helper), *grandma* (lowest driving gear), *mule* (small warehouse tractor), *cowboy* (reckless driver), *gypsy* (independent driver), *holstein* (black and white marked patrol car), and *load for the Pope* (a load carried free).

Wellerisms interested Donald M. Hines and his "Wry Wit and

Frontier Humor—The Wellerism in the Inland Pacific Northwest" (*SFQ* 35:15–26) deals with curious phrases often used as fillers. Hines defines a wellerism as "an initial remark, an ascription to a person or an animal, and then an incongruous scene." Hines collected some thirty-five examples of these expressions. One follows: " 'So I'm told,' as the church bell remarked when it heard of the villager's death."

Patricia A. Mastick's essay, "The Function of Political Graffiti as Artistic Creativity" (*NYFQ* 27:280–96), quotes graffiti from the Watts district and the Ackerman Union in Los Angeles. The examples given are often chaotic or overwritten, but in general they seem to plead for a new order and an end to social and political oppression. People write graffiti, it seems, to prove themselves, to insult others, to excite readers sexually, to communicate an opinion, or simply to be amusing.

In "The Genre of the Folk Sermon" (*Genre* 4:189–211) Bruce A. Rosenberg, already the author of a book on the American folk preacher, discusses the folk sermon and finds its origin chiefly in the rural South. Structurally it is indebted to spirituals and New England sermons, but in linguistic form it often resembles the traditional work of the Yugoslav *guslars*. Rosenberg points out that there is usually no manuscript, that sermons vary greatly in length, and that even though they lack alliteration, rhyme, and conscious imagery, they often turn out to be true poetry. He makes an interesting allusion to the sermon delivered by the Reverend Shegog in the final pages of Faulkner's *The Sound and the Fury*.

The late Gordon Wilson contributed a two-part article to the *Kentucky Folklore Record* entitled "Origins of the People of the Mammoth Cave Region as Shown by Their Surnames and Regional Words" (17:10–18;31–39). Wilson selected from linguistic atlases words once current along the eastern seaboard and then found many of them still alive in Kentucky. From such evidence he deduced the geographical origins of the speakers.

Several articles have appeared in recent years revealing the peculiarities of "Boontling," an esoteric language invented by the inhabitants of Boonville in Mendocino County, California, probably for the purpose of mystifying outsiders. Although familiar today to only about two hundred people and possessing a very limited vocabulary, Boontling has excited more interest than its currency might suggest.

Charles C. Adams, in *Boontling, An American Lingo with a Dictionary of Boontling* (Austin, Univ. of Texas Press), has provided a word list, definitions, and suggested origins of the terms employed.

Two studies of pejorative epithets in common usage, which incidentally often make use of identical evidence, provide entertaining reading if one has a fairly thick skin and does not belong to any of the groups victimized by these *blasons populaires*. Alan Dundes, in "A Study of Ethnic Slurs: The Jew and the Polock in the United States" (*JAF* 84:186–203), theorizes that many of our conceptions of racial groups come from proverbs, songs, and jokes rather than from personal contact with individuals. He cites A. A. Roback's 1944 study of "ethnophaulisms" and quotes examples. The chief part of his discussion, however, centers on ethnic slurs directed against two groups. Jews are generally depicted as materialistic, addicted to sharp business practice, motivated by an excessive desire for status, and physically marked by big noses. Poles, on the other hand, are depicted as poor, dirty, stupid, inept, and boorish. Dundes discounts the accuracy of these stereotypes and laments the fact that they do exist. He also observes that such slurs take some of the heat off a group previously victimized in the United States, the Negroes. Mariana D. Birnbaum, in "On the Language of Prejudice" (*WF* 30:247–268), uses material from the Roback volume more extensively and devotes much of her essay to European slurs directed against each other. But such common expressions as French leave, to be in Dutch, castles in Spain, the French disease, mad as a Finn, and drunk as a Swede (or a Russian) suggest wholesale export across the Atlantic. Causes for such deliberate derogation of one's neighbors might be excessive nationalism, a country's attitude toward immigrants, and the plight of minority groups. In the United States the Jews and Negroes are the targets of the largest number of ethnic slurs, with both religion and race proving to be vulnerable factors. Curiously enough the American Indian has had only a few barbed remarks directed against him (Indian giver, for example).

Shirley L. Arora's "More Spanish Proverbial Exaggerations from California" (*WF* 30:105–18), a sequel to a previous article, might be said to include ethnic slurs too, but the proverbial expressions given in Spanish here were gleaned from Spanish speakers and commonly refer to Latin Americans. They are grouped by subject matter: thinness, stinginess, ugliness, and stature.

Another group of proverbial expressions was compiled by Bonnie Brinegar in "Metaphorical Expressions from Adams County, Mississippi" (*MFR* 5:124–31). She lists 124 examples of what she prefers to call "metaphorical expressions" rather than proverbs. The speakers were both black and white and many of their phrases are generally familiar.

vi. Folk Heroes

The gallery of American folk heroes continues to recruit unlikely members, though to be sure some of the newcomers seem ill at ease in their new roles. Nevertheless, their credentials are valid. Merlin P. Mitchell in "Tales of Bone Mizell" (*SFQ* 35:34–43) collects anecdotes about a south Florida cowboy roughly contemporary with Buffalo Bill and adept as prankster and worker. Mizell was once jailed on the charge of "drunk and disorderly [conduct] and urinating on a public doorknob" but generally he managed to stay out of the law's clutches. Mitchell recites a number of tall tales about Bone Mizell but supplies little biographical data. John M. Vlach covers very familiar ground in "Fenimore Cooper's Leatherstocking as Folk Hero" (*NYFQ* 27:323–38) and strives to link Natty Bumppo with popular conceptions of the frontiersman. Vlach's contention that *The Pioneers* is rich in folk materials such as proverbs, details of material culture, social customs, and regional speech will surprise no one. Jan Harold Brunvand's "Reputatia, Repertoriul Si Stilul Unui Münchausen American" (*REF* 16:375–90), published in Roumanian with a French summary, presents data about Len Henry of northern Idaho, a local storyteller who adapted traditional tales to his own purposes and often presented himself as the hero.

Two articles imply that certain craftsmen might well be accorded folk hero status. Mac E. Barrick's "David Stoner: Notes on a Neglected Craftsman" (*PF* 20,ii:16–21) describes a Pennsylvania Mennonite farmer who was extremely skillful in carving wooden farm implements, notably rakes, forks, and brooms. His products retained utility until steel tines replaced wooden ones in the twentieth century. Anne Marsh and William Aspinall, Jr., in "Harold E. Leightley: Portrait of an Auctioneer and His Craft" (*KFQ* 16:133–50), not only depict vividly a successful auctioneer of Centre County, Pennsylvania, but sample auctioneer's jargon and explain some of the ges-

tures or signs commonly used by bidders. If public exposure and
public interest can identify a folk hero, surely an auctioneer qualifies
as one.

The false heroics of both lawmen and desperadoes stimulated
Gary L. Roberts to examine their biographies in "The West's Gun-
men" (*AW* 8,i:10–15,64). It is well known that the early writers who
recorded the lives of Wild Bill Hickok, Wyatt Earp, and Billy the Kid
not only romanticized their subjects but were neither accurate nor
thorough in their researches. Roberts points out that as a consequence the books are full of inflated claims and fabricated incidents.
Today revisionist biography is difficult because much of the original
source material has vanished.

Neal Lambert makes a case for the unnamed protagonist of a
famous Western novel as a folk hero in "Owen Wister's Virginian:
The Genesis of a Cultural Hero" (*WAL* 6:99–107). Lin McLean,
Wister's other cowboy figure, was too much the vernacular hero; the
Virginian, both frontiersman and gentleman, became a cultural sym-
bol as well as the paradigm of all Western fiction.

Such figures have aroused speculation about what really constitutes a folk hero. Michael Owen Jones in an article entitled "(PC
plus CB) $\times$ SD (R plus I plus E) $=$ HERO" (*NYFQ* 27:243–60)
proposes a formula to identify folk heroism. Translated, his symbols
might read: Personal Charisma plus Credulous Biographer times
Social Definition including Recognition plus Imputation plus Expur-
gation produces HERO. Jones adds that the biographer must delete
certain objectionable traits and that he must impute to his hero
qualities which have no basis in fact: namely, charitableness, truthfulness, and reform. Among the examples he cites to sustain his theory
are Billy the Kid, Jesse James, Gib Morgan, and Barney Beal.

vii. Cures, Beliefs, and Superstitions

Folk medicine and primitive cures have always fascinated the folklorist, who continues to accumulate evidence from various parts of
the country. A Philadelphia ophthalmologist, Edward S. Gifford, Jr.,
in "The Evil Eye in Philadelphia" (*PF* 20,iv:58–59) reports that he
still sees patients who believe in the power of the evil eye despite
the absence of any logical or scientific basis. Amulets for sale in Phila-

delphia such as small gold figures of a hunchback, a fish, and a crescent moon are supposed to be efficacious in breaking this malign spell. Another physician, Paul W. Schedler, in "Folk Medicine in Denton County Today: or, Can Dermatology Replace Dishrags?" (*Hunters & Healers*, pp. 11–17) testifies that Texas rural dwellers still believe in ancient traditions. Raw meat on a patient's head will break a fever, standing barefooted on a newspaper will relieve leg cramps, and rubbing a wart with a dishrag which is then buried will remove the unsightly growth. Louisiana Acadians profess similar beliefs. Anna M. Boudreaux in "Les Remèdes du vieux temps: Remedies and Cures of the Kaplan Area in Southwestern Louisiana" (*SFQ* 35:121–40) lists cures supplied by some fifteen residents, most of them with little formal education. The illnesses listed include bronchitis, eczema, and snake bites, none of which entail surgery but all of which supposedly respond to family remedies. The familiar ingredients of turpentine, soda, vinegar, castor oil, and grated potatoes bulk large in the family pharmacopoeia.

Several Mississippi collections merit notice. Ella R. Hall in "A Comparison of Selected Mississippi and North Carolina Remedies" (*MFR* 5:94–113) compares the folk medicine of two states using as a basis the extensive list in the *Frank C. Brown Collection of North Carolina Folklore*. She presents 195 remedies from Mississippi sources, 78 of which had no clear parallel in the North Carolina compilation. Panaceas for warts, arthritis, and the common cold were most numerous. In "Folk Recipes of the South" (*MFR* 5:1–9) George W. Boswell lists a variety of student-collected recipes under the headings of inedibles, staples, and soups and drinks. Included are instructions as to how to make lye soap, hominy, vinegar, milk soup, and last but not least moonshine. James E. Spears in "Negro Folk Maternal–Natal Care, Practices, and Remedies: A Glossary" (*MFR* 5:19–22) presents representative Negro cures for such ailments as boils, bronchitis, nose bleeds, insect stings, and earache (child's urine wrung from a diaper is recommended!).

Wayland D. Hand chooses two particular items to make a case for transference from one continent to another. In "Anglo-American Folk Belief and Custom: The Old World's Legacy to the New" (*JFI* 7[1970]:136–55) he discusses the dumb supper and various beliefs associated with bees. Oddly enough he finds the ritual of the dumb supper more common in the United States than in England, while beliefs about bees (despite the familiarity of Whittier's poem "Telling the Bees") seem more prevalent in England.

In "The East Texas Communal Hunt" Francis Edward Abernethy comments on hunting customs in the wooded areas of East Texas (*Hunters & Healers*, pp. 3–10). He discusses the function of the driver and observes that young hunters still have deer's blood applied to their faces as a sign of maturity. If the hunt is successful the actual deerslayer is awarded hide, head, and feet, but the driver is given the liver, traditionally the seat of strength and courage.

A 1970 volume which demands notice even though it is a revision of an earlier publication is Harry Middleton Hyatt's *Hoodoo, Conjuration, Witchcraft, Rootwork* (Washington, D.C., American Univ.). This two-volume compilation, the lifework of an Episcopalian minister seriously interested in superstition, is probably the most ambitious thing of its kind ever attempted. The material comes almost entirely from Negro informants and antedates World War II. The work is loosely organized, has no index, and is difficult to use; moreover, there is almost a complete lack of information about Hyatt's informants. But the flood of material on cures, potions, charms, and witchcraft practised by Negro "doctors" has no parallel in American folklore compilations. Hyatt's original book dealt with the area of Adams County, Illinois. The later edition covers a much larger region.

viii. Literary Use of Folklore

An increasing number of articles dealing with the literary use of folklore confirms the growing interest in the appearance of folk themes in American imaginative writing. Criticism has ranged from surveys of individual authors to analyses of folklore in specific works.

Wolfgang Mieder in "Behold the Proverbs of a People" (*SFQ* 35:160–68) examines the use of proverbs in Carl Sandburg's poem "Good Morning, America." Beginning with the definition of a proverb as "a concise statement of an apparent truth that has currency among the people," Mieder quotes the eleventh section of the poem and italicizes the proverbs. He observes that Sandburg's examples are generally nonmetaphorical and often derive from the world of business. Like Franklin before him Sandburg altered the familiar adages and often quoted only parts of the original. George Carey in

"John Greenleaf Whittier and Folklore: the Search for a Traditional Past" (*NYFQ* 27:113–129) emphasizes the fact that Whittier, well known as a Quaker and abolitionist, was also an important folklorist. *Legends of New-England in Prose and Verse* (1831) provides striking evidence of the poet's early concern with the Indian heritage and with witchcraft and demonology. Later poems like "Mabel Martin" and "Abram Morrison" reflect Whittier's knowledge of rural and maritime superstitions. Carey's article is comprehensive and convincing. Michael Owen Jones, in " 'Ye Must Contrive Allers to Keep Jest the Happy Medium Between Truth and Falsehood': Folklore and the Folk in Mrs. Stowe's Fiction" (*NYFQ* 27:357–69), contends that Harriet Beecher Stowe did her best work in writing about New England themes. Her talented storyteller Sam Lawson, based to some extent on Calvin Stowe, is an expert blacksmith, mechanic, carpenter, barber, and clock repairman but he seldom works; instead his rambling monologues in *Oldtown Fireside Stories* are rich in popular belief and Yankee idiom. Labelled by Mrs. Stowe as the village do-nothing, Sam Lawson is by turns amusing, aggravating, and moralistic but in any event an unforgettable character. He is also the narrator of some of the author's best stories, such as "The Ghost in the Mill."

Two well known stories elicited articles. William E. Powell in "Motif and Tale-Type of Simms' 'Grayling' " (*SFQ* 35:157–59) argues that Simms's story, because of its exploitation of such themes as "murder will out" and "murder made known in a dream," should be listed in the appropriate place in any index of North American folk tales. In "Of Snakes and Those Who Swallow Them: Some Folk Analogues for Hawthorne's 'Egotism; or, the Bosom Serpent' " (*SFQ* 35:336–46) Robert D. Anser cites several factual accounts of persons who apparently swallowed snakes and suffered serious discomfort but concludes that Hawthorne probably had no single source in mind for his tale. To Anser the story specifically "depends upon a folk motif for its point of departure." In another treatment of the same subject, "Bosom Serpents Before Hawthorne: The Origins of a Symbol" (*AL* 43:181–99), Sargent Bush, Jr., examines an extensive list of serpents entering the human body. He summarizes evidence from early medical documents, newspapers, and even Spenser's *Faerie Queene*. Hawthorne undoubtedly had a wide variety of material which he might have used although the moralistic interpretation was largely his own.

In "From Folklore to Mythology: Paul Green's *Roll, Sweet Chari-*

ot" (*SLJ* 3,ii:62–78) Howard D. Pearce surveys Green's career as a dramatist and stresses his use of superstition, belief, and rural idiom in the early folk plays. Green's symphonic dramas diverged from his initial work, but *Roll, Sweet Chariot* presented the transformation of John Henry from a folk hero to a confidence man and spiritual leader. Pearce implies that Green's exposure to the German-Jewish theatre and the Japanese Kabuki theater, both highly stylized, unfortunately led him away from the simple, elemental folk drama in which he excelled.

Folklore in the fiction of Charles W. Chesnutt is the subject of Richard E. Baldwin's essay "The Art of *The Conjure Woman*" (*AL* 43:385–98). One of the most important early Negro writers, Chesnutt described Southern plantation blacks who used "goophering" as a means of bringing about their aims. The Negro ability to employ folk belief for practical ends comes out especially in stories like "Po' Sandy," about a man conjured into a tree, and "The Goophered Grapevine," about a spell used to preserve a threatened vineyard from destruction. In many ways Chesnutt's character, Uncle Julius, has the cunning and deviousness of the more famous Uncle Remus.

In "The Fiction of Jessamyn West" (*IMH* 67:299–316) John T. Flanagan assesses Miss West's craftsmanship and points out her careful use of rural colloquialisms and folk comparisons. The Indiana Quaker stories collected in *The Friendly Persuasion* and *Except for Me and Thee* are particularly rich in traditional locutions of the Ohio Valley.

Critics also observed the incorporation of folklore in several minor novels. In "Myth & Folklore in *The Ordways*" (*Hunters & Healers*, pp. 133–45) Patrick Mullen examines William Humphrey's 1965 novel of East Texas. A narrative of family history, *The Ordways* deals with an immigrant pioneer and his search for identity. Mullen points out various myths employed in the story: the past, the family, the quest both physical and spiritual, the cowboy, the American West. Folk anecdotes and tall tale elements reinforce the folkloristic content of the novel. Dorothy Weil in "Folklore Motifs in Arna Bontemps' *Black Thunder*" (*SFQ* 35:1–14) discusses a 1936 novel about a Virginia slave insurrection. Many folk elements are identified: good luck and bad luck charms, conjuring, burial customs, omens. Bontemps is praised for his use of folklore not only as colorful detail but also to present a believable, mostly black world. James T. Bratcher and Nicolai Von Kreisler, in "The Popularity of *The Miller's Tale*" (*SFQ* 35:325–35), discuss the comic elements in one of Chaucer's narratives and point out the occurrence of substantially the same situation in George Milburn's novel, *Old John's Woman.*

North Carolina novelists seem particularly adept at using both black and white folklore in their fiction. Harry C. West in "Negro Folklore in Pierce's Novels" (*NCarF* 19:66–72) contends that Ovid Williams Pierce's use of Negro folk speech as well as black sayings and superstitions contributes substantially to the success of his three novels of eastern North Carolina. Joseph D. Clark, in "Burke Davis as Folklorist" (*NCarF* 19:59–65), praises *The Summer Land* of 1965 and then tabulates the kinds of folklore inherent in it: folk songs, folk speech, proverbial expressions, customs associated with horse trading and picnics, and such practices as coon hunting and soap making. John Foster West finds in "Mrs. Morehouse's *Rain On the Just*" (*NCarF* 19:47–54) that the novel published in 1936 is "a minor classic of local color and folk literature." Kathleen Morehouse, he asserts, was especially successful in capturing local idiom and terminology, despite her New England ancestry. Similar claims are made by Cratis Williams in "Linney's *Heathen Valley*" (*NCarF* 19:55–58) and W. Amos Abrams in "*Time Was*: Its Lore and Language" (*NCarF* 19:40–46) for novels written by Romulus Linney and John Foster West.

An excellent essay by Guy Owen, himself the author of four novels and many tales, deals perceptively with the novelist's attitude toward folklore and the dangers sometimes inherent in it. In "The Use of Folklore in Fiction" (*NCarF* 19:73–79) Owen describes his evocation of a mythical Cape Fear County (very much as Faulkner invented Yoknapatawpha County in Mississippi) and an imaginary town, both of which have close actual counterparts. Striving to write entirely in Southern dialect, he did research on tent revivals in order to get his details correct, and he used both regional incidents and speech localisms. He sensed early in his career as a novelist that folk songs possessed peculiar power and charm. But Owen was aware that too much dialect would frighten away readers and narrow his audience, and his essay is a valuable corrective for those who believe that folklore per se will make any piece of fiction a popular success.

A rather different type of traditional lore is the subject of Susan Dwyer Shick's article, "Baptist Autobiography as a Folklife Source"

(*PF* 20,ii:22–30). She admits that the chief motive behind most clerical reminiscences is hortatory but finds them richly informative about such matters as dress, drinking habits, trades and crafts, early schools, leisure activities, and even folk architecture. A useful short bibliography is included in the essay.

ix. Material Culture

Scholarly interest in material culture of folk life continues to diversify and ranges from beekeeping and food customs to furniture and architecture. A staff-written article, "Beekeeping," in *Foxfire* (5:161–73) discusses the trees frequented by bees, the identification of bee trees, the making of a hive out of sections of "beegums," and such natural enemies of bees as bears, skunks, and moths. One rural apiarist insisted that bees had specific functions: some carried water, some made honey, and some cooled the honey.

The famous Concord wagon stimulated S. Blackwood Duncan to write "The Legendary Concords" (*AW* 8,i:16–17,61–62), in which he traced the career of Lewis Downing and described the basic features of one of the most celebrated of American vehicles. Not only was the Concord coach strong and durable, but it was gaily painted and proved serviceable for the hotel trade, mail carrying, and stage lines.

Interest in regional food habits produced several informative essays. Charles R. Mangam in "The Magic of the Black-Eyed Pea" (*NYFQ* 27:236–39) recalls the tradition of eating black-eyed peas on January 1 to guard against danger or ill luck in the coming year. In his view the custom almost becomes a fertility rite. The entire winter issue of the *Keystone Folklore Quarterly* is devoted to papers on food habits, two of which merit special attention. In "Soul Food and the Sambo Stereotype: Food-lore from the Slave Narrative Collection" (16:171–78) Charles W. Joyner contends that for the most part the slaves were well fed on corn pone, sow belly, greens, sweet potatoes, molasses, and occasionally whiskey. Today "soul foods" not only perpetuate this diet but have become symbols of black identity although poor people of both races eat them. Roger L. Welsch in " 'We Are What We Eat': Omaha Food as Symbol" (16:165–70) discusses the dietary habits of Omaha Indians living in the Missouri River bottoms. More farmers than hunters, they harvested blue corn, squash, and grapes while they put arrowroot, Jerusalem artichokes, and milk-weed to good use. With such foods certain eating rituals developed which were sometimes involved in the peyote cult.

Two articles in *Pennsylvania Folklife* also reflect this interest in food habits. Gregory Gizelis's "Foodways Acculturation in the Greek Community of Philadelphia" (20,ii:9–15) points out that Greek regional cookery has survived despite an obvious trend toward simpler methods of food preparation. Familiar Greek dishes still enjoyed in America are dolmades and baklava. Don Yoder in "Historical Sources for American Traditional Cookery" (20,iii:16–29) gives bibliographical material on Pennsylvania Dutch dishes and suggests that cookbooks, travellers' accounts, federal reports, newspapers, local histories, letters, wills, and even legal documents can yield evidence. Nor should iconography be neglected, since drawings and pictures can be very helpful.

Other aspects of folk life in Pennsylvania also attracted attention. In "The Use of Amulets Among Greek Philadelphians" (*PF* 20,iii: 30–37) Gregory Gizelis traces briefly the history of amulets and stresses their supposed value as protection against both the evil eye and the ordinary hazards of life. Howard H. Wedmann and Monroe H. Fabian in "Pennsylvania German Fraktur: Folk Art in the National Archives" (*Prologue* 2[1970]:96–97) call attention once again to the decorative art found on birth and baptismal certificates and identify at least one of the artists. Carroll Hopf in "Decorated Folk Furniture" (*PF* 20,ii:2–8) observes that the traditions and techniques of painted furniture often go unnoticed. Raw wood in a wood oriented culture easily became monotonous and familiar; sometimes it needed concealing. The author gives an interesting account of the sources of pigments and the astonishing results often achieved. A gracefully written article by Earl F. Robacher and Ada F. Robacher, "Flight of the Distelfink" (*PF* 20,iv:2–8), discusses the slow disappearance in Pennsylvania of the distelfink or American goldfinch and moves on from that to various bits of avian folklore. Bird motifs frequently appeared in art (vases, toys, fraktur, plates, molds) but the distelfink, usually made "for pretty," became a symbol of the whole Dutch country even though the folk artists seldom gave a literal impression of the bird. Folk architecture is studied by Amos Long, Jr., in "Bank (Multi-Level) Structures in Rural Pennsylvania" (*PF* 20,ii:31–39). Pennsyl-

vania farmers showed a tendency to build barns against or into hill-
sides both for warmth and convenience. Some of their multilevel
structures still remain.

A different kind of folk architecture in Indiana was the subject of
an interesting article by John M. Vlach, "Joseph J. Daniels and Joseph
A. Britton: Parke County's Covered Bridge Builders" (*IF* 4:61–88).
Parke County contains some thirty-six out of the state's 130 covered
bridges, most of them erected by two carpenter-builders. Vlach discusses the methods and materials used for the bridges and provides
detailed drawings. To him the covered bridge "is a bona fide folk
item in the material culture of Indiana."

Several articles by Michael Owen Jones deal with the economics
or the aesthetics of folk craft, and all derive initially from Jones's
doctoral dissertation at Indiana University on chairmaking in Appa-
lachia. In " 'I Bet That's His Trademark': 'Anonymity' in 'Folk' Utili-
tarian Art Production" (*KFQ* 16:39–49) Jones discusses the need to
identify such objects as gun stocks, dulcimers, and chairs as the work
of individual craftsmen. Fellow artists can often do this but the
purchaser is concerned only with the utility of the object he buys. In
" 'They Made Them for the Lasting Part': A 'Folk' Typology of Traditional Furniture Makers" (*SFQ* 35:44–61) Jones distinguishes between craftsmen who make chairs for use and those who are concerned about the aesthetic appeal of their products. He feels that it
is desirable to differentiate the attitudes of folk artists. In a long,
protracted, and redundant article, "The Concept of 'Aesthetic' in the
Traditional Arts" (*WF* 30:77–104), Jones discusses Western elite
aesthetic theory and analyzes six points propounded by Alan P.
Merriam. By the time Jones gets around to his Appalachian chair-
makers at the end of the article the reader has lost the point of the
discussion.

A clearer and more provocative article about folk and popular
culture was contributed by Bruce R. Buckley to *Country Cabinet-
work and Simple City Furniture*, edited by John D. Morse (Charlottesville, Univ. Press of Va. [1970]). In "A Folklorist Looks at the
Traditional Craftsman" (pp. 265–76) Buckley begins by briefly defining folklore, folk life, regional ethnology, and listing their connota-
tions. Borrowing from the anthropologist Edward Hall he enumerates
three levels of culture: the informal (folk), the formal (popular), and
the technical (classical or academic). Folk learning, he argues, is

learning by imitation, popular learning is learning by precept or admonition, and technical learning is one-way learning from the teacher, specialist, or scientist. Two families of furniture makers, previously discussed at the Winterthur Conference of 1969, exemplify his distinctions. The Dominy family of East Hampton, Long Island, makers of clocks and furniture, are true folk craftsmen faithful to tradition despite their proximity to New York City; the Dunlaps of New Hampshire, famous for chairs, tables, desks, and chests, are influenced by the fads of Boston and become as a consequence less traditional and more popular. Country versus city furniture, Buckley concludes, is a less significant distinction than the folk versus the popular.

x. Obituaries

Several obituaries or memorial tributes to distinguished folklorists which appeared in 1971 have value beyond the purely biographical. Wilson M. Hudson's tribute to Mody C. Boatright (*JAF* 84:242–43) stresses Boatwright's editorial services for eighteen years to the Texas Folklore Society as well as his own books on Gib Morgan and oil industry folklore. Felix J. Oinas's notice of the work of Vladimir J. Propp (*JAF* 84:338–40) is of value to American folklorists even though Propp's work was done entirely in the Soviet Union and dealt primarily with Russian fairy tales and *skazki*. Probably no single book of folklore theory has won wider recognition than Propp's study of the *Morphology of the Folktale*, published originally in Russian in 1928 and made available in an English translation by Laurence Scott some thirty years later. Joseph D. Clark's "Richard Jente as Folklorist" (*NCarF* 19:191–93) commemorates a North Carolina professor of German whose specialty was the proverb. Jente's collection of paroemiological volumes was bought by the library at Chapel Hill, and Clark describes representative titles and cites the manuscript compilations and analogues which Jente left when he died.

The summer 1971 issue of the *Keystone Folklore Quarterly* (16: 51–113) is a memorial to George Korson, the indefatigable collector of Pennsylvania coal mining songs and lore who died in 1967. Among the memorialists are Archie Green, Wayland D. Hand, and Gerhard Heilfurth. Green's tribute is the fullest since it incorporates sections of his 1972 book *Only a Miner* and places Korson against a back-

ground of field collecting and library annotation. All the writers agree
that Korson succeeded so well in his work because of his strong interest in the miners as people and because he met them on their own
ground. Korson's volumes, *Coal Dust on the Fiddle* and *Minstrels of
the Mine Patch*, both reprinted since their original appearances, have
become classics of mining lore.

University of Illinois

18. Themes, Topics, and Criticism

G. R. Thompson

The materials for this chapter remain recalcitrant. Although I have attempted to impose an order, that order is embarrassingly arbitrary and selective. But on the principle that much of the value of such a review as this lies in the perceptions of the critic, I have emphasized certain matters that seem to me especially significant. The major of these is the continuing development of a theory of criticism, and I have given special consideration to this curious and provocative activity.

The development of recent critical theory in America may be described in terms of a simple Hegelian dialectic. Out of a basically romantic matrix, a divided stream of idealistic thought about the nature and function of literature has emerged. On the one hand, literature is conceived of as a body of organic aesthetic objects reflecting the ideality, or archetypal resonances, of the artist (himself a microcosm of the perfect cosmos) through heightened language and evocative natural symbols—a perfect form of forms. On the other hand, literature is seen as reflective of the fallen, imperfect world in which men live but which they must strive to improve by enjoining morality—a concrete exemplum of ameliorative action. In the first case, "universal" value resides in the deep, internal expression of the artist; in the second, universal value resides in the external confrontation of the artist with the problems of men in society. Both assume some attainable vision of perfection: on the one side, almost spiritual perfection of aesthetic form; on the other, pragmatic perfection of social institutions. Both possess strong undercurrents of romanticism, and both are implicitly messianic in concept.

For thirty years now, the aesthetic rather than the cultural version of American critical idealism (the New Critical stance that an art work is an autonomous aesthetic object to be perceived primarily if not exclusively as a structure of formal design in and of itself) has

dominated literary theory in this country. But the dialectical process
continues; with the political turbulency of the later fifties and the
decade of the sixties, a theory of politically and culturally oriented
criticism has again come to prominence. This time, however, it is
reinforced by a European formalist methodology that not only looks
outward to the culture but also simultaneously inward to the designs
of the work as aesthetic object and, as well, to the very processes of
creation itself. Mention of this "structuralist" activity has been made
earlier (see *ALS 1969* pp. 331–36, 337–43). Despite crackings and
strainings, redundancies and disjunctures, a collective articulation of
a critical theory integrating the obvious validity of both the cultural
and aesthetic approaches to literature seems on the verge of cogent
expression.

Two dialectics may be observed. First, there is the aesthetically
oriented criticism of archetypal myths associated with the work of
Northrop Frye complementing the culturally oriented structuralist
analysis of social myths derived from the work of Claude Lévi-
Strauss and applied to literature by Roland Barthes, Jacques Lacan,
and others. Second is the tendency of the scientific approaches to
language, represented by the attempts of Noam Chomsky and others,
to study the norms of the structures of language, the transformations
from these structural norms that may be called style, and the semantic
load they bear, to end up approximately where another school of
literary structuralism has arrived from a different point of departure.
Both the linguists and the "Geneva" school of existential structuralists
(see *ALS 1969*, p. 334n) conclude by positing what Chomsky calls
the "deep structures" of human consciousness (a bedrock of logical
apperceptiveness built into the brain akin to such basic physiological
structures as bilateral symmetry) in some kind of objective interaction with the subjective perception of the data of the external world.
Thus, both the basic mode of human communication (our language
patterns) and the individual manipulation of that medium (our
style, our rhetoric) represent a verbal artifact, a fossil imprint, of
the act (or structured series of acts) that is the intersection of the
mind of the artist with the external world. And, just as in American
critical thought, behind all the complexities of the intersecting systems of expression there lurks a transcendentally romantic conception of the ultimate unity of all phenomena. Several of the works
relevant to American critical theory to be discussed here attempt to

deal with the theoretical complexities of such a conception of the artifact that is literature, of the act of creation, and of the act of reading.

Four recent essays on the development of various aspects of "formalism" are helpful. George H. Douglas in "Croce's Early Aesthetic and American Critical Theory" (*CLS* 2[1970]:204–15) argues that although it is the subjectivist and expressionistic theories of Croce that are now best remembered in America, he actually stands at the head of modern formalist criticism in this country, his ideas having been "implanted on American soil very early in the twentieth century" (p. 209). When Croce discussed the human spirit and human culture in its totality, the "expressive element was dominant"; but when he turned to literary criticism it was the "presentational, symbolic element that became dominant." René Wellek's criticism that Croce was not concerned with the "objective verbal structure" of a work but only with the feelings, attitudes, and "leading sentiment" of an author is grossly misleading. Croce's early aesthetic provided a "logically consistent foundation for a formalistic or phenomenological approach to art. In his early aesthetic Croce . . . developed a theory of intuition [the primal form or deep structure of human experience] which lends itself to a style of criticism that focuses on works of art as self-contained and unified entities" (p. 213) without necessarily confining them to that alone. For Croce was also a historian and "phenomenologist of culture." Thus he combined both a concern for the inner human content of a work of art and its intrinsic formal relationships with a concern for its place in culture.

Ewa M. Thompson's "The Russian Formalists and the New Critics: Two Types of the Close Reading of the Text" (*SHR* 4[1970]: 145–54) compares the orientation of the American New Critics with that of the Russian Formalists, whose work is identified with the decade following World War I. Although slight, Thompson's article does offer insights, including a revelation of the dialectical nature of New Criticism as compared with the "systems" conception of Formalism. In Ransom, the form and content opposition takes the shape of "determinate meaning" (rational argument) colliding with "determinate metre" (style) to produce that "indeterminate" meaning and metre that are the "texture" or "tissue of meaning" in the work; in Brooks, the dialectic of the poem results in unity generated by the tensions of irony and paradox; in Tate, it is extension and intension.

The Russian Formalists, however, whose views are like those of the early Kenneth Burke, viewed the structure of a literary work as containing "layers" or systems. Roman Ingarden, for example, suggested four basic systems interacting: (1) the sounds of language; (2) the meanings of words and phrases; (3) the material objects presented; (4) the inner characteristics of persons and philosophical ideas presented by manipulations of point of view. Thus, for the Formalists, literature is composed of "staircase" progressions of structures similar to the schema of linguistics (the Prague Linguistics Circle developed out of Russian Formalism).

Arthur K. Moore, in "Formalist Criticism and Literary Form" (*JAAC* 29[1970]:21–31), surveys various modern theories of literary form as an introduction to his essay on a "newer" theory of the concept of form and of such newer "formalist" criticism. In his survey, Moore argues that common to all theories of form is the fact that perception of the form of an aesthetic object is not perception of the object itself but only of aspects of its form. The concept of form as an "isolable entity" which can be perceived in whole is invalid, and the "newer" formalist critic creates a "working model" of the aesthetic object. This model is created in an attempt to make practically assailable the form of a specific work by showing the work as "a complex in which premises are modified in relation to each other and to the object of perception." The critic's model of the work is a product of his intuition of the whole work and subsequent recreation via critical discourse. This model-building, in a sense, falsifies the work because certain aspects of the work necessarily must be excluded. Critics do not pretend to exhaust a work in their critical acts, but they do "claim implicitly that their models embody all significant relations." Yet what is significant in a work varies according to the consciousness of the critic; no completely uniform observation of a specific work is possible. Because a new formalist critic makes use of the potentialities of language to recreate in a model the form of the work that he individually perceives, the act of criticism is an open-ended, infinite series of perceptions as opposed to the older formalist conception of the work as the closed form of an autonomous object.

A similar argument is implicit in Joseph N. Riddel's "Against Formalism" (*Genre* 3[1970]:156–72). Taking as his starting point Sarah Lawall's *Critics of Consciousness* (Cambridge, Mass., Harvard Univ. Press [1968], Riddel surveys the basic assumptions of the Geneva school of structuralists about the internal "world" of the author and of the critic. Poulet, for example, stresses the exclusiveness of the *cogito* or basic structuring force of the author's consciousness and insists on an initial division of subject and object. The critic is "preoccupied with a subject that precedes language, with the mind before it unites itself 'to an object to invent itself as subject'" (p. 159). Finding that Lawall has failed to explore the "foundations of thought from which both American formalist criticism (especially contextualism) and French structuralism react against a criticism of consciousness," Riddel proceeds to undertake a brief exploration himself. Literature for the critics of consciousness is an act of consciousness manifesting itself in language. Literature is not characterized by its external structures (forms, genres) but by its "inner necessity," by the structuring force that is the author's obsessive way of seeing relationships. The context of literature therefore lies in an author's total pattern of consciousness, and includes every scrap of his writing. American New Criticism, however, separates literature from experience and posits the autonomy of the individual work. (The implication, as I see it, is that New Criticism has no rationale for the study of more than one work of an author in terms of that author; a New Critical analysis of "Melville" makes no sense; only a study of this work, and that work, and that other work makes sense.)

For the critics of consciousness, the particular form of a work loses its priority in the critic's interest; instead, the critic's choice of an author reflects a value placed on that author's pattern of consciousness by the critic. Whereas the American New Critics have tended to see literature as more complete than experience, the work of art resolving itself into a "completed form, an autonomous whole to be contemplated in and for itself" and becoming a "constituted object which transcends itself," the critics of consciousness see the act of criticism as an almost mysterious empathetic alignment of the mind of the critic with that of the author. They argue that consciousness lives in "constant pursuit of itself in perpetual self-renewal, self-reference, and hence self-creation" (p. 161). Although such a process leads inward upon itself, the intersection of the inner structuring force with the external world is embedded in the medium that consciousness employs to articulate its consciousness of itself. The author takes the language he inherits and reorders it into his own thematic structures, creating that imaginary subject which is his own consciousness, a "linguistic world-within-world." When a critic seeks the author's *cogito*, he "catches the author's 'style,' the pulsations of his feeling-thought" (p. 170).

The theoretical problems attendant on the analysis of autonomous aesthetic objects by formalist methods, on the intersection of the patterns of consciousness of the writer with the external patterns of his world, and on the critical act are the basic subjects of Geoffrey Hartman's *Beyond Formalism: Literary Essays 1958–1970* (New Haven, Conn., Yale Univ. Press [1970]) which collects twenty-one essays into four sections—on the state of literary criticism, on the novel, on poetry, and on literary history. In his preface, Hartman writes that when literature joins in the quest for objectivity transcending the literary work, the critic becomes akin to a philosopher in quest of some truth. Regarding literature as "engaged reflection" on the consciousness of consciousness," Hartman tells us that in order to respect the formal study of art he had to go "byond formalism" and to "define art's role in the life of the artist, his culture, and the human community" (p. ix). The notion of literary form as "organic" or "unified" has become a reductive concept in the hands of American critics, whereas European critics too often neglect literary form and "dissolve art into a reflex of consciousness, technology, or social process" (p. xi). New Critical emphasis on "words" too readily becomes a narrowing concept unless it guides us to "larger structures of the imagination," not only to "forms like drama and epic, but also to what Northrop Frye calls 'archetypes' and Lévi-Strauss 'mythemes.'" In America, our obsession with "value-free" techniques of exegesis of what we conceive as an "objective" or autonomous work has considerably shrunken the once grand art of interpretation. Thus, the ensuing collection of essays represents Hartman's attempt to blend New Critical exegesis with the larger, outward-moving methodology of both the cultural structuralists and the critics of consciousness.

The first three essays set out his critical orientation in more detail. In "Structuralism: The Anglo-American Adventure" (pp. 3–23), Hartman claims that the structuralist activity is entering into its own era of dominance.[1] Structuralism as he defines it is a method of "medi-

1. This essay is reprinted in a useful compendium on *Structuralism*, edited with an introduction by Jacques Ehrman (Garden City, N.Y., Doubleday, 1970), pp. 137–58. Another useful collection is *Introduction to Structuralism*, edited by Michael Lane (New York, Basic Books, 1970).

ation" in the search for the relations of relations. It is an organic criticism that has switched from the particle theory of the New Critics to a field theory. The emphasis is now on wholes as opposed to parts. These wholes are systems of relationships within specific works that are within the greater system of a body of work or field of works. Northrop Frye, G. Wilson Knight, and Marshall McLuhan are offered as the foremost English-speaking proponents of structuralism. In "The Sweet Science of Northrop Frye" (pp. 24–41), Hartman's discussion of Frye's quest for the universal structuring principle (archetype) of literary art both reveals his fascination with Frye's thought and his sense of its limitations, a subject he takes up again at the end of his book. What Frye has come up with is an "anatomy of romance" that suggests the "total form" of art as essentially "comic." Descents into death or chaos are always followed by ascents out of death or chaos. The cyclical descension/ascension pattern is analogous to the visit to and from the underworld in ancient mythology, but the essential difference is that in ancient myths gods are the subjects whereas in modern literature (as romance) men are the subjects. In the third of the theoretical essays, "Beyond Formalism" (pp. 42–57), Hartman explores further the "human context" of syntax, metaphor, myth. His ostensible purpose is to defend formalism from the attack of F. W. Bateson on what he called "Yale formalism." Taking as his main targets Brooks, Wimsatt, and Wellek, Bateson had "defined *formalism* as a tendency to isolate the aesthetic fact from its human content." Hartman, however, defines it "as a method: that of revealing the human content of art by a study of its formal properties" (p. 42). Hartman then moves (somewhat too rapidly) from an example of the interpretation of Wordsworth to a discussion of the concept of *cogito* posited by Georges Poulet. This interaction of the *I am* with the *I think*, is defined by Hartman as a "continuously generated relation linking thought to the world." By this he means approximately what we earlier called a basic structuring force or habitual mode of seeing relationships and expressing them (as in metaphor) that is part of a writer's structure of consciousness (see also *ALS 1969*, p. 333). Reiterating his belief that the study of forms must lead outward to the mythos of the world, Hartman concludes the piece with a railing against the present "whore" of explication, followed by an injunction for us to "raise exegesis to its former state by confronting art with experience" (p. 57).

The thirteen essays that follow, on works by Milton, Blake, Wordsworth, and others, while frequently instructive, do not to my mind satisfactorily demonstrate as applied criticism the grand claims of the theoretical essays. In the last section, however, in "The Voice of the Shuttle: Language from the Point of View of Literature" (pp. 337–55), Hartman does offer a demonstration of the larger evocative meanings of words (of the "archetypal potential" of metaphor, for example), moving from what he considers the limits of rhetorical analysis to the concept of the "zero value" of juncture or space and the "redundancy" of the phonetics of words to the redundancy of puns (a pun, by way of analogy to linguistics, is the "smallest literary unit"), to "tmesis" (an intruded juncture in a word continuum) to tmetic breaks in syntax to larger kinds of "desynonymization" (Coleridge's word) or "binary opposition" (the structuralists' word) that exist in and around such works as *Oedipus*, from metaphor and rhythmic pause to philosophical conception. Thus, when we come to the last essay, "Toward Literary History" (pp. 356–86), we are prepared for a revelation. This essay has a subsection called "Toward a Theory of Form" in which we are to be presented with an overview of twentieth-century critical activity; and Hartman outlines some general affinities of Marxist criticism with Frye's archetypal criticism, commenting on the opposition presented by the inadequate elitist stance of New Criticism, and proceeding to two kinds of structuralist criticism. The first is Lévi-Strauss's attempt to use myth analysis to analyze social consciousness (myths resolve cultural conflicts); the other is the ritualistic resonance of I. A. Richards's "participatory theory" of literary form as the act or process of reconciling tensions. This overview then leads to another subsection called "Toward a Theory of Literary Vocation" in which we are to see a link between the form of the artistic medium and the artist's historical consciousness. But Hartman never really goes beyond the call for a theory "toward" articulating and demonstrating such a link, and the argument blurs, runs, and dissolves into mystical rhetoric about "becoming," "appearing," "Genius and genius," much like the incantatory references to irony and tension that he criticizes the New Critics for. As a collection of essays by an alert intelligence, this is an engaging book, but finally only an exploratory essay into a theory of literature.

A polemical version of this concern for literature as expression of the self's becoming, and a variant on the concern for literature as both individualized verbal form and cultural expression is Richard Poirier's *The Performing Self: Compositions and Decompositions in the Languages of Contemporary Life* (New York, Oxford Univ. Press). What we should respond to in literature, according to Poirier, is the "performance," that is, the artist's consciousness confronting the "cultural, moral, psychological premises" that define what "many people still regard" as the "essence of literature as a humanistic enterprise." But these humanistic and liberal traditions are the very forces threatening to wither the life energy in literature. Representative of the repressive forces acting against this sense of energetic life are academic criticism of literature and the sophistries of political rhetoric (another kind of "performance"). The first three essays of the book deal with a body of literature that Poirier regards as evading analysis by being exhaustively self-analytical; the next three essays suggest ways of locating "energies" in literature and the popular arts; the last three essays attempt to explore the "political and cultural equivalents" of the literary proposals of the first two groups: how, that is, men delude themselves into thinking that they are dealing with the real problems of contemporary culture.

The life energy of a work resides in that "self-discovering, self-watching, finally self-pleasuring response" to the "pressures and difficulties" of the writer engaged in the struggle to keep himself from being smothered by the "inherited structuring of things." Thus in Poirier's theory, as in the others considered so far, the artist is put squarely back into the middle of what literature is and does; and his "performance," or creative act, is the message in much the same way that for Marshall McLuhan the medium is the message. Poirier writes, for example, that the drama of *Ulysses* is only incidentally that of Stephen, Bloom, and Molly! "More poignantly" it is the drama of "Joyce himself making the book." Poirier finds in modern criticism an "alarming" tendency to analyze the structure or "stage" an author utilizes and to treat such a structure as if it were the author's message. He writes of *The Sound and the Fury* and *Light in August* that "Faulkner needed his structurings the way a child might need a jungle gym: as a support for exuberant, beautiful, and testing flights" (p. xv). The "flights" themselves are far more important than the "jungle gym." Yet a prerequisite to "performance" is that the performer, the poet, novelist, musician, or painter must properly sense and express the "multiple sounds" which comprise the elements of reality (p. 46). Authors who try too hard to be literary, to conform to set standards, present too narrow a scene. In *The Confessions of Nat Turner*, for example, William Styron "is unable at any point to give Nat a voice distinguishable from that of the elegantly rhetorical narrator." Authors who hear and record many voices, many sounds, such as James, Frost, and Eliot, are not only more actively engaged in writing from reality, but they actively participate in history while they create. In *The Waste Land*, Eliot keeps his own voice entirely submerged. Only the voices of others express the reality Eliot himself senses. The idea of "composite sounds" is thus part of Poirier's contention that literature, culture, and politics are inseparable issues. Anyone who truly performs, from the Beatles to Norman Mailer, must hear all sounds and must find "an energy which is its own shape," which "de-creates" inherited structures, both artistic and political, and "redefines their components." But the final impression of all of this rhetoric is that the theorizing is shallow, if not confused.

Another treatment of "performances" is found in the spring 1971 issue of what may well be the most ambitious undertaking in literary history and theory today, *New Literary History: A Journal of Theory and Interpretation*, edited by Ralph Cohen. As Cohen remarks in "A Preface to 'Performances'" (*NLH*, 2:363–66), each issue of the journal "examines a theoretical problem which, while specifically literary, has ramifications or analogues in other disciplines. Each issue offers a commentator who analyzes and comments upon the contributions. This procedure imitates an actual interdisciplinary symposium. The subject matter of Volume 2, Number 3, is "performances" in drama, the arts, and society, with Marshall McLuhan's "Roles, Masks, and Performances" (2:517–31) masquerading in the role of the performance of a critique. Although few of the articles thus far published in *NLH* have an American focus, several of them are important for contemporary discussion of "newer" criticism, a theory of genre, literary history, and the intersection of culture and literature. Thus, in Volume 1 (1969–1970), no less than eight of the thirty-four essays published can be recommended to the student of American literature as worth his attention: J. M. Cameron's "Problems of Literary History" (7–20), D. W. Robertson's "Some Observations on Method in Literary Studies" (21–33), Georges Poulet's graceful and engaging "Phenomenology of Reading" (53–68), Leo Marx's "American Studies—A Defense of an Unscientific Method" (75–90), Robert Weimann's discussion in "Past Significance and Present Meaning in Literary History" (91–109) of how a "break with the formalist dogma of the autonomy of the work of art" is leading toward a synthesis between literary criticism and historical scholarship that "reveals the extent to which the virtues of close textual analysis can survive the decline of formalism" (p. 101); Henry F. Mays's "The Problem of the American Enlightenment" (201–214); Richard Harter Fogle's discussion of American romanticism in "Literary History Romanticized" (237–47); Cushing Stout's discussion of Henry Adams and William Dean Howells in "Personality and Cultural History in the Novel: Two American Examples" (423–37); and Arnold Goldman's "Dos Passos and his *U.S.A.*" (471–83). In Volume 2 (1970–1971), in addition to articles already mentioned, one might well consult Hans Robert Jauss on literary history as a "challenge" to literary theory (7–37), Michael Riffaterre on the stylistic approach to literary history (39–55), Jan Brandt Cortius on the relation of literary history and the study of literature (2: 65–71), Stanley Fish on "affective stylistics" (123–62), Alastair Fowler on the life and death of literary forms (199–216), Seymour Chatman on the definition of "form" (217–28), and Warner Bertoff on the place in literary history of *The Autobiography of Malcolm X* and Norman Mailer's *The Armies of the Night* (311–27).

The last essay is reprinted in a book-length collection of essays that, from its title, sounds as if it were in a mode of the newer criticism. The six essays comprising the first part of Warner Berthoff's *Fictions and Events: Essays in Criticism and Literary History* (New York, Dutton) purport to deal with the "more general phenomena of literature" in connection with "different kinds of reality." But although three of the initial essays deal loosely with reality and literature in terms of the "rites" of "communion" that an author must "perform," Berthoff's orientation is basically old-fashioned with an overlay of structuralist rhetoric that never quite comes clear. Moreover, the second part of the book (seven essays, the last of which is comprised of a series of brief book reviews) centers on a rather traditional conception of "traditions and talents" in American literature from Emerson and Melville to Edmund Wilson, Van Wyck Brooks, Wallace Stevens, Hart Crane, and others. Thus, while we are led at first to expect something akin to a structuralist demonstration of the relation between literary "performance" and social "performance," what we actually find is Berthoff celebrating the "passing" of "the Age of McLuhan, Inc." and the "recovery" of a great tradition of the "classic" and the "historical" that bears only the most general resemblance to any of the structuralist modes of thought.

In "The Study of Literature and the Recovery of the Historical" (pp. 15–29), Berthoff attempts to enumerate the elements of an "ideal" literature and criticism. Literature shows how a "collective wisdom" operates within a "single intelligence" and becomes part of a new "cause," a "change," a "transcendence." The "fundamental pattern of the *historical*" revealed and embodied in literature is the sense of a "generic progression" which belongs to man alone, which "defines his coming into existence," and which leads to his "freedom." The study of literature in this (romantic) sense is, Berthoff feels, ignored by the present traditionless and "antinomian" age. In order to develop a genuine body of lasting work, Berthoff claims, the writer must perform three basic rites or communions: the "rites of association," the "rites of propitiation," and the "rites of power"; these phrases refer respectively to a work's "communion with its audience," its "communion with the world of subjects and materials," and its "progressive communion with itself" (pp. 27–28). Berthoff tries to explain these rites further in the same essay and returns to them (by implication, at least) in "Literature and the Measure of Reality" (pp. 56–72). In this latter essay, we learn that "reality" is always a "factor of consciousness" and always "symbolism." Although one sees the parallel between the three "rites of communion" and the triadic statement that literary reality causes the reader to participate actively in it, corresponds to experience, and causes a recognition of the reality of other beings, the significance of it all remains rather cloudy.

In "Fiction, History, Myth: Notes Toward the Discrimination of Narrative Forms" (pp. 30–55), Berthoff renews his claim of a current "drying up of invention." Thus, it is the responsibility of the critic to expand into the study of human event and possibility through extraliterary knowledge; in particular, Berthoff recommends to our attention the conceptions of myth held by Claude Lévi-Strauss and Northrop Frye. In a misleading parallel with the triads of the earlier essays, Berthoff suggests that it is through the three narrative forms of fiction, history, and myth that "new" knowledge may be presented. Berthoff's main thrust is toward the reestablishment of a narrative vessel for the "new" studies of psychology, epistemology, sociology, and so on, in the hope that these disciplines, when combined with a formal study of literature, will produce a new era of "classics."

Two final essays reveal Berthoff's true critical orientation. In "Modern Literature and the Condition of Exile" (pp. 73–101), Berthoff treats the writer's estrangement and isolation from his own nation and reading audience. In many instances a writer's exile is in actuality a "pilgrimage for self growth." In the essay "Witness and Testament: Two Contemporary Classics" (pp. 288–308), reprinted from *NLH*, Berthoff argues that in a revolutionary age, with civil rights in the center of the turmoil, "witness and testament," are not only valid, but also well-chosen narrative forms. He attacks Richard Gilman's contention that books like *Soul on Ice* or *The Female Eunuch* ought not to be subjected to literary criticism, arguing that all good fiction should be "an act of creation and definition of the self" and that Gilman's suggestion is merely patronizing. Indeed, it is the act of considering Mailer's *Armies of the Night* and Malcolm's *Autobiography* as literature that leads Berthoff to call them "classics." Both works boast the balance between private and public engagement which Berthoff praises in any literature: although intensely personal, they share a "broad common awareness." In discussing the somewhat occasional nature of the subject matter (contemporary civil strife), Berthoff says of the two books that "they give us what our major literary tradition, as we find it in Franklin, Emerson, Whitman, Melville, Henry James, Robinson, Fitzgerald, the Stevens of the *Letters*, has always propounded . . . and that is the saving counterforce of personality." Thus, while he shares many of the same concerns as the structuralist critics, Berthoff's real critical matrix is New Humanism. It is as if *Fictions and Events* represented a none too orderly point of intersection between the over subtle complexities of structuralist criticism and the literate and lucid simplicity of humanist criticism, to which we shall now turn.[2]

2. Other recent books relevant to the state of criticism in America include the following: *Readings in American Criticism*, edited by Thomas E. Berry (New York, Odyssey Press, 1970), is a useful anthology of reprinted essays. *The Quest for Imagination: Essays in Twentieth-Century Aesthetic Criticism*, edited by O. B. Hardison, Jr. (Cleveland, Ohio, Press of Case Western Reserve University, 1971), collects twelve essays on critics and their critical backgrounds. E. D. Hirsch's *Validity in Interpretation* (New Haven, Conn., Yale Univ. Press, 1967) is a work attuned to the intricacies of newer criticism in a way that Monroe C. Beardsley's *The Possibilities of Criticism* (Detroit, Mich., Wayne State Univ.

A good exemplar of the insight and lucidity of the liberal humanist tradition is Malcolm Cowley. Now we have fourteen of his essays —on Hawthorne, Whitman, Horatio Alger, James, Dreiser, Anderson, Pound, O'Neill, Frost, Van Wyck Brooks—and on American naturalism, three cycles of myth in American writing, and the function of criticism—gathered under one cover as *A Many-Windowed House: Collected Essays on American Writers and American Writing*, edited with an introduction by Henry Dan Piper (Carbondale, So. Ill. Univ. Press [1970]). The title is taken from the last essay in the volume, "Criticism: A Many-Windowed House" (pp. 244–52), in which Cowley rejects the various systems of criticism for a common-sense eclecticism: "Instead of dealing critically with the critical critics of criticism, I have preferred to be a critic of poems and novels, or at most a literary historian." When he examined the "big critical works," he says, he found that they usually were "so badly written as to reveal a sort of esthetic deafness," that many were "contemptuous of writers and writing," and that most were "episodes in the battle among critical systems, one or another of which we were being cannonaded into accepting as the only true critical faith" (p. 244). But each system, whether historical, biographical, psychoanalytical, expressionist, moral, political, or formalist, led to a "different but equally specialized and partial standard for judging works of art." Cowley comments on the "let's-pretend" quality of each and offers a wry defense of the "purified subject of the system known as textual or integral criticism or less exactly . . . as the 'new' criticism": in this system, the critic naively "pretends that every work of literature is completely autonomous, and then judges it by the complexity of its inner relations. He could find worse standards." First published

---

Press) is not. Two works by Philip Hobsbaum, *Theory of Criticism* (Bloomington, Ind. Univ. Press, 1970) and *A Theory of Communication* (London, Macmillan, 1970) are wearisome but rewarding, the latter containing among its eleven chapters a useful "Critique of Linguistic Theory." René Wellek's *Discriminations: Further Concepts of Criticism* (New Haven, Conn., Yale Univ. Press, 1970), in addition to discussion of theories of comparative literature, of genre, and of literary history, also contains essays on stylistics and criticism, on the literary theory and aesthetics of the Prague School, and on the state of contemporary European criticism that gives perspective on the structuralist critics. Two mutually illuminating books that do not at first glance seem related are Northrop Frye's *The Stubborn Structure: Essays on Criticism and Society* (Ithaca, N.Y., Cornell Univ. Press, 1970) and Kenneth Burke's *The Rhetoric of Religion: Studies in Logology* (Berkeley, Univ. of Calif. Press, 1970).

over ten years ago, this caveat regarding New Criticism antedates some similar criticisms of Richard Foster and Lee T. Lemon, as well as anticipating the current desire for a recovery of historicism in literary analysis. Cowley observes, for example, that it is obvious that the "study of any author's language carries us straight into history, institutions, moral questions, personal stratagems . . . ." He concludes with a statement of his own critical principles. Criticism should be defined simply, as "writing that deals with works of art." Criticism is not a science but one of the minor literary arts, subordinate to rather than superior to its subject matter (the major literary arts, poetry, drama, fiction); thus it should be written in the language of the culture and not in some variety of philosophical, medical, or social-scientific jargon. Moreover, the critic, as a part of the act of criticism, should select works of art that are worth writing about. Finally, Cowley remarks of his own method that he starts "innocently" with the text itself and with as few preconceptions as possible, then moves outward to other works by the same author, to the author's biography, to questions about audience, occasion, intent, and so on. And the reprinted essays of the volume reveal the clear mind looking through these various windows.

But the attempt to achieve literate simplicity can lead to shallowness. Marius Bewley, whose earlier writings on American literature, *The Complex Fate* and *The Eccentric Design*, were more than occasionally insightful, continually teeters on the edge of plunging, as it were, into the shallows in the twenty essays and reviews collected as *Masks & Mirrors: Essays in Criticism* (New York, Athenaeum [1970]). The reprinted reviews, however useful, remain just that—reviews. Such essays as "The Heroic and the Romantic West," and "James Fenimore Cooper: America's Mirror of Conscience" offer little that is new—though the essay on "The Land of Oz: America's Great Good Place" is a delight to read. Perhaps Bewley is at his best in the last section, which is focused on poets and includes Stevens and Emerson, Eliot and Pound, and Hart Crane—but even here one senses a kind of introductory quality to the essays.

Quentin Anderson's *The Imperial Self: An Essay in American Literary and Cultural History* (New York, Knopf) runs something of the same risk, though it comes off better initially. It begins simply enough as an attempt to trace the displacement of a social consciousness in American literature and culture by a kind of territorial imperative of the self, conceived as an unusual configuration of the transcendental and the Freudian. Anderson argues that Emerson, Whitman, and James disavowed the inherited notion that individual identity is an inherited fatality (presumably of a Calvinistic sort) but instead saw the self as an agency of renewal, growth, and change. This is hardly a startling or overly complicated proposition. These three writers Anderson puts in contrast to Hawthorne who felt that it is only in society that we "become human," whereas Whitman, Emerson, and James saw the celebration of individual identity as the means of making "new versions of the self." Thus a dialectics of generating "new selves" may be observed in these three writers; each was possessed of a tendency toward self-abnegation in the face of the cosmos counterbalanced by a compulsion to assert the importance of the single self. So far, the argument is familiar, but it is to bear some strange fruit. One strand of Anderson's argument has to do with the "transitive, genital" personality, which is either a very abstruse concept or a fancy way of saying something very simple. I am not sure which, because in a readable explication of "Crossing Brooklyn Ferry" Anderson offers a provocative example of how such a personality constructs its symbols. We discover that Whitman "genitalizes" the face in other poems and that the confluence of light and water through and around the reflected face in the water of "Brooklyn Ferry" implies semen. This symbolic resonance is what makes the phrase about individuality within a larger context, "struck from the float," so "powerful." Linking up various other sexual innuendoes in the poem, the image is the objective correlative of that center that is the self and to which and from which vital energies flow. Although one may (or may not) accept this reading as suggestive, he is likely to resist the extrapolations of the last chapter, "Coming Out of Culture" (pp. 201–44), where, with plentiful reference to Norman O. Brown, Anderson offers other versions of the "genitalization" of the self. More and more the meaning of key terms becomes elusive. A book which commences with simple observations and clarity ends in obfuscation.

Lucidity, however, is the hallmark of a little book of collected works by Austin Warren called *Connections* (Ann Arbor, Univ. of Mich. Press, 1970). Five of the nine essays are on American writers, Cotton Mather, Hawthorne, Emily Dickinson, Paul Elmer More, and T. S. Eliot. The essays on Mather, Hawthorne, and More are in the mode of biographical sketches, and the same mood prevails in Warren's alert literary biography of the characters of *The Scarlet Letter* and of the poetic persona of Dickinson's poetry, as well as in his tracing of the development of Eliot's critical ideas. As Warren comments in his preface, the "connections" are of various kinds, the responses of later writers like Whittier, Mrs. Stowe, and Hawthorne to Mather, friendships among authors, the relationships among religion, knowledge, and literature that Warren believes act in concert. "As a literary critic, I have no 'method,' no specialty . . . but, confronted with the situation of 'practical criticism,' I look through my repertory for the methods and the mixture of methods appropriate to the case before me—in consequence of which the proportion of stylistic analysis to biographical, or biographical to ideological, will be found to vary from essay to essay" (p. ix).

Connections is also probably a better term than *themes* for two other general books on American literature that need mention here. Harold P. Simonson's brief *The Closed Frontier: Studies in American Literary Tragedy* (New York, Holt, Rinehart, and Winston [1970]) draws connections between the Turner thesis of the significance of the frontier in American history and the metaphoric significance of such a concept to the literary imagination. Simonson deals with what he calls the eschatological aspect of this symbolic "walling" in such figures as Howells, Mark Twain, Rolvaag, and Nathanael West, concluding that against the background of a closed frontier the actions and dreams of American writers took on meaningful configuration and beauty. The book is almost never opaque, but neither are there any complexities to endanger its simple clarity. Indeed, the significance of the frontier is much more sharply etched in a book that draws connections between the Hudson River School of painters and two modes of "pictorialism" in the earlier American romantics. In *The Pictorial Mode: Space & Time in the Art of Bryant, Irving, & Cooper* (Lexington, Univ. Press of Ky.), Donald Ringe observes that the prairie frontier pictured in the writings of Bryant and Cooper (drawn in part from the sense of the immense scale of things in Thomas Cole's paintings) often expressed a "vision of a despoiled nature." "It is but a step from this picture of a ruined landscape to a view of the prairie as a foretaste of the kind of earth Americans may leave to their children" (p. 51), as, in fact, these early writers warned. Later, having drawn connections between spatial dimension in painting and literature, Ringe observes that a symbolic mode had to develop from

the problem of expressing a "temporal dimension in a single landscape." The painter had to do it through detail; "the blasted tree or
ruined monument could, of course, suggest the desired effect, and
each became a part of the landscape convention" (p. 206). The writers, having the suggestive power of language at their disposal, had an
easier time than the painters, but the techniques of Irving, Cooper,
and Bryant also began to tend toward symbolic representation of, or
evocation of, space and time to suggest such things as the eternity
and infinitude of God and the smallness of the observer. A later generation of writers (especially Whitman) was to perfect this technique
in literature and to develop a romantic theory of perception that went
well beyond what the earlier writers conceived.

Two essays on the dialectics of American romanticism, though not
equally insightful, nevertheless are broadly suggestive in both a
literary and a cultural way. Richard P. Adams in "Permutations of
American Romanticism" (*SIR* 9[1970]:249–68) argues that although
Emerson, Hawthorne, Thoreau, Melville, and Whitman used metaphors of organicism to describe literature and the universe, the concept of dynamism is more important (followed to its logical conclusions, organicism is a static system). A mechanistic conception of
things reasserted itself in the latter part of the nineteenth century
and the first part of the twentieth, giving way once more to a new
variant of dynamism in the works of Hemingway, Faulkner, Stevens,
Frost, and others. Jesse Bier in "The Romantic Coordinates of American Literature" (*BuR* 28[1970]:16–33) claims that we can easily
codify American literature by asking the question whether our writers are unwilling or unable to accept a realistic measurement of human limitations. Two-thirds have not been able to accept such a
concept of limitation. The American romantic, moreover, goes either
to an extreme of optimism or an extreme of despair, refusing (except
for Hawthorne and Melville) to inhabit a realistic middle ground.
The "historical extensions of the facile romantic extremes in American
history have been either puerile or ominous": from Transcendentalism came Horatio Alger; from Poe came horror and literature bent
on subverting the individual. (The argument here is, at the least,
strained.) On the other side, our avowed realists have been "circum-
spect" and "cowardly," and the result has been an "imperfect realistic
literature." In a vaguely implicative conclusion, Bier predicts that
the prominence of romanticism will not continue.

Related to the romantic impulse of American literature is a set of dialectical propositions about optimistic idealism and pessimistic nihilism focused in the figure of the hero. Three works present this pattern. In *American Dreams, American Nightmares*, edited by David Madden (Carbondale, So. Ill. Univ. Press [1970]), Madden categorizes American dreamers in a triad: those who say "yes, in thunder" are the true believers who help make and remember heroes; those who say "no, in thunder" are atheists and who help make and encourage victims; and arching over the true believers and the atheists are the agnostics. who say "maybe." The agnostic "contemplates the interaction between dubious heroes and their vulnerable witnesses" (p. xvii). The nineteen essays of the volume are offered as a collection of criticisms on writers who have responded variously to "the American experiment," in an attempt to answer the question of why the American Dream turned into a nightmare. Several of the essays on American fiction have been discussed in last year's *ALS* (see pp. 224 ff.), but the larger concerns of the volume have not. Among the general essays are Robert B. Heilman's "The Dream Metaphor: Some Ramifications" (pp. 1–18), Leslie Fiedler's "The Dream of the New" (pp. 19–27), Louis Filler's "Machiavelli for the Millions: Some Notes on Power Structures" (pp. 28–44), Maxwell Geismar's "The Shifting Illusion: Dream and Fact" (pp. 45–57), Irving Malin's "The Compulsive Design" (pp. 58–75), Oscar Cargill's "Gift to the World" (pp. 204–13). Two examples will suffice to indicate the thematics of the book.

Irving Malin contends that heroes in American novels are often subjected to harsh authoritarianism with which they are unable to cope: "They try to construct a design—a pattern to master their environment—but it becomes an inflexible measure which eventually destroys the self. The design . . . dominates them and becomes their sole, godlike authority" (p. 58). Cooper's Ishmael Bush and Irving's William the Testy are early prototypes, but Poe was the first to create a real psychological study of the phenomena. The dreams end in nightmares. The attempts of Poe's heroes, of Hawthorne's Hollingsworth, of Melville's figures, of Hemingway's Nick Adams to master the environment rob them of self-mastery. They become things. Leslie Fiedler, in "The Dream of the New," argues that the cultural drive to make things new contains a self-destructive element. Americans will rebel and attempt to destroy anything which cannot be made

new. This effect in literature causes the repudiation of tradition and
the advent of parody and pop art. Fiedler believes that American
writers parody previous writers, consciously or not, and that they also
parody themselves, as may be witnessed in James, Faulkner, Mailer,
and a great many other writers. Of Poe (a "key figure in the whole
process"), Fiedler writes that "despite the appalling seriousness with
which he took himself, he was the inventor of at least two pop forms:
the detective story and science fiction" (p. 23). Although Fiedler feels
Poe was "saved" by turning to pop art, he is less certain about the
whole of American literature: "by the act of self-destruction the
American novelist makes his fiction dream rather than art, what
passes rather than endures, an experience almost as satisfactorily
transient as television itself. The Art of the New is totally nihilistic,
but it is joyously so; which may explain why our most authentic books,
however tragic the lives of their authors, are if not quite blithe, funny
at least" (p. 27). This presents a rather striking parallel with a recent
book on nihilism and humor in American literature.

Richard Boyd Hauck's *A Cheerful Nihilism* presents a more elaborate and suggestive dialectic of heroic optimism. Taking Sisyphus
as an image for the absurd hero (someone who assigns meaning to
a struggle without intrinsic value, and who is capable of creating
alternatives to being destroyed by a sense of the absurd out of a
double or paradoxical perception of dilemma of meaninglessness),
Hauck stresses the act of literary "creation" as an act of "confidence"
in the face of perplexing ambiguity. Many American writers have
chosen to create a framework by which to live in the midst of chaos;
such a framework is an arbitrary act of faith. Furthermore, some
writers proceed to joke at their own inability to see beyond the relative; and they laugh in the face of absurdity. It is the arbitrary choice
of humorous stratagems that chiefly concerns Hauck.

Although not humorists, such writers as Wigglesworth and Edwards were among the first to discover the inadequacy of man's
artistic or intellectual attempts to solve the problems of ultimate
meaning. Franklin's life and writings show arbitrary acts of faith to
be counters to existential despair, and he was one of the first American
writers to choose humor as a response to uncertainty. The creation of
the ambiguous narrator began in the "absurd frontier" of such Southwestern humorists as Thomas Bangs Thorpe and Johnson Jones
Hooper. Melville continued the absurdist tradition, with humor ap-

parent even in many of his bleakest stories; Mark Twain, of course, draws heavily on Southwestern humor; and there are "subtle shifts back and forth across the thin line between the ridiculous and the terrible" in Faulkner. Variations in the tradition are traced in the contemporary fiction of Heller, Vonnegut, and Barth. Although some of Hauck's assumptions and methods are questionable (his tendency to merge the strategies of the writing with the personality of the writer, for example; or his assertion that the device of an ambiguous narrator began in the tall tale), the book is a lively critical performance.

In a forthright preface to *The Heroic Ideal in American Literature* (New York, Free Press), Theodore L. Gross states that his goal is to trace the moral configurations of the tension between "idealism and authority" or "conception and reality" in American literature through five eras. There is a dialectical progression represented by the Emersonian hero, the Southern hero, the black hero, the disenchanted hero, and the quixotic hero: the heroic optimism of the age of Emerson and Whitman is countered by the shallowness of the heroic ideal in the nineteenth-century South; this gives way to the violent optimism of twentieth-ceutury black writers, which contrasts with the pessimism of Hemingway and Fitzgerald, which in turn gives way to the low-key optimism of more current writers.

The Emersonian hero emerges rather than appears, with the preternatural qualities of an epic figure. Hawthorne first cast the shade of reality upon the ebullient, self-reliant optimism of Emerson and Whitman. Melville studied the "nature of authority" and James was transitional and increasingly modern in the period between *The American* and *The Ambassadors*. The Southern writer (Simms, Page, and a few lesser-known contemporaries) was something of a straw man. Since their work is ethnocentric and partisan, productive tension between the ideal and authority is absent. In the case of the black hero, the one American most qualified to view the world as absurd refuses to do so. Gross finds the idealistic strand in the explosive works of Wright, Ellison, and Baldwin. This idealism, pitted against the destructive authority of white America, generates a conflict of idealism and authority which creates truly credible heroes. In the fiction of Fitzgerald and Hemingway (the disenchanted hero), idealism is "retrospective" and realism "omnipresent." The terrible wound which afflicts Hemingway's heroes applies also to society; the deterioration of Fitzgerald's characters serve to denounce America and the world. With the quixotic hero (the work of Bellow, Salinger, Mailer) there is a new direction of quiet optimism. Here the conflict between the ideal and authority is within the hero. Gross maintains that he wishes to avoid the kind of distortion that often results in a theme or type study such as this, especially reductiveness to a single set of characteristics. In the main he has—and in prose that is readable, clear, and energetic.

Such works as these, then, are illustrative of two major styles of academic literary criticism and literary history as now practiced in America. The one is complicated and over-subtle, but provocative even when approaching incantatory jargon. The other strives toward simplicity in the best sense but often demonstrates similar tendencies toward obfuscation, and sometimes toward simplistic rather than simple expression. For the present, we shall have to wait for the major scholarly work that is a true synthesis of these critical approaches— a work, that is, that combines the very apparent sophistication of the newer criticism with the rather different sophistication of the older.

Washington State University

I wish to thank the Department of English of Washington State University for a summer grant-in-aid which enabled Mr. Roger Steinmetz to assist me in the compilation of data for this review.

Index

This index gives references to literary and historical figures who are referred to throughout the book, as well as to authors of the literary scholarship therein surveyed. Works are cited only for those authors given chapter coverage. Literary movements and genres are not indexed as such, since the organization of the book makes pertinent pages clear for most such studies.

DATE DUE